Yago de la Cierva

GW00468972

Leading companies through storms and crises

PRINCIPLES AND BEST PRACTICES
IN CRISIS PREVENTION, MANAGEMENT
& COMMUNICATION

IESE
Madrid, 2021

Yago de la Cierva
IESE Business School
Camino del cerro del águila, 3
28023 Madrid (Spain)
www.iese.edu

Translation: Jamie Lynn Black & Philip Muller
Cover Design ©2017: María del Mar Chapa Hammeken, www.variopinto.com

Ordering Information: www.iesep.com
Quantity sales. Special discounts are available on quantity purchases by corporations, associations, and others. For details, contact the "Special Sales Department" at the address above.

Leading companies through storms and crises/Yago de la Cierva — 2nd ed.
ISBN 978-1-78726-427-4

In his classes on corporate governance, my dearly missed colleague Prof. Luis Manuel Calleja often used to say that chairpersons and CEOs should dedicate all their attention to three things: exceptions to the rules, crises and the company's future. I fully agree: if there is a crisis, top management is responsible and should be involved. If not, either it is not a real crisis, or it is a sign that top management is not thinking strategically.

Managing a crisis involves a lot of communication, because its consequences for the organization's reputation could be much more damaging than material harm alone. Most crises require us to act on two planes: fixing the problem and communicating what is going on to the company's stakeholders. Both tasks are intertwined: without ensuring the goodwill of my stakeholders, I will not overcome the situation.

We will move between two areas, the science of management and the art of communication. Knowing how to face a crisis is a basic element of management, and the ultimate test of the communicator's competence. As Antonio Hernández Deus, one of my mentors and my boss for a couple of decades, says; «the only true communication is crisis communication», because only then do many bosses pay attention to communication; survival often depends on communication.

The prudential principles of crisis management and communication should be put into practice... with prudence. More than answers, they provide many questions for leaders to ask themselves. One cannot always "take the safe route", for example, because that might lead a company to do nothing (and in any case, not all crises can be avoided). The same applies to assuming full responsibility for your actions, or keeping your stakeholders updated. "Nothing in excess", Solon of Athens, one of the seven sages of Greece, used to say, twenty-seven centuries ago. This aphorism also applies to prudence itself.

This book draws on four types of sources. The first is monographs in the field of crisis management and communications, a discipline that has been around for fewer than fifty years but is now coming of age. Case studies on crises suffered by different corporate and public institutions are a second source. Organizations that have allowed researchers to access and study what they really experienced have contributed decisively to the progress of

What to expect from this book

We live in turbulent times. These first few years of the third millennium are full of painful accidents, disasters, political turmoil, and corporate crises in all economic and social sectors, involving all types of organizations, on all continents. No one can feel safe because no one is safe.

At the same time, people have high expectations from managers and political leaders. They demand that big corporations, small businesses and public institutions conduct their activities in safe mode, preventing incidents that could harm people and property. They also expect them to be prepared to cope with unexpected problems.

In these turbulent times, when social trends like European integration seem to be halted and thrown into reverse, and countries like Spain, though united for more than five centuries, are now struggling to stay together, what we really miss are true leaders.

This book is an attempt to help prepare the ground for the emergence of such leaders. Crisis management and communication is not a theoretical discipline – it's a practical one. Its guidelines come from experience: learning points from good and bad crisis management. This book's leitmotif is the principal virtue of leadership: prudence. The prudent person, drawing on a background of practical knowledge and an ethical approach, will be able to take the right decisions with the limited information available and in the short time frame that crises grant to managers.

Index

management theory. We should be grateful to managers who have made the courageous decision to opt for transparency and social responsibility. A third source is applied scientific experiments, which are increasingly being used in crisis management and in other social disciplines. Finally, my own personal experience in the field as a crisis consultant for companies and non-profit organizations.

Crisis management is deeply related to ethics. The principles and values of individuals and organizations are put to the test by failures and bad news much more than by successes and good news. In a crisis, what really matters are people's needs and expectations. So much so that a crisis represents the moment of truth for both people and institutions: moments in which it is possible to see what stuff they are made of. Crises are the time when we discover heroes such as Chesley "Sully" Sullemberg, the pilot who, in 2009, landed his damaged plane on the Hudson River saving all the flight's passengers and crew; or villains such as Francesco Schettino, the captain of a cruise liner that capsized in 2012 because of his imprudence, killing 32 people.

That is why the word "ethics" is one of the most repeated terms throughout this book. Let me be explicit and transparent about my views on ethics. When I speak about right and wrong, just and unjust, I follow the classical approach, in which ethics is the science of moral duty, an inner sense close to but different from what is useful, convenient for the majority of people involved, statistically normal or legally binding. This school of thought includes in its ranks philosophers such as Aristotle, Aquinas, Pieper, McIntyre, Spaemann and many others; it considers ethics as a normative wisdom, establishing norms of unconditional value and universal range.

While writing this book, I had in mind MBA students and corporate or public managers participating in IESE executive education programs. My goal was to make them think and act systematically. There are many wonderful books with a more practical approach, listing the immediate decisions to be applied as soon as a crisis hits the organization. I preferred another point of view: to improve the decision-making process. That's why we first study the principles that should inspire the corporate response to a crisis, and then present those best practices in their real context. My real goal is to help present and future leaders find out how their leadership and managerial skills could take advantage of these situations and improve.

Addressing this book to such an audience inspired me to choose a direct style that would make the book easily readable, even if the result is less academic. For that reason, I have left out the usual bibliographical support: maybe I am wrong, but I doubt anybody would benefit by knowing where to find a quote. Nevertheless, whoever is interested in reading more will find those references at the end of the book. Instead, I have used footnotes to add examples of real crises. I think these stories are meaningful examples of good and bad crisis management. They convey the important message that even intelligent and experienced leaders of respected and well-managed companies and organizations have to cope with severe crises.

I would like to express my gratitude to my colleagues Miguel Ángel Ariño, Juan Pablo Cannata, Marc Carroggio, Marilú Esponda, Mireia Las Heras, Juan Manuel Mora, Rafael Rubio, Guido Stein, Antonino Vaccaro and Julián Villanueva, who made significant suggestions that improved the book. I feel also obliged to my students; I hope I learnt a lot from their comments in class. I also thank Philip Muller, who revised my poor English. They deserve most of the merits the book may have, and I solemnly declare them innocent of its defects.

Yago de la Cierva
ycierva@iese.edu
Valletta, 16 August 2020

CHAPTER ONE

Our world

A society prone to crisis

We are living in a social context that is predisposed to crises; extraordinarily powerful technologies - nuclear, chemical, genetic, and many others; densely populated communities in highly dangerous geographical areas - think of the millions living on the San Andreas Fault in Southern California; failure of political and cultural integration, causing social complexity and tension; unequal globalization, provoking massive new migrations; clashes of civilizations resulting from wars of short-term interest... all of these factors combine to create a new global environment in which any issue that pops up anywhere in the world can somehow have major, immediate repercussions in our own neighborhood.

Ideological factors are also playing a key role in making crises happen more frequently. Our civilization is inherently *hypercritical.* One of the most important characteristics of contemporary political philosophy - in contrast with classical thought, which always sought harmony - is that it sees conflict as society's natural condition. Today's wise men prefer criticism to consensus, viewing conflict as the engine of progress. As the French say, *du choc des idées jaillit la lumière* — light is born from the clash of ideas.

This perspective is not necessarily wrong. The fact that Western societies create and respect procedures that protect social harmony and conflict resolution should be a source of pride. We should value the pluralism and multiculturalism of our societies because these characteristics are a positive source of innovation. Nothing is less modern than a unanimous consensus. «We are all wary of situations deprived completely of any type of conflict: they remind us of the peace of a cemetery», writes Navas.

We are in a level society, where nobody is more than anybody else. Everything is subjected to judgment, and any one opinion is as valid as any other. We go to ridiculous extremes: a football coach is asked for his opinion on a decision made by the health authority, and a newspaper tries to find out if the popularity of the Pope has risen this year ...

An unprecedented political polarization is taking root in this level society, accentuating emotional conflict and reducing rationalization. Whoever assumes the identity of a group uncritically accepts the position of the group and rejects everything that comes from the adversary. In these circumstances, dialogue ceases, moderates are denounced by both parties as being unprincipled and lukewarm, and mediators are traitors. And any excuse is enough to start a crisis.

This tendency may have something to do with the discredit which the basic principle of authority has suffered in Western societies. In many environments, the ruler or leader is viewed suspiciously and their power is judged to be a threat to personal freedom. In fact, one of the most worrisome trends today is the level of mistrust with which people view governments and international political institutions. The Edelman trust barometer ominously shows that the level of confidence not only in governments and media, but also in companies and NGOs has declined every year for the last twenty years.

Distrust goes hand in hand with increased regulation. Today, public organizations think that their mission is not to promote progress but to regulate it, and to this they dedicate their best efforts. Everything must be regulated! In addition, each regulation is accompanied by its own body of inspectors, who never suffer budget cuts.

However, government inspectors are far from being the only monitors looking over our shoulders. There are more **and more** social vigilantes carrying out the role of district attorneys, overseeing any and all institutions that are present in their sphere of control. The way that power in Western democratic societies is wielded encourages the growth of interest groups and activists, who are more than willing to exert pressure on institutions through a wide range of actions to mobilize public opinion.

Public regulators and social watchdogs also have new technological instruments which allow them to monitor us. At frightening speed a growing number of States and multinationals are becoming the Big Brother George Orwell described in his novel *1984*. For now, legal protection of the privacy of communications saves us, but I shudder to think what will happen when the traffic police gain direct access to the speed data provided by my car's navigator.

Additionally, sociologists underscore the fact that interpersonal ties are growing weaker and weaker. For millennials and the later generations, the relationship between employees and employers is much weaker than before. Life-long employment, the ideal for so many Westerners until only a few decades ago is outdated and job-hopping is perceived as a plus for personal growth and professional development. Furthermore, consumers no longer have any ties to their brands; in fact, the offer of goods and services far exceeds demand. Particular companies which were indispensable in the times of our grandparents now find themselves completely replaceable.

Lastly, the fact that crises tend to happen every single day has eliminated the exceptional character that the term had in the past and is now used to describe a wide array of "problems" such as a massive layoff, a drastic drop in income, or a major alteration in our normal activity. Yes, sir, in this sense there are more crises than ever.

Without any doubt, the inter-twining fabric of our society — that Bauman has so aptly called "liquid times" — and the ever-present divisions at all its levels (individualism, family disintegration, the collapse of traditional political systems – and globalization) weakens the relationships among people and promote volatile, uncertain, complex and ambiguous environments: a paradise for crises.

The media as crisis catalyzers

It is essential to fully grasp the importance of the media in the contemporary social and cultural context. In Western societies (and progressively in other cultural areas), the media *present themselves as guarantor of the common good.*

The period in which they claimed to be unbiased witnesses to what was happening in front of their own eyes is, purely and simply, history. They now feel that they have a *sacred mission* to fight against all and any political, economic, military or religious powers and to hold a stake in a broad range of issues. They are no longer simply witnesses of what is happening in the world, but rather vigilantes of all institutions. In fact, the media are one of the most effective forces in fighting corruption, scandals and all the "mistruths" of the establishment.

In many countries, investigative journalism has brought down governments and unmasked white-collar criminals, more effectively than the police, the Treasury or the central bank. From witnessing change, they have become its promoters. They foster ideas and try to shape society according to an agenda which influences the approach and content of their reporting. In the media today there is an undeniable social activism.

Furthermore, as technology allows them to cover any event anywhere in the world in real time, their role of control has a multiplied effect. Faced with an accusation, the institution no longer has 24 hours to respond, but has to do so immediately, because online news sites are updated by the minute.

Secondly, news is now a synonym of conflict. You only have to take a quick glance at the headlines in any daily newspaper or listen to the first few words in any newscast to realize how true this is. «Conflict is the motor fuel of any story», says John Allen, and journalists are «at heart story-tellers, and conflict is what makes their stories work. Without some struggle, some tension, some uncertainty about the outcome, stories simply don't work. This is an insight into drama at least as old as Sophocles, and the basics haven't changed much since his day».

The good news, on the other hand, seems less relevant: the outbreak of a war generates more news than the signing of peace. As an old Chinese saying goes, «a falling tree makes more noise than a growing forest». Moreover, positive events, to be news, are presented in a context of conflict. Something negative must be added to them, although this element is, from the quantitative and qualitative point of view, absolutely marginal.

Additionally, the mix between information and entertainment has influenced the tone of even the most reputable of news sources in the last few decades and has created the hybrid *infotainment*. The term "news" no longer refers to facts, which are too serious and objective, but rather to the buzz, which has six triggering factors: taboos, something that is unusual, or something that is enormous in scope, a rarity, newsworthy and/or secret.

Nevertheless, this is not the reporters' fault: it is ours! The public — in other words, us, you and me — are more interested in any bad news than we are in good news. As Mark Twain once said about one of his characters, «There is a lot to say in her favor, but the other is more interesting». The media exert major influence on society, but we should also point out that societies have the media that they deserve.

The media have assumed that one of their prime tasks is to monitor public authority, and more specifically the *people* in power, and this has many consequences in a reporter's mind set: it makes them tenacious, insistent, suspicious by nature, and hyper-critical. As Kerchner said, only half-jokingly, «if reporters smell a rose, they look for a coffin». In fact, the relationship between those in institutions and the news world is not always easy. For *The Washington Post* ombudsman, «Journalists know that a company/institution/government has the expertise and money to spread its good-news message. Newspapers think it's their job to make sure people hear the other side» In this sense, there is a conflict of interest between journalists and institutional communicators.

In addition to this hurdle, we should also bear in mind that many organizations are less than transparent. They employ all means possible to hinder the reporter's task. Quite often, an institution will pressure a journalist or launch rumors and misinformation campaigns, in order to benefit its own ends.

Therefore, the media have a major effect on organizational crises. A single journalist could transform an accident or a disaster into a crisis. In the minds of many executives, a crisis is not a crisis unless the media finds out. The situation does not become critical until reporters begin to call. Many feel that without independent media, there is no reason to fear any crisis whatsoever; and so, censorship is such a strong temptation to those in power.

The impact of technology

The nearly ubiquitous presence of social media in our daily lives, have led to the emergence of a new type of person, the *digital native*, who thinks, feels, desires and acts completely differently than a *digital immigrant* (someone from the older generation, someone like me!). This type of *anthropological mutation* has major consequences in respect of how people relate to each other, their relationships with organizations and, indeed, within the configuration of a different society.

For millennials and the following generations, the key factor is the content generated by users. The value of this content is not as feedback but rather in the legitimacy for users to decide for themselves the subject, the approaches, and the messages that they want to convey.

Each one of us has always felt that we are the center of the universe. Moreover, in today's internet world, we really are. New citizens generate content about themselves. According to the Pew Research Center, the driving force behind the explosion of the number of blogs is what is called "creative self-expression" (the vast majority of what is posted in blogs is about the author of that specific blog). People want to be seen, known, and be famous. There is a new social category, that of the celebrity, which is even contagious: if your cousin happens to be a well-known actress, there is no reason that you cannot be well known as well, in the category of "somebody's cousin." «Fame is no longer the prize of a long life of merit, based upon easily proven accomplishments. A couple of interviews on TV is more than enough to reach this desired level of being "famous"» says Navas.

The internet has totally changed our social rules, because the board and the pieces in this new game (the society and its players) are brand new. Matud observes that the structures of political, economic and social power are being transformed into structures based upon powers that are relational, more liquid but no less real.

But this is also true, not only of the structures, but of people's daily lives. We live in an era of distractions or, as Michael Harris described it in 2014 constant connection produces absence and lack of focus. According to a 2018 research from RescueTime, people generally spend an average of 195 minutes on their phones every day (and that number does not include the hours spent on their laptops, nor watching Netflix). What's more, on average, we pick up our phones 58 times a day. Those numbers are so close to an addiction (we are «hackable animals», Noah Harari says – tracked by algorithms that "know us better than we know ourselves") that there are more and more books and coaches charging a lot of money to help you quit smartphones...

This *digitodependence* is stronger among young people. The findings of a sociological research project carried out by the Future Foundation in the UK in 2013 in respect to the 16-34 age group showed nearly 50% review and reply to their professional emails while lying in bed; and 68% never turn off their cell phone. It is quite obvious that the dividing line between what used to be the place where we worked and the place where we lived has been blurred. The director of this Future Foundation research project stated, «The time we spend in bed is no longer meant to rest but rather it is viewed as being a period of time where we are connected to another device». I am sure that five years later, this phenomenon has increased, not decreased.

The social media are critical here for three basic reasons: they have dramatically changed the relationship between citizens and traditional media; they have altered the balance between people and institutions; and they promote a lack of representativity.

Firstly, *the weight of traditional media in crisis management is being greatly reduced,* because its mediation capabilities are no longer exclusive. It is true that newspapers, radio and TV are still media; but they are no longer the only media and their control over social debate is being, and will continue to be diminished.

This is not necessarily beneficial for institutions, neither in general nor in a crisis. It is true that reporters' perseverance and aggressiveness may end up being a real headache, but at least they tend to follow rational, professional criteria (they double-check their information, confirm sources, listen to both sides of the issue, etc.) and act within a legal framework — aspects which tend to be ignored in social media.

The social media have now reduced a large portion of the time that viewers used to devote to the traditional media. Statistics show that this "second screen" has reduced 64% of TV viewing, 23% of the time we used to spend reading the written media; and even 17.7% of the time we used to spend listening to our favorite radio station. The impact of social media is compounded when we consider that in the time that we are listening to the radio or watching TV, we may also be on Facebook or another one of our favorite social media, in other words, on the second screen.

Secondly, citizens can be listened to in much more widespread ways. The digital revolution is the prime factor that enables users' opinions to be considered by both companies and public institutions. Social media in particular support these co-creation processes by providing stakeholders that have never met offline with unprecedented opportunities for joint brand-related interaction. Nowadays, citizens have at their disposal a valid instrument to be used against organizations' abuses that they have never had before.[1]

They can not only make their voice heard: social media enables people to use digital platforms to easily mobilize against any institutions perceived as a social threat. *Netizens* supervise companies more intensely than any regulator, public controller or investi-

---

[1] In spring 2008, the Canadian musical group "Sons of Maxwell" were on tour across the Northern part of the USA. At O'Hare Field they saw how United Airlines personnel were casually tossing their luggage around like tiddlywinks, luggage that happened to be carrying their precious guitars worth US$3,500 and ended up causing the instruments a lot of damage. Over a full year, the lead singer threated to sue United and when he finally realized that the Airlines had no intention of reimbursing them, he did what he had been promising: he made a musical video about his experience as a United customer and posted it on YouTube. In less than 24 hours the video had gone viral and in 3 days had been viewed by millions of people all over the world. It seems that the episode taught the airline industry a lesson because in 2011, Delta reacted quickly to avoid such a crisis when American troops returning from Afghanistan became angry with the airline for demanding US$200 for each and every extra piece of luggage. The soldiers posted a video in YouTube telling the world in general what had happened, and it was downloaded 250,000 times in a few hours. Delta immediately changed its conditions and decided to accept all the extra luggage for free.

gative media, and they check whether what they say is true or mis-leading, and demand action from the authorities. Online activists pay special attention to corporations perceived as lacking ethical standards, and cunningly track their activities and denounce their wrongdoings.[2]

---

[2] An example of this could be the Baidu healthcare scandal. In 2016, Wei Zexi, a 21-year-old college student diagnosed with Synovial Sarcoma – a rare cancer with no effective treatment – posted his experience online. He found on Baidu (the Chinese version of Google) a hospital that would "guarantee the effectiveness of the treatment." One of the doctors even promised him at least 20 years of life. What Wi Zexi did not know was that the search engine was not bona fide information but a paid ad. After several months of treatment and spending 200,000 RMB (around USD 30,000) the cancer transferred to his lungs, and he died a few days later. Posts and media reports began to question "who killed Wei Zexi", and uncovered several mal practices in that hospital. But public anger also pointed the finger at Baidu. This giant Chinese company already had a bad reputation: many thought it played dirty tricks against Google and was responsible of its competitor's quitting the Mainland China market; and it was also accused of infringing copyright, selling administrator positions in its Chinese version of Wikipedia, and its "pay-for-performance" (P4P) business. Unlike its competitor, Baidu not only disguises paid ads and shows them as a normal search results, but – as a CCTV exposé showed – search results are the consequence of a bidding process between advertisers. If a company is No. 1 in natural results but refuses to participate in the bidding process, Baidu will block its site. After Wei Zexi's death, an official investigation team demanded that Baidu be reformed. Baidu's response was questionable: it blocked the term "Wei Zexi" in its wiki so it was impossible for anyone other than Baidu to edit it; it announced on its Weibo account (Chinese Twitter) that it had contacted Wei Zexi's father to send its condolence, shielded the hospital and stated that Baidu had no legal responsibility in this incident. After a strong public reaction against the company, Baidu changed its strategy: the company said they had contacted regulators, hoping the government would investigate the hospital. Again, nearly all comments were negative. Afterwards, Baidu expressed its willingness to reform its P4P business, but did not do so: Netizens showed they stopped doing so only in relation to "Synovial Sarcoma" but continued "selling" other medical terms. What made people angry was the fact that Baidu never apologized, either for what happened to Wei Zexi, or for the misleading information; and that they had lied, and knowing the risks involved in P4P business, Baidu didn't reform itself until forced to by the investigation team. Baidu took legality as the only standard in decision making and didn't have any commitment to eliminate danger for patients.

It is significant that the evolution of social relationships is such that Time magazine chose The Protester to be its 2011 "Person of the Year". If society at the end of the century was already prepared for the crisis, the digital world we are living in has further strengthened this tendency.

In this sense, the new digital environment is characterized by its capacity to give more power to individuals than to institutions. As González Herrero and Smith say,

> Currently, stakeholders demand a new relationship with the organization, a new tone and attitude from corporations that need to adapt themselves should they want to be successful in today's crisis management. [...] Organizations must interact with their audiences well before any crisis arises. This is not a new principle in crisis management. What is new and requires a cultural shift for many organizations is that the engagement is now public.

Finally, the massive creation of fake personalities on networks (because that's what bots are) and their coordination to transmit self-serving messages distort public opinion. Fake news not only manipulates content, but also the way in which it is spread.

Bigger and more vulnerable institutions

Never in the history of the world have there been, as there are today, enormous companies and institutions that are actually more powerful than whole countries, as Norman Jewison foresaw in the 1975 movie Rollerball; and yet, at the same time, our troubled social environment and today's economic development model render these giants rather vulnerable.

As we have briefly explored, there is no shortage of external causes for crises: technological, cultural, political, demographic, and the inherent speed of our world. However, the internal causes are just as important. The root of the global financial crisis in the last decade and many other problems is the fact that many major multinational companies are led by a new type of CEO, who is charismatic, fearless, heterodox in his management style and motivated by huge compensation packages. These people, and the copy-cats that follow them, are more than willing to break the rules, and have led their once rock-solid companies to the brink.

Other global tendencies make these risks more acute. We are a society where efficiency, cost, and short-term profitability rule.[3] The large-scale, highly centralized, tightly coupled systems make organizations, communities, nations, and the world highly prone to crises.

Nevertheless, leaders tend to view crises as abnormal or infrequent events that happen only in extraordinary situations and that are therefore not worth planning for beforehand. This approach lacks any sort of logic, according to Nassim Taleb; failing to pay attention to the unusual is simply creating a new vulnerability at the back of our leaders' minds. «Our world is dominated by the extreme, the unknown, and the very improbable (improbable according to our current knowledge) — and all the while we spend our time engaged in small talk, focusing on the known, and the repeated».

All of these factors together may explain why organizations are suffering crises so often: these are difficulties which very severely affect an institution and jeopardize its prime objective and even its very survival as an institution. Crises are not those problems that have to be addressed on a daily basis, but rather major, extraordinary obstacles that create a serious danger due to the severity of their effects, the speed with which they take place, the uncertainty about how they will evolve and the confusion that provokes the need to make immediate decisions without even having all of the information available.

A crisis may happen to anyone (even to the best of us): *there is not a single institution anywhere in the world which is immune* to crises. It is impossible to foresee and eliminate all risk factors: from the physical point of view, there are unforeseen catastrophes; and from

---

[3] Ulmer uses an eloquent example regarding our food system. «Hog farms in Asia may now have over 1 million hogs on a single farm. A food-borne illness crisis in the old days of a more decentralized food structure may involve a few thousand people. With our current highly centralized system, foodborne illness crises impact millions of people throughout a country very quickly.»

the human point of view, human freedom is an unlimited source of surprises. In this sense, organizations may be classified in two groups: those that have already undergone one or more crises, and those which have not suffered one yet.

In general terms, vulnerability in the face of a crisis depends on three types of factors: the institution's social context (the more variable, dynamic and competitive it is, the greater the risk will be); its governance style (a one-man, top-down style is deemed to be a greater risk factor); and the institution's specific characteristics and corporate culture (the type of activity, size, the profiles of their staff and the relationship that those employees and others have with the organization all contribute to a variety of vulnerabilities).

These factors call for relevant changes in the organizations. First, change within: set up around a corporate purpose that determines what it contributes to its context in clear terms shared by staff. Enterprises should be sustainable in respect of the environment, in respect of society and in the way they are governed, if we follow the ESG (Environmental, Social, Governance) trilogy that is redefining organizations.

Then, change towards the exterior. Bridgeman recommends that corporate speaking during a crisis should sound more like a conversation than a statement, more an engagement than a pronouncement: it's all about engaging with your stakeholders. As Ogilvy explains, the goal of relationship-building with your public is to strengthen their loyalty to your brand so that they will defend you even in a crisis.

To achieve this in the online world, dialogue and conversation are as important as the message itself, and even more important than rights.

Additionally, the digital world has been a great information and authority leveler, continually changing the border that separates the public and private spheres. The situation in which only the "owner" — and no one else — is privy to information relevant to a decision-making process, is less common than ever in private interactions and is practically non-existent when dealing with institutions. All it takes is one person with a smartphone at a private party for everything to become open to public scrutiny.

Legitimacy may be vaguer than legality, but it is also more demanding. Organizations do have obligations to the society in which they operate, obligations that are not limited to simply obeying the law. Organizations base their legitimacy (their *social license to operate*) upon the services that they render. Because of this, they have the additional obligation to respond to the needs and legitimate desires of society and its members in situations where their services are relevant. As Cohn said only half joking, «What right do others have to tell you how to run your business? Well, the reality is that we are now living in a world defined by social conscience. Today, companies have to be nimble and integrate social concerns into their business». [4]

Living in harmony with your environment, in symbiosis with the surrounding society, is a strength for any institution. All institutions should have a positive and beneficial impact on their environment. This is valid in any circumstances, but much more so in a crisis. This is the moment to show the institution's social responsibility and its coherence with its mission. If, for example, a river overflows and destroys half of the city, the local organizations absolutely must do something to help those who have been left homeless. It is not enough for the public institutions to offer temporary housing in basketball arenas: private parties (individuals and/or corporations) also have the obligation to do their part in solving the problem.

---

[4] In March 2010, the environmental group Greenpeace launched a social media attack on Nestlé's Kit Kat brand for using palm oil. According to the activist group, the oil came from a supplier that was destroying Indonesian forests and, as a consequence, putting orangutans in danger. Nestlé's initial response took a legal form: the company's legal department notified YouTube of the video's copyright infringement of the Kit Kat brand, and YouTube pulled the video from the platform. Only 1,000 viewers had watched it. Greenpeace's reaction was to post the video on other websites, and launched a campaign against Nestlé's Facebook page, criticizing its lack of environmental sensibility. The video went viral, it was shown on major news channels across the world; and some broadcasters even put it on their own websites' front pages. The video was again posted on YouTube and this time was ranked number one. But the worst aspect of Nestlé's corporate response was their official posts on Facebook: so harsh and ironic that they exasperated the audience and made the problem bigger. So, when Nestlé decided to change strategy, they had not only to suspend buying from the Indonesian supplier, but also create the new post of global head of digital and social media, to change their marketing and communications approach.

Another significant aspect of social obligation refers to people's perceived *right to know*, which leads to organizations having a certain obligation of transparency. Organizations exist to fulfill a social function to the benefit of all people. As people have the right to information about organizations' activities, these organizations, in turn, have an absolute obligation to inform.

So, what are we supposed to do? In general, nobody has any qualms about shouting about their own successes; I do not know any organization which is shy about informing when things are running smoothly. But when they are having trouble, suddenly everything is different. When people slip and fall down, it is quite common for them to look around to see if anyone has noticed. This is true for institutions as well. In fact, when an institution "slips and falls," the first thing it does is to try to hide it. This instinctive reaction should not surprise anyone. Public knowledge is so relevant in any crisis that you could say that the only real crises are the public ones — in other words, those that the institution's stakeholders are aware of.

In reality, what is at stake *is not the right* to not reveal the problems the institution is having, but *the legitimacy of acting* in that way in respect of those who feel that they have a right to know.

The response to this depends directly on the type of relationship that exists between the institution and its stakeholders, and on the effects of any problem on the latter. If the bond is sporadic in nature and the stakeholders are minimally affected by the consequences, it does not seem necessary to communicate a problem. However, if the relationship is deeper and more stable, and the consequences are potentially severe, it would be necessary to inform them.

The key is mutual trust. Ask yourself whether communicating the problems to your stakeholders who are legitimately affected will strengthen your ties with them. Alternatively, imagine what the stakeholders their reaction would be when they find out from a third party that the institution has hidden the problem from them. That will clarify whether the stakeholders feel the organization has the obligation to inform or not.

What makes crises fascinating is that they *show the institution's soul and its real internal culture.* If management feels compelled to serve its stakeholders, both internal and external, it will provide complete and precise information, even if by doing so the organization seems to lose in the short-term. On the other hand, if it prioritizes its own interest over social benefit, the attitude will be perceived as self-seeking rather than collaborative. When the problem is revealed, the stakeholders will help those organizations who are considered beneficial for their environment and will turn a blind eye to their mistakes. With the others, people will be tough on them, or even worse, they may try to get even.

This book is about relations

Let me begin with a declaration, which openly states the framework of this book. For me, institutions are no more than a set of human relations structured around a purpose and intertwined with theoretical knowledge and skills, experiences and emotions. I take it as an axiom: it does not require any proof. If you do not agree, find another book or another enjoyable way to spend your day. However, I would like to make this perfectly clear from the beginning, as the consequences of this approach will arise several times throughout these pages.

I underline the relational aspect in any enterprise, beyond any material or productive aspect, because people are the most important element in any organization. The manufacturing process for a product of any sort — be it shoes or pianos — or the workplace — be it a factory or an office — are indispensable elements of an institution, yet they do not render a true portrait of the enterprise. That is most effectively done by describing the relationships that it has with its employees, owners, sales network, clients (current and potential), neighbors, etc. The map of stakeholders (who they are, what they think about the institution, how we communicate with them, etc.) is the best description of any organization.

From this point of view, crises are grave threats to the relationships that an institution has with its priority stakeholders: those upon which the very identity of the institution is built. Thus, if I had to summarize the critical factor for an institution's resistance or vulnerability in the face of a crisis into one single concept, the key word would be unity A united organization is one in which values and strategies are shared, where everyone has the same goals, and where the various roles are carried out with a vision of the whole. This does not refer to a monolithic or static union, meaning a total lack of separation or fracture, but rather a dynamic reality, lived out by a group of people who share a common project. This sound foundation is the result of a reciprocal exchange — top-down, bottom-up and horizontal — of information and values, of data and emotions.

In this sense, the stronger the ties between the institution and its stakeholders, the less vulnerable it is to a crisis. Furthermore, an external obstacle may even strengthen these existing relationships instead of damaging them. An external aggression against a warring institution filled with in-fighting may have dire consequences, while that same aggression could actually forge even more cohesion in a united organization.

This approach also indicates the way out of the crisis: taking measures that strengthen our ties with the public and build consensus around them. In a crisis, the manager (of a company, government or whatever other institution) who only cares about fixing the mess and asks "to be left alone to fix it", has not really understood the situation. His attitude must be the opposite: he should let operatives do what only they can and know how to do, and then guide, persuade, unite, create consensus on how to resolve the problem, reinforcing relationships with everyone: with employees and customers in a company; with the opposition and business, union and social leaders in a country; and with benefactors and volunteers, in an NGO. We will come back to this because it is crucial.

Knowing how to properly deal with a crisis implies, in short, knowing well the stakeholders of the institution and communicating with them. And all this from an integrated point of view: that of senior management. Only those who know how to respond in an integrated way to all their audiences will be able to manage a crisis well, because they will know how to determine priorities and transmit in an orderly manner messages appropriate to each one of them, but not contradictory to each other. On the other hand, when the relationship with stakeholders is distributed among different people and offices, giving a unitary response as an institution is not impossible, but it is much more difficult.

Thus, crisis management and communication are a microcosm of all corporate management. This includes leadership and communication with your personnel, your public authorities and regulators, your clients and providers, your investors and your local communities. And all from a single, unitary point of view, avoiding any contradictions and inconsistencies.

Is there a "crisology"?

The goal of this book is clearly oriented towards managerial activity. Its main contents are practical principles and best practices in crisis management and communication. Nevertheless, it won't hurt to explore briefly its scientific status, as a conclusion to this first chapter. At least it will help to evaluate the strength of its recommendations. However, if you are not interested in epistemology, just jump to the next chapter.

I dare say that crisis management and communication have a clean bill of health in practice and are progressing quite well when viewed from a scientific perspective; yet the subject is undergoing a phase of profound debate when we look at its epistemological foundation. This is so true that Kouzmin, somewhat sarcastically perhaps, wonders if crisis communication and management are both in crisis.

Traditionally, crisis management has advanced with case studies: analyzing big problems suffered by companies, the corporate response and the results: what worked and what did not work and why. From those studies, we proceeded towards lists of best practices. In recent times, applied research has put those best practices to the test and has confirmed most of them.

Nevertheless, from a scientific perspective, this is not good enough. There are many gaps: the sample of crises is not accurate (the case studies refer mostly to big companies, with an open-minded management that allowed researchers to find out what exactly happened); empirical research cannot reenact the complexity of real situations; and worst of all, there are no case studies of problems solved before they became crises, which are the best practices of all... In fact, we study anatomy from the narrow viewpoint of a traumatologist.

For these reasons, scientific research on crisis management has ventured into more advanced sciences in search of the proper methodology. Yet, we may wonder if, indeed, a sort of "crisology" could ever be created around crises themselves.

According to Ricoeur, crises may be viewed from four separate perspectives. One is to study them from a medical perspective: the turning point in the evolution of this specific disease, when its pathology becomes apparent and when we see if the result is going to be favorable or unfavorable. This was the starting point when crisis communication was first studied, as was mentioned earlier.

The second approach is based upon psychology and psychiatry and underlines the unrest created when transitioning from one phase to another within our lives, breaking away from our past. This change creates uncertainty yet opens the door to a new life, and, in this sense, the comparison is especially suitable for describing corporate identity crises.

The third perspective is epistemological in nature and views a crisis as the transition between two paradigms, understood as sets of coherent assumptions and axioms regarding the world in general. This transition takes place whenever something happens that cannot be explained by the reigning scientific or cultural assumptions and, hence, the existing paradigm must be replaced.

The fourth perspective is economic, contemplating the advances of humanity by looking at on-going, never-ending cycles. This vision, rather cold and basically objective, as is the science of econometrics, provides clear results whenever it is applied to larger events that are taking place over a long period of time, yet tends to fall short whenever it has to try to explain a specific crisis, in much the same way that statistics are valid to describe the traffic flows within a large metropolitan area and yet are practically useless for a driver on a specific day.

These four perspectives do actually provide an excellent view of crises, yet none of them individually sheds much light on their full complexity. As Topper & Lagadec affirm,

> Normality is our natural nest, stability our beloved home and certainty our paramount aspiration. Decision makers ask for action, but properly mapped. Businesspeople ask for risk, but properly controlled.

Wild weather is the friend of no one. Academics — sons of Descartes, enchanted with the mathematics, on account of the certitude and evidence of their reasonings' — are eager to understand the world and its laws, but within proper limits. As Alvin Weinberg put it: "Science deals with regularity; art deals with singularity".

Thus, for many crisis communicators, the field should be dealt with as an art rather than as a science.

For many years, crises have been studied as unusual events that interrupt the tranquility within our normal world. Facing these events, we tend to ignore this hiccup in the graph and focus on the standard curves. The question that has always been viewed as being irrational is whether it is worthwhile to study something that we fail to understand. It may be even less logical to try to establish some sort of theory about these unusual, unlikely events: it would be a contradiction in itself, inconsistent and highly suspicious in nature.

The fact that crises have become more commonplace and tend to happen more frequently has forced management to pay greater attention to them. Thus, by the beginning of the 21st century, many varying cases had been studied closely and a series of best practices for addressing crisis situations have been established, and numerous theoretical models had been generated to define a series of outlines to describe the possible evolution of practically every type of crisis.

Nonetheless, there was an underlying doubt whether this scientific research with all of its models and theories was in fact limited by its methodology. It is reasonable to conclude that what we learn about the development and management of past crises may have limited value for improving the management of tomorrow's crises.

Nowadays, factors such as climate and environmental change, the constant overhauling of production chains, globalization, greater usage of fragile technologies, the ever-present and threatening emergence of worldwide terrorist groups, citizen unrest in many countries around the globe, and troubling economic downturns, etc. are provoking crises that have never been seen before.

Major, large-scale crises have been replaced by others on a much smaller scale; we have gone from highly complex situations to those that are simply impossible to grasp; from events that have a wide range of interrelated factors to others that are totally interdependent in nature. "High- speed" is a thing of the past: in today's world everything happens at the same time and is reported all over the world within a fraction of a second; what used to be seen as being local is now universal in scope. The OECD rightfully states that we are living in a period of mega shocks: events that have a major and unpredictable future effect, that cause a major shake-up in industrial, social or geographical terms. .

Within this new social scenario, crises are not only faster, more intense and more commonplace than in the past, but society is in a much more fluid situation, social and intellectual foundations not being nearly as solid as before; therefore crises are no longer the exception but rather have actually become the rule.

These events and changes create doubt as to whether we will ever be able to fully understand crises and develop laws with 'non-crisis' categories such as cause-effect, etc. So, some may ask whether or not the time has come to change the paradigm itself and apply a new epistemology, better suited to this objective and not borrowing the concept from a normal world.

For instance, Topper & Lagadec have proposed that we should assume fractal geometric as the proper scientific model for crisis research, because it is better suited to explain events such as the recent financial crises which are highly complex and volatile and have peaks and valleys in their timelines.

Let us look at an example in order to be able to more clearly see how it applies. Within the scope of this fractal theory, as it has been developed by Benoît Mandelbrot, economic models are based on a bell-shaped curve and may be used to explain as many as 95% of cases. Yet, for standard economic theory, the extraordinary events represented by anything that falls within either extreme of the curve are not considered, as they are considered too rare or impossible to quantify. Therefore, it is simply impossible to study them.

In this sense, the traditional theory does not properly reflect reality in its entirety, but rather 95% of it; and what if our own situation falls within that 5% that is not explained? If we want to safely cross a stretch of water, is it enough for us to read in the weather forecast that there is a 95% likelihood that the water will not be choppy, although that means that there is a 5% chance of huge waves? Furthermore, as Mandelbrot points out, this 5% of extraordinary events may have more damaging consequences than the remaining 95%. Therefore, it is quite obvious that the theoretical gap is indeed relevant.

Regarding crisis communication as a science, there are four reigning theories within the field:

The *Image Restoration Theory* developed by Benoît. For this author and his followers, organizations are under siege when they are held responsible for some act that is viewed as being offensive; and their response could adopt six different types of defensive strategies, from accommodation to full resistance. This analytical model leads to the best responses being adapted to the specific type of crisis and to the priority stakeholders in a specific situation.

The *Situation Crisis Communication Theory* proposed by Coombs studies the factors that define the public's perception regarding the organization's responsibility, classifying the numerous situations in which it may find itself (as a victim, as an accidental cause or as a legally responsible cause) and suggest the most suitable response in respect to each situation.

The contingency theory, as developed by Wilcox and Cameron, explains that communication between an organization and its stakeholders may be managed with strategic criteria, differentiating the evolution of the problems in four separate phases: conflict management, risk management, crisis management and image restoration. This approach will lead to a positive attitude in promoting the corporate reputation.

Finally, the stakeholder-centered approach in crisis communication comes from research into strategic management and is based upon the development of permanent, win-win relationships with the varying stakeholders. Its main proponents are Ulmer and Mitchell. This type of approach leads to more solidly ethical crisis communication.

Each of these theories provides a different model to be studied from a theoretical point of view and a systematic framework for its empirical experimentation, yet the specific measures recommended for the varying situations and the best practices established do coincide. Indeed, though they are different in nature, they are not incompatible, and a lesson may be learned from each of them. A detailed study of each would only be worthwhile from an academic point of view and so we will not give them further attention in this book.

So, let's move on from this overview of our field's basic foundations, useful indeed for its gnoseological status, but much less relevant for our readers who are more concerned about being well prepared to manage and communicate during a period of crisis.

Story: why people don't trust companies

Since 2006, patients with a severe and unknown lung disease increased in Korea. In 2011, a pediatrician at the Asian Medical Center in Seoul, surprised by so many cases among young people and pregnant women, called for an investigation into the growing number of patients across the country with severe lung conditions (according to an unofficial source, 6,210 casualties, including 1,359 deaths, had been confirmed by November 2018). Official research confirmed the connection between dozens of deaths from lung pathologies and chemicals used to sterilize household humidifiers.

The main company involved in this scandal was Reckitt Benckiser (RB), a British multinational cleaning products company. In 2001, RB acquired the Korean brand Oxy that used the substance PHMG to produce a humidifier sterilizer called Oxy Ssak Ssak. The company advertised that PHMG was approximately five to ten times less toxic than other disinfectants and was used in innocuous products such as shampoo. However, it had not conducted studies on its toxicity when inhaled. In addition, because humidifier disinfectants were classified as industrial products, safety standards for food or drugs were not applied.

The first investigation took just a few months to confirm that the sterilizer was the cause of the lung disease. In July 2012, the Fair Trade Commission accused the four companies of describing their disinfectants as «safe for humans». The first was Oxy-Reckitt Benckiser, which enjoyed 80% of the market in Korea. Oxy RB denied any illegality and hired the country's largest law firm for defense.

Victims and social groups planned to take the British company to UK courts, but RB first denied all ties to Oxy RB, until it was discovered that in fact it owned 100% of Oxy RB. Then the highest-rated television shows in Korea dealt comprehensively with the scandal, airing terrible testimonies of the suffering of the victims, and deliberating on the responsibility of corporations and governments.

While the Korean authorities were investigating the case, Oxy RB removed hundreds of scientific articles on the side effects of those sterilizers available on its website since 2001 (demonstrating that they knew and did nothing, and then tried to hide evidence); they changed the company's legal status to dodge all legal responsibility; they bribed the director of the scientific team at Seoul National University researching PHMG to manipulate the results; and their executives answered often all official questions with «I don't remember».

Only when the Seoul Attorney discovered all this, on April 21, 2016, did Oxy RB Korea apologize to those who had become ill as a result of their disinfectant and to relatives of the deceased, and promised financial compensation. The British matrix also published a similar apology.

This late and cold apology did not convince anyone: «The apology was not for the victims, but for the prosecutors», one victim said. That's why South Korea's victims and major civic organizations promoted a boycott. Large supermarkets and other major retailers stopped selling all RB products.

In addition, the media found that the UK parent company had already acknowledged that it had conducted a US study on the sterilizers of its humidifiers, which stated that they could be lethal to humans.

On 12 September 2016, a special rapporteur of the United Nations High Commissioner for Human Rights said the British company should "ensure that all victims receive a sincere apology," and called for more efforts to compensate victims who had not yet been identified.

From a legal point of view, in January 2017, a Seoul court found the former Oxy RB first executive and 15 other employees guilty of criminal negligence and mislabeling. In September, Oxy RB announced that it had decided to stop production in Korea due to the boycott. According to RB's annual results report, Oxy RB had paid about 300 million pounds in compensation to victims.

CHAPTER TWO

Leadership, communication and ethics

Crises: basic concepts and features

In common everyday language, the word *crisis* clearly has a negative connotation: a severe problem that is affecting a person and/or an institution and creating hardship. Corporate crises cause damage and leave victims; they are expensive and require seemingly endless hours of overtime; and quite often, the finger is pointed at those who are managing the institution involved, accusing them of wrongdoing or negligence.

The origin of the term is medical: crisis is the turning point in the development of an illness. From this point, some are fatal, some go on to recovery; and the others develop into another form of problem. More than its consequences, what make a crisis critical is the uncertainty and confusion, in which time seems to come to a halt awaiting the outcome.

This concept applies not only to people's health. Institutions also go through threatening situations, in which it is uncertain whether the danger will become a reality or not. The Greek root of the word, *krino*, means precisely to distinguish, to decide, to exercise judgment in the midst of a dilemma.

A crisis can also produce positive effects: it offers opportunities for change. In crises, heroes are born, changes in the organization are accelerated, latent problems which had been postponed for better occasions are faced, company personnel are renewed, new action strategies emerge, alert systems are developed that did not exist previously, new competitive aspects appear, etc.

Since President J.F. Kennedy first used it in 1959, it is now commonplace to cite the eastern etymology. He explained that the Chinese symbol for the word crisis, called wēijī, is actually a combination of two words, danger and opportunity; and his interpretation has become quite popular.

In reality, it seems that wēijī does indeed mean "crisis" and that the wēi syllable of wēijī conveys the notion of "danger", but the jī syllable of wēijī does not in fact signify opportunity, but something like the crucial point when something begins or changes. Thus, a wēijī is indeed a genuine crisis, a dangerous moment, a time when things start to go awry.

Herman was the first to define corporate crises as events that are characterized by three basic elements: surprise, threat and short response time. In this sense, the main trait is the second threat. Ulmer, Sellnow & Seeger emphasize that every crisis has the potential for positive communication activities and results. Including both threat and opportunity in the definition of crisis broadens an organization's response framework to a crisis.

Not all threats are crises. An organization may find itself involved in a wide variety of extraordinary situations, and the terms that we tend to use are quite similar indeed, yet they are certainly not synonyms: emergency, incident, disaster, and conflict.

Emergency is an unexpected physical threat that requires a quick response — it tends to be technical in nature — yet it does not have any direct or immediate consequences in respect to the organization's relationship with public institutions. For example, a breakdown in a hospital's electrical installation may lead to a major emergency that requires an urgent technical intervention on behalf of the maintenance team.

Incident is a mistake or a breakdown, more or less severe, of one of the physical elements within a complex system, yet this malfunction does not impede the general operations of the whole. For example, we could call a breakdown in the rail services between two nearby cities due to a collapse of a bridge that did not cause any personal injury "an incident". The obstacle may be resolved by simply providing bus services for passengers. (Yet we should be careful: quite often an institution will call something an "incident" when it really is a true crisis, precisely to try to play down its severity).

Disaster is the failure of a major physical element, causing the system to stop completely. There is no longer any uncertainty about the consequences, which have already occurred, and therefore the situation is Game Over. It would be the case, for example, of a chocolate factory without any type of insurance which completely collapses due to the overflow of a nearby river.

Conflict is a partial variation in the organization's social circumstances that jeopardizes its daily operations but does not fully impede them. For example, the disagreement between the faculty and the administration at a university about how overtime should be paid. The academic setting is affected, and the conflict blocks other decisions but as long as the crisis does not explode (the faculty going on strike, for instance), classes are still being given.

A *crisis*, on the other hand, is a major variation in the organization's social circumstances. Its primary traits are the uncertainties in respect to what may happen next, the speed with which everything occurs, and the extreme urgency in implementing measures, there not being enough time to thoroughly discern the best approach. In this sense, emergencies and incidents require first of all a technical response. Maybe later (or almost at the same time) the organization will have to face the consequences on its stakeholders, and that would be the crisis, which has to be handled by managers, not technicians.

Furthermore, crises are attributed to human causes rather than to a force majeure. The concept of crisis is always closely linked to the concept of someone being blamed for it and being held responsible for either originating the problem itself or failing to have properly responded to it once it happened. In fact, an outbreak of food poisoning is not in itself a crisis but may become one if it happened through a lack of hygiene or if the support provided for the victims was poorly managed.

This system of classifying these events has many practical consequences. Defining a problem which is being addressed as an emergency, an incident, a disaster, a conflict or a crisis will be useful in determining who should be handling the event and what the institution's initial response should be.

Definitions

Many authors have tried to define the essence of a crisis. The most famous is by Fink: a «decisive and unstable situation that runs the risk of: 1) increasing its intensity; 2) be subject to inspection by the government or the media; 3) interfere with the normal development of the business; 4) endanger the positive image of the company or its managers; 5) cause damage, in some way, to the bottom line of the company's results».

The two I personally like most complement each other. From a corporate point of view, González Herrero tells us that a crisis is «a situation that threatens the organization's goals, upsets its existing relationships with it and requires an extraordinary intervention of the company's top management in order to avoid, or at least minimize, any and all possible negative consequences».

On the other side, a sociologist like Elizalde defines crisis from a subjective perspective, as a situation, in which a person or an institution is immersed, consisting of four basic elements: a major threat to its scope of power and autonomy; a lack of sufficient time to resolve the problem by applying normal procedures; intense emotions; behaviors that are out of control, both within and beyond the walls of the institution.

Summing up, we could say a crisis is an unstable, uncertain situation that runs the risk of triggering severe damage to the institution's material and immaterial assets and primarily to its existing relationship with its main stakeholders because, in one way or another, these stakeholders will reach the conclusion, rightly or wrongly, that the institution itself is to be blamed for what has happened.

Classifying institutional crises

At first glance, we may think that each crisis is unique. As Caponigro says, each crisis is like a fingerprint: there are no two identical crises. Yet an examination of their origins and the way they evolve reveals a series of elements that are common to all crises. Thus, Elizalde affirms that «it is true that a crisis is to some extent unpredictable and contains elements of indeterminacy, but these components tend to be more related to the tendency that men have not to think about what can go wrong than with the structure of a crisis».

Discovering and analyzing these common elements will help us see past the apparent unpredictability and recognize the useful familiar patterns, foresee and prevent crises that could affect our organization, and – if we are unable to avoid them – at least we are able to reduce their negative effects.

Academia has classified crises according to different criteria: frequency, type of cause, avoidability, etc. This is not just an academic question: classifications are needed to anticipate decisions in planning the handling of a crisis. In this book, we will follow Lerbinger's classification, because it gives concrete hints on how to react in each case. He splits them into the following groupings:

Natural crises: there are no human causes and, hence institutional responsibilities are strictly limited to the reasonable expectation of having taken the logical measures to foresee the crisis, of having implemented the required steps before the crisis happened and of having provided a suitable response.

Technological crises: these are caused by misusing industrial technology: a leak in hazardous products, collective food poisoning, etc. The consequences are severe indeed, because stakeholders will always blame them on human errors. Additionally, emotions usually run high in this type of crisis.

Confrontational crises: triggered by a person or a group that publicly confronts the organization and tries to mobilize other people to either impede or drastically change the institution's activity.

Malicious crises: provoked by external illegal or criminal actions: this would be the case in the kidnap of a manager and/or employee, a hold-up, industrial espionage or sabotage, an attack by hackers, etc.

Crises triggered by corporate mistakes: these crises happen when top management make wrong decisions through lack of prudence, prioritize short-term performance over long-term goals, or run the company for their personal benefit, to the detriment of the organization's other stakeholders: for instance, when a corporate executive committee decides to drastically raise their own stipends while reducing security-related expenses in their factories, or when the board does not fulfill its supervisory responsibilities.

Crises triggered by corporate wrongdoing: someone in the company, probably an executive, commits a crime or a serious act of misconduct in the exercise of his or her job: for example, an adult mistreating underage workers who are reporting directly to him or her, embezzlement, forging documents, etc.

The bibliography on crisis management tends to use industrial accidents and criminal attacks as the best examples of crises. Nevertheless, year after year, statistics provided by the *Annual Crisis Report* prove that the real cause of the vast majority of crises are decisions that have been made by management on its own; they do not appear out of the clear blue sky but could have been foreseen relatively easily.

At first glance, these statistics may seem to be unsettling. However, they tell us that most crises give warning signals, and that we do not usually have to fight against colossal and blind forces of nature but against our own mistakes. If we are able to improve the way we make decisions, we will guarantee an effective crisis prevention procedure.

Statistical analysis

Mark Twain popularized the well-known words of wisdom, «There are three kinds of lies: lies, damned lies, and statistics». To make things worse, the best-selling book covering this topic is *How to Lie with Statistics*, by Darrell Huff, a brilliant work on how to defend oneself against the misleading usage of what is called "creative statistical explanations."

At the end of the day, the problem does not lie in the data itself but in the way this data is used. Therefore, as an introduction to the subject, it will be worthwhile to specify some data that will give us an idea about the dimensions of this area.

Which are the most frequent crises, those which are unexpected o or those that are foreseeable? According to the Institute for Crisis Management (ICM), in 2020, 27% of crises were unexpected while 73% were smoldering cases, which began with a minor issue that could have and should have been identified and properly resolved long before it developed.

Are there many institutions that are affected by a crisis? According to the *European Communication Monitor*, seven out of every ten corporate communication directors who were interviewed stated that they had had to handle a crisis within the previous year.

What is the most frequent cause? According to the same ICM report, the most frequent causes were found to be management mistakes (19.6%), cybercrime (13.3%), discrimination lawsuits (11.9%), labor conflicts (10.6%), whistle-blowing (8.1%), white-collar crime (4.3%), defective product recalls (2.6%), natural disasters (2.3%), environmental damage (2.3%), executive dismissal (2.2%), consumer activism (1.8%), violence in the workplace (1.6%) and class action lawsuits (1.2%).

Which type has increased the most? Those that grew the most compared to previous years are complaints of sexual harassment (twenty times more than two years before), hacker attacks (2019 tripling 2017) and disputes over labor issues, which doubled, and whistleblowing, which grew by 43%.

Who should be blamed for the crisis in most cases? The responsibility for nearly 51% of all crises falls directly on the shoulders of the organization's management; 32% on its employees; and the remaining 18% on external causes: natural disasters, consumer and client-related issues, conflicts with public authorities, activist attacks, hackers and IT-related crimes.

Do crises only affect those companies and institutions that have younger, inexperienced managers? In list of the most severe crises that took place in the 2017-2020 timeframe, we find some of the most iconic institutions in the whole world, such as Apple, BBVA, Bayer, Boeing, Credit Swiss, Deloitte, Dolce & Gabbana, Facebook, Goldman Sachs, Google, Huawei, Marriott, McDonalds, McKinsey, Odebrecht, Petrobras, Procter & Gamble, Target, United and UPS- companies which are all most definitely being led by mature, highly-experienced managers.[5]

Are corporations the only ones who suffer crises? Not at all. In the last five years, many public organizations and persons have been hit by severe crises. We could mention such prestigious organizations as the IMF (International Monetary Fund), the Bank of England, the Israeli Prime Minister, the Mayor of Toronto, the CIA, the Organizing Committee for the Brazilian 2014 Soccer World Cup, the International Olympic Committee and the NBA; the British and the Spanish Royal Families; NGO's such us Greenpeace, Doctors without Borders, the Red Cross and the Boy Scouts; and major Universities such as Penn State, Syracuse, Duke, Virginia Tech, Oxford or the Madrid Complutense.

Do crises actually hurt an institution's intangible image or is the damage limited to that of a tangibly economic nature? The drop in a corporation's stock market capitalization can be as much as 50%. The Gulf of Mexico oil spill caused by British Petroleum's oil rig explosion, triggered by its desire to save money — by not spending half-a-million dollars for the proper safety valve — caused damages which reached over $20,000,000,000 (yes, that's right — there are 10 zeros in that number) that BP had to pay out to the victims and spend on the environmental clean-up. In 2007, Merck, the pharmaceutical giant, had to pay a $4.5 billion settlement to the fami-

---

[5] In 2017, United Airlines suffered a traumatic reputational crisis due to the way a passenger was violently removed from flight 3411 from Chicago to Louisville, after refusing to accept a change to the next day's flight and USD 1,000 in compensation. Videos filmed by other passengers and posted on social media were very damaging not only because they showed unnecessary violence but mainly because they contradicted the first official version that it was the passenger who was impolite and aggressive; and even the second response, in which United's CEO defended its personnel in an internal memo that was then leaked to the media. This episode shows that crises and mistakes also happen to good companies and good leaders. In fact, United's CEO Oscar Muñoz was doing a great job: he took over a company in crisis (in 2005, United had been permitted to default on its pension obligations after filing for bankruptcy and had slashed the retirement plans of many of its 134,000 current and former employees. His predecessor had to resign because of corruption); he was able to reach an agreement with the unions and put the company back into profit. He even won the PRWeek prize "Communicator of the Year" in March 2017.

lies of 3,100 people who died of heart attacks or strokes allegedly caused by Vioxx. Facebook was fined 5 billion dollars for the systematic violation of the privacy of its users. . According to the 2019 report by IBM's Ponemon Institute, the average cost of a cyberattack is nearly $ 4 million (an average of $ 150 for each individual piece of data stolen).

This negative economic impact also affects non-profit organizations: the sexual abuse crisis cost US Catholic dioceses and religious congregations $ 3 billion (about 1 billion of which went to lawyers).

How long could the effects of a crisis last? Crises leave deep and long-lasting scars. Their effects can last many, many years, especially when they leave victims and were not well resolved.[6]

---

[6] The Bhopal disaster, a gas leak from a Union Carbide pesticide plant in India in December 1984, is considered the world's worst industrial disaster. The official immediate death toll was 2,259. The government of Madhya Pradesh confirmed a total of 3,787 deaths related to the gas leak and 558,125 injured. The cause of the tragedy remains disputed: the Indian government and local activists argue that slack management and deferred maintenance triggered the disaster, while the Union Carbide Corporation (UCC) maintains it was caused by an act of sabotage by a disgruntled employee. The factory's owners were UCC (50.9%) and Indian Government-controlled banks and the Indian public holding (49.1%). In 1989, UCC paid US$470 million to settle litigation stemming from the disaster. The company stated that the restitution paid "was US$120 million more than plaintiffs' lawyers had told U.S. courts was fair" and that the Indian Supreme Court stated in its opinion that "compensation levels under the settlement were far greater than would normally be payable under Indian law." Union Carbide also undertook other steps to provide continuing aid to the victims of the Bhopal disaster: they contributed US$ 90 million to the building of a local hospital for the treatment of heart, lung and eye problems; a US$2.2 million grant to establish a vocational-technical center in Bhopal, a US$5 million donation to the Indian Red Cross after the disaster; and it developed a Responsible Care system with other members of the chemical industry, designed to help prevent such an event in the future. Despite all that, more than 30 years have passed and the wounds have not healed.

Managing and communicating in crisis

As Pérez Latre has written, a crisis is not a communication problem, but one of governance and management where communication can contribute effectively to its solution. Crises are the responsibility and competence of the one who governs the organization, not of its communications director.

Crisis management can be described as a systematic way of analysis and work that allows a crisis to be faced in the best possible way: identifying the weak points of the organization in time, introducing the necessary changes so that the weaknesses do not turn into crises, planning the institutional response by communicating with the organization's stakeholders during the crisis and, finally, evaluating the response of the organization and leading the post-crisis recovery.

González Herrero and Pratt have defined three causes, which have led to the ever-increasing importance of communication in crisis management. The first cause is the increased attention which the media pay to scandal, polemics, and disaster situations of all kinds. Second is the increased likelihood that a business may be accused by a whistleblower and that such accusations will be received with credibility. The third cause is that the wrongdoings of other managers and corporations within the business community have had a detrimental impact on the reputation of the business community as a whole.

There is a close link between crisis communication and crisis management. Crisis management are described by Gigliotti & Jason, as «an organization's capacity to quickly, efficiently and effectively roll out the required emergency operations to reduce the public health threats as well as any and all security issues for individuals, the loss of public or private property or the negative consequences upon the company's normal operations.»

On the other hand, crisis communication is *a systematic analysis and procedural approach* that enables companies to face the relational aspects of a crisis with its stakeholders. Crisis communication aims to reduce, or even eliminate, the negative effects on the relationship with the organization's priority stakeholders. This requires an ability to communicate the institutional response to a crisis quickly and effectively.

The concept of crisis management is much broader than that of simple crisis communication, yet we should not consider them separate activities, as the informational task (communicating the facts and the measures that have been taken) is one of crisis management's most essential elements.[7]

Moreover, if the aspect that defines the crisis itself is precisely the threat that exists to the existing relationship between an institution and its stakeholders, solving the problem and communicating the solution to the problem are two elements that must always go hand-in-hand.

To sum up, both extremes must be avoided: you should not underestimate the role of communication by neglecting the stakeholders and attempting to resolve the problem without them; but nor should you prioritize the protection of the corporate image even over the first task of solving the problem.

In the first case, the mistake lies in overlooking that even if the problem is a technical issue, the relationship with the institution's stakeholders is not; a crisis will never be overcome without the consensus of the stakeholders (and quite often indeed, their active participation in the solution may be required), and this will never be reached unless there is a constant communication flow.[8]

---

[7] An example of how communication is a decisive element when facing a natural disaster was evident during the tsunami on December 26, 2004 that affected 11 countries and left more than 225,000 dead. The 2005 Red Cross annual report on disasters in the world stated that the scientists in the area had the technology to register the force that triggered the tsunami but lacked the means to inform everyone on how the situation was going to develop and how to respond. On the other hand, communication was the determining factor in respect of worldwide donations and offers of help and support for the victims.

[8] In the summer of 2006, New England and some parts of Canada suffered a severe electrical blackout. It was, obviously, a technical crisis and as such the power utilities were responsible for fixing it; but the most relevant aspect was that which dealt with the personal consequences, especially those people living in urban areas. From this point of view, and far from overlooking the problem resolution, the public authorities spent much of their time and resources in citizen communication to avoid the pitfalls that could have been caused by a lack of information and which could have had far-reaching effects, much more severe than the technical aspects themselves.

The second mistake is being worried mainly by the consequences of the crisis on the corporate reputation, and thus communicating that the problem is resolved or is near resolution to soften protesters and gain some time, when in reality it is not. Unfortunately, there are many institutions that, when faced with a crisis will deny the evidence itself and downplay its true importance. This mistake comes more often from a management decision rather than one taken by the communication department. When corporate communication is poor, it is because the corporate governance is weak. Crisis management is the responsibility of those that are managing the institution because it requires decision-making that is directly related to the institution as a whole. The institution's top management should handle a crisis: the corporate CEO, the SME's managing director, the medical director of a hospital, the president of a university.

Certainly, they must delegate everything that is technical (it does not make sense for the CEO to join the rescue teams), but they decide the scope of operations ("spend what you have to spend, but save those people"), and they lead the communication initiatives.[9]

Who should be in charge of communication during a crisis? In general, terms, we would say that it should be the communications director. In fact, this responsibility tends to be one of his primary roles. To effectively perform this role, he or she must be in permanent contact with the authority and have full access to any and all information. However, as the relationship with stakeholders is a primary factor in the solution of this specific problem and a single, agreed-upon action plan is indispensable, it would be more precise to state that crisis communication is also one of the crisis manager's main tasks, at least in the most important aspects within that specific crisis. In other words, *crisis communication really is in the hands of the institution's maximum authority and cannot be delegated.*

The institutional authority would be making a major mistake if more attention is given to the technical aspects of a crisis than to

---

[9] Going back to the blackout case we mentioned above, while the technical solution was entrusted to the experts, citizen communication was managed directly by the Mayors of New York City and the other major metropolitan areas affected by the situation.

the communication aspects. Herein lies one of the main difficulties in crisis communication: its guidelines are set or defined by institutional communicators, but to put it in place effectively requires authority and power that go well beyond the competencies of any communications department. This is especially valid when we are looking at crisis prevention. How could the communications director of a bank prevent leakage of news about the improper use of funds by the bank's chairman, considering that it is not in his or her hands to avoid such misconduct? Most probably, he or she learnt about it only through the media...

To solve this dilemma requires top management to be directly involved in ordinary communication activities, and even more so in times of crisis. As Schmertz — a corporate manager, not a communicator — says, «Communications is a management aspect which is far too important to be delegated to lower level employees».

From this perspective, in which the emphasis is placed on prevention, crisis management looks towards the future, trying to anticipate the dangers that could affect the institution. If you had to sum up its essence in a slogan, you could say that *crisis management is about preparing for the worst.* Its purpose is to anticipate, prevent and anticipate; that is, to identify the risks, determine the probability that they may trigger a crisis, reduce them, and determine the responses for each crisis situation.

In this sense, the preventive management of a crisis combats ambiguity -one of the main enemies of managers-, presenting measures of immediate application, previously approved by the management. In fact, the institution can only respond effectively to the problem as soon as it arises, through a clear and articulated distribution of the responsibilities of each one, preparing plans of operational solutions for crisis circumstances and information on available resources.

Ethics and crisis management

As we explained in the introduction, crisis management and communication are a practical science, based upon prudence and common sense, with a foundation of solid professional and ethical principles. It requires a certain amount of intellectual preparation by those who are familiar with the organization, its context and the specific problem. Crisis response plans are operational guidelines, not a series of automatic measures to be applied immediately in all cases without deliberation.

As in any practical science, it is based on the experience gained from real cases that demonstrate the benefits of following a few guidelines and the painful consequences of ignoring them. Its strength resides precisely in this point: these guidelines work, and their efficiency has been proven time and time again in many real crises.

At the same time, in a way, these guidelines establish the rules: the rules of managing and communicating in a crisis produce results because they are in harmony with the ethical nature of the human being and human society. *They are useful but the source of their value does not come from their usefulness.*

For example, the "never lie" principle is based on the experience which has been gained from living through many, many crisis situations in which a lie, even the apparently most innocuous , may have represented a very serious mistake that was never forgiven. Nevertheless, the strength as a set of rules does not arise from the negative consequences of having broken the rule but rather from the moral requirement of always telling the truth. In the same way, "protect your people" is another basic principle of crisis management, and if it is not practiced, the reaction of the employees will be very negative; but we do it not out of fear, but out of conviction.

In short, crisis management and communication best practices work because they are based on human nature. It would be wrong to regard them as a selection of coercive legal or regulatory guidelines created by political or professional consensus, and, worse still, as a series of techniques adopted according to a mere criterion of effectiveness. Certainly, some of these guidelines are also required by law, and many are also very effective. But their binding force does not derive from the norm or utility, but from ethical foundations based on moral common sense: avoid doing evil to others, respect their rights , do not lie or cheat, comply with the law, obey authority, help those in need, be upright and fair, assume responsibility of your acts, etc. For this reason, they should be put into practice even when the law does not impose them or even when it might seem more useful – at least in the short term – to act differently.

What Covey explains about people can perfectly apply to organizations of all types:

> You always reap what you sow; there is no shortcut. This principle is also true, ultimately, in human behavior, in human relationships. They, too, are natural systems based on the The Law of the Harvest. In the short run, in an artificial social system such as school, you may be able to get by if you learn how to manipulate the man-made rules, to "play the game." In most one-shot or short-lived human interactions, you can use the personality ethic to get by and to make favorable impressions through charm and skill and pretending to be interested in other people's hobbies. You can pick up quick, easy techniques that may work in short-term situations. However, secondary traits alone have no permanent worth in long-term relationships. Eventually, if there is not deep integrity and fundamental character strength, the challenges of life will cause true motives to surface and human relationship failure will replace short-term success. Many people with secondary greatness — that is, social recognition for their talents — lack primary greatness or goodness in their character. Sooner or later, you will see this in every long-term relationship they have, whether it is with a business associate, a spouse, a friend, or a teenage child going through an identity crisis. It is character that communicates most eloquently. As Emerson once put it, «What you are shouts so loudly in my ears that I cannot hear what you say».

Ethically based behavior will give companies considerable advantages. Firstly, your stakeholders will recognize this. Many crisis managers have experienced that a virtuous response usually helps generate more support during a crisis, and cooperation for rebuilding and renewal afterwards.

Secondly, even reporters, who in the midst of a crisis often seem to be out for blood, will eventually respect those who have assumed the mission of doing things the way they should be done above all else.

Later, this type of behavior creates a good precedent, which is admired and imitated: it is the *exemplarity* so eloquently defended by the Spanish philosopher Javier Gomá, which is essential to lead a change.

Lastly, ethics gives consistency to my response to a crisis. I do things according to principles, which are not mine: they are engraved in people's hearts. If I do this, others – from employees to customers – will know what I will do next, and that is very reassuring. Deep down, ethics is like the keel: perhaps it weighs and prevents me from anchoring close to the beach, but it is essential to be able to set the course when the wind is not coming from the stern.

Ultimately, an ethical response to the crisis is more likely to help the organization to survive, and it also has the quality of promoting internal renewal. As Schwartz, Cragg & Hoffman put it, «The success or failure of the crisis response is not just a matter of technical expertise, but also of the extent to which you have a solid ethical foundation». This is especially valid in crises due to unethical behavior: ethical behavior is the best prevention, while behavior without moral references favors the crisis; and the most effective way to learn from a crisis is moral regeneration. [10]

On the contrary, companies and organizations where a fundamental ethical duty is violated normally end up discovering an endless string of irregularities. [11]

---

[10] In the section dedicated to statistics, we mention the explosion of an oil rig in the Gulf of Mexico due to an ethical error: wanting to save half a million dollars while putting the platform's security at risk. To respond to the crisis, BP launched a serious and profound ethical reform, an essential requirement to really turn over a new leaf.

[11] In 2013, a *Los Angeles Times* investigation of the US bank Wells Fargo revealed intense pressure on its managers to achieve sales with extremely aggressive and even mathematically impossible goals. After publication of the article, the bank made only nominal efforts to reform the company's sales culture, but it maintained its reputation. In 2014, *The Banker* named Wells Fargo the World's Most Valuable Banking Brand for the second year in a row; and in 2015, the company was ranked the 22nd most admired company in the world and the 7th most respected company in the world. The real problems began in September 2016, when the Consumer Financial Protection Office announced

Nevertheless, the ethical decision is to do the right thing above all else, even if the consequences are hard. As Bennis has pointed out, «It is not enough for a leader to do things right; he (or she) must do the right thing». Doing what is good simply because of its practical benefits is an ethical contradiction.

Herein lies one of the perplexing aspects of crisis management. Paraphrasing the title of Alistair MacIntyre's outstanding book, *Three Rival Versions of Moral Enquiry*, we could say that there are three rival versions of crisis management and communication based on the philosophical foundation of each (in other words, its vision of human beings and of the world). One version has a pragmatic root that prescribes behavior that works (or describes behaviors that have worked). The second has a more legal nuance, its recommendations are based on the law or, at least, on the social consensus as stated by public opinion. The third, which we will be explore and recommend in this book, has an ethical basis – that is, related to the nature of human beings and society.

It may seem that all three approaches are in harmony because there are many cases in which, in the end, they result in the same practical suggestions. Yet each of the approaches bases its suggestions on very different reasons, and only one is a moral compass. We must ask ourselves: what should we do when they do not coincide? What is my primary goal: to do what I have to do, do what the law requires, or to meet the expectations of my stakeholders?

In this book, we defend the idea that doing good for utilitarian reasons or legal reasons is not good enough. In other words, if in a crisis, my spotlight is utilitarian, or my focus is compliance, I

---

that the bank would be fined for illegal activities. The regulator discovered that its employees opened more than 1.5 million savings accounts, half a million credit cards and thousands of insurance policies, without the authorization of clients, to ensure their bonuses. The consequences were dire: in fines, settlements and reimbursements, in 2018 Wells Fargo paid out nearly $ 3 billion, 5,000 commercial agents were laid off, its CEO was forced to resign, and the Federal Reserve prohibited it from increasing its assets due to years of misconduct, until the bank resolved its internal problems. In December 2018, the company's Standard & Poor's credit rating was A-, while in 2007 it was the only bank with an AAA rating.

will most probably focus on short term benefits and completely fail in my ethical duties.

But I don't hide the fact that there are 'other' approaches. At the opposite end of this spectrum, quite a few crisis managers resemble one of the characters in John Grisham's best sellers, who describes himself with these words: "I'm an agent, a contractor, a freelancer with a specialty. I get hired by big companies to put out fires. They screw up, they realize their mistakes before the lawyers do, so they hire me to quietly enter the picture, tidy up their mess, and, hopefully, save them a bunch of money. My services are in great demand. My name may be Max Pace and it may be something else. It doesn't matter. Who I am and where I come from are irrelevant. What's important here is that I have been hired by a large company to put out a fire."

Throughout this book, we will encounter many ethical dilemmas: what to do when I realize that a batch of one of my products is toxic or defective; how to react if I find out that a boss is abusing an employee; who to speak to if I discover a criminal accounting irregularity that nobody has detected yet; and so many more cases taken from real life. The answer will be different depending on who I am and what my corporate culture is.

This ethical approach is deeply related to the organization's culture. Crises are moments of truth: situations in which our stakeholders see something which was covered-up and unknown. As Dezenhall & Weber stated in a humorous fashion, «if conventional public relations has been disparaged as telling pretty lies, then crisis management should be praised as telling ugly truths. » However, it is quite difficult to change course on the spot and start acting ethically when the organization's culture usually proceeds in the opposite direction.

Corporate culture and reputation

The culture of an organization is formed by the set of written and unwritten rules that indicate the correct way to think, evaluate and act, and constitute the basis of corporate identity. The stronger the culture, the less important rules and organization charts are: everyone knows what to do in an unexpected situation because they have interiorized criteria and priorities and can apply them to the case even without receiving specific guidance.

An examination of the institutional culture is useful because it reveals that some are more crisis-prone than others. For example, those in which power is concentrated in just a few hands, or those that are overly bureaucratic in nature, governed by strictly written rules and endless procedures, are more vulnerable and fragile.

The success or failure of any crisis response will always depend on how well it fits into the organization's culture. Hence, managing to avoid a conflict at any cost may not always be deemed as successful crisis management. Sometimes it may be absolutely unavoidable to face a conflict or a crisis in order to defend the institution's very identity. The ethically responsible attitude does not consist in trying to avoid all conflicts, but rather in giving equitable solutions to such cases. If a situation were to be considered unjust, the most desirable conduct would not be simply to sit back and take no action, but rather to publicly say what we should stand for and actively promote change.

Furthermore, in those cases in which the reigning values are felt to be unjust, it is absolutely necessary to actually provoke the crisis. «Breaking this type of consensus will be the greatest service that one can provide to the overall cause of human dignity. Breaking this apparent harmony may create problems for us with the current public opinion. But it is more important to feel comfortable with our own conscious and with God himself, » as Navas reminds us.

Some vulnerabilities also have to do with local cultures. Social sanction for a lie, or the importance of social hierarchy vary from country to country. For instance, there are places where superiors have to confirm the decisions of subordinates: the harmony of the group is more important than the expression of individual opinions, and there is a strong sense of shame at losing face. These traits can result in a corporate culture imbued with obedience and loyalty to the organization.[12] Such a configuration could compro-

---

[12] In 2009, the Toshiba Corporation appointed a new CEO. His predecessor had changed Toshiba's original corporate culture, in which respectful disagreement was welcome, into a managerial style where the pressure to meet unrealistic goals was enormous, communication was

mise the internal system of accounting checks and balances. But it is not the country to blame but the company: external influence can be substantial, but it never eliminates freedom.

For better or for worse, a crisis may be what has to happen, finally leading to reforms that, although long-viewed as necessary by all, have never been carried out.

In these situations, crises are golden opportunities, because they unveil serious problems nobody wants to admit. [13] In addition,

---

strictly vertical, and disagreement was banished. The new CEO put even more pressure on his subordinates to achieve higher profits. In January 2015, following an anonymous tip, the Japanese financial regulator FSA launched an investigation into Toshiba's accounting. Toshiba's first reaction was to initiate an internal investigation, which concluded by saying that «accounting irregularities had been detected (...) in relation to certain company projects,» so it decided to establish an independent investigation committee. The committee found emails indicating that wrongful accounting practices were voluntary. When this finding was released, Toshiba's stock price fell 40%. Two months later, the independent report concluded that between 2008 and 2014, during the tenures of the three CEOs who had departed from Toshiba's original culture, the company had overstated its earnings by approximately € 1.2 billion. All three were accused of pressuring managers to achieve goals so high that they could not be achieved without committing fraud. The investigation panel concluded that Toshiba's corporate culture, which required obedience to superiors, was an important factor allowing fraudulent accounting practices to emerge. The culture operated at the level of the business unit heads and at all levels of authority. After the resignation of most of the top managers, other errors were exposed; as a result, on August 1, 2017, Toshiba was officially removed from Nikkei 225, the stock index of the best Japanese companies.

[13] Didi Chuxing is the largest taxi company in China, with 30 million daily trips and around 450 million users in more than 400 cities in China. Late at night on August 24, 2018, a Didi taxi driver killed a young female passenger on her way to a birthday party. It was the second murder committed by a company driver in three months. The young woman had time to send a distress message to her friends, but the company refused to give the requested information either to them or to the police, arguing that they are only obliged to do so 4 hours after a disappearance. Shortly after the police detained the suspect, Didi posted a public apology letter on Weibo. This apology, rather than helping, further aggravated the problem. First, people realized that Didi was

they reverse the burden of proof: everyone agrees that something bold must be done. Crises enable the launching of reforms that would otherwise meet insurmountable resistance.[14]

Identity also has consequences in communication: the two are intimately entwined. Paraphrasing the old philosophical adage, we could say *comunicare sequitur esse*, the way of communicating depends on the way of being. Communication emanates from corporate identity and culture, since its essential objective is that the public image of the institution should faithfully reflect reality.

At the end of the day, communicating in a crisis is the litmus test for corporate communication. Its raw material is the corporation's reputation, understood by Fombrun & Rindova as "the collective representation of a firm's past actions and results that describes the firm's ability to deliver valued outcomes to multiple stakeholders. It gauges a firm's relative standing both internally

---

simply copying the last apology letter they published after the first murder in May (which Didi had removed so that no one would notice the copy and paste). Second, Didi lied by saying that the suspect forged the car's license number, so as not to have to take responsibility, but this was refuted by local police. Third, Didi executives took three days to make a public apology, but only in writing and via Weibo: the company did not contact the victim's family or make a public appearance. Finally, Didi's refusal to give information to the victims' friends or to the police was an indication of a bad corporate culture. This kind of reform could and should be undertaken without waiting for the authorities or the pressure of public opinion to make it happen.

[14] In 2011, McKinsey faced a serious reputational problem, when a leaked recording of a telephone conversation demonstrating that a former CEO, already estranged from the firm, was trading with privileged information. Dominic Barton, CEO since 2009, took advantage of the scandal to solve the underlying problem: the company had grown so much and so fast that it had lost what had made it great: the five principles that Martin Bower had coined 50 years ago: «1) Put the client's interests above those of McK or the consultant; 2) Adhere to the highest standards of truthfulness, integrity and trust; 3) Protect confidential customer information; 4) Maintain independence of judgment; and 5) Provide only services that add value.» Despite notable internal resistance from partners, Barton preferred to eliminate practices that contradicted those principles and to preserve the firm's reputation, even if that meant earning less.

with employees and externally with its stakeholders, in both its competitive and institutional environments."

Crisis communication is therefore the concrete way of preserving reputation when it is in danger. Reputation is what my actions say about me, not my image. Sometimes, to be consistent, we have to maintain our reputation, who we are, and at the same time harm our image: do what we have to do, because that is what someone who discovers a criminal in the company does: report it, even if it will be in the newspapers. I will try not to have it appear in the media, of course, but I'm not going to let the perpetrator get away with it, so it doesn't get in the press.

On the other hand, those who consider communication (in times of peace and in times of crisis) as corporate makeup, a purely aesthetic exercise, betray the true nature of communication as a manifestation of social responsibility towards stakeholders.

This is precisely the link between ordinary communication and crisis communication: to be aligned with and united to the culture of the organization. Crises test the robustness of the seams between communication areas that are not linked internally. For instance, when investor relations, media relations and internal communications are not under the same umbrella, disagreements and cacophonies are inevitable.

Emphasizing the unity between ordinary communication and crisis communication also serves to reject the practice - illegitimate, in my view - of using different methods and standards for each case. Some companies, for example, behave with rectitude in normal life, but when faced with a serious threat, they follow the "anything goes" rule; and to avoid contaminating their internal staff, they subcontract to an agency that solves the problem without asking how, but only how much. The flaw is not in the hand that wields the wrong instrument, but in the mind that directs it.

The Story: acting and communicating[15]

The Chipotle Mexican Grill restaurant chain started the "new fast food" system. Under the motto «Food with integrity», and using high quality fresh ingredients, classic cooking methods, distinctive interior design and friendly employees, they serve a menu focused on burritos, tacos and salads. In 2015 it had more than two thousand restaurants in the United States, Canada, the United Kingdom, France and Germany, and revenues of $4.5 billion.

On September 11, 2015, 64 people fell ill with salmonella in Minnesota, and 45 cases were attributable to the consumption of tomatoes at local Chipotle restaurants. The intoxication passed unnoticed by the media.

A month later, a regular client became ill after eating a bowl of chicken, made with 21 fresh ingredients. The doctor told him that he had a bacterium called "E. coli 026" and that he could have contracted it with one of those 21 ingredients. It wasn't the only case: 46 more people who had eaten in Chipotle days earlier got sick too, and 20 of them had to be hospitalized.

As a result of this contamination, in early November Chipotle closed its 43 restaurants in Oregon and Washington State to try to identify the source of E. coli and to disinfect the premises. The media had a field day with this story.

On December 21, the U.S. health care agency announced that it was investigating an outbreak of what appears to be a different version of E. coli that had affected five people in the states of Illinois, Maryland, and Pennsylvania who had also eaten in Chipotle.

After some research, Chipotle discovered that one of its major suppliers was the origin of E. coli. These microbes can be transmitted to crops in irrigation water, or when animals defecate in fields, or if manure is not processed effectively. When food is cooked at sufficiently high temperatures or disinfected properly, the bacteria disappear, but because many of Chipotle's ingredients such as tomatoes, lettuce and coriander are fresh, the cleaning process is more difficult.

---

[15] Episode documented by Marcela Girón.

Chipotle was very diligent in its research, but the company had difficulty in identifying which batches of raw materials went to each store at any given time. The problem was traceability from the farm to the point of consumption. The chain decided to implement a stricter and more sophisticated food safety plan that went beyond compliance with industry standards and laws. They hired a specialist, who recommended changes at every step of the Chipotle system, and was intended to help their suppliers test DNA for products prior to collection in order to discover potential pathogens. The recommendations also allowed for early preparation of food and in more easily purifiable places other than places of consumption, and a stricter process of washing, disinfecting, controlling, cutting and packaging. Some tasks were moved to centralized kitchens, etc.

When the plan was ready, the CEO of Chipotle attended *The Today Show* and apologized to the people who had got sick. He did the same on Facebook and Twitter, and described the strict new food safety program. A week later, Chipotle placed a full-page ad in the newspapers signed by the CEO that read: "The fact that someone got sick from eating at Chipotle is completely unacceptable to me, and I'm deeply sorry. As a result, we are committed to being known as food safety leaders, as we are already accredited as the fast-food chain with the highest quality ingredients".

According to Grabowski, what makes the Chipotle crisis unusual is that most companies « speak loudly» but their actions are not as loud as their words, and Chipotle did the opposite. «His actions were blunt, but they communicated them poorly»-

Chipotle was right to make a sincere apology, but he made it late. He waited until December to appear on television, social media and newspapers rather than from the first moment that the bacteria infected the first customers; furthermore, company representatives never met the victims. Communicating your decisions is an inseparable part of your response.

CHAPTER THREE

Principles

Nothing is more practical than a good principle. In this chapter we shall be looking into the principles that provide meaning and sense to the best practices which will be further developed in the following chapters. These principles are the origin of the practices' strength as well as the criteria to which they should be applied. Understanding them will also help the manager to be — and not simply to act as — a good crisis manager. In the heat of a crisis, it is vital to make the right decision about which way to proceed and not simply because one has learned the tactic to be used, but rather because it is a way of being.

Address perceptions more than facts

To properly understand a corporate crisis, the most critical perspective is to *accept the stakeholder's point of view*. By doing so — and only by doing so —will you be able to properly evaluate the facts. The facts alone are relatively important, but the manner in which your stakeholders perceive these facts is even more important. With this in mind, a time of crisis often necessitates that greater weight be given to the stakeholders' perception than to the actual facts themselves. It is often public perception that causes the crisis.

This does not mean that a crisis is a completely subjective event. A crisis, a true crisis, is triggered by some specific event that leads to the ensuing public uproar. Here I would like to stress that the perceptions themselves should be considered as hard facts, in the same manner as all other physical, tangible and measurable facts. The term "fact" includes both the material and the sociological events, in which the context plays a major role.[16]

By applying this approach, you will avoid making the common mistake of judging that the facts are favorable for your institution, and thus conclude that it is not necessary to communicate with all thestakeholders, nor address the false facts as baseless accusations. When, in reality, by failing to communicate, you may actually trigger a real crisis.

This happens especially in crises in which a person is involved: such crises happen because there is an actor determined to create a state of public opinion contrary to a specific institution, and seek his own political, economic or ideological gain. As long as there is an accusation in the air and someone defending it, the organization needs to defend itself. It doesn't matter that the accusation is false, what should stimulate our response is that the accusation is credible (that there are people who believe it): in other words, it is a perception, not a fact.

Whether it is accurate or not, the stakeholder's perception is reality for him. If the public believes a risk exists, it can be expected to act according to that belief. Seeger recommends that if the public believes that a crisis is severe, it is also important to acknowledge that belief and respond accordingly.. In addition,

---

[16] In 1999, several groups of Belgian youngsters fell ill after drinking Coca-Cola. The company was heavily criticized for not having reacted quickly or effectively enough. In experts' opinion, the prime factor that led to the adverse reaction was how they misjudged the doubts that the general public had regarding food and beverage companies. According to Dezenhall & Weber, «Coca-Cola attributed the illness to causes ranging from contaminated carbon dioxide to psychosomatic hysteria. On the clinical level, they may have been right. On an emotional frequency –the wavelength that matters in times of crisis – they were wrong. [...] Coca-Cola failed to appreciate the degree to which resentment can trigger a witch hunt. The mightiest institutions ironically become the most vulnerable under such conditions.»

Lukaszewski, one of the gurus of our field, has even dared to break it down into percentages, and in what he calls the *mathematics of reality*, 15% corresponds to the basic facts and data, and 85% to raw emotions and perceptions.

In this sense, *the severity of a crisis is directly proportional to its public perception.* Public opinion is formed by perception, not reality. Regardless of what is really happening internally, the way the public perceives a situation becomes the reality which a company has to address.

There are cases in which stakeholders may not take an extremely grave fact seriously, as it has not been perceived as such. Conversely, something of much lesser impact may explode into a full-blown crisis, if – rightly or wrongly – it is perceived as such by the public. For instance, if a tax inspector, a journalist or a stock market analyst sees some suspicious accounting in an institution's books, the company's management cannot fail to respond immediately even though no unlawful acts have been proven. It would be totally unacceptable to stand back and watch when such an abnormality occurs, even though the institution may feel it is unsubstantiated. The problem is real from the very instant in which people consider that it is real, regardless of its true impact before that point of time.

The same is true of the corporate response. Its effectiveness is not only measured by objective criteria, but also by the way it is perceived by different audiences.[17]

Bear in mind that a crisis implies significant uncertainty regarding the future. Your stakeholders wish to know what is going on and why it is happening; but they are just as eager to find out

---

[17] The Malaysia Airlines Flight MH370 accident, which we will discuss in detail later, shows how important it is to take into account the perceptions of victims. The airline made a great logistical effort: it provided room and board for all victims' relatives in Kuala Lumpur and Beijing while the search continued. However, by sharing few updates, withholding relevant information, and failing to highlight the victims in its public statements, Malaysia Airlines created the perception that they were a secondary consideration, and that the company was more concerned with how the accident would affect business and their relationship with the authorities.

whether it may happen again, in that same institution or in any other in that same sector. It is in this direction that a solution must be designed and applied, easing people's fears and expectations. In fact, the public will not be able to move ahead and finalize their perception regarding the crisis until they feel reasonably sure that this troubling episode will not repeat itself in the foreseeable future. Only then will people be able to get this incident out of their minds and consider forgiving those they blame for the crisis.

Perceptions are also important because the notion of risk is closely related to the feeling of uncertainty. The perception of risk as perceived by the stakeholders is subjective in nature. It depends on a wide range of factors: age (younger people see themselves beyond any danger), intellectual level (generally speaking, the higher the intellectual level is, the more likely people are to reject superstitions) and gender (scientific research has shown that males tend to have a lower perception of risks than females). In addition, the frequency of the risk itself and the sensation that it is voluntary or controlled also have a subjective impact.

The two key parameters for risk assessment are familiarity and control. When activity involving risk is an everyday occurrence, the danger is perceived to be less. For example, many people are afraid of flying but drive their car without due care, despite the fact that statistics show the risk of an accident is higher for those who travel by road than for those who travel by plane. The same happens with domestic accidents: they are more frequent than work-related accidents, and yet no one feels in danger at home.

Second, control. When we think that we are in control of what we do, we feel more secure in do in doing it, even though in reality we are not. The more control we have, the safer we feel... not based on facts. Many inexperienced drivers feel safer when they drive than when someone more skilled is at the wheel.

There must be harmony between the corporate response and the public perception, but this is often complicated by the organizations' natural tendency to assess risks based upon their own objective and/or even scientific criteria. It is much easier for organizations to rationalize processes and focus entirely on their standard set of measurable statistics and indicators, than to consider all the varied appraisals, which change from one person to the next. In fact, most risk reports tend to be based upon measurable facts rather than anything tied to perceptions at all.

Nonetheless, a multitude of catastrophes caused by human calculation and error have dampened a once-hearty trust in the ability of science to forecast and solve problems. Nobody, be they our employees, our local communities, our clients or the media addresses any crisis based upon objective scientific criteria. Thus, scientific risk assessment should always be measured from a human judgment angle.

Furthermore, science is seldom unanimous in a crisis. The covid-19 pandemic has once again made manifest that science is not certain. Wise people with Nobel prizes on their shelves defended contradictory positions based on scientific data; and media experts (perhaps not very profound but dangerously good disseminators) had more followers than true savants.

Accepting uncertainty and ambiguity is one of the best practices in crisis management and communication. Inevitably, one should accept the fact that critical situations are full of uncertainty and confusion. Companies should follow Seeger's advice:

> Crises and disasters are, by definition, abnormal, dynamic, and unpredictable events. Crisis spokespersons, however, often feel a need to be overly certain and overly reassuring. This may be largely a consequence of a belief that the public cannot accept uncertainty situations and needs certainty in the face of a crisis, even when information is simply unavailable. However, overly reassuring statements in the face of an inherently uncertain and equivocal situation may reduce a spokesperson's credibility. This is particularly the case as a crisis evolves in an unexpected, unpredictable way. In addition, over-reassuring statements that lack credibility may even create higher levels of alarm.

Therefore, forthrightness in dealing with the public implies explaining the facts as they really and truly are. A best practice of crisis communication, then, is to acknowledge the uncertainty inherent in the situation with statements such as, "The situation is fluid," and, "We do not yet have all of the facts." This lack of assertiveness allows the communicator to refine the message as more information becomes available and to avoid statements that are likely to be proven inaccurate later in the day.

Take care: the most ethical approach requires us to be assertive when we can, and recognize our lack of information when that is the case, because it contributes to the complete understanding of an issue by posing alternative views that are based on complete and unbiased data that aim to inform. Ambiguity is unethical if it poses alternative interpretations using biased or incomplete information that aims to deceive.[18]

If the situation is muddied, it is far from honest to assert clear statements when nothing at all is really clear.

Listen to protesters

When a local community begins mobilizing against a polluting and toxic industry, it all starts with doubts about whether health hazards are real or just unfounded assumptions. At that stage, people seek the opinion of doctors, scientists and other experts, and meanwhile anxiety and fear predominate.

That situation, Herbert says, is not eternal. Soon fear turns into anger, and the protest begins to mobilize. This change from calm to protest is gradual: people overcome fear by taking an active stance, and raising their voices, first for their own benefit (to convince themselves that at least "they are doing something") and then by fighting.

One of the most surprising aspects within the scope of crisis management is finding yourself unexpectedly in front of an ugly crowd. Why are these people so upset? Why are these reporters asking personally insulting questions? Why are our employees attacking us this way? Why are the posts in social media so aggressive-

---

[18] More than 20 years ago, Ulmer, Sellnow & Seeger documented intentional ambiguity and therefore clearly dishonest practices by the American tobacco industry regarding how nicotine is harmful to smokers' health: they commissioned false scientific reports and financed associations that defended the tobacco industry under the guise of being unbiased, lobbying, etc. Unfortunately, this is not a unique case.

ly against us? These are bewildering experiences, especially when we haven't done anything wrong or maybe it is only the first time we've done something wrong. Understanding how to handle yourself in front of a group of people who are fiercely against you is one of the most necessary steps to be able to communicate effectively during a crisis.

Please bear in mind that the public in general may not be willing to favor our institutions. Even if it is the very first time that our organization has made a mistake, we must realize that the public has most likely suffered negative consequences of similar mistakes made by others in our own sector. The public has every reason to be upset. Corporations, companies and both local and national authorities have tried to cover up mistakes, kept all the potential risks under cover, misled and even brazenly lied to them. Therefore, people feel that they have had the wool pulled over their eyes more than once and are simply not ready to trust anyone anymore.

The following statement is a fact: even if most companies clearly state their commitment to serve their employees, clients, shareholders and local communities, and want to establish a win-win relation for all parties, when something bad happens many of them do exactly the opposite. They tend to resort to complete silence, hiding any evidence, launching smoke screens and thinly veiled threats of ceasing sponsorship or advertising on particular media, and other initiatives they have in their bag of dirty tricks.

There is a wide variety of reasons for these different approaches: remaining silent because their lawyers have recommended to do this; pretending that nothing has happened or that there is no reason to be so upset; trying to retain or destroy information (ignoring that sooner or later the truth is going to come out anyway); presenting their own stance as a scientific or independent fact, perhaps even by having it certified by some imaginary organization; stating simply that they have nothing to do with the issue, or blaming it on someone else — maybe a recently fired employee is made out to be the scapegoat, or an innocent third party.

Even more drastically, organizations sometimes react by creating authentic media wars using anything and everything in their power, licit or illicit (who cares?) to distract people's attention, to either silence reporters or to usher them onto a bandwagon, thinking that the "fan effect" will work: if everyone is involved, none of us is guilty. These sad, yet frequent, cases of abuse obviously explain why none of us trust institutions anymore.

The sole alternative to these tactics requires, to start with, *a thorough understanding of why a stakeholder is upset.* Knowing, not "judging", is the first step to formulating the most suitable response.

In these kinds of situations, it is possible to witness true ire. Webster's Dictionary defines ire, as "very violent anger in which one loses self-control and commits violence, be it verbal or physical in nature." If someone is out of his mind, it is better to know that before you start arguing him, because he (or she) is certainly not going to calmly defend his or her own position; he will react angrily, actually even to the extent of damaging his own position. Nothing is more dangerous than an angry opponent, because their ire makes tem unpredictable.

In real terms, ire is a self-defense response to pain or the threat of pain that one feels, even when the threat may simply be perceived rather than real. In dealing with these situations, the distinction between rational and irrational ire is irrelevant.

First, those who are extremely angry feel their fierce attitude is reasonable, and their anger is likely to intensify if others react to their outrage as though they are irrational.

Second, one must not entertain the feeling that the person who is so angry lacks either information or intelligence. This assumption will prevent us from looking at the real causes of that person's anger. It is much easier to blame the anger on the person rather than investigate any rational basis for his seemingly irrational behavior. Our self-sufficiency whispers in our ear, "I know what is wrong with him", so we do not look for the true causes.[19]

---

[19] In May 2013, a Business Insider report comparing various fashion brands noted that Abercrombie & Fitch did not manufacture plus sizes for women, and recalled a statement from the CEO, Mike Jeffries in 2006, in which he stated that his clothes are not for everyone, but for cool young people, and he concluded: «Are we exclusive? Absolutely!» The online reaction was immediate. On the same day, *Change.org* launched a petition to Jeffries: «Stop telling teenagers that they are not beautiful; You must make clothes for teenagers of all sizes!". Its #FitchTheHomeless campaign calling for a boycott went viral. Other entities, such as the National Association for Eating Disorders and

Not infrequently, the powerful underestimate the position of the weak, without realizing that feeling defenseless does not diminish anger at all, but, on the contrary, increases it. "Beware the wrath of the meek," says a Spanish proverb. Asking about the causes of anger can help unmask those who use aggressiveness as a mere ploy to intimidate the adversary.

If one party fails to make an effort to understand the other, they are more likely to adopt an adversarial stance, and thus, they will find it much harder to identify the common interests that may be used as the jumping-off point for an eventual agreement. Unfortunately, say Susskind and Field, «when the lack of a conciliatory spirit prevails, even the search for a dialogue or the proposal of alternative solutions to the absolute annihilation of our adversary are deemed as being treason»- In such circumstances, a spiral of ire is created and its very first victim is the truth itself, regardless of who is right or wrong.

Thus, the angrier the public is, the greater the effort we must make to really listen to them. These people have suffered the aggression directly either by losing equity or by being threatened and they need to vent strong feelings before they are ready to listen. When people are upset, they have a passion to be heard. "Having something to say" is a single-minded state that focuses all of one's energy and attention. It may seem counterintuitive but a person who knows how to listen is, in a sense, a good conversationalist because listening closely is an effective way to be listened to. Only once the stakeholders have been listened to will they hear the institution's side of the argument.

America the Beautiful Teen Empowerment, protested vigorously. The brand was silent. The crisis ended with the resignation of Jeffries (who in his 20 years as CEO had transformed a small 36-store firm into a colossus with more than a thousand stores), and a profound reform of the firm's values. The boycott's success was due to the media's support for the protests, giving it the conceptual framework that explained A & F's profound error: ignoring that one of the most deeply felt social problems today (in the affluent world) are personality disturbances and eating disorders among adolescents.

Tune in emotionally

In the same line as attuning to public perception is to be able to give the proper weight to the world of emotions. Crises, as seen from the angle of those who are suffering the consequences, are highly emotional situations due to the inherent risks involved and the lack of time to solve the problem and hence uncontrolled behavior tends to take place both within and outside the organization.

The institutional response in a crisis should not be limited to simply publishing the cold facts, with no emotional commitment whatsoever, but rather it should show signs of sensitivity, understanding, humanity and real feelings. In a nutshell, you should show the facts as closely as possible to the way in which the average person would describe them. There are intellectual issues and emotional ones and each one should be dealt with separately. When someone speaks coldly about an issue that triggers passion, he or she generates rejection and his or her words become less relevant. Ailes suggests we bear in mind "that the facts provide information, but emotions provide the right interpretation."

It is impossible to overstate the importance of communicating with compassion and empathy in crises that have hurt people. This is the recommendation of James Lee Witt, director of the Federal Emergency Management Agency (USA):

> You can empathize with their pain and embarrassment at being helpless. You can make adjustments to the recovery process based on their need for dignity. You can make sure they have shelter and a hot meal. You can listen to their stories and acknowledge their concerns. You can hug them and let them cry on your shoulder. You can say to them as I do, "we will never be able to bring back your memories, but we can help you build new ones".

In order to achieve this, it is necessary to know how to interpret the state of public feeling: fear, uncertainty, ire, pain, rage, pessimism, and sadness. If, for example, a radio station reveals that one of the main benefactors of an NGO has been arrested during a drug trafficking operation by the police, that NGO's spokesperson should show the proper feelings in accordance with the circumstances: shame, disbelief, concern for the person involved and his family, respect for the ongoing police investigation and a lack of overall information about the whole issue. In other words, the spokesperson should behave while in contact with the media as if they were talking about a life-long friend. This is not the moment to accuse anyone (and certainly not the police), but rather the time to show concern and disbelief. Nothing else is required during these first few hours of a painful episode: only feelings because the public would like to be in the shoes of those who are suffering this tragedy and see what type of people they are. Eventually reporters will be asking who was aware of the problem and if the income incurred from such drug trafficking ended up in the NGO's books; but all this will happen sometime down the road.

Communication is a relation that is established between people, not some sort of anonymous mechanism used to spread ideas. As Mora stated, our society is overpopulated with broken hearts and perplexing intelligences. We must approach physical and moral pain with extreme care. Empathy does not imply renouncing our own convictions but rather putting ourselves in the other person's shoes. In today's society, those responses which are based upon feelings and humanity are the most compelling.

If empathy must be developed in those cases in which the institution has done nothing wrong, it is even truer in those cases when there are actual responsibilities. True feelings are required to be able to effectively communicate in situations in which people have been hurt.

Social media are a wonderful thermometer in measuring public emotions. Online reactions are often superficial and rash. I agree that they should be taken with slightly more than a pinch of salt and no one should react too rashly based on what they have just read on some blog. Yet the danger that they represent for major institutions is most likely the contrary. Many institutions at a time of crisis simply ignore them as being too superficial to deserve any credit or attention whatsoever. In my book, that is a big mistake.

We also should consider the vast gap between generations. Younger people are less likely to be convinced by rational arguments: their own personal experiences and their friends are the main reference points that make up what they perceive as being their values. Common sense has changed and to be able to even start to get through to this generation, you have to use completely different pitches that both begin and end with emotions.

For older people, especially for those who have developed their own personalities in an environment based upon austerity, personal effort and meritocracy, this concept may simply sound like pure sentimentalism, and behaving in this way means treating people as if they were mere teenagers. The problem is that our new generations have developed their own personality based on another set of parameters and it should not be assumed that they would automatically control their emotions. Moreover, self-control is no longer considered a plus, and the socially predominant theory nowadays is that controlling your emotions is perhaps not perceived as being an upside. Younger people seem to think that letting your emotions control you is the best approach. One wonders if Oscar Wilde would be shocked to learn that his famous comment that "the best way to avoid temptation is to fall for it," is no longer a funny line but rather a common practice.

In this sense, institutional responses should avoid any inkling of being condescending to others or showing signs of excessive self-confidence. The institution should never forget that they are always one of the main suspects in a crisis and they are the ones who have to win the affect and trust of all stakeholders. Ogrizek & Guillery underline that those who have experienced several crises know that it is modesty that is needed more than anything else.

Reacting with compassion, concern and empathy with all the stakeholders is one of the primary best practices in crisis management and communication. Sociological research shows that people react positively to a spokesperson who recognizes the concerns and shows human compassion when faced with damage that may have happened; in this way, their credibility and perceived legitimacy are strengthened before, during and after the incident. "Some crisis spokespersons — comments Seeger — may be reluctant, however, to frame their statements with expressions of concern and empathy for fear of appearing unprofessional. These efforts to maintain professionalism are often perceived by the public to be cold and uncaring. The resulting perception may undermine the message and credibility of the messenger."

Public opinion, emotions and feelings are of capital importance in a crisis. A cold and apathetic response to what is perceived as being a human problem will only end up with the institution being considered Public Enemy Number One. As Cohn stated, «the public understands that problems or accidents can happen, but what they won't accept is the semblance of insensitivity on the part of their leaders».

That is why it is so critical to use a more moderate tone and gentler expressions. There are some words that in themselves sound like a slap in the face and others that come across like a pat on the back – words may either be harmful or medicine that cures wounds. Uncertainty about how a crisis is going to develop tends to trigger tensions, which often lead to disproportionate reactions. Lukaszewski explained it quite well: "keep your testosterone under control because the minimum amount of negative energy that you let go of, will boomerang by at least 5 or 10-fold."

Therefore, the corporate response has to express vividly how calm they are feeling. Nobody should ever insult anyone else nor respond to any insults that they may have heard. Emotional tuning and moderate language are critical and should be carefully chosen so as to properly convey your message. The tone of a response is an integral part of the message itself. Verbal violence represents a huge obstacle to pacification.

Acting this way is never easy. In public debates about ideological subjects, it is quite common to hear one person insulting another. For instance, the suffix "phobic" (e.g., homophobic or islamophobic) is an easy way to disqualify your opponent as irrational with a minimum mental effort. Being aware of such manipulative tactics beforehand will help you handle such an accusation, take a deep breath and respond calmly, even when your opponent is insulting you. The right tone in your message must be accompanied by a polite presentation.

Bear in mind that in communication the non-verbal element is just as important as the verbal. Even more, according to Craig, verbal elements represent a mere 7% of the whole communication process while the other 93% depend entirely on other aspects beyond the words themselves: 38% on the paralinguistic aspects (the tone, sound of your voice, the pace) and 55% on your body language (facial expression, gestures, visual contact, and your way of moving). Therefore, the way you present yourself, your personal style, and the way you treat others is extremely important.

It is even more necessary to be humble when the parties in conflict are a major institution against one single person or a very small group, as has so often been the case, when the general public automatically takes the side of the underdog.[20] The bigger the organization, the more important it will be for it to demonstrate humility and humanity.

In closing, one more tip. While you should not overdo it with humor, nothing is better than a quick joke to reduce the level of tension. I mean a friendly, sincere and honest joke, but not sarcasm or irony, which some may deem as being offensive (perhaps laughing at yourself is ok). Not taking yourself too seriously opens the door to dialogue and shows respect for the other party. Plays on word, symbols and situations all have their place. However grave the circumstances may be – or precisely for that reason – a joke may help to lower the tension in the conflict and is impeding any reasonable progress.[21]

Argument from the other person's point of view

A corporate response should strike the right emotional tone, but let's not exaggerate. You should behave with feeling, but you should not decide based on feeling. Your decisions and your communication should be rational.

---

[20] I found the following *El Mundo* headline quite educational: «[the Spanish bank] Bankia has reported a lady with mental paralysis for vandalism in one of their offices.» You don't have to keep on reading to know which side any reader will be on.

[21] In February 2018, a few unrelated factors made chicken meat unavailable in the United Kingdom. Desolate Kentucky Fried Chicken (KFC) suppliers were unable to keep up with demand, and the fast-food chain had to close its 900 stores in Britain. The franchise's regulars reacted with anger and disdain. The company responded by inserting an ad in which the initials of the brand were seen in a different order (FCK) and apologizing. That creative and fun way was welcomed by clients and by British society. It is an example of using the sense of humor, in a place where being witty is highly appreciated.

Reasoning must be used and must be used frequently. Crises and controversies often trigger outright rejection of the other party's proposals and ideas, and mutate into prejudices and stereotypes. In order to not fall into this emotional trap, you must make a major additional effort to ensure that the voice of reason is being heard. My insistence of paying careful attention to public perceptions, understanding why people are angry and talking with the proper emotional tone are preconditions to creating the best environment for rational thinking.

Emotions themselves are not only problematic for those on the outside, but for those on the inside as well. For instance, if a manager is being heavily criticized on a daily basis by the local press, even though they may, in fact, be a calm-natured person, eventually this barrage of emotions will affect their behavior and even their own advisors will be acting under this pressure. Elizalde recommends that we use an external consultant who is not going to be affected by this type of emotional pressure during our crisis.

The fact is that excessive noise and overall confusion in a crisis environment is a major obstacle that often makes fluid communication practically impossible. Controversies create confusion in contents, tend to deform the message itself and pave the way to exaggeration which spreads all too easily. This confusion is greatly multiplied in time of crises as risks are perceived as being imminent and the time factor is so critical that people tend to act first and think later.

To overcome this reigning confusion, we first need clarity in our contents, meaning clear and easily understood messages for all. Questions that stakeholders are asking should be clearly addressed, putting ourselves in their shoes, thinking deeply about their ideas and weighing them up properly and then expressing them as simply as possible.

The perverse effects of scientific terminology (medical, biological, legal, etc.) must be avoided at the same time that you are communicating the inherent risk or trying to explain complex realities. Obviously, institutions are simply trying to provide precise, detailed and clear information, but people tend to get lost when terms that they do not understand are being used.

At the end of the day, what may end up happening is exactly the opposite of what the institution was aiming to accomplish.

People reach the erroneous conclusion that the institution is trying to hide something beneath all this technical jargon that they are unable to understand.

Clarity is achieved ... by being brief. In a crisis there is no time to read long messages; and if there is, what is lacking is attention to get to the end, or people read diagonally. Therefore, an effort must be made to be succinct in the key messages.

So, in times of crisis every effort must be made to ensure clarity and the use of everyday language. When it is absolutely necessary to use technical terms, they should immediately be explained in such a manner that anybody is able to understand them. Misunderstandings are the root of all communication evils.

A very effective speaking style is one that uses images. Visual information tends to allow any normal person to understand complex information and estimates more easily by using comparisons with units of measurement that they are already familiar with.[22]

Secondly, issues should be addressed in a positive manner. Our own opinions should be presented in an affirmative way, not as a rebuttal of the adversary. We should not take for granted that everybody knows our position even before we start speaking. On the other hand, if we treat the audience as if they are more intelligent than they may appear to be and know less than we think they do (although more than a few tend to apply the opposite strategy), we will obtain good results.

Thirdly, giving the proper importance to the public's perception also requires that the institution's response will have to be able to adopt that group's perspective. It must be relevant: in other words, it must deal with what people are really worried about, and it must be meaningful to our listeners and not simply meaningful to us.

---

[22] For example, to convey the seriousness of the humanitarian crisis that has been taking place in Syria ever since the end of 2012 we could give the figure of 3.5 million refugees that is increasing at the rate of 4 thousand people per day. But it would be much easier to explain the severity of this drama for a Galician like me if I say that it represents a third of the population of the whole of Portugal and that each and every week a refugee camp is being set up which is as large as the city of Santiago de Compostela.

Thus, by clearly showing its concern, the institution is not aiming to defend its own interest but rather the interest of those people it is serving. The public should be able to understand that the institution is seeking the overall good of the people and that it feels responsible to society in general and, above all, that it has a soul.

Differentiate between public opinion and the law

An organization's activity is scrutinized in two very different courts: that of public opinion and that of the law. Each one has its own sets of rules, procedures, pace, and sanctions.

Top management needs to receive advice in both domains. It needs lawyers and it needs communicators. But allow me to insist on the latter, because the former can be taken for granted. Neither serious companies nor their executives, when accused of any wrongdoing, will move a finger without the assistance of a good lawyer. The real risk is following their recommendations before even listening to a communicator about the possible consequences of all options on public opinion. Both types of advice have different content and vision, but their perspectives are complementary.

What members of the steering committee need to realize is that quite often while we might have the legal right to do something, it would not be in our best interest to do it. Corporations and people's lives often show that *you may have the right but not be right,* and we could end up — as McCann entitles his book — *Winning the Legal Battle, Losing the Public War.*

The court of public opinion has its own characteristics, which radically distinguish it from the court of law. First, in speed. Their sentences are immediate, because the public does not wait to have all the elements to convict or acquit, as judges and juries do, who usually need years to reach a sentence.

Second, the presumption of innocence does not protect those who remain silent: whoever is accused by the media is guilty until proven otherwise. One could almost speak of a presumption of guilt, because the maxim of the majority is closer to the saying, "wherever there's smoke, there's a fire."

Third, "all are equal before the law" is an almost universally accepted basic legal premise, but not all of us are equal in the court of public opinion. The specific situation of each individual plays a major role in a given crisis. The rich and powerful will always be perceived as being wrong and the weaker party will be heavily favored, even in those cases where the law favors the rich and powerful, as has been proven repeatedly in many crises. In fact, the public tends to identify the rich and powerful as being the bad guys. As Seymour & Moore wrote, «it appears that there is a natural tendency to think that everybody who has become rich have had to sell their souls to the devil».

Another version of "good guy vs bad guy" is "big guy vs little guy". Big corporations are not especially loved today, and people tend to link large companies with the bad guys. The myth of David and Goliath shows us that the larger organizations are always wrong and that the smaller individual who challenges this larger organization is always right.

This predisposition against the powerful is also seen in things that are perfectly legitimate for an individual but are perceived as being unacceptable for a large organization.[23]

Fourth: they also differ in penalties. The punishment in public opinion can be more severe than the deprivation of liberty or a pecuniary fine: the social discredit and the damage to a good reputation can be more onerous and lasting than a prison sentence. And not that's not all: sometimes even juries and courts pay more attention to public opinion than to the letter of the law.[24]

---

[23] L'Oréal, the French perfume giant, hired as its "campaign face" a very good-looking young Belgian lady who they happened to spot in the stands during the Brazil 2014 World Cup. However, they had to break the contract with her in less than 48 hours once social media had gone viral showing pictures of the girl's Facebook profile with an antelope and other animals that she had just shot. Hunting is a quite obviously legal and legitimate activity, yet it is completely out of place for any organization and their corporate image.

[24] On July 20, 2002, the newly opened Utopia nightclub in a posh Lima shopping center hosted a theme party to launch Zoo, a new Hugo Boss fragrance. As part of the show, they hired a circus, which would show a tiger, a lion, a horse, and a chimpanzee in cages. More than a thousand people packed the place. At 3 am, an artist lit a torch to get public atten-

Fifth, many norms which protect the accused in law don't function in public opinion. Perhaps the judge declares you not guilty due to a formal error, or because a judicial period has elapsed, but people continue to consider you guilty, and even more so precisely because the law has not convicted you. The same happens with another basic legal principle, that criminal law cannot be retroactive. The judge cannot convict a felon if the law prohibiting conduct was not in effect when the events took place. But in public opinion, you'll be guilty forever.

The last discrepancy with the court of public opinion, and the root of the other differences, is that the judge is obliged to respect the law. As the old Roman adage goes *Dura lex sed lex*. But people are not shy about discarding the legal solution because the rule does not adapt well to the specific situation. Elizalde comments: «In a crisis, it is a normal behavior to raise doubts about the applicability of certain legal norms. And if in the end the positive law prevails, people disagree and criticize the system as subjectively unjust.»

The court of public opinion – the opinion of our stakeholders – is driven much more by natural ethical criteria than by legal norms. Legality and socially responsible behavior are not synonyms. Some actions may be legally acceptable yet socially unacceptable and thus a lawyer's modus operandi should not be the only basis for establishing the corporate response to a problem.

---

tion, starting a fire. There were no fire extinguishers or emergency lighting, and some fire exits were blocked. Rescue teams found four people dead, another twenty-five died on the way to the hospital, and more than fifty were injured. The nightclub's owners did not want to assume any responsibility: they kept quiet and decided to wait for the trial. Instead, the mall preferred to negotiate with the victims. Sometime later, the general manager of Utopia accused the victims of just wanting revenge, of selling their forgiveness for $ 99,000 and thus obstructing the judicial process. Two years after the fire, in 2004, the general manager of the nightclub was sentenced to 15 years, while the president and vice-president of Utopia fled and hid abroad (Interpol captured them in 2018). The prosecutor requested a 7-year sentence, but the judge ended up giving them a 15-year sentence, probably due to public pressure. When the manager finally offered an apology, people did not accept it because it was too late and did not seem sincere.

Managers should make their decisions bearing in mind what is both socially and ethically acceptable. Overlooking this may lead to very unpleasant surprises indeed. For instance, public opinion considers that suppliers' mistakes are also the responsibility of their providers.[25]

This contradiction between the law and social consensus occurs quite often: for instance, when the law allows a person or an institution to behave in a certain manner, but public opinion deems that behavior to be anti-social. The law and public opinion (or in its ultimate extreme, social ethics) are completely different in scope and impose very different obligations. Another example is when a company applies rules which are out of sync with present-day values, ignoring the fact that times have changed.[26]

---

[25] In 2016, Samsung launched its new flagship, the Galaxy Note 7. A few weeks later, Samsung received 34 reports of battery burns, and very soon the company stopped production and sales, made an informal recall first, then two full recalls and finally recalled the product for good. Samsung had outsourced the production of the batteries of that model to two different companies, A and B, and the technical investigation found that all the problems were related to supplier A: their batteries had a design defect that in some circumstances caused the phone to overheat and even burn out. Samsung's answer was: It was not our mistake, but the problem is: people buy Samsung. For that, the company took full responsibility and never blamed anyone else. Samsung didn't even mention the supplier's name in public.

[26] In February 2015, NFL player Ray Rice and his fiancée Janay Palmer were arrested in Atlantic City (NJ). According to the Police report, Rice and Palmer struck one another with their hands when they were going to their room in the hotel's elevator. Rice's attorney called it a "minor physical altercation", and both were charged with simple assault. But the next day, the TMZ website released a video showing Rice dragging an unconscious Palmer out of the elevator. Later on, Ray Rice was indicted on aggravated assault. The NFL responded to the issue quite slowly, and in July, it suspended Rice (who, in the meanwhile, had married Palmer) for two games . This punishment was in line with NFL's previous treatment of cases of domestic violence, but it was widely considered to be completely insufficient. Because of these protests, in August the NFL issued a new, and more severe policy on domestic violence, and admitted they had made a mistake in the Rice's case. But in September, TMZ released the surveillance footage from inside the elevator that shows Rice punching Palmer in the face, knocking her unconscious. Within hours, Rice was suspended indefinitely. The lesson from this crisis is that companies and organizations should update

This dichotomy between lawyers' advice and that of communicators advice happens both ways. Sometimes a communicator suggests an action plan as being the most appropriate, because it is in line with the stakeholders' perceptions, yet it may have serious negative legal consequences due to the major legal responsibilities involved. On the other hand, it is also possible that the most appropriate actions from a legal angle will have devastating effects on public opinion. These conflicts appear quite often, for instance when illicit behavior that generates social alarm is being tried: public opinion will demand a more severe sentence than that which is required by law.

We should not be surprised that in specific cases the head of the communications department and the legal affairs director seem to be on opposite sides of the fence. If for instance, the corporate CEO has been accused of tax fraud, the former would automatically propose calling a press conference, while their legal team will probably be in favor of silence as, at least among United States lawyers, there is a general consensus that during a crisis, the client should not say anything.

Communication advisers are also useful when dealing with political authorities. Rob Rehg, from the global firm Edelman, stated that one of the biggest challenges he has encountered is convincing a company that has never dealt with a PR firm to follow its advice over that of a lawyer. For Rehg, lawyers are completely counterproductive in the political arena, which is an important stakeholder community when foreign companies start their operations in the US. In speaking to that community, the key is to translate what contribution a company can make to the U.S. economy in terms of jobs, tax contributions and philanthropy.

Organization management always has the need, and especially in times of crisis, to have excellent advice from their teams of consultants, in both law and communication. Experience shows the

---

their policies to stay in line with social perceptions. The two-game suspension was in line with previous punishments, but domestic violence is now deemed to be a graver criminal conduct than in the past. The NFL showed itself to be disconnected from public opinion because of its slowness in tackling the issue: it took four months to decide on the first sanction, and they didn't investigate the facts at all.

validity of listening to both from start to finish in a crisis, overcoming the temptation to leave one of the two on the sidelines to avoid internal struggles. Which would be more dangerous: losing millions of dollars due to a legal sentence or a long-term loss in credibility and your corporate reputation? In fact, in the vast majority of cases, there are not two completely different interpretations of the case but rather complementary opinions that should be integrated by taking into account both opinions and reaching an agreement about the best approach to be agreed upon and applied by both sides.

In this sense, Caponigro tends to advise top management to study the problem jointly with their legal team and their communication experts, who have experience, objectivity and, at the same time, flexibility: «Do not make the mistake of hiding critical information from one or the other, solely as a means of avoiding conflict and confusion. If you are lucky enough to have both an excellent lawyer and an excellent communicator, let both of them share in the information gathering process and in the decision-making itself.»

This integrated approach will enable top management to avoid the two extremes: imprudence and naïveté. It is recommended to take into consideration all the possible legal consequences that could be incurred by any specific public declaration.

If I may digress, I would say that communicators sometimes face a problem of proof: legal risks are often easier to quantify and present a more short-term threat, while reputational risks are long-term and more complicated to evaluate with certainty. For this reason, legal reasons can stop an institution from acknowledging any responsibility, even against hard evidence to the contrary, with devastating consequences on public opinion.

The challenge must be solved by the communicator with a managerial mindset: learning to quantify these damages, or at least showing their impact on the relationship with their stakeholders, and the consequences on the business.[27]

---

[27] In the summer of 2019, Spain suffered the largest listeria outbreak in its history, with more than 222 confirmed cases in five regions. The outbreak caused three deaths and seven miscarriages. The cause was the shredded meat of the La Mechá brand, produced by Magrudis, a

Good results are easily achieved if corporate lawyers and communicators work together long before the crisis explodes. In fact, the lawyers in an organization may be converted into communication allies. This is especially true in the case of prevention: they both share the mission of advising top management regarding the on-going trend in respect of security and all safety precautions (legal compliance and due diligence), and may foresee the adverse consequences of a potential crisis on the corporate reputation. Thus, the specific moment to begin to work hand in hand is in jointly writing up the crisis scenarios and the response drafts (where they will provide details about the crisis management plan); in this way a certain degree of consensus already exists when the crisis hits.

In chapter 9 we will delve into the coordination of legal and communication aspects when it is necessary to go to court to defend the corporate position.

Follow your conscience

A crisis uncovers the institution's soul and reveals its corporate culture. An unexpected event for which a standard response has not been foreseen reveals the company's true objectives, the

---

family business from Seville. As Patricia Núñez has documented, the company's reaction could not have been worse: first, they lied by saying that the laboratory tests prior to packaging were negative (and when fatalities began, the laboratory notified the police that they had alerted the company); later, the company withdrew the questioned products from the market, but concealed from the authorities that they also commercialized shredded meat under other brands, processed at the same facilities; they did nothing for the victims; and in their statements to the media they tried to minimize the problem and never assumed any responsibility. The official investigation also found that Magrudis did not meet sanitary standards, had illegal labor, and had committed creditors fraud. So, the owners of the company went to prison, and the company closed. It hurts to say this, but it is hard to believe that it was all the fault of the owners: the law firm that advised Magrudis to handle the problem in that way must bear some proportion of responsibility.

strength of its moral principles and its real internal cohesion. A crisis is the best test of leadership, bravery and creativity for an organization's management.

The way leadership is carried out during a crisis underscores an organization's concept of social responsibility and ethical values and what it considers to be its service to society: «It is often when corporations are confronted with what is for them a most unexpected event, to which they know how to respond, that they reveal their true purpose in our society, sometimes being able to introduce courageous policies, free on this occasion of the artificialities of a fixed industrial image – a phenomenon which never fails to surprise journalists and employees alike,» comment Ogrizek & Guillery.

In a crisis, the voice of conscience suggests three behaviors: always tell the truth, respond to your actions and work professionally. Let's look at them one by one.

Always tell the truth

While we do grant a high degree of relevance to all the subjective aspects involved in a crisis, we are certainly not going to underestimate the value of the truth of actual facts. I would like to emphasize that crises are intensely emotional situations in which the prime task is to restore public trust in the institution itself and in its leaders. There is no way to bring a crisis to a close when those responsible lack authority and credibility.

There are many types of authority in an institution: power, position, seniority, experience, performance... It is a fact that crises trigger such major uprisings in organizations that the only authority that is accepted is that which is based on trust. Moreover, trust is only obtained by telling the truth. «Tell the truth —recommends Henrici —, this simple imperative is the most evident and basic principle involved in communications ethics ... truth is the norm.»

Honesty and sincerity are recognized as the best practices in crisis management and communication. Truthfulness is indispensable in gaining credibility. Telling the truth in difficult situations will establish the basis for future cooperation with both the authorities and the other stakeholders that are directly involved. On the other hand, by being silent the only thing that would be gained is further distrust and moreover it serves no useful purpose. Silence may help at the very beginning but, in much the same way as a boomerang, social negative reaction is bound to come back stronger and unexpectedly. In today's world, it is virtually impossible to assume that the truth will not come out.

Respect for the truth is especially important in a crisis as the temptation to hide it is so very strong. Revealing a negative fact that clearly hurts our case is deemed as being negative in any circumstances and do so precisely during a crisis may have very grave consequences indeed. Why reveal aspects that will otherwise not be in the public domain? For this reason, people quite often prefer to lie; the risk of being caught is less serious than accepting that we goofed.

In other cases, people justify not telling the truth in order to protect others: «Often, crisis managers believe that, by withholding information, they are operating in the best interest of the public. By so doing, they risk reducing trust. Maintaining honesty, candor, and openness in spite of the impediments is a fundamental exigency of most crisis communication,» recommends Seeger.

On other occasions people lie spontaneously, without premeditation. . A corporate spokesperson is asked a question and he or she is unauthorized to reveal that data (perhaps for good reason). Feeling the need to say something or having doubts about what to say, they end up by giving an answer that is less than 100% truthful. It is as if the lie was the most suitable reply to an illegitimate question. The justification for anyone who has done this is simply "you did not have any right to ask that question". Obviously, this type of behavior should not be compared to those who systematically fail to tell the truth but, in any case, the fact is *a lie is a lie.*

We must admit that this total and absolute rejection of telling a lie is less than universally accepted. In some cultures, there is either no major moral sanction or the odds of politicians, top-level business people being taken to court are so low that nobody is surprised that they lie, and if they were to be caught, nothing would happen anyway, so they do it all the time. Nevertheless, if the institution is present in a wide variety of cultural contexts, the most prudent approach is to follow the strictest rules.

Lying is always wrong and in the midst of a crisis, it could be the most serious of all possible mistakes. Personal and business relations are based on trust and we all know that trust is gained little by little with lots of work involved, while it can be thrown out of the window by one stupid mistake. Public trust in an institution may be retained even though a serious accident has taken place, but it will be totally lost if the error has been voluntary in nature and a lie will always be deemed as a voluntary error. In this sense, as we will see in a moment, a lie will turn a crisis into a full-scale scandal, the most serious problem that an organization can face in the field of communication.

Beyond this, as we have already seen, we should not overlook that lying – in any of its multiple forms – is, most surely, the worst possible behavior in the eyes of any Western reporter. So we should certainly not be surprised that the mere suspicion of covering something up, instead of leading the reporter astray, will only make them more determined to learn more.

In this respect, all communicators agree that no one should ever lie in any case whatsoever. There are no "white lies" or "benign lies" and much less "legitimate lies." You should never say something that you know to be false - ever.

In addition to the ethical standard, which prohibits lying, there is a pragmatic reason not to lie. You will lose all your credibility with everybody (employees, investors, clients, the press), and when that trust has been lost it may never be recovered.

I think this way of acting is right, but we should go much further: it is necessary to emphasize that we cannot lie and that lying is wrong, not because of the fact that it triggers negative consequences. Even when lying could go undetected because the stakeholders have no way of knowing the truth, a lie is an unacceptable communication tool in general and much more specifically in crisis communication.

All the information released by an institution to all its stakeholders and through whatever channel it may choose must be truthful in nature. This way of acting is the only responsible behavior that an institution may use within the scope of its obligation to society as a whole. This rule is not based on reasons of efficiency but is more of a moral imperative.

Obviously, respecting the truth does not mean that you are obliged to give a long-winded answers to each and every one of the questions that may be raised by your employees, reporters, clients, etc. There are cases in which it is legitimate and proper to not provide all of the information that is being requested. Consequently, there is no ethical obligation to provide all the information that is requested, when for example, providing that information would be breaking the confidentiality rights of a person, be they a manager, an employee or a third party.

A specific sign of prudence is that which refers to information regarding the health of top management. Looking at a specific case in which the CEO of an organization had a serious illness, Barton gave the three following pieces of advice:

- Take each case by itself depending on its circumstances without trying to apply a general rule. It may be worthwhile looking at how other institutions have managed their communications in similar situations, but the only true guidelines are to apply a communicator's own wisdom and expertise.
- Keeping a secret is a double-edged sword: it gives power to those who know the secret and protects the feelings of the people involved, but it is an unstable situation that can blow up in any moment and certainly leads to distrust.
- Keeping a secret is very hard indeed and, when the truth comes out, the consequences tend to be devastating for those responsible.

You should not provide too much information about an ongoing issue, nor regarding a negotiation that is taking place because it may influence the way things unfold and even create an obstacle in that negotiation. In the following chapter, we will look much more closely at the way to cautiously communicate during a conflict in order not to damage the results of a negotiation.

One may also provide a succinct response when the reporter or their newspaper/magazine is publicly against the institution or when past experiences have been negative and there are many reasons to doubt their evenhandedness. Ethical rigor is halfway between trying to keep a secret and being naïve when faced with someone who refuses to accept the evidence: some reporters misuse their profession and the best approach which a serious institution should apply with this type of journalist is to keep them as far away as possible.

The cases we have just been discussing are the *exceptions to the rule*: the information that is provided should be complete, if there are no serious reasons to justify limiting the general rule. As Soria explains,

> *The truth should always be the complete truth.* As the German philosopher Hegel stated, "Only the whole is true." Partial truths, precisely because they are partial, may be completely false. This does not mean that for a statement to be true it has to say everything that may be affirmed in respect of the matter; it may affirm in terms that are perfectly correct about one single aspect of the truth. But when this declaration is used to communicate, it will only be true if its context is evident and clearly indicates that it is merely a partial declaration.

Additionally, in those cases where you have the right to not tell the whole truth this fact does not authorize you to state something which is false. This is the time to explain why it is not possible to respond: because it breaches a person's confidentiality; because this information should be released by some other organism (a law enforcement agency or a judge, for example); because it is being negotiated and therefore it is impossible to provide information until an agreement is reached; because it is sensitive data which could destroy a competitive advantage that has been achieved by the organization if disclosed, or simply because the information is not available at this point in time and will be released at the appropriate moment.

These may appear to be "non-responses" but at least they do provide a certain amount of orientation and respond to the other party's desire to be informed. Regardless of the formula used, the most important aspect is the attitude being shown, not the specific expression used: the same words may be used with good of evil intentions. The important thing is that what is said actually corresponds to a sincere desire to inform with the truth.

So, is there an obligation to tell the whole truth? Soria maintains that you cannot expect corporations to call the media in relation to any bad news that affects them. Nonetheless, you can demand that they present these facts honestly whenever they are so requested by reporters or when they do so of their own accord, in those cases that the facts may have repercussions on the stakeholders which the organization is directly related to.

Therefore, certain ideas – like "the public is predisposed to panic" – are nothing more than prejudices, and should be rejected: «One of the impediments to an approach leading to successful dialogue in a crisis is the myth that the public will panic if it has accurate information about a crisis. This myth is not supported by the available research, and, in fact, there is some reason to believe that withholding information from the public decreases the probability that it will respond appropriately,» says Tierney.

At the end of the day, it is a matter of being levelheaded and well balanced. When the news is bad, the organization in itself is an interested source of information and, due to this, it does not have a radical obligation to provide all the details involved of its own accord. Yet, it is also true that the stronger they defend their own interest, the less credibility they will have with others. Thus, organizations that know how to overcome their own short-term self-interest when the time comes to communicate their own mistakes, will end up gaining a more solid and lasting degree of credibility.

Scientific research conducted by Arpan & Roskos-Ewolden has proved that the proactive strategy called "stealing thunder" gets good results: «when an organization steals thunder, it breaks the news about its own crisis before the crisis is discovered by the media or other interested parties.» Their empirical analysis shows that this strategy reinforces the organization's credibility and is well received by their stakeholders, much better than any excuses that may be given once the facts have been revealed.

It is therefore fundamental to learn how to release bad news and a sign of leadership is the ability to change an organizational culture before the crisis happens. In this manner, when the crisis appears, the organization will already be vaccinated, with a robust employee relationship.

If there is a slight insistence here in the need to always tell the truth, it is because the temptation to take short cuts by lying is very strong indeed. Danish philosopher Kierkegaard once wrote, «Men are by nature more fearful of truth than of death.»

Answer for your actions

Ethical obligations are not limited to simply telling the truth, but to taking action and assuming responsibility for what has happened as a consequence of the institution's activity. This response has three elements: to immediately stop doing what is causing harm to people; to recognize the implications of what has happened without pretending to be unaware of the situation or blaming others; and to accept the responsibility to repair any damage that may have been caused.

The first step consists of immediately stopping whatever it is that is being done wrong, interrupting the cause of the problem, and eliminating the public risks being caused by the organization. The first step in crisis management must be removing the causes of the problem. Only after this has taken place, the communication can play its role: informing about the actions that have been adopted, so your stakeholders accept and support them, and instructing them how to put these measures into practice. Bear in mind that the actions themselves are much more important than words will ever be.... Actions speak very loudly indeed.

Sometimes this attitude will imply major expenses: closing down the factory for security reasons; recalling a toxic food product; covering the medical costs of affected employees; terminating the pursuance of a promising line of pharmaceutical research; replacing brand new equipment that may be dangerous to our clients, etc. However, it is the only way to prove to our stakeholders that they really are the institution's prime concern and that the institution is managed on solid, long-term criteria.

Cohn states: «When a company discovers it is making a defective product and orders a recall, it is taking responsible action. When a company is caught hiding a problem, its response is perceived by press and public as "damage control" — the focus is on self-defense instead of the customer's well-being. Consumers never reward bad corporate behavior.»

This interruption does not mean admission of guilt, but assumption of responsibility. With that goal in mind, companies should stop an assembly line to remove the corpse of a deceased worker, assume the cost of rescue teams, transport the injured to the hospital, and take care of the victim's families.[28]

Secondly, it is absolutely necessary to publicly accept your own responsibilities for what has happened, when that is the case. This includes assuming responsibility for what a subsidiary did, without using the subsidiary as a shield.[29]

The opposite attitude would be to try to create confusion, directing attention towards other people in order for your stakehold-

---

[28] On 6-14-2016, Matt and Melissa Graves were enjoying a vacation with their two-year-old son Lane at Disney World Park in Florida. That night, while they were strolling along the shore of the Seven Seas lagoon, an alligator seized the boy and carried him away before the horrified gaze of his parents. His father jumped into the water to try to save his son, but to no avail. More than fifty agents in helicopters and boats, a team of divers, trap experts and an alligator radar system were deployed in the lagoon. They captured four alligators, but when they were sacrificed, they found no human remains inside. The boy's lifeless body was not found until the next day. Those rescue efforts, which implied no small expenses, although the chances of finding the victim alive are practically nil, were the correct line of action: Disney owed it to that family.

[29] On March 2015, a Germanwings flight from Barcelona to Düsseldorf, with 144 passengers and 6 crew members on board, crashed 100 km north-west of Nice in a mountainous area inaccessible by road. The reason for the accident was that the co-pilot – who was suffering from severe mental problems, although he had successfully passed all the official examinations – deliberately crashed the plane. The official investigation concluded that the pilot was the only person responsible for the crash and declared that the accident could not have been prevented because of the security measures implemented in the cockpit doors after the 9/11 attacks. The corporate response both in taking care of the families and assuming the social responsibilities of victims' relatives, launching a formal investigation, releasing only confirmed information (without commenting on rumors), and withdrawing advertisement campaigns, was very professional and compassionate. It was key that Lufthansa, the parent company of Germanwings, decided to step up to the crisis. Although this could have had negative short-term implications for the Lufthansa brand, in the long run, it reinforced the brand's image and reputation. Also, for the victims' relatives, knowing that a leading airline was responding and offering logistic and immediate no-strings-attached financial support for short-term expenses created a positive perception.

ers to place the blame and/or responsibility for what has happened on someone else's shoulders.

This type of reaction, totally lacking any ethical basis, is what is known as spin. This means intentionally misleading people as a technique. The people who use spin as a tactic are fully aware of the weight of perceptions and symbolisms, they know how to make a journalist eager to publish a piece of news (or not publish it, whatever the case may be) and without the journalist realizing that he or she is being manipulated, without his or her consent.

Spin-doctors sell their expertise and unlimited creativity to any cause, be it holy or illegitimate. They do not lie, in the sense that they do not say a single thing that they know not to be true; yet they mislead everyone with a series of false hints and smoke-screens, using a series of grammatical tricks and expressions such as "perhaps" or "I would certainly not discard the possibility that...", in order to avoid any accusation later on of misconduct. Without any doubt, this way of acting is exactly the opposite of how socially responsible organizations should behave.

It would be even worse to directly accuse someone of having performed certain actions: this should never be done, not even when we are absolutely certain that a third party is responsible for what happened. If the institution is in no way involved with the actions pointing its finger at those who are really to blame is quite risky. There are three basic reasons for not to doing this:

A private institution should not be doing the job of the state prosecution — accusing someone of wrongdoing. The institution should certainly provide the local law enforcement authorities with all the information they have, but should only disclose publicly that information that proves that they are innocent.

During a crisis, companies should act and be perceived as acting calmly. An accusation is a clear sign of aggressiveness and is usually interpreted as typical of a lower moral category. Stakeholders do not react well towards institutions that blame others. The only thing that should be done is to put the information on the table: people are smart enough to know how to interpret this information.

Moreover, the worst thing you can do in the midst of a crisis is to create an enemy. If there is a public debate about who is truly responsible, you can bet that both parties will inevitably end up with mud on their face, even though sometime down the road it is proven that the institution itself was truly innocent.

However, some companies prefer a blunter action, and shift the blame to another organization. In their eyes, it seems more effective to say, 'We are not responsible, but we know who is,' rather than just saying, "We did not do it." In fact, the results could be less favorable. When organizations cast accusations at one another, trying to place blame on the other party for the crisis, this scenario quite often heightens uncertainty about who is responsible for the event, and the accusation affects both of them.[30]

Thirdly, and lastly, the institution should accept its obligation to repair any personal and/or equity damage that has been caused to any individual as a result of the company's activities. It is like saying, "if it is our fault, we'll pay for it".

Obviously, that does not mean that the institution should immediately accept the obligation to make any specific monetary compensation, as will be seen later on, but rather simply recognizes that the damage that has been incurred should be repaired in the most convenient manner possible, when the institution is proven to have been involved. Their legal advisors should also approve this type of open commitment previously.

In summary: these three declarations of corporate responsibility and accountability by an institution underscores once again that facts are more important than words. The institution's credibility and prestige are not based upon a series of declarations of principles or on any code of ethics, but rather on its day-to-day practices, and on how it reacts when hit by a crisis.

These guidelines are valid both for managers and for communicators. However, they do not apply to them in the same way, since managers lead, and communicators follow. What if the top management decides to follow other priorities, and pursue a short-term goal (i.e., overcoming the crisis whatever it takes)? What

---

[30] This is, according to Venette, Sellnow & Lang, what happened between the presidents of Ford and Firestone, who mutually accused each other of being responsible for a series of accidents. This public debate not only ended up destroying a long-term business relationship between the two companies that had lasted for 95 years but also seriously damaged the reputation of both companies.

would be the ethical response of a communicator, who disagrees with that approach?

In my opinion, communicators should do as any manager with solid principles would: do whatever is in their hands to change the situation and, if that is impossible, find the right moment to leave that company. We are not talking about minor problems, but a real crisis: companies using underage workers, selling defective products that cause harm, distributing forged goods, or discriminating against personnel because of their race.

However, the responsibility of communicators is higher, because corporate communicators, as Soria puts it, should act as the «organization's conscience. This is a very suggestive idea and raises multiple ethical challenges.» To a certain degree, they consider themselves the guardians of the organization's social responsibility: they act as the company's ambassadors with its stakeholders, and vice versa: the stakeholders' ambassadors to the board. Thus, their first moral obligation consists of effectively defending correct decisions before the board. If that does not work, they should start thinking about resigning their post (or of not accepting the role in the first place), if and when they are asked to communicate something that is, in ethical terms, incommunicable. In this respect, Ross has stated, «if you are not willing to renounce a contract or a post due to your principles, there is no sense whatsoever in claiming that you are a member of a young and constructive profession as, in all reality, you are really only a member of the oldest profession in the world.»

These three specific statements (stop the damage, publicly accept responsibility, and repair the consequences when it is proven) are the starting point and cornerstone of the institutional response. Yet this is far from being enough to define a suitable response. I should also wonder how much responsibility I must admit, to what point I should emphasize my concern for what has happened, and to what degree I should make excuses.

Tough questions indeed. One thing is to be concerned and share people's pain for a terrible event; it is quite another to state, directly or indirectly, that the institution you represent is responsible. Anyone may sincerely share someone else's suffering and try their best to do everything in their power to help them, but at the same time, not accept any responsibility whatsoever for what has happened. The ultimate ethical question, what I should do here and now, is never more strongly felt than in this situation.

The first way of responding is assuming a pragmatic approach: what is going to work best? Within the scope of this line of action, there are those who immediately recommend that you should apologize. In crisis management, apologizing has become commonplace. Many people — top executives, athletes using steroids, politicians stealing public money, actors and singers who have not paid taxes for decades, kings and queens who have been caught cheating — do it every single day. All you have to do is watch the daily news and see for yourself. Apologizing has become a very popular technique, eliminates all evil, and guarantees you will be forgiven for all your sins.

Strangely enough, we have gone from never wanting to say "we are sorry", like in the Roman Empire, which used to say, *Senatus non errat et si errat non corrigit ne videatur errasse* (The Senate is never wrong and if it is wrong, the mistake will not be corrected in order to ensure that no one sees it was wrong), to the point in which we are apologizing when nothing wrong has been done as a clear strategy to be viewed as really being nice people. The problem is that apologizing as a tactic is simply not believable.

A second way of approaching this issue is to look at it empirically: base your decision on which is the most suitable response strategy in each type of crisis upon experimental deduction. Within the scope of this criterion, crises may be split into three types: one in which the organization is the victim of the crisis, not to be blamed at all; a fortuitous crisis in which there is a relatively low degree of responsibility for the organization; and crises that are intentional, in which public perception attributes full responsibility to the organization for what has happened.

This empirical approach suggests linking the institutional response to the social perception of responsibility. In the first case, companies do not deny the problem but reject any responsibility for what has happened, stating that it should be blamed on another player or some other external factor (negotiation strategy); in the second, the company tries to minimize corporate responsibility for what has happened by explaining that the acts that triggered the crisis were "unintentional" (diminishing strategy); and in the third, the organization accepts full responsibility and publicly apologizes (reconstruction strategy).

In accordance with this approach, in a crisis in which they are victims, companies must use a negotiation strategy; in an accidental crisis, a diminishing strategy; and in an intentional crisis, use a reconstruction strategy. This is the prime school of thought for most experimental research in crisis communication, and its statistical results are very favorable. It provides useful insights about how to decide on the best response, but — in my opinion — it has failed to reach its full possibilities. An action plan may not be defined simply because it works from a statistical point of view: what if it does not work in my own specific case? Can we decide what the best option is by simply looking at the law of probabilities? Moreover, does it really matter whether we are or are not guilty or if it all depends on public perception?

As is true with the rest of ethical dilemmas related to crisis management, the response that I feel to be the most solid and efficient is to base actions on truth and justice. With that foundation, companies should apologize when there is something to apologize for, and not to apologize and strongly defend their stance, when and if the accusation is false. This is the true sense of the word "apology": the defense Plato used with Socrates, showing why his teacher was right and not apologizing at all to those who had unjustly condemned him to death. In those circumstances, defending oneself is an obligation.

It is very easy to understand how many consultants may recommend a conciliatory stance, even in those cases in which the organization has no responsibility whatsoever in order to lessen the current level of tension and hoping that in such a way its enemies will be less aggressive in their actions. Yet it may be seen as being a sign of weakness and end up strengthening those who are attacking it and the actions they are taking.

Hence, perceptions and reality should be carefully studied. When the company has clearly done something wrong, or the reason for the dispute itself is so minor that it is not worth fighting for, you can apologize and accept full or partial responsibility. However, sometimes the best approach is to defend the organization against an unfair attack and steadfastly refuse to apologize. Dezenhall & Weber suggest: «Companies in trouble need to do the right thing, but sometimes that includes going on the offense, whether that means pushing back at detractors or simply reminding people why you're worth supporting in the first place.» The best decision does not have to be the nicest one.

Be prepared

Telling the truth, ceasing to do whatever is wrong, accepting your own responsibilities and repairing the damage are not the only ethical principles in crisis management. There is another ethical norm that is also present and should be considered: be prepared to act with professionalism. Both managers and communicators have a moral duty to perform with the maximum professionalism possible while carrying out their work. Professionalism, expertise in the task to be done and a competent performance make up professional ethics. «Working poorly, not working enough, working without quality and without the required techniques are the main attacks on this ethical code,» says Soria.

Professionalism in the manager: being prepared is a must in today's world, where crises are frequent in all economic sectors. All managers should know what to do if a crisis happens, because improvising is the best path to failure.

The same with communicators: their mission has been righty described by Verčič as that of *cultural interpreter*. Communication with the various stakeholders is not something that should be done by amateurs but requires expertise, an intellectual background, a solid grasp of the techniques to be used and the communication tools, a strategic mindset, governance and teamwork skills and people management: skills that most certainly cannot be improvised.

Professionalism in communicating is a serious ethical duty for both managers and communicators. Professionalism certainly includes technical skills, but its most important aspect relates to content: knowing how to formulate the message in a clear, eloquent, friendly and unequivocal way. I insist on this point, because many crises have originated from inexperience and the lack of professional preparation when facing the challenges and risks that are implicit in any communicative action: ambiguous terms and equivocal expressions due to precipitation; challenging attitudes to the media during press conferences; self-reliance and not asking for advice from whoever could give it; excessive confidence in one's own capacity for improvisation... And the same applies to marketing, in fact even more so: intentionally provocative advertisements, which provoke rejection; frivolity when touching on sensitive subjects, which, with no such intention, cause hurt out of sheer bewilderment ...

It would be necessary to overcome the vision that communication is a set of techniques without a soul, and that persuasion – the objective of any communicative action – is an amoral activity. To think that way means to confuse good manners with the hypocrisy of some highly educated people. Certainly, any technique can be used in an abusive way, but the spontaneity of rudeness is not exactly a value.

The laws of rhetoric are within the reach of all pockets, and behind the great speakers of the past and present there is always a meticulous preparation, a tireless effort to improve and an extreme attention to detail. For example, Steve Jobs' parliaments come to mind: as his biographers have shown, inspiration came to him after many hours of perspiration.

For those who regret that they have been caught by surprise, one would like to remind them of those words that Shakespeare's Julius Caesar uttered: «The blame, my dear Brutus, is not in our stars but in ourselves, we allow ourselves to be inferior beings.» We let the crisis catch us unprepared.

The Story: a Panama paper[31]

On 3 April 2016, based on information leaked by the Panamanian law firm Mossack Fonseca, more than a hundred media outlets, associated with the International Consortium of Investigative Journalists (ICIJ), published reports on numerous offshore companies owned by major public figures from several countries.

Among the incredible number of politicians and personalities around the world who allegedly had assets in those offshore com-

---

[31] Episode documented by Ragnar Gudmundsson.

panies was Sigmundur Daví-Gunnlaugsson, Iceland's prime minister and former journalist. He had won the election by being very
tough on the foreign creditors of Icelandic banks, which had collapsed in the financial crisis that had hit those institutions a few
years earlier.

A few weeks earlier, on 11 March, the prime minister had accepted an interview with a Swedish national television reporter.
According to the request made by the reporter, the topic of the
interview was to review the aftermath of the 2008 financial crisis
and the current state of the economy.

The interview began with general questions about the confidence and credibility of the government, etc. Gradually, the questions became more personal and direct. The journalist masterfully
led the prime minister to declare the importance of credibility, the
responsibility of paying taxes in one's country, etc. The prime minister explicitly denied any personal or family connection to offshore companies. The journalist then challenged him, showing
him documents proving the direct involvement of the prime minister and his wife in an offshore *company* in Panama.

The shocked and confused prime minister choked on a couple
of questions and left the interview abruptly.

The interview was not aired immediately, and over the next
few days the journalist repeatedly asked for additional comments.
The prime minister refused to add anything else, unless his remarks were treated as confidential, which the journalist refused.

Four days later, before the interview was published, the prime
minister's wife revealed on *Facebook* that she had a stake in an offshore company, incorporated in Panama, and that all taxes had
been properly paid. She noted that the company was her property,
although she had made a mistake registering her husband as a 50%
owner; but she hoped that would not lead to misunderstandings
that could harm her husband's credibility.

The revelation fell like a bombshell on the political scene in
Iceland. Soon, the media also discovered that the company owned
by the prime minister's wife had open claims worth 3.5 million
euros against the failed Islandic banks. The prime minister, who
had been one of the staunch adversaries of international creditors,
was one of them.

Finally, on April 3, a report on Iceland's national television on the Panama Papers, viewed live by nearly 65% of the Icelandic citizens, showed that three ministers had been involved in offshore companies, although the prime minister's participation was by far the most important. The show also aired an interview with the Swedish journalist. Icelanders watched in shock as the prime minister brazenly lied and how he finally became infuriated, got up and left the set.

After some political maneuvers and other desperate attempts to survive, Gunnlaugsson resigned on 6 April. This episode shows how the media can be very effective at uncovering corruption; but above all, whoever lies and is caught has no public redemption (except in banana republics).

CHAPTER FOUR

Stakeholders

Classifying criteria

Any organization — as we emphasized in the first chapter — is a set of human relations structured around a mission and intertwined with theoretical knowledge and skills, experience and emotions. The best way to understand an organization is through a map of its stakeholders: who they are exactly, how much they share its vision and goals, what their expectations, fears and perceptions are, etc. The more we know about them, the better: and this is valid for employees, clients, local and national authorities, investors, suppliers, media, etc.: with everybody involved. Unless we know who we are talking to, any effort to have a meaningful relationship is bound to fail.

The map of stakeholders is a fundamental instrument for management. The science of governance pays much attention to this approach - the stakeholder management theory- since it is a reality in the corporate governance of many well-managed companies, and there is an increasing number of books and research papers devoted to it. We have left behind the approach advocated by Milton Friedman (and many others), who argued that the first duty of management is to maximize the shareholder's profit No credence is given nowadays to the ideas of Edward Freeman, who emphasizes that the company must be beneficial to all its stakeholders, and the manager's duty is to ensure that the company is the place where their interests can be maximized over time.

This book is not the right place to examine this trend, but its rise is easily explained: in our world, organizations depend on each and every stakeholder. The rules of the game have changed, and the company must strengthen relations with each one and give an account to each one, because all are indispensable. We are in an ecosystem in which if the bees perish, the lions end up dying. Opposition by any stakeholder can cripple any organization.

The map tells us who our stakeholders are: people who have a stake or interest of any kind on our company. Differentiating in homogeneous groups is vital, because their interests vary a lot from one group to another, and some are more important than others.

In addition, the clearer the delimitation of a group, the easier it will be to establish a good relationship.

The ideal must be to create personalized relationships. In many cases, this remains a mere desideratum: because when the institution is related to many people, it is not easy to personalize so much. I highlight it as an objective, and to distinguish as much as possible between people and divide the interlocutors into homogeneous groups with which to interact.

Aside from dividing them into homogeneous groups by interest, we need to know how they relate to the organization, and their own characteristics: their qualitative traits (sociodemographic data, lifestyles, interests, preferences) and relational (previous experience, relationships with relevant personnel, etc.). As Capriotti says, we collect the data for these three categories – interests, channels, and profiles – in an orderly fashion.

Having a CRM is not enough for our current and potential clients: we need an instrument that covers all stakeholders and their mutual relationships.

Classifying criteria

Stakeholders tend to be classified as either internal or external. This traditional way of separating them has certain limitations. Some feel that this distinction is misleading because it artificially creates a boundary between the two groups while insinuating that the relationships with those *on the inside* and with those *on the out-side* should be dealt with separately. In reality, the key words in today's world of communication are *integrated communication*. Additionally, in many organizations it is practically impossible to define what is internal and what is external, and relationships may even change according to the topic being discussed.

Matrat suggests another classification, that splits them into four levels: decision making (groups that must give their authorization in order for the organization to carry out its day-to-day activity), consultative (groups that should be consulted by the organization before it carries out its day-to-day activity), behavioral (groups whose actions may either favor or hinder the institution's actions) and those with an opinion (those who influence the environment whenever they publicly express their point of view).

In this book, we will follow the approach proposed by Alfonso Nieto, that separates stakeholders by their priority for the organization: *participants* are those who have a solid relationship with the institution and thus proactively affect the institution's activity and its communication; and *stakeholders*, who are a set of people and institutions which are all passive in nature with respect to communication.

Having said that, what really matters is not the scientific model, but the classification (the stakeholder map) of a specific institution in a specific crisis.

Participants are the most important stakeholders: their internal or external presence is absolutely necessary for the day-to-day activities and their absence would imply the end of the institution. The term implies that, in a time of crisis, managers should consider participants as an integral part of the organization, although from a legal point of view they may actually be external parties.

Beyond these two general categories, participants and stakeholders, we are going to add two more: the mediators with public opinion (journalists), and the people who could potentially be harmed by the institution (the victims). Let's begin with the latter group, because whenever there are victims, they should have top priority.

Victims

Many crises cause harm to both people and their property. Actually, a sign that we are in the middle of a crisis is that the company's operations have caused someone harm, or at least there are people claiming they have been hurt by our organization. As Lukaszewski stated, «creating victims is what makes a crisis a crisis.» In a nutshell: our stakeholders will judge the organization according to the way it has treated its victims.

The relation with those who have suffered harm is the most delicate challenge in crisis management and communication. Any relationship with hurt individuals is complicated; in addition, managers are not trained for this situation, so they don't know even what they don't know, and consequently they rarely ask for advice.

Incidents with greater or lesser material consequences take place every single day, but from the very second that a victim is involved, everything changes. One single human victim is enough for public perception to be multiplied tenfold and easily surpass the threshold of what defines a crisis.

Over the last few decades, there have been numerous accidents that have caused grave personal damage, by either pure negligence or even by criminal conduct.[32] There is a long list of terrible stories.

The media will pay extra attention to this type of incident because they are dramatic in nature and full of conflict; they grab people's attention and are even morbidly fascinating. Just look at the audiences that have listened to or watched interviews with those who have been hurt or relatives of those who have been killed in some sort of tragic accident. The media love this type of

---

[32] Every country has its tragedy: in France it was the case of the contaminated blood that, due to a lack of proper health controls, caused numerous deaths in 1992. French Health Authorities discovered this contamination and were informed about the potential risks involved but preferred to do nothing, because to come clean about it *was too expensive* in terms of their own image. In Italy, the leak from a chemical plant in Seveso provoked malformations in newborn babies; in Spain the so-called "aceite de colza" scandal, an industrial type of oil which was mixed and sold for human consumption; etc.

news and will give it hours and hours and pages and pages for what seem to be weeks on end... and the story will last forever.[33]

Because of this, legislation and jurisprudence have evolved to handle these cases with increased severity. Causing victims puts the organization into defense mode in front a court of law and in the court of public opinion. It is very difficult for a company to emerge with its reputation unharmed even if it is innocent and has proved its case. Public perception thinks, "The victim is always right". Even when the victim has acted imprudently or even in bad faith, corporations are up against the current.

Let us recall that major media coverage should not be the prime reason for institutions to take care of their victims. The focus, as we have seen earlier, should be on making the right decision towards them, accepting our own responsibilities, and responding to our true priority stakeholders, who are not the media, but rather our own personnel, our clients and neighbors and the public authorities.

Finally, a terminological precision: the terms *victim* and *survivor* can be problematic. Those involved may want to be called one way or the other. It is preferable – as Coleman suggests – to use the term they prefer. In this epigraph we use *victims* to underline the responsibilities of the organization, but we will have to stick to how those people want to be called.

Main mistakes with victims

In dealing with people who suffered harm, the following mistakes are common:

Taking too long to meet with victims. Obviously, it is not going to be a pleasant encounter. In some cases, the corporate representatives may not even be welcomed. Whatever the case may be, try to meet with the victims as soon as possible and face-to-face, and never send a person who could be seen as a lower level executive.

Thinking that it is a matter of money. If you assume that the main topic of conversation with the victims will be the economic compensation, you are wrong. The first thing the victim wants is to be

---

[33] For instance, every anniversary of the oil spill caused by the Exxon Valdez in Alaska as far back as 1989 is still considered newsworthy.

heard. After that, the second priority of the victims and their families is to know the whole truth about the situation: Who was responsible for it? What were the causes? It is a mistake to feel
obliged to immediately offer a monetary settlement. Even though
the desire to take measures to undo the damage may be considered
honorable indeed, there is a danger that it may be interpreted as an
attempt to buy off their silence - something which will further
exasperate the victims. Public opinion — and that of the victims
themselves — tends to feel completely deceived if the company's
initial reaction is to offer them a check. The time to put a dollar
and cents value on the damage will come much later.

Considering it a private matter. Many institutions agree to apologize, but only out of public view. That is a mistake, because when
an action causes victims, it is a public issue. Once you have listened
to the victims closely, companies should apologize both in private
and in public: explaining to them what has happened and telling
them how you are more than ready to accept the consequences.
Express your solidarity with the victims, and distance yourself from
the causes that triggered the incident. This is much more critical
when a member of the institution has caused the damage voluntarily. In these cases, the institutional stance must be very clear indeed
and leave no room for misunderstandings.

Trying to fix things in secret. Organizations sometimes attempt to
avoid damaging their reputation by reaching outrageous out-of-
court settlements with the victims, which include confidentiality
agreements. Experience proves that these secrecy clauses are actually ineffective and may easily be violated, with devastating consequences. Once these stories are made public, people tend to feel
that the victims have been doubly mistreated, once by the original
abuse and later by having been silenced with money.

Falling short in finding all victims. Companies may consider victims solely those who have suffered physical injury and ignore
those who claim to have suffered psychologically. Those who have
suffered psychological damage are fully entitled victims. People's
psychological stability may be traumatized even when there is no
physical impact whatsoever. Both the law and jurisprudence demand companies handle both physical and psychological damage,
and provide victims with medical and psychological assistance,
even if there was no physical trauma, and use all professional help

that may be required as long as there is stress and general discomfort.

Guidelines in dealing with victims

There are five fundamentals that should be applied in dealing with the victims: be proactive, prolong the attention as long as necessary, involve the victims in the problem-solving process, evaluate the damage from the victims' perspective, and use a third party to set a fair compensation.

Firstly, *the institution should take the initiative.* It is necessary to establish contact with the victims, give them information, even though they may not have expressly requested it yet and set up the proper channels to answer all their questions (free telephone numbers, for example), meet all their needs and ensure that they feel that they are being listened to.

Secondly, *victims should be given immediate, substantial, and prolonged attention.* It is insufficient to simply provide them with information and listen to their stories immediately after the incident. You should continue to offer them full consideration and take any and all measures that may be required to guarantee that the quality of the personal care being given does not decline due to a lack of concern or experience. If so required, a person from the company should be assigned full time and fully resourced.[34]

Thirdly, *the victims should be treated as being protagonists in the solution.* They are not simply the recipients of the institutional care,

---

[34] On August 5, 2010, the access tunnel to the San José Mine collapsed and 33 miners were trapped underground. The 121-year-old copper and gold mine is located 800 kilometers north of Santiago, the capital of Chile (the story of their rescue is magnificently told in 2015 by Patricia Riggen in her film *The 33*). Beyond the technical and political success of the operation, I would like to underline how the authorities did the right thing with the families, prioritizing people, although responsibility fell on the owner of the mine. They were put together, separated from the public and housed at the Campamento Esperanza (Camp Hope), where they could be alone and meet privately with the rescue team and authorities. They were almost always given information first before it was released to the press. The families also received food, water, etc., and were supported by a psychologist.

as if they were children but rather active players in the process it-self. The organization should ask them for advice and authoriza-tion in respect of any public decision that affects them. Nothing should be done without having consulted them first.

Fourthly, *the damage should be assessed from the victim's perspec-tive, not from that of the institution.* It is far from unusual to find cas-es in which the first consideration of the organization that is re-sponsible for the damage is to estimate the maximum amount that they were planning to pay for an overall settlement. However, the proper approach is to study this point by listening to the victims first.

There are times when victims will feel that it is justifiable and legitimate to demand compensations that are well beyond reason. Instead of having a knee-jerk reaction, it is more practical to find out whether these requests were made in and are compatible with good faith. As Elizalde has suggested, «It's worthwhile knowing whether there is willingness on their part or if the victims are act-ing in bad faith, either of their own accord or while under the in-fluence of advisors who in turn are acting in bad faith. In this case, we are able to anticipate that communication with this type of people will be very limited indeed and quite possibly the best way to negotiate with them would be through third parties.»

Lastly, we should definitely *use an unbiased third party to deter-mine fair and just compensation for any and all damages* that have oc-curred. It seems obvious that the party who has caused the damage should not be the one who assesses the amount of compensation. The judgment capabilities of the damaged party may obviously be less than clear and could lead to a much greater or even in some cases a much lesser demand. This third party could be a govern-mental authority (a court of law) or perhaps an arbitrator chosen jointly by the two parties. Unless a third party is used, it is more than likely that any decision that is taken will never be considered "final" and thus the conflict may never be closed.

Participants

As we explained earlier, we call participants those stakeholders who take an active and direct part in the institution's structure and activities. They are normally classified in five groups: managers and employees, who have a labor relationship with the institution itself, in some cases as employees and in others as freelancers; partners who have invested either capital, goods or rights so as to be part of the corporate ownership structure (an equity share); public authorities; clients or those who normally receive the goods and services provided by the organization. Some types of organization have other participants: alumni in universities, benefactors in cultural foundations, parents of a high school, etc.

Managers and employees

The characteristic that defines managers and personnel as participants is their stable work relationship. Traditionally communication with middle managers has been radically separated from communication with employees. However, the organizational tendencies of today's world have flattened companies, making them more horizontal in nature. The decision-making process is no longer solely in the hands of top management but has trickled down to all levels; this makes it difficult to distinguish between managers and employees.

Jointly studying communication with managers and employees does not imply that we deny the differences between both groups, but rather emphasize the aspects which tie them together. As we will see later, companies should act with concentric circles, within the scope of the specific structure for a given organization, starting with the group that is a priority in each specific case.

As Seitel has said, «the hardest function in institutional communications is internal communication, or, in other words, communicating with your employees.» As was seen in chapter 1, there are a number of reasons for this: legal, economic, political, ideological and cultural factors can all weaken the connection with internal stakeholders. Maintaining fluid and well-implemented communication with our personnel has enormous advantages. By improving the flow of information, decreasing the likelihood of conflict, encouraging creativity and clarifying the role of each person within an organization, internal communication generates trust among our employees and coordination in order to achieve our common goal.

Both practitioners and scholars agree that in those cases in which there are no victims, the internal stakeholders represent the communication priority in the midst of a crisis. Obviously, when this principle is stated, the type of organization and the type of the conflict should be borne in mind. But it is worth mentioning, because during a crisis many organizations pay much more attention to the media, public authorities and those who control them, while overlooking their own employees.[35]

In critical circumstances, internal communication may be the most complex and difficult of all for four basic reasons:

Firstly, communicating with our personnel is essential because in ordinary circumstances *the crisis affects them most directly.* If the crisis has caused victims, it is more than likely that among those who have been affected there will be some of the organization's own employees. However, even when there has not been any personal damage, a crisis can seriously affect employees in a number of other ways. If the crisis has economic implications, it is quite likely that pay-raises and internal promotions will be frozen, and some positions may even be in jeopardy. At the very least, a crisis automatically implies a major increase in employees' workload and, inexorably, unpaid overtime.

Stress is inevitable in any crisis and this can increase conflict and decrease teamwork between both people and divisions or business units. Lastly, if the stakeholders perceive that the organization is really to be blamed for the crisis, its personnel will try to distance themselves from the organization. They will be embarrassed by what has happened and this embarrassment will create a

---

[35] A good example in which the employees were placed at the very, very top of the list of priorities was the action plan of American Express in 2001. At that point in time, the main Corporate Headquarters were very near the Twin Towers in New York City. After the 9/11 terrorist attack, the Amex CEO decided that his first concern was to evacuate all company employees as soon as he possibly could. That was his first message and defined the company's priorities for the whole external crisis. Only when he had been told that all personnel were safe did he move on to the second stage: informing shareholders, investors and employees based in other locations that all was well and that the company was able to continue providing its services at its usual level of quality.

gap between them and the organization, and will weaken their loyalty and sense of belonging to the institution.

Remember: crises are not technical facts or variables, nor laboratory experiments, but events that leave deep scars on people. As Elizalde states, «behind any organization that has been damaged or has actually gone under, there are people who suffer the consequences of unjustified criticism, any emotional control or a lack of a proper prevention system,. Companies survive, countries are reconstructed but people do not have enough time to restart their lives or reconstruct their own identity after a public crisis.»

Secondly, *internal stakeholders will seek and demand more information than anyone else*. They want to know exactly what has happened and what to expect and they are convinced that they have every right to this information. Those who have been working loyally and hard for years and years think they have earned the right to be kept in the loop. In a certain sense, they feel that they are in some way the owners of the institution itself and want their voice to be heard in these critical moments.

Thirdly, *employees become the main source of information for other stakeholders*. Without any doubt, they are reliable sources for their relatives, friends, neighbors, and business colleagues, public authorities – police officers, judges, etc. – and quite often even for traditional media and the social media. What they post in their blogs and other platforms may be unofficial, but they are considered trustworthy spokespeople for the institution.

In a crisis, this role is further accentuated. They are asked questions by other stakeholders, who consider them experts and first-hand witnesses to what has happened. And after a crisis, they are the main source of information for internal and independent reports.

Fourthly, because *their full commitment is more needed than ever*. It is critical that members and employees retain a high morale and be willing to do more work than normal and even make sacrifices for their company. They should trust their bosses and be excellent ambassadors for their institution. Thus, communication with its personnel should always be an organization's top priority, and not just in times of crisis. A good relationship with its employees is always required and *not just because a crisis may happen*. When there is a good relationship, everything always runs more smoothly.

In addition, good communication during a crisis period is the best way to strengthen this relationship. It's in bad times when you find out who your real friends are.

Fifth, *the consequences of not taking good care of them are really damaging.* All institutions are vulnerable to possible actions by their angry employees or members. There is no worse enemy than that of an employee who is out for revenge.[36]

So, the organization should always be aware that if an employee is upset that means that there is a problem that has to be solved (not that it may create a crisis, but rather that it is a sign that something is not working) and so this element should be included in a strategy of prevention.

Sixth, *do not underestimate the role of former employees.* The same can be said of former employees: when they think they have nothing to lose, some react with a grudge, and the company can hardly defend itself from their payback.[37]

---

[36] Theranos, the pharmaceutical startup founded by Elizabeth Holmes, went bankrupt in 2018. The havoc began with a *Wall Street Journal* article whose main source was Tyler Shultz, who had been in Theranos for eight months. Fed up with what he had seen, he wrote an email to Holmes complaining that the company had falsified the results of laboratory experiments and ignored the fact that quality controls were continually failing. What made him explode and expose the fraud was the ironic and offensive response of the president of the company to his respectful emails.

[37] In Formula1 2008 season, two-times world champion Fernando Alonso and rooky Nelson Piquet Jr. drove for Renault. The team leader was Flavio Briatore, and Pat Symond, director of engineering. The cars weren't competitive: in the first 14 races they had achieved only one podium, and even that had been through sheer luck. So Renault's victory in the Singapore Grand Prix came as a surprise, thanks to a fortunate combination of starting with low fuel, refueling early and ... being benefited by an accident and the consequent exit of the safety car, which prohibits the drivers from refueling. The crashed car was Piquet Jr.'s Renault. The following year, Briatore decided to terminate the contract with Piquet due to poor results. It was not a friendly ending. A few days later, Piquet Jr. reported that his team had forced him to crash his car in Singapore for Alonso to win the race. Following the investigation, in which Renault did not contest the charges nor respond to questions, the International Automobile Federation announced the disqualifica-

As Jáuregui writes, a key aspect to assess the maturity of an organization is how well its former collaborators speak of it. Regardless of who took the initiative in disengagement and regardless of what motivated it, it is relevant to maintain at least a good emotional relationship with former collaborators.

As the case of current employees, we do not treat former employees well because they can help us in a crisis, but because they deserve it (at least, *in most cases*). You can learn a lot from them if you do surveys to find out the reason for their departure and, if it were the case, avoid the same mistakes in the future. But it is a good thing to go further, and maintain more or less intense active communication , and speak well of them, no matter what happens.[38]

If we do this, former collaborators could be more persuasive ambassadors in a reputational crisis than current collaborators: their independence will make them more credible. Otherwise they will be fearsome enemies.[39]

---

tion of the Renault team for two years, the indefinite suspension of Briatore from Formula One, and a five-year ban on Symonds.

[38] In 2019, Antoine Griezmann, one of Atlético de Madrid's best players, left for Barcelona FC in an inelegant way, and Atlético fans were very unhappy. Asked about this, Diego Pablo Simeone, the Atlético Head Coach, said: «I am grateful to the footballer, to the player that we have had these five years. I have only words of gratitude for what Griezmann has given us, for what he has grown as a footballer. [...] I have learned in life that I shouldn't judge others. I understand that you, the media, have the mission of giving your opinion, but I understand that in life you do not have to judge other people's decisions. And even less when someone has given everything: the club did, I did, and Antoine did as well. From the sporting point of view, it's unnecessary to say what an extraordinary footballer Antoine is. He came at a certain time and now he's taking a step towards a new goal in another position as a footballer. We took part in all this growth. He is one of the top scorers in the history of Atleti, they have been five wonderful years. I am grateful because he has given us everything and I do not judge anything, no one.» I consider that press conference (5-17-2019), accessible on YouTube, to be a magnificent example for all types of organizations.

[39] On 3-10-2019, an Ethiopian Airlines Boeing 737 Max bound for Nairobi crashed soon after take-off from Bole, Addis Ababa airport, killing all 157 passengers and crew. This tragedy triggered one of the most

Lastly, *crises produce power vacuums precisely when an operational chain of command is more important than ever.* In these circumstances, the immediate supervisors are inaccessible, quite often communication channels are blocked, and the company's personnel feel isolated. Precisely for this reason, it is crucial that employees share the institution's core values and priorities.[40]

Management should always inform personnel in accordance with their expectations, both in respect to the content of the message as well as its tone and form, in person, by letter, by phone, in full company or divisional meetings, etc. Paraphrasing what is a valid ethical norm in any culture, Caponigro points out, «this is the best of all possible advice: *"Communicate with employees the way you would want to be treated if you were in their shoes"*. You will almost always do well if you follow this guiding principle.» This principle establishes a valid paradigm: «treat your employees as you would like them to treat your best clients», reminds Covey.

---

serious corporate crises of the year, which lasted more than a year. The official investigation determined that the cause was faulty software. Media reports attributed this to the fact that the software had been developed at a time when Boeing had laid off its experienced engineers and entrusted their work to recently graduated foreign employees. Their sources? Mark Rabin, a former Boeing software engineer who was fired in 2015, told reporters that he remembered a meeting where a Boeing manager had claimed the company did not need senior engineers because its products were already mature. Rick Ludtke, also a former Boeing flight controls engineer who was fired in 2017, explained that the company "did all kinds of things" to cut costs. A Boeing spokesman denied these statements, but his credibility was questioned.

[40] Two opposite examples can help to underline this . The first one was in Florida: when the city had been hit by a terrible hurricane, the local manager of a chain store helped all she could to those in need. When asked why she did so, her answer was: «During a crisis, you must throw out the budget.» She shared fully the corporate culture and did not need any instructions from headquarters. The negative episode was the work of a Starbucks' employee who forced a team of ambulance personnel to pay for the bottles of mineral water that they had handed out to the victims on 9/11. Calls to management were initially ignored – until the story was published, stirring up an internet-based consumer boycott of Starbucks. Only then did the ambulance workers get their money back and the CEO apologized.

These explanations are just common sense and any experienced manager will have already thought in that way. Nevertheless, when a crisis comes up, many managers prefer to solve all the problems by themselves, behaving with a total lack of trust toward the rest of their teams within the company and even trying to act behind their backs. The negative consequences of this behavior towards employees or members and associates – as it is virtually impossible to hide everything from them during a crisis – are very serious indeed and long lasting: unhappy employees have excellent memories.

In this sense, the worst thing that could happen in a crisis is that an institution's employees find out what is happening by watching the news on TV or reading the local newspaper. At least the same degree of information being provided to the media should be given to personnel. At least as much, if not more.

The experience in all types of crises and in a wide range of places shows that *middle managers and personnel in general respond excellently* when they are properly informed. [41] To achieve this, we

---

[41] In December 2008, the most popular evening newscast in an Italian town opened with the tragic news of an accident in the workplace in which a 20-year-old employee had been killed. The news included an interview with a co-worker, who instead of blaming the company, said that it was a very sad event indeed, but the company did not have any responsibility as it always paid very close attention and provided resources to prevent accidents in the workplace. This reaction was not isolated. A representative of the trade unions also stated that the company, «is one of the most careful in respect to on-the-job safety and has invested lots of money in recent years in this area»; and another employee came out and said, "the accident happened due to the lack of experience of our colleague, even though he had attended a safety course of over 170 hours: but when you are busy working, experience is the key factor." Even the local parish priest was on the company's side and in his homily at the funeral said, «it is very sad indeed that such a young life had been taken,» and he thanked the company for the support given to the victim's family." As Mazzei, Kim & Dell'Oro point out, those favorable reactions towards the company were not a matter of good luck, but the consequence of very good internal relations. The company had a total commitment to ensuring a safe working environment by investing in safety measures, security training and internal communication without trying to save a few cents here and there: an intranet, a monthly letter from the CEO to all employees, audiovisuals and events for the staff, etc. This episode reflects how the reaction to

must provide specific information for our employees, without taking for granted that they will already have heard the information through the inevitable grapevine: and adopt an attitude that will reinforce our mutual ties and trust.

It is equally necessary to not simply inform but rather indicate what is to be done and why. During a crisis, you should request employees' collaboration; explain why their help is important, and follow-up with a sign of gratitude. Briefly, *tell them what is going to be expected of them.*

In addition, social media bring a new channel for employees to help their companies. They may be even more effective than official spokespeople.[42] According to González Herrero & Smith,

> In a world that deeply values two-way communication, corporations and governmental organizations need to adopt a new attitude and open their cultures to allow employees to communicate online by using the available social computing technologies. Not necessarily so that they represent the official voice of the organization, but empowering them to convey a similar voice to that of the organization's with bloggers, in online forums, etc. [...] For companies used to one-way communication, a "many to many" dialogue may seem a huge step forward, but by building open and honest relationships with the key influencers establishes a company's credibility and may help to prevent crises or, at least minimize the damage they can do.

---

the tragic accident was also very well managed: in its content, its tone, the choice of communication channels with the varying audiences, in the way it supported the victim's family and in the emphasis it placed on reviewing procedures to ensure that accidents of this type would never happen again.

[42] In July 2013, an Asiana Airlines plane crashed at San Francisco airport. Victims and their families, witnesses, other travelers and general public commented about it, but the company was unprepared and remained in silence for eight hours. This silence caused the airline great harm to its reputation and on the stock market. Only later was it discovered that Asiana had prohibited its employees from mentioning on social media that they worked for the company.

Organizations should carefully consider the best strategy on these channels: the most effective instrument, the most suitable tone, the most appropriate interlocutor, the right frequency, etc. Additionally, the more thorough the information being received, the greater the trust in that response and the sense of responsibility is generated, and thus fewer rumors will fly around.

What is certain is that the company should reach employees before they hear the news from some other source. If possible, information should reach all parties involved at the same point in time, as a sign of respect for them and as a way to avoid the message being misconstrued; a single source will always be deemed as more trustworthy. However, in those cases when this cannot be done, our communication should be organized in concentric circles, to reach everyone in an orderly fashion and ensure that no one is left out.

To ensure the consistency of messages, channels, and timings, it is important that the internal communications department is integrated within the corporate communication division. When it depends on Human Resources because it is seen as an administrative tool, the corporate response in a crisis will be less strategic and more vulnerable to errors, dysfunctions, redundancies, and black holes.

In summary, the golden rule is *to treat all internal stakeholders as they expect to be treated*, both in the contents and in the style. There is some news that employees will never accept favorably if received through the media or from a co-worker over a cup of coffee, and this is especially true of bad news. In these cases, it should be the boss who delivers the news in person, regardless of how bad that news happens to be.

Lastly, let us point out that a crisis is certainly not the best time to gain the esteem and respect of your staff. We can take advantage of the goodwill that has been gained during a period of ordinary circumstances. If, in good times, management has built a constructive working environment, internal stakeholders will most likely react well during the storm and play a major role in overcoming the crisis.

On the other hand, if the climate in the workplace is cold and hostile, or if employees feel detached from the organization, in a crisis their contribution will be lukewarm: that type of environment leads to shoulder-shrugging, resistance and even sabotage.

Obviously, a crisis is not the best time for an organization to suddenly start being concerned about internal communication.

Having your "goodwill-tank" full with each stakeholder is the best strategy of prevention. If your employee communication is being carried out properly, internally they will react positively, maintaining their prior commitment, not taking advantage of the crisis for their own benefit, and informing management of any risks and threats that they may be aware of. Outwardly too, they will defend their company, countering false accusations that are made against it and doing their best to enhance the corporate reputation.

Furthermore, whenever employees perceive that they are being well treated, they tend to defend the company in public and not to over-exaggerate top management's mistakes, nor disclose secret information. Committed employees will always give their organization the benefit of the doubt, even in those cases when their bosses' actions may be questionable.

In conclusion, employees are the most effective defense for a company's reputation and, in time of a crisis, employee support plays a major role. Internal communication is a key factor that should be leveraged to prevent a crisis, lead to the proper reactions, minimize damage and produce positive outcomes.

Shareholders and partners

In this category, we include those who have invested capital, rights and tangible and intangible goods in the company, to provide it with the equity it needs. In accordance with the institution's nature and their own contribution, they may be defined in a number of ways, as founders, promoters, shareholders, partners, patrons, etc. It will be necessary to look at the specific profile of each institution to be able to define the characteristics of its shareholders. For example, it is quite commonplace for the partners to also be managers and in those cases, we should apply the points included in the previous section.

The relationship between the company and these *participants* is characterized by two features: they own the company but do not run it. Therefore, this category of stakeholders does not include the owners-and-managers of commercial enterprises, nor the managers of cooperatives or family-owned companies, although many of these guidelines would certainly be applicable in those cases as well.

Shareholders, especially in the case of a company listed on the stock market, are stakeholders with their own attributes. On one hand, they are the real owners of the company and should be considered an institution's internal stakeholder. On the other hand, in many cases, they are variable in nature: they do not feel tied to the company, beyond the simple economic value of their shares and the dividends that they receive quarterly, and so in many cases they are more than willing to sell their shares at the first sign of what they regard as a serious problem that is not being properly addressed. Furthermore, you should differentiate between major and minor shareholders, as both their attitudes and decision-making power vary greatly.

It is a common doctrine that shareholders are not the priority public in a crisis nor should they be treated as such. *In crisis, people before benefits.* They may be nominally the owners, but the managers' priorities in crisis response should be, first of all, the victims, if any; and then, the staff, because they are the ones who will get the company out of the crisis. Shareholders can aggravate the situation by selling their shares en masse, but little else. For this reason, guiding the institutional response to the crisis based on the interests of the shareholders is wrong, because it puts financial aspects above all else in respect of the rest of the organization.

As mentioned before, the traditional view that the top management's main objective is to maximize shareholder value is obsolete. That view has been superseded by a holistic approach, in which companies should be valuable to all stakeholders. Developing the corporate response based on stockholders' interests is, in my opinion, a huge mistake, as it places financial aspects above all else.

Generally speaking, and with the comments added in chapter 8, shareholders are mainly concerned about the company's financial value, and in times of crisis, shareholders will focus their attention on the economic consequences that could take place. Information towards them will be more effective if it underlines the financial benefits of acting ethically. Managers should explain that dealing with a crisis requires prevention and communication with a wide range of stakeholders, and that trying to hide the problem or to deny responsibilities is not the best path also for economic reasons. Mistakes due to not taking the right decisions are costly.[43]

Certainly, reasoning with your stockholders in purely economic terms does not mean you close the door to an ethical approach. Ethical behavior is a highly positive value in the activity of any institution and more and more corporations seek to establish a solid ethical foundation as a competitive advantage. As Fombrun has stated: a solid *reputational capital* helps to minimize or lessen the impact caused by negative events and/or attacks.

An organization with a good reputation, a track record of aiding its social environment and with leadership that practices what it preaches will always get the benefit of the doubt. This prestige has a clear dollar and cents value for any company. On the other hand, a company's reputation is tarnished with when it fails to show signs of social responsibility and this will often lead to a sharp drop in their stock market capitalization.

Let us insist once again: shareholders are a public of secondary importance when compared to an institution's staff, the institution's priority public both in times of calm and in times of crisis. Behaving in any other way, as is unfortunately seen quite often, may lead to short-term benefits; but as Rockefeller has pointed out, «it is very sad indeed to see how a company's quotation in the stock market rises at the cost of its employees». Yes, sir — the epitome of 19th century capitalism.

---

[43] In January 2013, the cruise Costa Concordia sank off the Italian island of Giglio. The ship, after having collided with some rocks, partially sank and in the chaotic evacuation of its passengers, 32 people died. According to González-Herrero, the poor handling of the accident and the ensuing communication (for example, although it was front-page news all over the world, the shipping line's initial press conference was held 58 hours after the boat had sunk), ended up creating more than $139 million in quarterly losses for Carnival Corporation, and they were forced to set aside $515 million to cover the loss of the ship. The lack of proper preparation by the company also led to a major loss of trust by both its current and potential customers. In addition, Costa Concordia's captain was sentenced to 16 years in prison.

These comments refer to the role of shareholders as a stakeholder in the framework of a general crisis. There are situations in which shareholders are the priority stakeholder. We will analyze them in chapter 8.

Public authorities and regulators

Authorities are those individuals that are above the organization and, in some way, regulate it. In general terms, we consider all of them to be participants because their role in a crisis is extremely important; but please bear in mind that there will be cases in which the authorities will be nothing more than a secondary public, important but certainly not primary.

As a general rule, communication with authorities is determined by their role as public servants. The way a company deals with authorities in a crisis reflects the responsibility that company feels toward the society which those authorities legitimately represent. Additionally, authorities often intervene and decide even the minutest details, especially when public funding is involved. Communication with authorities will also depend on the degree of interest that they show in a moment of crisis, and that – as we know – depends greatly on the social perception of the eventual consequences. As has been stated earlier, the organization should act in accordance with the social perception of the crisis itself. The authorities depend enormously on what is perceived as public opinion as well as the opinion which appears in the press; they do not act solely in accordance with objective, scientific or statistical criteria, but are more frequently moved by emotional, symbolic and ideological criteria.

In this sense, communication with the authorities should be based upon not only their political positioning but also on *the pressure being exerted on them by society in general.* Some crises have relevant political aspects, and in these circumstances, the public authorities will feel that they are compelled to intervene. In other cases, the crisis may affect a country's national interests, and companies must follow government's decisions.[44]

---

[44] This was the case in the BSE (mad cow disease), which was caused by the neurotic spasms that it triggered, and which caused the death of

A good experience is to ask yourself: whose is this problem really? The fact that the crisis has happened in my facilities should not induce me to respond that it is my responsibility. All matters that have to do with crimes and violence, national security, public health, etc., are by their very nature the responsibility of the State. Thus, the company must immediately inform the competent authority and accept its leadership. The only exceptions are containment measures, if they are urgent: sounding the alarm, evacuating a factory, etc.

For example, if we suspect that a manager or employee committed a crime, the institution's duty is to report the facts and cooperate fully and without hesitation with the authorities. It would be wrong to interpret the special relationship with the accused as a reason to avoid or delay contacting the police, and much less to help him or her to escape justice.

In such circumstances, launching an internal investigation is out of place. We naturally need to check whether the evidence is plausible or the accusation credible, but the rest is up to the police. And to achieve this, protocols are useful, so that the organization does not go beyond its responsibilities. For instance, in a case of sexual harassment in the workplace, the company is not competent to carry out a criminal investigation, only collaborating in what they are asked to do.

Sometimes this is difficult, because it contradicts solid instincts: as it happens within my headquarters and it is going to affect me, I may be tempted to take the reins in the affair. No. The usual guidelines for bank branch personnel during a robbery are

---

over 50 people. The mad cow crisis began in 1986 in the UK. Four years later the number of cases had multiplied tremendously, yet the precautions being adopted by the authorities were few and far between. In 1988, several countries vetoed British beef and this embargo was unanimous throughout the European Union a year later. The European Commission, under pressure from Member States, gave greater weight to the concept of free movement of goods rather than public health and its preventive measures proved to be totally inefficient as the disease appeared in France and other countries in 1991. The full embargo was not implemented until 1996 after the first human fatality. This crisis, which lasted for more than a decade, demonstrated the lack of (and the urgent need for) of a Pan-European protocol to manage this type of crisis in which people's health should overrule any other factor.

inspired by this principle: don't play the hero, give the robbers whatever they want, and don't endanger anyone.

The same goes for health issues. If, for example, there were a meningitis epidemic among the students of an Islamic school in the city, the authorities would see it – and rightly so – as a public health problem, not as a private matter for the Muslim community.

Putting myself at the command of the authorities includes communication aspects. I cannot inform the public without their consent, when the people's reaction may affect the management of the crisis. Returning to the example of the school, it will be the health authority that decides how, when and who to inform. The opposite could aggravate the problem: thousands of people collapsing the emergency services of hospitals and spreading the contagion ...

A different situation happens if the authorities' interest were to be heightened by a bitter clash between two private institutions. Regulators feel that their intervention is required to ensure the common good and social peace. In these cases, communication with the authorities becomes a decisive element in gaining the support of public opinion, a critical element in itself in respect of solving the problem.

Properly informing the authorities — or even better, collaborating with them — is the best approach for getting them involved in the solution. It is true that this active role implies sharing the power and the decision-making, but that is the inevitable price you have to pay for sharing overall responsibilities.

A crisis that is the direct consequence of a conflict between an organization and the public authorities calls for another kind of response. Ordinarily the institution has little chance of winning, irrespective of the validity of the authorities' claims, as it will be perceived to be the aggressor against the common good, which is justifiably represented by the said authority. Hence, the best strategy in this case is to reduce the conflict by using a moderate tone and acting with consideration of public opinion to modify its perception. The path itself will be longer than just imposing your decision, but the result will be better for you.

This is not a matter of establishing who has more power. The same recommendation will also be valid when the private organization's position is stronger than that of the authority they are arguing with. Think, for example, of the controversy between Apple and Copertino, the Californian town where that computer company has its corporate headquarters; or between Inditex, the world's leading textile company, and the Galician municipality of Arteixo.

Being right or wrong does not depend on how big you are or how thick your wallet is; as has been pointed out earlier, everybody – and first of all, journalists – will always be on David's side and against Goliath.[45] Therefore, we recommend choosing a dialog and consensual approach; this will be further discussed in the following chapter.

However, when the company is caught between the conflicting interests of a priority stakeholder and the authorities or supervisors, an accurate analysis has to be made. The company has to figure out which relation is more important in that case.[46]

---

[45] On June 2012, the city council of the Scottish town of Argyll and Bute banned a nine-year-old primary school pupil from updating her blog, "Never Seconds", with photos of lunchtime meals served in the school's canteen and offering ratings for their nutritional value. The photo of a nice little girl made headlines in the main British media outlets and some international media as well. The blog started receiving an immense number of views due the ban, and the story spiraled into one much bigger than it had ever been before. The furor forced the local authority to reverse the ban, with the leader issuing a statement to say there was "no place for censorship" on the council.

[46] On December 2015, a terrorist attack in San Bernardino, California, killed 14 people and injured 22. The police recovered one of the attacker's work phones (an iPhone 5G) but it was locked with a four-digit password and was set to eliminate all its data after ten failed password attempts. The FBI wanted Apple to create a new software that would unlock it, but Apple declined. The FBI convinced a court in California to issue an order to comply with the request, and a hearing was scheduled for March 2016. On the same day, Apple's CEO Tim Cook released an online statement to Apple customers, explaining the company's motives for opposing the court order. He also stated that while they respected the FBI, the request they had made threatened data security by establishing a precedent for the U.S. government to force any technology company to create software that could undermine the security of its products: "The United States government has demanded that Apple take an unprecedented step which threatens the security of our customers. We oppose this order, which has implications far beyond the legal case at hand. This moment calls for public discussion, and we want our customers and people around the country to understand

Clients

Clients, consumers and habitual users of the products and services provided by the organization, particularly those with whom it maintains a relationship and those who participate directly in its day-to-day activities, are also participants in the organization.

Customers are not an accessory to a company, but one of its main assets. A well-known and loyal client portfolio allows an enterprise to create new product lines, implement service personalization, etc. That's why the customer database and its corresponding CRM is the true treasure of relational marketing and – as Chiesa states – digital systems have become one of the areas where companies are making the largest investments.

Marketing vs. Communication

Before entering the matter, let us delineate the fields of action of marketing and communication. Certainly, both departments pull in the same direction, towards reinforcing relationships. And yet their goals are different. While communication (or PR) tries to ensure stakeholders' approval, by reducing conflict and improving cooperation, marketing tries to increase sales, market share and overall revenue. As Czarnecki describes it: «Marketing adds value by increasing income. Public relations add value by decreasing expenses that become necessary when issues have been ignored.»

Both disciplines are growing closer and closer, since marketing pays more and more attention to the value of relations (for instance, regarding co-creative processes with the stakeholders involved in brand creation), and communication uses more and more marketing tools to measure, segment, and plan. But they are different.

Second, and in accordance with the majority opinion among communicators, consumer relations are part of corporate communication. This is how Fronz explains it:

---

what is at stake." The case was not settled in court because a day before the hearing was supposed to take place, the government obtained a delay, saying they had found a third party able to assist them in unlocking the iPhone. But it shows how important is to understand who your primary stakeholder is.

While communication strives for stakeholders' acceptance, marketing strives for emotions to increase a company's market share and revenues. In other words: while from a marketing perspective a consumer consumes products and services, from a communication perspective the consumer consumes information about the organization and its environment.

In a crisis, marketing and corporate communication should work hand in hand, especially in those cases in which customers may be affected. However, communication should take the lead in a crisis, because of its nature: a threat which could damage the relationship between an organization and all its stakeholders, not only customers. Crisis management and communication demand an integrated vision of the company, in which the priority stakeholders are victims and, after them, employees.

Therefore, in a crisis there should be more communication than marketing and advertising. What is primarily at stake is the company's reputation and not its quarterly sales or profits. As Ries has stated, to create a company's reputation, communication comes first; advertising and other promotional activities follow.

Furthermore, marketing campaigns – Cocker states – have a very limited impact on the repairing of a company's image damaged by a crisis. When the organization is suspected of wrongdoing, consumers view advertising as less convincing and persuasive, and it may be misinterpreted and actually strengthen the negative feelings against the brand.

Who is a client and who is not

The key word is *habitual*. Simple consumers or occasional users are not participants, but rather those who have a stable relationship with the institution. The monetary aspect is secondary: those who do not pay for a company's services and products are also priority.

The lack of a monetary transaction does not impede us from classifying them as participants. At all costs, we should avoid making the mistake of thinking that those who do not pay do not have any rights, nor may they demand anything (in this case, information): for instance, beneficiaries of CSR initiatives, recipients of NGO programs, etc. are truly participants.

At first glance, it may seem that non-profits do not have clients/consumers, since their partners, benefactors and members look more like internal and not external stakeholders. Nevertheless, many of these practical guidelines regarding *consumer relations* are perfectly applicable in newsletters for parents and/or the relations of non-profits with their benefactors, etc.

All of us coincide in that clients are a critical public for the institution ("the basic reason for a company's existence" is a mantra we hear every day), but when a problem arises, it is no longer so easy to respond to the following question: should we tell our clients about it? There is no one right answer to this question; sometimes our clients will find out even before the organization does; in other cases, it will not be necessary to tell them about it, because it does not affect them and, lastly there will be cases in which it is necessary to tell some of them about it but not all.

Asking yourself the right questions may help you identify the best reaction to address these situations, which should be approached with extreme care: will the clients find out about the problem even if we do not tell them about it? If I were the client, would I like to be informed by the organization before hearing about it from some other source? If I don't say anything and they realize that something has gone very wrong, what will they think about my silence?

The response to these questions will often help you determine the best way to inform your clients about what has happened: how, why, when and what effects it has had on the organization; explaining to them what has been done to remedy the problem and to ensure that it will never happen again; demonstrating that the situation is fully under control; showing that you are more than available to answer their questions; explaining what is expected of them; and expressing your gratitude for their ongoing support and understanding.

Secondary stakeholders

In addition to participants, whose relations with the company are absolutely essential to its normal operations and even for its survival, the organization maintains rapports with other stakeholders, although with a lesser degree of importance: the so-called secondary stakeholders, or simply, stakeholders. In this group we tend to find neighbors, competitors, suppliers, institutions of civil society, experts and influencers in that particular industry, and people in general who have some sort of interest in the organization, regardless of how vague this interest may be.

People who may become participants at one point of time or another are also within this category: potential managers or employees, occasional consumers who may later on become habitual consumers, etc.

Nonetheless, assigning a person or a group to the category of participant or that of a secondary stakeholder is not clear-cut. There are no *primary or secondary stakeholders in themselves*: they are one or the other depending on the type of organization and the circumstances of the case. For instance, for an industry located in an uninhabited area, the relation with its local community will certainly be secondary while it would primary for an antique shop on Main Street.

By including all kinds of external stakeholders among the company's *stakeholders*, we further emphasize the social changes that have taken place over the last few decades. In its original sense, *stakeholders* referred to those who had a moral interest "at stake" in the organization, but lacked any sort of legal ties with it, as opposed to *shareholders*: "owners of a certain percentage participation, stockholders," according to the Dictionary. Nowadays, however, more and more people feel the organization's activity affects them in one way or another, and so they think they have a legitimate right to be listened to. Again, public perceptions go beyond legal rights and duties.

Neighbors

One of the most neglected stakeholders are neighbors and yet, their importance – at least in Western societies – is growing steadily. For instance, the opening of a new corporate headquarters requires a communication plan with its neighbors, and not only with the City Hall, who have to approve the new facility. It is a well-known fact that new business facilities tend to create problems for the neighborhood and trigger adverse reactions in local communities. Preserving an untouched urban environment, a nice suburb or a summer resort area that is still "human," are tasks that are carried out with passion and creativity. This social rejection phenomenon is what sociologists call the NIMBY (not in my backyard) Syndrome. Glaberson describes it very well:

> NIMBYs are noisy. NIMBYs are powerful. NIMBYs are everywhere. NIMBYs are people who live near enough to corporate or government projects — and are upset enough about them — to work to stop, stall or shrink them. NIMBYs organize, march, sue and petition to block the developers they think are threatening them. They twist the arms of politicians and they learn how to influence legislators. They fight fiercely and then, win or lose, they vanish.

Social rejection favors and even triggers, true crises. People are highly sensitive about any conceivable health or environmental risk, they can easily be mobilized against such initiatives they perceive as harming the status quo and — as everyone knows all too well — their protest marches always get wonderful media coverage. Conflicts are colorful and full of surprises, often purposefully so. Other times the news may be centered on some major disagreement with the authorities that could quickly turn violent.[47]

---

[47] In January 2014, riots broke out in Gamonal, one of the most populated neighborhoods in Burgos (Spain), where moving around was a nightmare. For this reason, in the campaign for the local elections of 2011, both the conservative candidate (PP) and his socialist counterpart (PSOE) promised a parking lot. The council elected at the polls put the project out to tender, which was evaluated by a jury with representation from residents and businesses in the area. It also promoted public exhibitions, conferences and neighborhood assemblies, and distributed videos and informative flyers about the project. And yet, the day after construction work began, citizens called on social networks for open resistance to stop the construction. After a week of violent street

Among the secondary stakeholders, we also find trade unions and political parties, professional associations, direct competitors, former members, etc. The relevance of these stakeholders is growing steadily, especially since the tendency of these groups to join associations and become activists increased, attracting the attention of the media as well as the intervention of the authorities in their policy making.

To be able to identify the stakeholders we must know who would be affected by the institutional activity. According to Grunig, we are currently in a period of frequent institutional crisis and only a third of them are triggered by natural causes: the other two thirds are the consequence of poor conflict management.

It would be shortsighted for a company to limit its interest to simply avoiding conflicts with secondary stakeholders. Organizations should be doing everything they can to turn these stakeholders into their allies. The best way to avoid a nasty argument with the neighborhood is by becoming active promoters of an on-going dialogue with the neighbors and community leaders. Trust is built on clear and open lines of communication. Surprises, on the other hand, generate anxiety which can quite often lead to disputes with local communities. In short: it's good to act as good neighbors.

It is absolutely necessary to keep them up to date about anything and everything that affects them and to be aware of any possible points of friction, in order to resolve them as soon as possible. Once the crisis has exploded, you should immediately notify them. We should apply the same criteria as we saw in respect of how you should approach your employees, by asking ourselves: What would

---

disturbances, the mayor announced the project would be scrapped. These popular mobilizations (which were not the first: others had happened in the previous months) aimed at excessive public spending at a time of a high unemployment , and at the negative consequences of that specific project: reduction of the width of the road, elimination of free parking slots, etc. But it was only the straw that broke the camel's back: the real cause of the disturbances was social exhaustion due to budget restrictions in respect of social work, previous public investments without social impact, and the construction of a new, privately managed hospital, etc. The case is interesting precisely because there was an attempt by the City council to share the project, which was clearly insufficient to build social consensus.

we want to know if we were in their shoes? How would we like to be informed? What tone would we like to hear?

The three basic rules of communication with neighbors and, in general, with the secondary stakeholders are as follows.

First, *be proactive.* We should not wait until these groups start to protest. We should go into the meeting aiming to inform them properly and facing the conflict with a constructive attitude. Experience shows that consensus building, which implies sharing power with others (not everything will be decided by the institution itself) will then lead to sharing responsibilities and common benefits. Seeking consensus rather than confrontation is always the best approach.

Second, *show a positive attitude.* Do not approach the problem as 'them against us', or as a legal dispute in which *mors tua vita mea*; be positive: what can my company do for its social environment? How could we contribute to the local community? Creating a good relationship with the local community is indeed a good long-term investment, and it will certainly pay off, in terms of goodwill and cooperation, when the crisis hits.

Third, *keep it out of the hands of technicians.* Putting corporate relations with the local neighbors in the hands of technical divisions tends to increase an organization's vulnerability. When the content and information channels are in the hands of either engineers or accountants, the whole conversation tends to be focused on aims and cold facts, lacking human connection. The same thing happens when legal criteria dominate: it tends to be misunderstood and give the impression that whatever is legal is the only thing that is legitimate.

In relationships with the local community, Barton has proposed ten things to always say to a community group: 1. I understand your position. 2. Let me restate your position. 3. We are willing to listen. 4. We will continue to work on this issue. 5. We share the desire for a good place to live and work. 6. We have differences. 7. We care about our host community. 8. We have common interests. 9. This dialogue benefits all of us. 10. You will hear from us.

The six opposite mistakes would be: 1. I agree with you. 2. You don't understand. 3. We need more time. 4. They're wrong. 5.

The media has distorted this problem. 6. This is a one-time request (or problem).

To achieve good community relations, the following has proven to be advantageous: analyzing new projects (opening of a new facility, for instance) from a broader perspective, that includes all the possible political, sociological and cultural factors. Best practice consists of integrating experts from the local environment into the project team. They will be able to share the local point of view, integrating the local elements (values, traditions, requirements) to develop a win-win approach for all. Once again, a good communication approach — a fluid and cordial relationship with all stakeholders — is the best conflict and crisis prevention measure.

The mediators: reporters

Many experts tend to include the media in the *participants* category, since they actively configure the institution's communication, both in general, and more specifically in crises. What is more, many crisis managers dedicate their best efforts to reporters, using the media to reach most of the company's stakeholders.

From my point of view, which is that crisis communication should be in sync with ordinary communication, the media are not always a priority stakeholder, nor a secondary public either. They are rather "mediators" with my stakeholders. They are not end recipients of this relation but simply a medium, or better, one of the channels I have to reach them (the others being direct communication channels).

In that sense, the media behave both as a stakeholder and as a communication channel with the other stakeholders, and so they are a unique kind of stakeholders. We will study them as a category in themselves to better understand their dual characteristics.

In the old days, journalism considered itself as a true picture of reality, objective and unbiased in nature. We saw in chapter 1 that reporters are no longer simply witnesses: they interpret, assess, analyze, give their own slant, and often try to persuade their audience. As Rodriguez & Sádaba state, «In the new communication framework we are in, in which the boundaries between information and opinion have absolutely disappeared, the media is playing a decisive role and one which is even greater in importance in conflict situations. [...] The press may actually either help to resolve these conflicts or do their part in making them last longer and longer.»

Another factor not to be underestimated is the economic crisis that news corporations are undergoing. From the point of view of their business model, today's newspapers are like the coal industry of the 1970s. The lack of resources influences the quality of information: newsrooms are short-handed; there are fewer experienced journalists and there is a greater dependence on agencies more information is covered by interns and there are concerns about the professional intrusion of netizen journalism... A small percentage of media is profitable, and without profit it is not easy to maintain editorial independence, which is essential for good journalism. It's a dog chasing its own tail.

Reporters: it may be worth recalling just for a moment the main characteristics of information professionals. Roger Ailes paints the following picture:

> Many people behave as if they were on some sort of a mission and perceive their work as a social service in the fight against lies and corruption; they feel they are obliged to demand the most from institutions and constantly be testing them (that does not mean that they are dead-set against institutions, they simply want to shake them up once in a while for their own sake); the most valuable prize is being able to uncover some scandal (although they are not always looking for one); many journalists place their profession above their own personal life: they believe it is their moral obligation to tell the whole world what they know, even if it means losing a friend, and are always looking for a piece of news, even running the risk of breaking up their own marriage, etc. They are full-time 24/7/365 reporters.

The media play an important role in any crisis. As we said before, many experts point out that some crises *would not exist without the media*. In their view, media relations are always a risky issue. Any minor mistake with a reporter may be the match that ignites the fuse of a crisis. Their attitude leads them to avoid journalists. They think that speaking with a journalist will either stir up or create issues that are not currently problems, or only exacerbate existing problems. For those who think along those lines, speaking to a journalist is always risky and the most prudent approach will always be to avoid risks.

The way a company approaches its relations with the media is far from being a theoretical question; it is a major strategic decision, with far reaching consequences. Some organizations find it tempting to deal with the media as simply one more means of self-promotion. The logical consequence of that approach is the attempt to 'control the information': persuade reporters to publish what reinforces my company's reputation and sales, and not to publish what goes against it. To achieve those goals, some are more skilled than others, some more ethical than others.

This is not the paradigm of desirable media relations which this book is trying to convey. Manipulation is the wrong approach for two reasons: Firstly, as is true in any communication relationship, its traits — says Grunig — should always be «reciprocal, trustworthy, credible, respectful, win-win in nature, and based on mutual understanding.» In much the same manner as in any other relationship, media relations has two sides, and if the features just mentioned are not put into practice by corporations, no one can expect the media to take them into account. Secondly, this approach may work in times of peace but if applied in a crisis, it could lead to disaster.

The leading principle for dealing with media within the scope of crisis management is crystal clear: the best investment is a *solid relation with the press which is mutually beneficial and has been established in smoother times*. Journalists will then treat the organization in the same manner as they were treated before the crisis.

Furthermore, one of the strategic reasons to open up a press office is precisely to get to know the journalists and to enable them to know you as well. This is a huge step in the right direction towards crisis prevention. Journalists will always ask tough questions — that is their job — but they will listen first to those with whom they already have a relationship of trust.

It isn't superfluous to state that the *media's interest in crises is legitimate*. Crises are one of the subjects that the public is most interested in, and journalists are capable of doing *anything* to tell that story to their readers, listeners, or viewers. In these circumstances, managers tend to feel they are being persecuted and react as if they were literally being attacked on all sides. This often ends up with the application of the age-old approach: "Better not to say anything than to make a mistake."

Langadec, one of the discipline's founding fathers, has described the managers' feelings during a crisis as follows:

> We feel that we are being attacked on all fronts: there are reporters everywhere we look. We seem to be the victims of a brutal wave of intruders who have taken over our organization and act as if it is newly conquered lands. [...] We answer their questions but then they tell a different story. It's an uneven battle: the journalist has the right to make mistakes but whenever we are wrong, we are severely judged, accused of being incompetent and condemned for having tried to maliciously misinform everybody.

This is why we *should turn the situation around long before a crisis hits* – do not take an "us vs. them" stance. It worth insisting once again: the first step in dealing with the media during a crisis consists in previously having established a professional, frequent, and win-win relationship with them. Crisis communication will inherit the pre-existing state of affairs. A crisis is certainly not the time to open up a new channel of communication and make new buddies; it's a moment when you either leverage a fluid relationship or you have to put up with a tense or non-existent one.

Different media outlets may present a crisis in different ways. The description of the facts themselves may be the same, but the way in which they are presented can determine if an accident is portrayed as an exceptional event or as evidence of something more sinister. Therefore, it is not a secret that some companies in crisis will prefer to take a shortcut and use measures to pressure editors to silence the matter. With a large dosage of realism, Ogrizek & Guillery write, «Some people do it and sometimes they are very successful.» But it is also true that when that silence is broken and the news comes out, or when the relationship is broken, the effects may be devastating for both the organization and its managers. There are no safe secrets anymore.

While this is not the right place to examine the principles and practices of media relations, let's just recall the guidelines that are especially crucial in crises:

1. Bear in mind the various interests of the media (deadlines, formats, audience) and provide them with whatever they need. For example, TV reporters need information AND images, so it is a good idea to allow them to film the scenes.

2. Ensure that top management are available to the media. During a crisis, the press always prefers to meet with those responsible in person, giving a face and name to the company while avoiding any conversations with lower level spokespeople. This does not mean that the best candidate is the CEO (although in some cases it may be) but just a qualified person directly related to this case.

3. Every journalist deserves the utmost attention. There is no such thing as a 'hardly important reporter' or a 'nearly irrelevant media outlet'. Excellence must be sought at all times, avoiding the assumption that managers are so prepared and skilled that they can be interviewed without serious preparation.[48]

---

[48] In March 2013, the Canadian-based Lululemon, a textile company specializing in yoga apparel, substituted the fabric used for their yoga pants for another of lower quality. Many yogis began complaining that when they bent over, their yoga pants were became transparent. When the complaint reached 12%, the company took notice. They recalled the leggings, offered full refunds to their customers, informed their stakeholders and fired the CEO and the Chief Product Officer. After the recall, in spite of a decline in revenue of approx. $67 million, everything was back to normal. But in November, Lululemon's founder and chairperson was interviewed on Bloomberg TV. Asked about the sheer pants, he said: «Quite frankly, some women's bodies just don't work for it... Even our small sizes would fit an extra-large. It's really about the rubbing through the thighs, how much pressure is there.» These comments outraged consumers: they found them offensive, and they protested both in person and online. Part of the problem was that this interview happened when the chairperson was on holiday in Australia, with no internal support or preparation for easy and difficult questions. Media relations are not informal relations at all.

4. Take the initiative, becoming the prime source for up-to-date information as soon as you possibly can, act creatively throughout the crisis, control the size of the problem to ensure that it is not blown out of proportion and properly manage the timing. If the news is negative, journalists should hear it first from company sources.

5. Many times, the media are much more interested in uncovering what is being hidden than in the information itself: *press releases are published in the appropriate section while secrets are front-page news.*

6. It is hard indeed *to beat* the media: if the relationship is approached as a bare-fisted fight, you may win the battle and lose the war. Therefore, it's better to adopt a constructive, respectful approach seeking a win-win outcome for both parties. If later on you realize that the reporter is not buying in, the best solution is to simply walk away rather than getting into a heated argument.

7. Remind the media that they have a social role to fulfill: explaining the debate to their stakeholders, articulating the public discourse, reaching a social consensus; information related to a rumor that may trigger a huge fall in the stock market or about an unconfirmed epidemic may create grave social alarm, etc.

In short, communication with journalists is indispensable in reaching the organization's stakeholders; but this is neither the first nor the main channel for the company. Actually, one of the main tasks of any corporate communication division is to maintain and feed direct channels with each priority stakeholder. If this is the case, the media are relevant regarding only those who don't know you. If a crisis hits a company which has good relations with its stakeholders and good communication channels to listen and talk to them, whatever the media publishes will have a limited impact.

Remember what we saw in chapter 1: social media have broken the monopoly that the traditional media had in mediating in the field of social dialog. The digital environment offers institutions the possibility of creating direct channels to communicate with its stakeholders without using the media.

On the contrary, organizations get in trouble when they do not have good relations through direct channels. If that is the situation, whatever the media say, even if it's misleading or plain wrong, will have a devastating impact in the company's reputation.

Story: Safety and self-driving cars

On May 7, 2016, a forty-year-old businessman from Ohio, USA, became the first man to die in a self-driving car accident His Tesla sedan was in autopilot mode when he crashed into the side of a large truck that was crossing lanes irregularly and by surprise on a Florida highway.

Tesla's challenge was to combine a compassionate response towards the victim while defending their product with data and competence. Not an easy job, because perceptions of new technologies aren't just based on science.

Tesla's chairman reacted quickly, releasing a statement on his blog titled A Tragic Loss. However, his following comments were more objective, focusing on traffic accident statistics, and comparing them to Tesla autopilot cars. These posts also included detailed information on autopilot functions and technology. Following the blog's publication, crisis management experts, the media and the general public criticized Musk's and Tesla's response to the tragedy.

Then Tesla's communication became confrontational. Elon Musk retweeted: «1.3 million people die each year in traffic accidents. However, 1 person dies in a Tesla on autopilot and people report driverless cars as unsafe.»

He also responded to a journalist via Twitter saying: «If you're worried that traffic deaths might alter the stock price, why don't you write about the more than a million deaths a year from other car companies?»

And to a Forbes article on the accident, Musk responded with a blog post entitled Bad Luck, which began by saying, «Forbes's article is fundamentally incorrect», and then continued in a defensive tone linking car accident deaths to autopilot technology.

Musk did not mention the deceased nor express his condolences to his family and friends. For this reason, many perceived the post as statistical, cold-hearted, and defensive.

In the following months, Musk continued to express his frustration with extensive coverage of the news of accidents involving autopilot. Comparing them to traffic accidents in general, he commented: «Musk reality is not reflected well in the media», and «a negative story dissuading people from using autonomous vehicles was effectively 'killing people' since the technology made driving safer.»

Independently of its communication style, Tesla did improve the system: it distributed a software update for the Tesla's onboard system in September 2017 (within three months of the crash), and a new one in December, to ensure the driver was engaged; these updates required drivers to touch the steering wheel more frequently.

From my point of view, every time a new technology appears, safety will always be a hot topic. Distortions in public perceptions can be eloquently challenged, but after a fatal accident, it is better not to get involved in an argument. You can be very eloquent and even challenge public assumptions, but after a fatal accident, it is better not to get involved in an argument. If you say, "the technology is right", it would be impossible not to be understood as "the driver was wrong".

A better approach would have been to send an apology after the accident, to accept responsibility in this tragedy and send clear signs of empathy to the victim's friends and family. Then, plan how to educate your stakeholders step by step, intervening often in various ways (including having others speak), knowing that it is a long-term task.

CHAPTER FIVE

Consensus and dissent

The curve of dissent

Institutions – we said in the first chapter – are ordered sets of relationships with their stakeholders around the corporate mission or purpose. An organization is incomprehensible if its value proposition is not known to its participants and stakeholders, which is the basis and foundation of its public legitimacy. In order to act in a specific context, institutions need social consensus.

Social consensus is the ideal setting for any organization: when it is known and appreciated for what it is, it grants the social license for the institution to operate. But what we are, how we are perceived, and the coherence of our purpose with social needs do not always match up.

When the organization's identity and activities are different from stakeholders' perceptions, then we have a communication problem. It does not matter whether the projected image is better or worse than reality: if they are different, we have a problem.

When the purpose does not coincide with social needs (that is, when the existence of the organization does not benefit the stakeholders), then we have an identity problem. We must change not our communication but our purpose: by making it more social and fairer. Or rather, we first have to change the institution's goals and activities, and then the way it communicates.

What often happens is that we only notice these problems by listening to the public. That is why we have to keep our antennae alert in order to properly discern the distance between perception and reality. We have to look at the institution's outward manifestations: whether there is confusion about what it does and what it defends, and whether there is discrepancy or confrontation with what it defends and its real activities, past, present, or future. Listening to our stakeholders' perceptions and confronting them with our reality will help us determine the best line of action: by clearing up the confusion with better communication and rectifying what is antisocial with internal change.

These two factors allow us to draw, according to Elizalde, a curve that unites the different situations:

- Confusion due to the existence of a risk, which alters the balance in the relations of the company with its stakeholders.
- Conflicts, where a participant or a public disagrees with the organization over some material aspect (the quantity, quality or timeframe of the product or service).
- Controversies, where the discrepancy does not refer to material aspects but to the principles and values that the company defends.
- Crises, which may arise from conflicts or controversies, to which is added the threat of serious harm and the urgency to resolve the issue.
- Finally, scandals, which are crises in which one of the basic principles of social coexistence has been violated.

The image of a curve also helps show that it is not a staircase with marked steps, but a gradual slope. That slope is clearly upwards, and the steeper it becomes, the more difficult everything becomes. Antipathy is worse than sympathy; suspicion is less bad than hostility, and hostility can degenerate into underground belligerence and from there into open warfare. Each step taken towards dissent makes the path of return more complicated, and also more expensive: when we are the bank's favorite company, we get a loan with fabulous interest rates, but when we are in a fight, it will either be denied or granted with very poor conditions attached.

Conflicts and controversies have one thing in common: the disagreement is not universal but concentrated on some specific point. Therefore, both can be described as a limited absence of consensus: a controversy will happen about values, and a conflict about interests.

This disagreement is limited, because not everything that an institution does or defends is rejected, but only one element. Or, it only affects one stakeholder, while the others remain on the sidelines because it does not affect them. For example, staff may be satisfied with salaries and safety conditions, but feel that break times are insufficient. Their claim is only of interest to employees, but customers, suppliers and other stakeholders remain relatively indifferent.

The same happens with crises and scandals: both can be described as a global lack of consensus: they affect all or almost all stakeholders, because they can cause the company to fall apart. The difference centers on the severity of the conduct attributed to the organization, which in a scandal is so offensive and unjustifiable that it cannot be forgiven. For this reason, the scandal can be labeled as a "superlative crisis."

For that reason, in this introductory section we will simplify and talk about the difference and similarities between conflicts and crises, as generic categories.

An essential difference concerns their frequency. Conflicts are the daily bread of institutions. Managers' main occupations are putting out fires, inside and out. On the other hand, crises are always extraordinary situations (except for professional tightrope walkers, who always walk a fine line).

This habitual nature means that in every organization there are procedures for the resolution of conflicts. The institutional response to a conflict follows ordinary channels, which can be accompanied by more or less tension, but always within what is rational. On the other hand, the response to a crisis is always accompanied by tensions exacerbated by the insufficient time available to solve the problem, and for this reason they become unstable situations, causing behaviors that are difficult to control.

As Elizalde emphasizes, «in a conflict the adversary is known and I have legitimacy to act, oppose, etc. In crises, on the other hand, there is a multiplicity of actors and their positions are not defined. For this reason, managers in a crisis experience loneliness – that is, dissent and lack of support – not only from opponents, but also from other agents, the uncertainty w as to whether they are with me or against me.»

Crises are eminently public phenomena, under the spotlight of the media. Instead, conflicts are better resolved by negotiating with the other actors in private, to reach a mutually beneficial agreement. This book is about crisis management, but we deal with conflicts because they are usually the main door through which crises arrive. Most crises signal their arrival through more or less serious conflicts, but always discernable to a well-trained eye. Prevention-based crisis management deals with how to prevent conflicts from degenerating into crises.

In the following sections, we will study each of these stages of dissent separately and in detail. However, this introduction is intended to highlight that all the manifestations of social dissent that an organization may suffer in its relations with its stakeholders have a common root. The fear of the neighbors of a chlorine factory, a conflict with a trade union, a controversy over the design of a shirt that looks Nazi, a crisis after worms are found in cans of fish, or the scandal of an NGO that hired prostitutes for their managers in an area hit by an earthquake, are not disjointed phenomena, but are linked by a common thread: the breaking of the consensus and trust that previously united the public with these organizations.

This diagnosis indicates that the strategy to combat all of them is the same: to reinforce relations with our stakeholders. Regardless of the seriousness and extent of the problem, the key to solving it lies not in techniques, but in re-establishing trust in the organization.

Regaining trust takes time. Results may not come immediately. But if trust in the institution is not weakened and public consensus recovers, that institution has a future.

Creating and managing consensus

The main objective in crisis management, as we have mentioned several times earlier, is to avoid conflicts becoming crises. An organization in permanent conflict with one or several stakeholders is not in a stable position; the conflict may drag others into it, provoking a crisis. Anyone who feels they are being mistreated will never be satisfied with the solution proposed by the other party. On the contrary, they will always be waiting for the chance to get even and recover that which has been taken away, and to soothe the terrible memories of suffering. Without consensus there is no long-lasting peace but at most a temporary suspension of hostilities.

Although it is impossible to avoid all conflicts, companies with a long-term vision and willingness to establish solid relationships with their stakeholders will try to resolve them fairly and justly, proposing win-win solutions and using persuasion more than sheer power. Susskind and Field, from the Harvard Mediation Institute, have proposed a systematic methodology to reach consensus, called the Mutual Gains Approach. The six key points within this program are as follows:

Recognize the other party's concerns

One way to achieve this is by having each side explain the viewpoint of the other, particularly highlighting the areas of common ground, and being able to explain the conflict in a way that is satisfactory to the other. If in a negotiation each of the parties manages to understand and explain the other's point of view, the probability of finding a consensual solution increases exponentially.

For this reason, Bazerman & Neale recommend that each party begins by summarizing the other position and underlining common points. Paraphrasing creates the conditions for a constructive discussion.

For example, in a conflict between a hospital and those living in the vicinity, the hospital director should begin a public address by publicly accepting the concerns of those living nearby: ambulance sirens at all times of day and night, parking issues, etc.

Promote a joint gathering of information

Avoid additional tension arising from distrust by using a third party to collect relevant data about the facts in contention.

In a climate of confrontation, the data and evidence collected by only one party is not usually considered credible by the other party and, therefore, reasoning based on that data may well be rejected. On the other hand, if the data is collected jointly, or at least entrusted to an independent investigation, the discussion starts from a solid basis which is shared by both.

In the previous example, research covering noise levels, parking spaces, and so on, should be done by jointly appointed third parties.

Offer specific actions to minimize the damage

Offer specific actions to minimize the damage that may have been caused and promise that compensation will be paid for any inconvenience properly proven. (Obviously, later on promises will have to be kept.)

Phrases like, "no worries, nothing will happen", "nothing has happened," "everything is going to be OK," etc., based on no hard evidence, are not credible and ruin trust.

Accept responsibility and share power

Accept responsibility, admit your mistakes, and share power with others. Aiming at a consensual solution implies that the organization should not make any major decision by itself. The other party will feel more integrated and responsible, more "ownership", if it has been made part of the decision-making process.

Therefore, something is wrong when managers feel *defeated* because others have modified the original proposal: the more the project belongs to everyone, the fewer conflicts there will be!

Using the same example, we should check if a better approach might be moving the Emergency Room entranceway for ambulances to another spot which does not affect residents, etc.

Be ethical

Always act honorably and respectably. Honesty is the best policy. Avoid any false attitudes, manipulation, bribery, etc.

Work for the long term

Propose establishing and strengthening a long-term relationship as your main goal. It is hard indeed, considering the amount of pressure that is being exerted to accomplish immediate results;

but working with a long-term perspective is the only way to success-fully maintain the institution's reputation, credibility and results in a two- or three-years' period. Conflict resolution should always lead to new opportunities of greater collaboration.

To compete or to collaborate?

I am perfectly aware – as Susskind & Field must be – that these tips have little to do with competitive negotiation methods and techniques. Some radical cases sing the praises of an aggressive negotiation attitude, one that refuses to give even a glass of water to the other - the "enemy"... A well-known book comes to mind (and a very good one in other aspects) entitled *Never Split the Differ-ence: Negotiating As If Your Life Depended On It*, by Voos and Raz.

In situations of tension and risk, collaborative negotiation ap-proaches are more effective, as recommended by my colleague Kandarp Mehta. This requires thorough preparation to understand what the other party is looking for; knowing how to keep control of our emotional states, avoiding threats and ultimatums.[49] «Dia-logue is the currency in a crisis – Mehta explains – and an open door is always better than a burned bridge.»

For this reason, if my negotiation is to have an impact on rela-tions with a group with which I want to build a long-term relation-ship, I am shooting myself in the foot if I don't achieve a mutually beneficial agreement. We should attach importance to creating a

---

[49] On November 2010, the Fiji government announced an increase in taxes on the extraction of mineral water from the aquifers of the archi-pelago. The raise multiplied by 45 what the US company Fiji Water was paying, and only applied to companies that extracted more than a cer-tain amount, a circumstance which affected only Fiji Water, so the company understood that it was a discriminatory tax. Its reaction was bold: it announced the closure of the bottling plant, the suspension of some services, and threatened to leave the island. Fiji Water's negotiat-ing position was weak: not only was its brand tied to the islands right down to the name, but it also paid less tax than it should have through irregular tax practices, and it did little to alleviate the poor economic situation of the country. In the end, Fiji Water had to g threat and ac-cept the tax.

stable collaborative environment, and not let short-term interests overshadow the long-term need to overcome a crisis.

Mehta also emphasizes that when concerns are intense, «it is important not to negotiate out of fear, but to generate hope. If we try to spread hope, we will get more hope in return, which will spread to society.»

Instead, we can employ tougher strategies if we are not in a critical situation, or if not reaching an agreement is not that relevant to us, or when negotiating with someone we will not see again, so the only thing that matters is here and now. Anyway, life has many twists and turns, so my recommendation is not to base negotiation on power, but on legitimacy.

Approaching negotiation as a collaborative endeavor starts from recognizing the beneficial effects of helping each other. If we get things into perspective, helping others is not only the right thing to do, but it's also the smart thing to do. In the face of collective threats, selfishness is the most impractical thing in the world, in addition to being morally ugly.

Ultimately, working for mutual benefit is not a technical formula, but principles of action that articulate an ethical vision. As Susskind & Field say, «leadership does not consist in managing your own team in order for them to do things well but rather for them to do good.»

The starting point is to apply a principle-based leadership approach, from which many operative consequences will flow: quantifying the damage that has been caused and the choice of mitigation and compensation measures; understanding the magnitude of the risk involved, and how to communicate this to all the interested stakeholders; defending our stance in appeals in the courts; the negotiation style to be used; etc.

Trust, the secret for consensus

We now run into another of those concepts that we use every day and with which we feel comfortable, but which turn into eels when we want to catch them: trust. As Baier says, «We perceive trust like the air we breathe: only when it is scarce or polluted.»

And yet it is fundamental, because trust is the key that allows co-operation, motivation, innovation, and change.

This has always been the case, but it is even more so now, where the new business models (Airbnb, Cabify, Spotify, TripAdvisor, etc.) are part of a collaborative economy. Our technological age, says Rachel Botsman, «is a new age, the age of trust.»

According to the Oxford English Dictionary, trust is the «firm belief in the reliability, truth, or ability of someone or something. » From an organizational point of view, however, an important nuance is added: when there is trust, we put ourselves into the hands of another. Here, we will accept the most common definition of institutional trust: «the intention to accept vulnerability based on positive expectations regarding another's conduct», say Mayer, Davis & Schoorman. In this sense, it is the tendency to ascribe virtuous intent to another individual or entity.

In emergencies, authority is exercised without question. If we are vacating a burning building, it is not the time to question the guidance of the firefighters. It is what happens at the first moment of an accident, or at the beginning of an epidemic.

In a crisis, however, the response must be urgent too, but there is time to think and to discuss. For this reason, crises pose a question mark regarding top management. Stakeholders wonder: can I trust the people leading the response to the crisis? The burden of proof is reversed: now it is the organization that has to regain the credibility that was lost or is at least under suspicion. If we simply say, "trust me", the answer we might receive is, "and why should I? What are you going to do to make me trust you?"

I list below some practices that favor the creation of trust in the midst of a critical situation. They all share the idea that people will trust us if we trust them first, with concrete facts.

Transparency in sharing information

When both parties take the same data as a starting point, it is easier to reach consensus. Before proposals begin, it has to be clear that the starting point is shared, both in the data and in its projections. For example, a workers' council will not accept the management's proposal to reduce salaries during a financial crisis, if they don't have the same data about income, expenses, sales projections, profits, etc.

First, define objectives

It is up to the institution to present its proposal and to discuss it. If the data on the situation and the premises on which the future projections have been made have been shared, proposals will be more easily accepted by the other parties. But it must be a proposal: we do not gain confidence by presenting a closed and indisputable formula. Dialogue and flexibility generate trust, rigidity and authoritarianism destroy it.

Respect stakeholders' priorities

Not all participants and stakeholders are on the same level in a crisis. We have to act in concentric circles. You should not inform your employees before your middle management: you have to work in a cascade, which is not always hierarchical because it should start with those most affected by the looming crisis that negotiations are trying to avoid.

Define policies

The specific ways in which the objectives will be achieved must also be agreed. Trust among different parties increases if, before a resolution is taken, those affected are listened to, and then detailed plans on how to develop the resolution are entrusted to cross-sectional commissions, which also include external parties, as experts or facilitators.

This way of proceeding not only favors consensus but also ensures that the plans are well made, because quite often those affected by the problem know more than the management about how to achieve the objectives, thus minimizing the damage.

Determine responsibilities

In a crisis, delegating and sharing power works better than trying to control everything from above. If the objectives and policies have been agreed, people must be held accountable, and allowed to make decisions about what are the best measures on the ground, that is, in direct relationships with stakeholders. This way of acting, which has been experienced many times in dealing with customer complaints, is even more important in a crisis, because it enables the problem to be solved without transferring it up to the senior management, just when they are saturated by other aspects of the crisis.

Trust people, to be trusted

These five elements are the operational translation of the principle we have just examined: sharing power to share responsibility. Life is too complicated to fit into a Soviet-style five-year plan. The organizations that best weather a crisis are those which are the most agile in making decisions to stay the course when the wind changes.

I emphasize this because, in a crisis, the temptation to authoritarianism and to take unilateral measures is stronger. It seems that, when faced with the fear that every crisis generates, people are more vulnerable and less able to resist those who act with despotic tics. For this reason, as I mentioned at the beginning, in crises you see the true face of people and organizations.

We come back to the same idea: it is not about winning but about convincing, if we want people to follow us of their own free will, which is the basis of any leadership. In crises, leaders are needed to bring the institution together, to create consensus (between employees and management; between competitors in the same affected sector; between the government and the opposition; between different countries), giving everyone a say. This is how Peters & Waterman describe leadership:

> It is the patient, usually boring, coalition building. It is the purposeful seeding of cabals than one hopes will reach the bowels of the organization. [...] It is altering agendas so that new priorities get enough attention. It is being visible when things are going awry, and invisible when they are working well. It is building a loyal team at the top that speaks more or less with one voice. It's listening carefully much of the time, frequently speaking with encouragement, and reinforcing words with believable.

Ultimately, as Handy recommends, «it is necessary to gain authority before it can be exercised.»

Communication strategy during negotiations

No negotiation strategy is complete without a parallel communication strategy. When a company is discussing an issue with another organization, private or public, we must be aware that there *is not one single negotiation table but rather two separate tables*: the one that exists between the parties involved in the negotiation itself, and the other pertaining to public opinion, primarily articulated through the mainstream media and online social media. The first is the more important, yet it would be a major mistake to overlook the role that is being played by the "second table" and how it influences the real negotiation table. Companies should always be seated at this "second table".

The two tables, each with their own set of players and rules, have different realms of publicity: one being private — while the other one is on view in public. But this does not imply that the dialog between these two parties at the first table is going to remain secret; on the contrary, everything which is said will end up being public, regardless of the clauses of confidentiality that have been agreed upon by all the participants. In short, *the two tables are different, yet both are public*.

Companies should intervene at the second table, that of public opinion, to *sway public opinion in favor of the solution which is being negotiated behind closed doors* or, at least, avoid any external interference with the first, negotiating, table.

The best way to achieve this is to speak throughout the negotiation with a single voice, using a neutral spokesperson, who will speak and act on behalf of the two parties. In this manner, instead of taking the dispute and placing it in the press, we will be able to increase the expectations of reaching a solution which is satisfactory for all parties, since we will be adopting a constructive attitude, leading to greater credibility for all parties and all the information that is being provided; in addition, as the information is less conflictive in nature, it will not most likely be on the front page as it is much less newsworthy).

Whenever this cannot be done, the parties involved in the negotiation are free to communicate with the press to express their concerns and convey reactions once the meetings have finished and proposals and counterproposals have been put on the table. Yet, they should refrain from giving the other party's point of view or quoting something that the others have said. In synthesis, *you can talk about your own position but not about the one of the other party.* In those cases, in which false news is being reported about one of the parties and the others who are involved in the negotiation are the source, the sooner the whole thing is denied, the better.

Finally, under these circumstances it is also useful to convey information about the issue at stake to educate public opinion (and the media). For instance, negotiating parties can produce a news bulletin, transmit the sessions on local TV or radio stations, create a website to both provide and receive information and opinions, publish the minutes of the negotiation sessions and publicly announce the agreements which have been reached, etc. The greater the transparency, the greater is the chance of consensus being reached.

Essentially, negotiating companies will benefit by pro-actively encouraging a climate of consensus, by assisting those participants who are not used to dealing with the media and by ensuring that nothing is said when tempers are flaring, which everyone would regret later on. It is true that everything would be easier if the whole negotiation were kept secret, because such a process without external interferences tends to be much more effective. Nevertheless, this is not always possible because there are times that the corporations that are involved have their own public persona or because the subject is of great interest to other social groups without a representative seated at the negotiation table.

Proceeding in this way in negotiations will also clearly show who is playing dirty and who is saying one thing at the negotiation table and then denying what they had said or perhaps saying the exact opposite at the public table. They may be using the public opinion table to turn up the pressure at the private table.

The Story: Consorcio Financiero and its stakeholders

Consorcio Financiero, or simply Consorcio, is one of the largest financial services firms in Chile. Very active in the insurance business in Chile and Peru, it owns 100% of Banco Consorcio and 25% of Larraín Vial Asset Management, one of the largest investment funds in the country.

On December 23, 2014, without prior notice, the Securities and Exchange Commission (the U.S. financial market regulator) reported that it was investigating Juan Bilbao, chairman and first shareholder of Consorcio (and board member of Larraín Vial and other companies), and Tomás Hurtado, IT director, for insider trading.

The SEC's indictment noted that both Bilbao and Hurtado had bought shares in CFR, a pharmaceutical laboratory of which Bilbao was also a board member, just before Abbot Laboratories made an OPA with a premium of up to 60% of the market price. According to the SEC, both executives bought shares in a period when Abbot's agreement was being discussed on the CFR board, but was not yet public. Its subsequent sale generated profits of $10 million for Bilbao and $500,000 for Hurtado. The SEC claimed that they used an overseas account registered in the Cayman Islands to avoid raising suspicions.

In the financial services sector, it is essential to build trust in investors and depositors. If confidence is lost, immediate withdrawal of funds can push the company into a liquidity crisis. Two precedents were fresh in the minds of the Consortium's executives. In 2013, Corpbanca, Chile's fourth-largest bank, suffered a liquidity crisis and went bankrupt. And two years earlier, the so-called "Caso Cascadas", a conflict-of-interest case in which senior executives of Larraín Vial were involved, hit the Chilean financial market. The company took too long to respond to the market, losing all institutional clients and many important customers.

Consortium's response to the SEC investigation was immediate. On the same day the news broke, Bilbao and Hurtado tendered their immediate resignation (although it was likely to have been "at the suggestion" of the board). The firm merely communicated it to the SEC and the Chilean regulator, while Bilbao made the following public statement:

I have made the decision to leave these directories with the aim of dedicating myself entirely to my defense in connection with the allegations of the U.S. Securities and Exchange Commission, as some media have published. I would like to state that these allegations refer to my personal activity and have no relation to any of the above-mentioned companies. On the contrary, they only refer to my private sphere, so my resignations also are intended not to affect any of these institutions, all of recognized and deserved prestige. They have no relation to the charges against me.

The next day, the company began meeting with its main private and institutional clients to explain the situation. The message was clear: Consortium had nothing to do with the facts under investigation.

That same week, Consorcio announced the appointment of a new president to replace Bilbao, and that of a new IT director to replace Hurtado. Both were people with extensive experience and recognized prestige in the country.

On 22 October 2015, Bilbao reached an agreement with the SEC. A $13 million fine ended the charges without the need to admit or deny them. A month later, Chile's Superintendence of Securities and Insurance fined Bilbao $3.2 million (Bilbao appealed, and at the time of writing, the Chilean Constitutional Court had not yet ruled).

Without getting to the bottom of the issue (privately, Bilbao insisted that he was innocent: when he became aware of Abbott's OPA by CFR, his stock purchase order was already active and he did not know what to do at the time), there are several lessons in the case.

First, the episode highlights the effectiveness of an immediate response. Consortium wasted no time, even though December 23rd is *almost* Christmas day, and the start of summer holidays in the country. In the course of that certainly difficult week, they had solved the problem.

Another lesson in the case is the importance of separating the defenses (legal and communicative) of the company from the accused. This is a good practice at all times, but especially when the incriminated conduct concerns the private activity of those involved, and not their performance for the company. The frame was clear: it's your problem and you have to manage it on your own.

Finally, it is worth noting the success of meeting immediately, and one by one, with its main clients, to inform them of the facts. Being a company of few but powerful customers, it was best to address them alone and privately. It would have been very different if it had been a commercial bank, with hundreds of thousands of customers.

The company never addressed the press. This is not surprising: it was a complicated story (insider cases always are), and generalist media wouldn't dedicate a lot of attention to its coverage: they are aware that understanding its implications requires financial knowledge, which is not available to most of their readers and watchers.

There is only one legitimate doubt: whether Consorcio should have announced an internal investigation to ensure that such practices had not taken place in the past, and to publicly reaffirm the ethical principles of the company, in which there is no room for any improper conduct. However, it is more than likely that they did communicate this... to their stakeholders.

Prevention: risks, conflicts and controversies

Previous chapters have summed up the key to successful crisis management as *be prepared* and *be prepared for the worst*. To be ready requires two activities: preventing crises and being prepared in case you cannot prevent them. We will study preventive measures in this chapter and leave crisis preparation for later.

Prevention includes two elements, the first of which is foreseeing the future. Companies should be fully aware of the risks involved in their normal activities. No operation is free of dangers, but this fact should not be a deterrent; any prudent manager needs to understand the risks and reduce them to the minimum. Therefore, prevention ends up applying the appropriate measures to eliminate risks and correct the organization's weaknesses. And one of these weaknesses is excessive self-confidence.[50]

---

[50] On April 20, 2010, an explosion at the Deepwater Horizon tower of British Petroleum's (BP) Macondo platform killed 11 workers, injured 17 others, and dumped nearly 800,000 tons of crude into the Gulf of Mexico. It was the worst oil catastrophe to date, costing the company 6.5 billion dollars. Subsequent investigations revealed the company's lack of prudence – not to say their outright arrogance. For example, in February 2009, BP noted in its Annual Exploration Plan and Environmental Impact Analysis that it was «unlikely, practically impossible»

The second element regards the internal and external context. The social, political and cultural environments change rapidly, and those changes demand adaptations and adjustments, both in management and in communication. Business leaders need what Anne Gregory calls "contextual intelligence", to understand those changes and take decisions to maintain the shared relationship between their company and its ecosystem. Listening to the company's stakeholders and to the social environment is paramount to avoid mistakes, or at least to correct them before they become a crisis.

Risk analysis and communication

Risks are the first phase on the curve of dissent. The feeling of being under a more or less serious threat creates a first fissure between the organization and its priority stakeholders. This happens when a company is at the origin of the threat; but also when it is affected by the risks produced by external causes, because they will have an impact on my relations with stakeholders. *Your risks are my risks*, we could say. Each type of risk requires a specific analysis and preventive measures; and the *institution's social responsibility implies that these risks must be explained to all of the affected stakeholders.*

Over the last few decades, risk analysis has become an important theoretical and operational discipline, especially in large industrial and infrastructure industries that require enormous, long-term investments, such as oil-drilling, long-distance pipelines, dams, etc. When these projects are carried out in unstable countries, known for their political, social or economic unrest, all of the parties involved (corporations, investors, major financial institutions and pension funds, governments) must study the risks in-

---

that an «accident leading to a giant crude oil spill» would occur in that well. That assurance led US regulators to exempt BP from a detailed environmental review of the exploration project. Executives turned a deaf ear to expressions of concern from their engineers, who warned that the metal casing the company wanted to use could collapse under high pressure. «This would certainly be the worst case,» warned a senior engineer in an internal report, but «I've seen it in other circumstances, so I know it can happen.»

volved in the operation very seriously, as any miscalculation might force an institution involved into bankruptcy, even though it were extremely sound financially at this point in time.

Additionally, corporations and organizations which carry out dangerous activities are obliged by law to have special preventive programs in place, all of which have major communication aspects and implications.

These rules integrate what we call *risk communication*, which may be described with Health & Abel as "the intentional exchange of information about health, environment, and any other risks among all of the interested parties." Nowadays, risk and crisis communication are becoming more and more closely integrated.

Risk analysis and crisis communication are part of a continuous and integrated process, which begins before the crisis and continues until the crisis is over, and in which the need to listen and report occupies a leading position. Seeger describes this process as follows:

> Risk communication has typically been associated with health communication and efforts to warn the public about the risks associated with particular behaviors. Drawing on the principles of persuasion, risk communication has largely been conceptualized as a problem of getting the public and/or specific target audiences to attend to identifiable risks, such as smoking, unsafe sex, or drinking and driving, and adjusting their behavior accordingly. Crisis communication, in contrast, is more typically associated with public relations and the need for organizations to repair damaged images after a crisis or disaster. [...] Recent efforts have been directed toward merging these traditions into a more comprehensive approach. This merged approach is, in part, a larger acknowledgment of the developmental features of risks and crisis, and recognition that effective communication must be an integrated and ongoing process.

This merge should not come as a surprise. When risk analysis is carried out with long-term vision and crisis communication focuses on prevention and developing long-term relations that will lead to successful collaboration during a crisis period, it is only natural for their respective measures to overlap.

Elements of risk management

Risk management has three components. The first is analysis, which is broken down into three steps: risk identification; description, both objective – with quantitative parameters – and subjective; and risk assessment (serious or slight, essential or dispensable, type of consequences, etc.).

The second consists of making decisions to minimize those risks, and to be prepared if they happen. The third and last is the communication of risk to the public.

The first two of those three components are eminently technical in nature. It is up to experts (in technology, medicine, food health, occupational hazards, etc.) to detect and assess the risks; and then make the contingency plan in case of an emergency. For example, a recall of contaminated milk is, fundamentally, a complicated logistics operation: how to locate the batches presumably affected, manage the return by customers to the stores, and from the stores to the company; and its disposal without risk to health or damage to the environment.

At this point, top management has only one objective: to put into effect the contingency plans. This is apparently easy, but it usually meets resistance. Some managers try saving an apparently avoidable expense (which goes directly against profits); others think it is better not to know certain things... Such attitudes reveal a lack of accountability and squalid ethics.

The next task for the decision-makers is to minimize these risks. *Zero risk does not exist.* Therefore, we enter the prudential sphere of governance. What is an assumable risk? In some industries, that is set by law: for example, the slow and complicated process that goes from a laboratory discovery to the distribution of a drug. In other sectors it is less regulated, and therefore the margin of autonomy of the company is wider.

In this field, the possibilities are innumerable, and for that reason I will limit myself to giving two pieces of advice, in line with the principles of crisis management we saw in chapter 3. First, companies will be judged not according to legal but to ethical criteria, which go well beyond the law. Business compliance is the minimum required, not the maximum. Second, to get your decision right, think about what you would do if that decision were known to your stakeholders. Nowadays, protecting a secret is a vain strategy, and the anger of the stakeholders when they learn that the company made no effort to avoid potentially serious damage will become a colossal gale.

Finally, risk communication has a management element and a technical element. Management is responsible for the strategy: transparency, the resources that are dedicated, etc. On the other hand, the elaboration of the message, the choice of channels and instruments, etc., are specific to the communication department.

The strategic part of risk communication is inextricably linked to risk management: it is the result and consequence of an emergency plan. Any plan includes communication measures, from the simplest (sounding an alarm) to the most complex (organizing a press conference).

Communicating risks

Let us look back at what was covered in chapter 3 about the differences between perceived risks and real risks. Public opinion is favorable to the scientific advances that have brought a better daily life, yet people tend to be more cautious when facing the unknown. Many factors affect this perception: the increasing influence of environmentalists, the impact of major dramatic events, people's own background and upbringing, etc.

Sociological research has shown us that "risk" is a multidimensional concept, shaped by objective damage, likelihood assessment and subjective cognitive and emotional elements. The final outcome is complex, because personal risk assessment is not fully rational. We all tend to underestimate risks related to our daily activities; one does not normally feel at risk at home, even though domestic accidents actually cause more deaths than toxic fumes. It is easier to accept something as a "reasonable risk" as long as we personally benefit from the action, our decision is free and the risk seems to be under our control. For example, when two people ride on a motor bike, the driver feels safer than the passenger because they feel in control, although statistics prove that the driver is in greater danger.

Dialog communication has proven to be an effective measure to in-form others about the inherent risks, as it conveys contents (scientific data), feelings and emotions, and feedback. Consequently, the use of interactive communication tools is highly recommended: conversations, press conferences, guided visits, open houses and other events. In addition, it is worthwhile to frequently stop and verify how efficiently the company's explanations are being received, and to check that the real message is reaching its recipients. This type of communication is similar to scientific information, as it explains complex concepts in clear, simple language which is understandable by us all.

Additionally, it is worthwhile to provide *useful information so that your stakeholders can reduce the risks by themselves.* These messages help to reduce the possible damage and produce the sensation that the situation is well under control. Seeger has summarized the requirements for these messages to be effective as follows:

> First, they recommend specific harm-reducing actions to those affected by the crisis. Messages might also focus on what can be done to help others (e.g., donate food or money, avoid the accident area and check in on neighbors). Second, messages of self-efficacy should also offer a range of activities. The CDC recommends, for example, including what should be done and what else might be done. Third, actions that may not have specific, demonstrable benefit may also be meaningful to the public. Displaying the U.S. flag following the 9/11 attacks was a powerful action that helped manage public anxiety. Finally, even those public responses to risks that seem disproportional may serve important social functions. Unless specific actions may actually serve to increase the harm, public officials should be cautious about discounting actions.

Messages of self-efficacy need to be constructed carefully so that the reason for the action is clear, to ensure that they are consistent and that the recommended action is meaningful. Without an understanding of why the action is recommended, stakeholders may misinterpret the message or give it an unintended meaning. Inconsistent messages, particularly when specific behaviors are being recommended, may create confusion, and reduce the chances of the desired action being implemented. Finally, the action should have both real and apparent utility in reducing the harm.

Then, when an emergency has occurred, companies must convey messages that show people how to protect themselves. Reynolds recommends offering several self-protection options that stakeholders may choose to apply according to the situation: minimal, average, and maximal. For instance, if city water is contaminated, he suggests, «Option 1: add several drops of chlorine to ensure that your water is safe to drink; option 2: boil your water for at least two minutes before drinking; option 3: drink mineral water. We recommend option 2.»

By using this system, we not only provide useful information but also reduce the degree of uncertainty among the general population, because we provide the means for people to feel that they play a critical role in solving the situation.

Informing your stakeholders about the risks that they are being exposed to is a challenge which has many internal hurdles: complacency on the part of managers who underestimate the possibility of a mistake or persist in thinking that something may is beyond their control; the fear of upsetting their bosses or co-workers or perhaps fear that if a risk is detected, it may create internal division; or lead people to think that consideration of the risk may distract people from the organization's goals.

Therefore, risk communication needs to be implemented within a strong ethical framework. *Its primary aim is not to diminish the stakeholders' perception of risk but rather to actually diminish the risk itself* through specific and effective actions. This is complemented with a neutral forum to gather information and make joint decisions (unilateral decisions do not resolve problems). Transparency and trustworthiness are also a must; a company's representatives should always keep their word and promise something only when they are absolutely sure that they will be able to keep that promise. Only a constructive attitude such as this can create a nonbelligerent social context in which the organization can carry on with its activities and avoid the radicalization of the differing positions.

The opposite of this socially responsible attitude would be to play elaborate games with the uncertainties of science or to practice different ploys of legal obstructionism. Such tactics, however tempting for companies, fuel the fears of the unknown among non-expert stakeholders. This causes them to become more entrenched in their point of view that, in the face of a substantial range of unknown factors, the only prudent course of action is to be extremely risk averse and to distrust anybody who plays down "their" risks.

It would not be the first time that business leaders were to succumb to this temptation and deny that corporate activity could possibly lead to any risk for others, when, in all reality, this danger does exist. This is why many, many people mistrust companies. Then it is hard to prove them wrong when they think that the only wise option is to strongly oppose and stand up to any possible risk created by a corporation. Only with a solidly ethical approach permeating the corporate culture will a company be able to establish strong relationships with both its own stakeholders and with society as a whole.

Issues management

Organizations are aware of the context in which they operate. They are also aware of the fact that the conditions that exist in their relationship with society lives are not solely, nor even mainly, established by politicians, but are rather the result of the interaction among all the social agents, including the institutions themselves.

The political debate in a democratic society is the arena in which the public sector (national, state/provincial and local authorities), the private sector (commercial companies and organizations) and the civil sector or third sector (NGOs, non-profit organizations, associations, etc.) interact to find solutions to society's problems. This process is fueled by the media and consists of a series of public debates leading to new legal regulation, unless these issues are voluntarily resolved by the private sector itself. Today's society is a highly complex environment.

Top management is constantly receiving information in one way or another about what's happing in their environment; they analyze and file this information away for future use. Some use it systematically, while others tend to make decisions based on their gut feelings; but, at the end of the day, all of them take stock of whatever may be beneficial or risky for their own institution and then calculate how they can fully take advantage of all these opportunities, while doing their best to avoid any possible risks.

The complexity in today's society leads many organizations to adopt a rigorous system to fully understand the context in which they operate. W. Howard Chase was the first author to develop a clear business model and apply a systematic methodology to this part of a firm's activity; and he was the first to put a label on this field, calling it *issues management.*

Concisely, *issues management* is the forecasting and planning system that enables us to study the inherent tendencies within a social environment and evaluate their impact on the organization; and on this basis to propose feasible operational plans. Its purpose is not theoretical; it does not seek to understand the context but rather influence it, in such a way that problems may be resolved from the very first moment they appear.[51]

Issues management is the first step in crisis prevention. It could also be defined as a forecasting technique aimed at identifying those events which could evolve into a crisis and limiting their evolution to avoid any possible negative effects on the organization. And, far from being a theoretical discipline, it promotes a proactive participation in the public debate before circumstances force such participation.

Many monographies explain how to conduct issues management in detail; interested readers will find some suggestions in the

---

[51] When Indra Nooyi was appointed Pepsi's CEO in 2006, she identified several tendencies, such as the global trend towards obesity and Type-2 diabetes as well as an upsurge in people turning to a healthy diet. She realized how these trends could have a major long-term effect on the corporation. Hence, the company designed a strategy to address these tendencies, investing in healthy products, in innovation and in acquiring food companies in emerging markets. These courageous measures, all requiring major capital outlays, do not normally show any positive effects for at least 10 years. In fact, in 2010, its main competitor had gained market share and its diet product had overtaken Pepsi's low-calorie drink. But Nooyi's strategy gradually began to bear fruit and by 2013 income and profits were performing much better than their main competitor's.

bibliography. For now, may it suffice to say that the various methods all include the following five elements:

1) Procedures to identify the birth and early development of a controversy through a well-defined detection system of social trends, which usually begins with a close monitoring of specialized publications.

2) Prioritizing action plans regarding those conflicts with a greater impact on the organization, either because of their probability or the severity of their effects.

3) Confidentiality: effective issues management should only involve very few people and be carried out with discretion.

4) Constructive spirit: analysis and discussions should proceed calmly, with a positive outlook and without panicking; they should not only consider dangers but new opportunities as well.

5) Lastly, specific proposals, which should conclude a clear list of concrete prevention measures and a timeframe to update these measures.

Evaluating conflicts in respect to their varying degrees of importance usually brings excellent results. In order to define priorities properly, we must ask ourselves the following questions: a) Will the controversy become more important? b) Will it affect our organization? c) Can the organization influence how this controversy will develop? d) Should we intervene, or would this action be counterproductive?

Based on the answers to these questions, conflicts may be classified either as those which must immediately be recognized and faced; or those which do not need to be addressed immediately, although the organization must be ready to address them sometime in the future. There are also others which must be carefully monitored but without immediate action.

In closing, it is worth mentioning that issues management is the right path for corporate communication practitioners to play a significant role in the decision-making process. Issues management actually should be one of the most relevant functions of any corporate communicator – at least as important as media relations, investor relations, public affairs, internal communication, institutional relations or CSR.

It is indispensable for communicators to realize they have a role to play in both identifying and preventing the problem. An organization must participate in the public debate before circumstances oblige it to. Czarnecki summarizes this with an image: «If business as usual is a road, then crises are potholes, washouts, detours, and speed bumps. Good issues management compares to a good road maintenance program and safe driving skills.»

Issue, Agenda, Agenda-Setting and Framework

Before going deeper into the subject, we should define the exact meaning of the key concepts within this subject: *issue*, *agenda*, *agenda-setting* and *framework*.

An *issue* is a controversial social problem in which there are two or more conflicting positions; and it is also a problem receiving a fair amount of coverage in the media. From a corporate point of view, Heath & Palenchar define it as «a point of dispute, a relative difference of opinion concerning a specific fact, value or norm, whose resolution has consequences both for the institution itself and its strategic plan and future success or failure.»

The *agenda* is the set of issues in a specific place and time, organized according to their degree of importance. They are the topics of discussion on the radio, by the people at the hairdressers, in a Whatsapp group, or among the fans at the soccer game during halftime.

The *agenda-setting* is the process in which some issues become the major subject-matter in media coverage and discussion, and — through the media — of public opinion and political action. As agendas are limited in nature, diverse social forces vie to include their issues in the public discussion.

Lastly, the *framework* is the conceptual background in which information is drafted and which to a large extent conditions its interpretation: its context, its argumentative approach, the way it is presented, pictures and graphics used to illustrate it, etc. In other words, the way a piece of news is presented is far from innocuous but full of pre-concepts. Once the framework is accepted, its conclusions are unavoidable. In this sense, framing is like a *second level of the agenda-setting*, where issues are selected and characterized.

Potential conflicts almost always follow the same itinerary. Take tobacco as an example: initially there was a discussion of a medical nature, about the impact of smoking on health. Little by little, technical reasons (medical, epidemiological, statistical) reached the layers of population most concerned about health, and at this stage organized groups (activist movements) began to demand X anti-tobacco measures from the health authorities.

Society began to become aware of the problem and its ramifications beyond just respiratory problems: the risk during pregnancies, impotence and the impact on public health in moments of scarce resources due to the economic crisis, etc. Those elements created public consensus on the harm caused by tobacco and norms were progressively toughened: prohibition of advertising, prohibition of smoking in state offices, in public places, in hotels, etc.

Finally, the consensus became almost universal (almost, because unanimity does not exist in democratic societies), and today pressure against tobacco is not only legal but also social: there is a general climate of public opinion against tobacco over and above personal preferences: it is thought that the right thing is to be against it, an attitude which goes beyond the law. Again, some activities completely legal are considered as unethical.

The conflict cycle

Research into how issues are born, grow and interact with other issues shows some of the common parameters that enable us to forecast their development. Specifically, the life cycle of an issue has four main phases: its birth; mediation and amplification; crystallization; and resolution.

In its nascent stage, some opinion makers try to create public awareness of a new, specific problem. As the promoters of the issue, they become the spokespersons for those who are aware of or suffering from the problem itself (or, if it has specific and well-defined interests, what is hidden behind it) and try to create a social consensus in support of their stance. In this first stage, the problem is only actually perceived by a small circle of industry experts and those people who are deeply committed to the cause. The subject is only discussed in private environments or in highly specialized media; the general public still hardly pays any attention to the issue, as it simply "does not affect us."

The second stage begins when some event triggers public attention. This event may be some sort of accident with mortalities, a dramatic story with great social impact, a well-known person publicly joining the cause, the protest of a highly publicized group of activists, etc. As of this point in time, the subject suddenly becomes of general interest, even though, as it is still relatively new, most people have not decided their own point of view.

In this phase, victims' voices are heard as well as those of the experts and those who are creating public opinion. The issue finds a place in the general media and the solution to the problem is beginning to be discussed: concrete solutions and working hypotheses are being properly proposed and commented.

Next, the issue crystallizes: the positions within the scope of the controversy begin to become more stable; stakeholders are being organized and mobilized to find solutions. Consequently, the general media begin to give time and space to the problem, political authorities are suddenly giving it serious consideration and taking the discussion to the various levels (local, national, etc.) at which actions and measures should be taken.

The last phase in this chain of events is resolution of the problem: political authorities decide what exactly the social good is, define the measures and sanctions to be imposed, set up the control organisms in charge of monitoring and supervision to ensure that these norms are being duly obeyed; and the courts are responsible for judging infractions. The problem still exists, but public opinion perceives that it has been addressed and what is good and bad for society has been clearly defined. From this point onward, the only thing which is left to be negotiated is how quickly the measures are to be applied, but there is no argument whatsoever about the essence of the problem itself.

The model that has just been described clearly indicates to the organizations involved in one way or another that the best time to intervene and to try to exert influence on the evolution of the issue is precisely at the very, very beginning. In fact, the greater the increase in public awareness, the lesser the organization's capacity to negotiate is going to be. If the organization does nothing in the earlier phases and waits until the last phase, it will not be able to do anything except suffer the consequences.

Intervening does not simply mean publicizing the organization's own opinion; it means becoming leaders in respect to social change and in overcoming the problem, and in showing their own public responsibility in the manner. They have to be part of the solution rather than part of the problem.

However, even though their intervention may be later than it should have been, the institution should never give up: things can always get worse. Let us look at the example of sugar again. In March 2014, the World Health Organization (WHO) carried out a campaign to recommend that we all reduce our sugar consumption. The WHO was following the same approach that had already been applied in numerous countries with measures in favor of a much healthier diet. Everything looked rosy and it was assumed that this campaign would be successful. The recommendation was that the total consumption of either free or aggregated sugars should never exceed 10% (50 grams) of one's daily intake, but the WHO announced, at that point in time, that they were planning to even further reduce the amount to less than 5% to obtain further benefits. Obviously, sugared soft drinks were their main target, as their consumption may lead to «an unhealthy diet, overweight, greater risk of non-transmittable diseases, even including dental issues like cavities.»

It is more than likely that sugar is going to become our next "tobacco issue". And, in much the same way as happened to the cigarette manufacturers in respect of the speed with which the anti-smoking campaign developed, the major multinational soft drinks companies have taken far too long to come out with an official stance, although they have stated that they are clearly in favor of the WHO recommendations, as they support NGO's such as *Action on Sugar*.

We will have to wait and see how this issue unfolds and who will be more active in their public statements: sugar-producing countries, sectors such as ice-cream, alternative industries, such as artificial sweeteners, or derivatives of the so-called "healthy sugars" that come from fruit, etc.

Acting with others, or even the whole industry working together, is much more effective than a single company going it alone. If a sector *defines a common policy/stance* regarding a common problem in due time, the controversy may be resolved in its favor, without harming their image and even gaining greater social benefits. On the other hand, if they sit back and let others resolve the problem, nobody is going to listen to their reasoning.

Unfortunately, many organizations wait too long, and they intervene far too late, when activist groups and associations have already framed the issue, and the media have called for new regulations. Many examples show that an issue which has been ignored will most likely become a crisis, and vice versa, a crisis that has been forecasted and acted upon it will never be more than an *issue*.

Monitoring

Organizations greatly benefit from paying attention to the nascent stages and the evolution of current risks in their social environment through detection and monitoring systems. These problems may stem from either internal or external causes and therefore systems to identify both types of sources must be set up and be seen to be functioning properly.[52]

---

[52] On 12-25-2015, a 24-year-old overworked employee of Dentsu, Japan's leading advertising firm, committed suicide. Her tasks had increased dramatically in the three months beforehand, and she fell ill. The young lady requested fewer assignments, but her boss refused. In desperation, she jumped from the third floor of the company's dormitory. It was the second suicide that year. Nine months after her death, the Japanese Bureau of Labor Standards ruled that it was an accident due to overwork. Under Japanese law, the name of the company in an industrial accident is not disclosed, so Dentsu thought that the suicide would remain hidden. Accordingly, they said and did nothing in those months. Days after the ruling, the victim's mother called a press conference, and the media began to investigate. On learning from the mother about her daughter's suffering (e.g., «I have no other wish than to go to bed, because I only sleep 10 hours a week»), people began to criticize Dentsu on the social media. Its reaction was to say that they were unaware of the Bureau's resolution. Immediately afterwards, the Ministry of Health, Labor and Welfare decided to investigate Dentsu without warning. Only then did the company begin to change. Following the investigation, Dentsu informed its employees of changes in the company's work style. A month later, it released its plans to prevent more suicides, announced the dismissal of the CEO and paid the victim's family an undisclosed compensation (about € 1M). This episode showed that Dentsu had failed to understand the changing trends: a new style of work among younger people, new policies in regulators,

Nowadays the key to monitoring lies in the digital world. A timely analysis of what is being posted on the Internet and social media may provide a perfect forewarning in order to be able to plan the right corporate response and avoid a crisis.

A quick response is fundamental. A less-than-immediate response could result in an organization losing control over a situation and could even cause some internauts to perceive that the issue is being hidden.

Another way of minimizing risks is to use today's IT systems such as SEO (Search Engine Optimization) and SEM (Search Engine Marketing) to ensure that the institution's website will always be first in any Google or other search engine's listings. In this way, if anyone is searching for information about your specific organization, the first listing of general content will emanate from your organization. Furthermore, both tools detect tendencies and new developments referring to whatever is being posted about a given institution.

It may be worthwhile to counter the widespread feeling that monitoring the digital environment is like the surveillance systems in a prison with video cameras and sensors everywhere. On the contrary, monitoring is much more like an ongoing conversation between parents and their teenage children; it involves much less talking and much more listening and observing. It is also true in much the same way as it is with teenagers: there is no need to necessarily respond immediately, nor to respond to every single piece of news that appears. Rerup gives the following advice to improve corporate listening:

> Expand your radar. Start by looking in different directions. Review your channels of information. Are you receiving information from many different sources? Invite criticism. Don't shield yourself from criticism — invite it. All too often, people close their ears to complaints about their products and services. Instead, have open conversations precisely with those unhappy customers. [...] Strengthen internal communications

---

who had begun to systematically investigate large companies, and the importance of emotions and empathy in the social networks.

channels. People need forums to talk about emerging issues. Involve younger generations, whose unique ways of looking at the world help identify potential problems and highlight areas that have never been considered before. A related idea involves appointing certain employees to serve as devil's advocates, whose job it is to argue the opposite point of view. Since many senior or middle managers are older folks, appointing younger workers for this role may help to counterbalance groupthink.

Every organization must develop its own tailor-made monitoring system, adapting it to its own circumstances. Larger multinational corporations, as Fronz pointed out, tend to classify their variables in four separate categories: political, economic, social and technological; other authors have added a fifth category, namely ethical variables. Smaller organizations should obviously concentrate their attention on one of these categories and leave the monitoring of global tendencies to industry-specific associations.

Digital turbulences

Today's digital world, as we described in Chapter 1, is a very risky environment. Its main traits — high speed, global range, intensely emotional, leveled, ubiquitous and eternal in duration – *all contribute to* make it highly unstable. Its predisposition towards conflicts and crises is such that **Coombs &** Holladay coined the term "paracrisis" to define Internet-based crises, because they are not truly crises, although they certainly seem to be.

This chapter, devoted to crisis prevention, is the right point to deal with digital turbulences. In these cases, the corporate response has the same aim: monitor, participate in the conversation that takes place in social media and intervene whenever necessary to ensure that the public consensus does not deteriorate.

Let's look first at the online dynamics of public perceptions and later on we will provide some guidelines for organizations of all types. But let me issue a warning to begin with. In this field, communication practice clearly precedes empirical research and we are still far from having a universally accepted doctrine. This novelty, together with its high frequency, justifies a broader study.

Online conflict evolution

The social media (in which we include any applications that have been developed around a general content or are user-managed, such as wikis, blogs, podcasts and social platforms) is a special area within a crisis and should be treated as such.

This environment certainly looks like a double-edged sword, because it enables us to communicate better, but at the same time, it broadens the risks involved. Others have pointed out its dual nature, as a crisis facilitator (it accelerates the crisis and broadens its geographical scope) and as a crisis trigger (it may cause a problem to become a crisis unless it is properly resolved at that earlier stage).

Additionally, it has been proven empirically that reactions within the digital world tend to be much more aggressive than those in an offline setting.[53]

For these reasons and also due to the fact that social media enable us to both listen more and better, Baron says that "public participation is the new norm in crisis management."

The dynamic in which digital turbulences tend to happen is articulated in the four following phases: its origin or initial reaction; its posting on social platforms; its appearance in mainstream media; and its consolidation as a real social media controversy. Let's look at these four phases one by one.

The first public reaction to any type of problem is always on digital platforms. Research regarding this aspect shows that the initial posts are usually highly subjective in their focus, with a dominant element of fear or anger, and respond to the need to find emotional support in critical or times of great uncertainties (as emergency situations) or a desire to receive guidance and not to

---

[53] In 2013, the CEO of the Italian pasta company Barilla made some improper comments regarding homosexuals in an interview. Reactions in the social media were much more negative than those of people following the affair through mainstream media. And curiously enough, the online call to boycott Barilla had no consequences on the company's sales.

face a problem alone (for instance, complaints about a defective product or service).

Some problems may spread through the digital sphere at a greater or lesser speed. The factors that are required to gain momentum are the degree of drama inherent in the story (or its humor) and the concurrence with prior negative experiences or a pre-existing negative vision of the company. In these cases, it is much more likely that the incident will provoke a mobilization against the institution. The situation may also worsen if the organization does not intervene or does so poorly. (A person who posts complaints on the social media expects the organization to be listening, and if the organization does not respond, he automatically gets angry and says, "They are not listening to me!" — One of the worst accusations that can be made on social media.)

A controversy which is raging in the digital world will eventually catch the attention of the mainstream media. At that point, the problem will have much greater public awareness, getting its own spot on the media agenda and becoming much more objective in nature.

In the fourth phase, the structure of the controversy is modified by the way it is being addressed in the mainstream media. There may even be a total shift: in a few cases, the whole situation may become much more intense and aggressive; but in most cases, the organization's approach may be adapted to coincide with the mainstream media's focus.[54]

---

[54] In January 2011, a chemical plant exploded in Moerdijk (the Netherlands). Initial reactions in the social media claimed that it had been a terrorist act, simply based on personal speculations and clearly with an emotionally based approach. Sometime later, the mainstream media started to explain exactly what had happened: what had caused the explosion, the number of victims, the real risks, the prevention measures that had been in place, etc. Very soon after that, once the media had given proper information about the incident, most social media participants decided to follow the media line. In the fourth stage, the social media once again took a different route from that of the mainstream media: while the latter continued to inform from an objective point of view, the social media focused on subjective aspects, were highly critical of the government's reaction and expressed doubts about the official information that was being published.

In this sense, the initial postings on social media tend to be highly critical, pointing the finger at those who are supposed to be responsible for what has happened; but the news gains further strength and credibility when it has been studied more deeply and seriously and is taken over by the mainstream media.

The mainstream media do not follow the same agenda as those who are involved in the social networks. They do monitor what is being posted in the digital world but then follow their own journalistic criteria, trying to gauge whether the information is newsworthy or not. Before publishing anything, professional journalists adhere to their discipline of verifying information with multiple sources and to their institutional memory to sense when things are more complex that they seem; and their judgment is of a higher order because it is honed by experience and specialized knowledge.

So, in order to know whether a digital conflict is or is not going to be published by the mainstream media, one should ask oneself the following questions: is there an inherent interest that is newsworthy, which may trigger the mainstream media to cover this specific news story? Is there some sort of controversy that has been brewing for some time? Is there any relevant stakeholder who could corroborate and join the protest? Do the primary stakeholders feel that the institutional response is being fair and solid and are hence fully supportive?

The transition from the digital world into the mainstream media is not necessarily bad for a corporation. What the mainstream media publish tends to calm the overall situation down and reduces the panic and anger that may have pervaded what is posted on the social networks. Hence, with the mainstream media involved, it is highly unlikely that the crisis will worsen.[55]

---

[55] Barak Obama is a staunch defender of the social media. That is why his message on the occasion of the first anniversary of the bombings at the Boston Marathon is especially significant. The then US president stated: "In this age of instant reporting and tweets and blogs, there's a temptation to latch on to any bit of information, sometimes to jump to conclusions. But when a tragedy like this happens, with public safety at risk and the stakes so high, it's important that we do this right. That's why we have investigations. That's why we relentlessly gather the

Guidelines covering the institutional response

So, what are companies supposed to do when faced with a digital turbulence? The first thing is prevention. It is essential that those who manage corporate profiles on the networks have a style book that helps them to submit to a discipline in respect of tone, content, retweet policies, etc.

It is also prevention, and good prevention that managers and employees know how to handle themselves on the networks, knowing that the border line between their professional activity and their personal area is very sketchy. Whatever they write in a private tweet, if it is controversial, will surely be attributed to the organization.[56]

The hardest thing to learn – and therefore the most necessary – is how to maintain a personal point of view while avoiding the two extremes: conflict and political correctness: how to be oneself without being offensive. This is the art of the "happy dispute", as Bruno Mastroianni calls it, that every manager should attain.

If the issue then arises on the social media, the same advice that was given in respect of conflicts is also applicable here: know your stakeholders, the characteristics of the various platforms, the opinion makers and influencers in those specific social media; integrate social media into the organizational communication strategy; and actively maintain an on-going flow of conversation with your stakeholders.

---

facts. That's why we have courts. And that's why we take care not to rush to judgment -- not about the motivations of these individuals; certainly not about entire groups of people." Indeed, the activity in networks during the hours and days after the attack of 15-4-2013 produced social panic and angry reactions of hatred against ethnic communities.

[56] The list of public officials who have had to resign because of an error on the social networks is probably one in which all the political parties are equally represented. That is why I will give an impartial example: the Spanish consul in Washington was dismissed by a conservative minister for having made fun of the socialist president of an autonomous community. Even diplomats, superbly skilled in good manners, screw up.

The first recommendation is to act fast. In networks, the speed with which bad news spreads is staggering. If you know you have made a mistake, don't hesitate: correct it immediately![57]

Second, the tone. Internet communication during a crisis period has to look more like a dialogue than a series of public statements. Presenting the corporate version is not enough; companies should engage in a conversation with those stakeholders active on social media.

This is certainly not easy. Companies tend to be reluctant to get involved in two-way communications; they do not feel that it is the straightest path to achieving their corporate goals, and, at times, it is nearly impossible to respond to the vast number of incoming messages. Nonetheless, this two-way communication is absolutely indispensable: you must reach everyone. Bridgeman explains it very well:

---

[57] Home Depot is the largest home improvement chain in the US. On November 7, 2013, a toxic tweet posted on its official account was immediately deemed racist and offensive. Home Depot removed the tweet very quickly, in fact within minutes, but it continued to circulate. Soon, the television networks spread it even further. On the same day, Home Depot responded directly to all negative comments with the same phrase: «We are so sorry for the stupid tweet. We have removed it». Later, the phrase was changed to: «We have zero tolerance for anything so stupid and offensive. We are so sorry. We have cut off the agency and the employee who published it». Home Depot sent it to all 80 people who posted negative comments. The apology tweets were received mostly negatively. Many people scoffed: «How long have you been copying and pasting that generic apology response @HomeDepot? Lmao». Home Depot did not respond further. In addition, its spokesperson told the Huffington Post: «We are also reviewing our protocols on social networks to understand how it could happen and make sure it does not happen again». Within a couple of days, the turbulence was over, and it had no detectable long-term detrimental effect on the business. Everything suggests that the public accepted it as a mistake and more or less agreed with the way the company solved it. My takeaway would be: digital turbulences come fast and also leave fast if we act quickly and proactively. It might have been better to interact with people and connect on a personal and emotional level, but the users captured what had happened, and they let it pass.

Forget about all the corporate mumble-jumble and the press agency's well-written prose. Get your senior executives out there in front of the audience, have them answer each and every one of the questions that people want to ask your company and tell them: I understand what you are saying and this is exactly what we are doing and this is the way that you have to do your part in solving the problem.

Companies that use an aggressive tone in their public communications or use scandal as a marketing tool are flirting with provocation to gain notoriety; they can easily make mistakes, and afterwards their apologies sound fake. This happens especially in the fashion industry, but also in areas.[58]

Corporate response must be *posted on the same digital platform* in which it is being discussed. Speaking up as soon as possible will halt the upward tension spiral and soften the general tone of the

---

[58] On November 21, 2018, Dolce & Gabbana was about to launch a luxury event in Shanghai, with 1,500 guests and more than 350 models. Three days before the event, the company ran an ad with a well-known local model trying to eat pizza and pasta with chopsticks, and a voice in the background said, «Is it too big for you?» Comments about the spot's racism and sexism flooded social media, and in less than 24 hours, the ad was removed, and the event canceled. Shortly thereafter, founder Stefano Gabbana intervened on his personal Instagram account with offensive comments, such as «China, dirty and stinky mafia.» Although Stefano later claimed that his account had been hacked, the boycott call took shape, and users began posting videos destroying D&G products. Sales fell dramatically in China: its Shanghai stores remained empty, major chains withdrew their products, and e-commerce platforms such as Net-A-Porter, Alibaba and JD.com sidelined the brand. It was not only consumers who reacted, but also China's state-owned media demanded the brand be respectful toward the Chinese market. Because of previous controversial ad campaigns (several analysts felt that his ad was intended to offend, to make the fashion show visible), his slow and lukewarm reaction, and the low quality of his apology video (not "D&G-ish"), many people did not believe him when he said that his account had been hacked. Chinese consumers acted as if they had finally broken off a toxic relationship that had lasted too long. In fact, the company's results in 2019 showed an increase in sales and profit in the global market, but a contraction in the Asian market, and it predicted that sales in China would decrease in the following year.

comments being made. In this new stage, the company has another opportunity to present its own reasoning. The Ki & Nekmat report covering the Fortune 500 companies shows that "companies that respond to their users' message managed to achieve a much more positive tone and approach in crisis periods." *A fast response mitigates the damage to reputation.*

The next step *is to deal properly with the media.* Journalists monitor what is happening on the social networks and as soon as they realize that a conflict is brewing, they will call those corporations to ask for confirmation, further information and their position on the issue. The reporters' role is crucial; they will provide the framework in which the conflict will be crystallized. The organization could be portrayed as a victim, as a negligent institution or as a company guilty of an intentionally illegal act. Obviously, this framing sets the stage for the whole future evolution of the conflict. Furthermore, reporters are often those who at the end of a crisis summarize the events, assign prizes and indictments, point out the lessons learned and give the definitive shape of the story that will become history.[59]

Empirical research has shown that in a crisis, social media postings comment much more often about the articles published in the mainstream media than other online content. People give the media more credibility and tend to quote what they read in the media more often than what is written on the institutional website, because – Sung & Hwang state – "the organization is not considered a credible source of information in a crisis."

Thus, organizations should properly diagnose the situation: the magnitude of the conflict, the degree of responsibility attributed to the organization, the nature of the stakeholders involved, the urgency of the threat, the impact on its bottom line and the real chances of being able to influence its development. The answers to those questions will tell us whether this is a "Para crisis" or actually the beginning of a real crisis. In addition, if the conflict had any

---

[59] In the above-mentioned case of the guitars broken by United Airlines, *The Guardian* described the airline as an inefficient operator incapable of safely transporting a simple guitar, noting: «United could have saved this public humiliation if it had followed its own customer service standards.»

sort of newsworthy content (human drama, a celebrity, etc.) it may be wise to pro-actively take the initiative with the media from the very first moment.

With respect to the fourth phase, when the conflict has dropped off the mainstream media's radar, companies still have to devote time to the issue. In the digital age, nothing ever goes away and dies. Mainstream media may decide to "end" a public discussion, but from time to time old news will surface online (and even rehashed and passed off as being new offline). Therefore, organizations still have to keep the online conversation going, using a blog or another direct channel.

Finally, a call to prudence. Respond quickly yes, but without affirming things that are not certain, simply because of intense external pressure.

In summary: the digital channels where these turbulences occur may be different, but the people involved are still the same. Therefore, conflict and crisis management in the digital world follows the same rules as those that apply in the real world. This is another reason why it so important to integrate online and offline responses.

Operational guidelines for specific conflict situations

Claim handling

Risk analysis uncovers aspects of corporate activity that may go wrong and therefore it is a very useful tool in crisis prevention. But there is another simpler way to predict what may go wrong: *the less important things that have already gone wrong.* I refer to complaints or other forms of protest by internal and external stakeholders.

Digital activism often uses Internet pages entirely dedicated to denigrating institutions, called anti-websites, rogue sites or sucks sites. There are hundreds of them, ordinarily created and maintained by angry customers or employees, and they use a mix of real grievances and ironies – sometimes really funny – that can be devastating. González Herrero and Smith say: «It is never easy and there is no consensus on how to approach these problems. The options range from starting a blog, if you don't already have one; asking for the help of other bloggers; launching an online information campaign; responding with a sense of humor or decide on legal action, depending on the specific situation.» The most effective option is prevention, buying the most significant alternative domains and even the anti-sites: it is cheaper.

Exasperated consumers are so numerous that not only pages against specific companies but also general complaint sites can be found on the Internet. An angry customer tells their story, the platform makes it public and contacts the company to demand that they answer the complaint; and it later reports on the progress of the complaint, giving statistics and rankings of the companies with the best and worst care services, etc.

Why do they do it? Not only because the address where you can direct your complaint are hard to find (not a few companies hide them on purpose), nor because complaining makes you feel better, but because it works. Many companies address those problems when (and only when) they are made public.

We keep coming back to our leitmotif: prevention. It is more profitable, in terms of reputation but above all in strengthening customer relationships, to make it easier for the dissatisfied customer to write, and to solve the problem right away or at least to explain why is not possible. In fact, what often triggers a customer's ire (or perhaps it would be better to call him an ex-customer) is not a faulty product or decadent service, but the evident lack of respect shown by not responding to a serious and polite complaint. It is not someone having a bad moment, but a bad strategy of the entire company.

Who should take care of complaints? At first glance, it may appear that claims related to defective products or services should involve either quality control or post-sales divisions. But, because they are of great help in identifying the tiny — and not quite so tiny — problems that could become a crisis, risk officers and communicators have to be in the loop. Most crises give off warning signs long before they mature, but unfortunately many companies do not take them seriously, precisely because they treat them as *insignificant malfunctions*. They have to be fixed, of course, but they could not possibly have any meaningful consequences.

So, the Claims Handling Department has a strategical importance in crisis prevention. All organizations may tell stories about dangers that have been prevented easily and cheaply thanks to someone calling attention to a small problem; or, on the other hand, major damaging incidents that happened precisely because warnings and small signals were not given due consideration.

Seitel proposes an acronym that defines the proper rules of claim handling: FRIEND, flexible, responsible, immediate, educational, need-driven & dedicated. It is particularly appropriate since being friendly certainly summarizes the right attitude that those who handle claims should have. In fact, even more important than these rules is the spirit with which the person dealing with claims should behave. Those handling claims are the institution's radar; every claim should be welcomed.

Obviously, it is not easy to receive a claim with a smile because the natural tendency is to be upset whenever we hear bad news. Thinking about the advantages that it presents from a "service excellence" perspective will make it easier to handle them properly. The attitude with which claims are received and dealt with truly reveals the institution's real relationships with its stakeholders. It is not an exaggeration to say that an institution's true face may be discovered by simply looking at those who handle stakeholders' claims and examining their attitude.[60]

In addition, in respect to in-house suggestions and complaints, it is critical to change negative attitudes; these messages must always be rewarded, and never punished. While no one wants to hear bad news, those who uncover problems within an organization are immensely valuable and should be rewarded not discouraged.

Managers should *want to know* what their organization's staff really think. The bosses are the ones who should be listening more than anybody else. They are the ones who have the most to lose if

---

[60] In 2005, a very influential blogger named Jeff Jarvis posted a complaint on June 21, about the poor technical assistance being provided by Dell. Many other disgruntled users followed his example, to the point that the blogger was receiving 10,000 visits per day. The antagonistic exchange between the blogger and the company lasted until July 11, but the subject was still red-hot all summer long, until the mainstream media published the news. At this point, Dell reacted decisively, strengthening its customer service department, and significantly revamping its user support processes, to the point that nowadays Dell is seen as one of the pioneers in online engagement. This confrontation ended up being a consumer relations' success story.

they don't. They should be brave enough to "face the music" when things go wrong. It is far from pleasant to hear bad news and complaints, but bosses should remember that it is equally unpleasant for the one who has decided to step forward and speak up to the boss.

Furthermore, bosses should have enough sensitivity to perceive these messages because they tend to be highly discreet and, more often than not, mere hints. Without overstepping the bounds of their position, the manager should be strong enough openly address the issues. Top management must consider an employee's willingness to be open about problems more as a sign of personal interest and commitment to the company than as a betrayal of their bosses and workmates.[61]

They should also avoid the temptation of not listening because the complaint is presented bitterly, impolitely or even offensively, for example when someone criticizes the boss in public and makes a fool of them. It is only natural to be upset and embarrassed in such circumstances, wondering why that employee could not have waited to tell me the very same thing but in my office, without humiliating me, or at least without shouting aloud. Yes, of course, he/she could and should have. Nevertheless, it would be a mistake to hide yourself behind that fact and defend your personal dignity. The wise advice is to lick your wounds and try to place the importance on the substance of the issue being addressed rather than on the form in which it has been raised.

Companies with rigorous procedures in place to ensure that top management will have full knowledge of all incidents and/or mistakes that have happened, and how they were resolved, will be able to prevent tiny problems from becoming immense crises.

Errors and rectifications

---

[61] In fact, according to Bazerman & Watkins, the prime cause of the two accidents in NASA, Challenger and Columbia, was because employees were afraid to speak up and the fact that there were no proper incentives to escalate problems and to take the appropriate measures to avoid a crisis.

Everyone — even journalists — know that from time to time the media publish news that are less than true. Even in those cases in which corporate communicators and reporters are highly professional and ethically rigorous, mistakes may still happen. Of course, it could be much worse if one party or the other, or even both parties, plainly lie or let other interests dictate what to publish or what not to. In those cases, the likelihood of mistakes increases exponentially.

Although this is not the right moment to go into greater detail, it is useful to recall that whenever false news about a company are not isolated cases but rather the normal situation, it is a clear sign that there is a latent conflict. The company needs to address this situation punctually and take the necessary steps to prevent the conflict from becoming a crisis.

My first comment regards the *normality of being criticized*. If the company is minimally important, some adverse publicity is almost inevitable. In fact, suspicions will be aroused if everybody praises someone or something: in our Western culture, unanimity is frowned upon, as if it were linked to a lack of freedom. Even people who are almost universally admired undergo personal attacks. Whenever someone voices a complaint against a prestigious public figure or institution, inevitably the media pounce on it and publish it immediately. The more prestigious the accused is, the bigger the news will be.

Secondly, companies should analyze lies and errors from one specific perspective: their credibility. *Lies are relevant only when they are believable.* In this sense, falsehoods that are not credible do not deserve to be rectified. As usual, the decision depends on the circumstances involved in each case.

Thirdly, *false facts should be rectified, but not opinions.* At the most, it can be proved that an opinion lacks any valid basis, but little more can be done. Everyone is free to express their own opinions and feelings. It is only when their statements are defamatory or even libelous that it may be worthwhile to defend ourselves, but even then, we should only rectify the facts which are wrong.

Fourthly and lastly, *there is a duty to defend the company*, and therefore organizations must rectify erroneous, incomplete or tendentious information and clearly re-establish the truth about their institution. If this is done, public opinion will cease to uphold the

negative judgments and perceptions which were caused by erroneous information and will avoid making such mistakes in the future.

When the mistakes that have occurred are relatively important, the truth must be re-established. But it is necessary to use
the proper tone in order to avoid making the rectification unpro-
ductive or even damaging. The company's short-term goal in dealing with the media is not that they should always publish favorable
news but rather that journalists know what the institution truly is
and what it does. Whether they publish a positive news story or
not depends on many factors; it is certainly not in the hands of the
company. Bigger stories, new ads and many other last-minute reasons change newscasts and newspapers' original plans every day. Of
course, companies are happy with favorable stories, but media relations are about... relations. A good relationship requires a good
deal of understanding by both parties. Hence, it would be a big
mistake to correct an error in a way which damages an existing
relationship. What good would it be to rectify a mistake, if, at the
end of the day the journalist becomes more distant from the company? It is vital to choose the right timing and the right way to
properly correct mistakes, combining clarity with a friendly and
courteous attitude.

We will now look at a number of best practices referring to
rectifications. They share a long-term approach: doing everything
possible to further strengthen the informative relationship with the
reporters covering a company and its sector:

- If the mistake is minor, it would be enough to make a quick
  telephone call to the reporter (or have a face-to-face conversation, taking advantage of an informal gathering), instead of a
  written rectification. At the end of the day, any rectification
  proclaims that the journalist has made a mistake and none of
  us like to publicly admit that we were mistaken. It is jokingly
  said that the *New York Times* sees the Roman Catholic Church
  as a «sister organization,» because it is the only other organization that claims to be infallible. The irony hides an element of
  truth about how many reporters consider themselves.
- An indirect rectification is often more useful than a direct one.
  For instance, publishing another news story in which the correct information is included but does not refer to the previous
  erroneous report. Bear in mind that a formal rectification

hurts the media outlet's reputation in the eyes of its stakeholders, colleagues, and competitors. Besides, it is better not to reiterate on the same controversial subject.

- If someone's statements have to be refuted, the first step is to confirm that that person really said what has been attributed to them. This step may seem rather obvious, but people often overlook this rather elementary precaution.

- Misunderstandings should be clarified at the same level on which they happened; they should not be escalated to the reporter's boss. If the local newspaper has made a mistake, the organization's local representative rather than a person from Head Office should make the rectification (a rectification made at national level would automatically give a national dimension to the problem).

- The tone and the style used are also part of the message. Rectifications, whether they are verbal or contain elements of body language, should never be sharp in tone or use harsh or ironic language. In particular, when the error is more a provocation than a mistake, every effort must be made to overemphasize the objectivity and politeness of the corporate response.

- Personal stories and first-person testimonies are much more effective than stark data and facts in correcting mistakes. Human faces communicate much better than simple images of buildings and manufacturing facilities.

- If the erroneous information generates social alarm, the organization should first show solidarity with the collective concern, and only then provide the facts and figures that refute the false information; furthermore, the information should be presented from the public's point of view.

- Lastly, an error is certainly not a sufficiently valid reason to completely interrupt your relationship with a media outlet. Perhaps you do not need to grant everything it requests, but you should still send the basic information provided to all media.

Nonetheless, there are reasons that can make it pointless or even damaging to rectify mistakes. These errors can be classified into three types: insignificant mistakes, errors in the context of a chronic conflict, and malicious errors.

a) Insignificant mistakes do not warrant a published rectification. Institutions should not expect everything that appears in the media to be absolutely perfect. Simplifications, for example, are always a less than exact version of the truth and never the full truth. In these cases, the institution should ask itself if a rectification would really be critical for the reader/spectator or, on the contrary, whether it could be seen as a sign of susceptibility and narrow-mindedness.

b) Nor is it necessary to rectify major mistakes within the context of a chronic conflict, when almost all media repeat the same misinformation. A corporate rectification is useful if it helps to make the company better known; if not, then it is better to pass. It takes a lot of prudence and patience to change a perception little by little, more by positive initiatives than by rectifications. Being in a rush to clarify everything is not a good idea.

c) Rectifications are also counterproductive when the errors are intentional: for example, when a journalist has a grudge against the organization; or an editor asks a reporter specifically not to inform but rather to attack. In those cases, when reporters call the organization, they do so not to check the information but as a mere formality: to be able to say that they did speak to "the other side of the story". This does not happen very often but unfortunately it is still more frequent than it should be. When a specific media outlet has declared itself to be the enemy of the organization, rectifications are worthless and other initiatives should be considered to correct the situation.

However, both in case of a chronic conflict and when a media outlet has declared its animosity, it may be is convenient to issue an official rectification, aimed mostly at third parties, to state that the organization, for the public record, absolutely and completely rejects the information published..

Alternatively, it should not be too difficult to find another newspaper, radio or TV station which is willing to criticize one of their competitors, especially if you are able to provide them with the evidence they need to prove that there has been a breach of the ethics of professional journalism.

To conclude, serious errors should always be corrected, but think first how. The key element is to reach those who read the information and thought it was credible, either through the same media outlet that published the wrong information or by other channels. Looking at the long term, a media outlet is like a well; if it is contaminated, you should not be worried about a dirty glass of water coming from the well, but rather about the source of the contamination. Being on bad terms with a relevant media is not good for any organization. You may seek external support or perhaps a mediator who is on good terms with both parties; but something must be done.

Rumors

The ever-increasing demand for information and the confusion that a conflict creates leads to an upsurge in what we might call informal communication, which goes hand-in-hand with rumor spreading. Contrary to what is normally believed, rumors are not an intentional method of misinformation. It is true that some rumors are created and spread intentionally, in the knowledge that they are baseless: a rumor might be used, for instance, to gauge public reaction to a hypothetical decision, to avoid someone from being nominated to a specific job, or to intentionally damage a competitor. But, normally speaking, rumors convey information felt to be true and are not disseminated with malicious intentions.

The most important thing in dealing with rumors is not trying to find out how they started but rather why they spread. Furthermore, experience — which has been confirmed statistically — tells us that, generally speaking, rumors are usually well based and that nearly all of us tend to pay great attention to them.

From the perspective of crisis management, rumors are one of the most effective channels for spreading negative information within a certain social group. They are also beyond the control of the company's authorities. The organization finds itself in a very difficult position: it has to either confirm or deny information which has already reached its audience, and which, quite often indeed, is highly distorted. However, the core of the accusation is: why didn't the company inform us? Even if the information were to be true, the fact that the company was late is enough to cause serious damage.

Rumors show us two things: that there is a certain demand for information (the rumor is only being spread among stakeholders who *wish to know more* about a specific subject) and that there is a lack of effective communication on the part of the organization. In fact, in those cases in which there is an abundant flow of information, there are hardly ever any rumors. On the other hand, an information vacuum is always going to be filled by mumbo jumbo, gossip, guesswork, 'somebody said'... These elements can destroy the best-developed reputation, bury the image of an organization and cause it to lose all credibility.

Moreover, in the case of a natural disaster of some sort, rumors may lead to major problems, because in situations of widespread panic, people tend to believe almost any rumor and that situation may lead to a real tragedy.[62]

At other times, rumors — information that has not been fully confirmed by at least two or three sources — are released by the media. That happened during the Katrina hurricane in Louisiana in 2005: radio stations and newspapers spoke openly about rape, murder and looting that later on were proven to be false, but the effect of this reporting was very harmful because it led to distrust and made many people reluctant to help others in need.

Davies led a sociological research project that examined how rumors begin and how they are spread. The two prime conclusions that are linked to conflict management are the following: firstly, *underlying any specific rumor, there is a prejudice*; quite often rumors reflect a latent problem that has not been properly addressed. Secondly, *there are some very favorable circumstances* that lead to rumors, such as the moments just before a change is announced. In fact, a rumor is the outward manifestation of social resistance to change. Therefore profound changes in organizations (mergers, for exam-

---

[62] On December 26, 2004, Aceh (Indonesia) was hit by a tsunami. The myth that "cadavers lead to epidemics" quickly spread and thousands of dead were buried in common graves. This only worsened an already dramatic situation: no one knew who had died and who had survived but were still missing. It heightened religious tensions as it was a clear obstacle for proper funerals and made economic compensation very difficult indeed as there were no death certificates. But biology clearly states that germs only survive for a brief period after a person has died.

ple) require an intensification of internal communication, in order to promote consensus.[63]

So, what are companies supposed to do then? Experts like Kapferer say that «there is no magic wand to keep a rumor from running wild.» Each case has its own set of specifics, yet the following rules can help in most situations:

a) *Rational arguments against a rumor are not always effective.* There are three situations in which reasoning does not work: when it is impossible to prove the truth; when the technical complexity of the case implies that a clear explanation will never be understood by the general public; and when the rumor is highly emotional in nature.

b) It is absolutely indispensable *to use a credible source of information against the rumor:* if the person/institution who is denying the rumor lacks credibility in the eyes of a specific public, everything that he/she says or does will be interpreted as simply being a confirmation of the rumor. In fact, when the spokesperson who denies the rumor is not trustworthy, Claude Cockburn's ironic statement comes to everybody's mind: «do not ever believe something until it has been officially denied.»

c) It may be tempting – but absolutely wrong – to feel that the rumor will somehow disappear by itself. No, Sir; the longer it's around, the more difficult it's going to be to deny it.

---

[63] In 2008, the Catalan company Gas Natural merged with the Galician electricity company Unión Fenosa, to form an international energy group with an integrated cycle. It had tried on two previous occasions to merge with other energy companies (first, with Iberdrola, and then with Endesa), but its attempts were truncated by political instrumentalizations and subsequent judicialization of the problem. To make the third attempt successful, it was vital that the employees of both companies should see the merger as a beneficial process for them and for their companies. In these circumstances, Gas Natural's communications director drew up a strategy the first step of which was that the internal communication department – which was in HR – passed to the communication division; the company thus addressed all its priority stakeholders in an integrated way. Systems were later created to learn what employees thought about the integration process, and their feedback guided successive steps.

d) It is even more dangerous to be sarcastic about the rumor, because many people will take the irony seriously and the "remedy" will just make everything worse.

The way an organization defends itself against a rumor will be
defined by the way in which the rumor is being spread, because
this will show us who is interested. The best way to fight against
the rumor is to saturate the interested public with a mass of information. Once everybody knows the facts, there will be no further
interest in spreading, or talking about, the other information, as
the oil that lubricates the rumor mill is precisely a lack of information. As Pinsdorf puts it, «Secrets encourage rumors and a rumor is always much more eccentric and extravagant than reality
could ever be.»

Saturating a public with information is not simply publicly
denying the error. In fact, it is not always effective to explicitly deny
a rumor, because once a piece of news has been published and the
exact opposite is said in rebuttal, the only thing that is achieved is
confusion, or even the consolidation of an association of ideas that
we precisely wish to avoid. Therefore, it is never a good idea for
someone who is the object of a rumor to repeat it.

In addition to this, there are no other fixed rules. There are
cases in which it is advisable to explicitly and clearly deny the rumor. When, for instance, it has triggered public alarm or has been
repeated by an authorized source; as from that moment on, what
was a rumor until that point in time has now turned into false
information that must be rectified. However this only happens in
an absolute minority of cases.

So, assuming that we are in the midst of a case in which it is
not advisable to directly deny the rumor, there are a number of
guidelines that have proven to be effective in properly (and indirectly) controlling rumors.

1) Disassociate yourself from the rumor, breaking the direct link
between your organization and the negative information that is
being spread around. Generic rumors, which are not attributable to anybody, are not damaging.[64]

---

[64] For example, if a rumor claims that "Fresh-Cola" has some ingredient
that causes cancer, the defense against this type of rumor could be to
prove that this component is also used in other soft-drinks as well as in

2) Do something which is very expressive and symbolic in nature. Its meaning must obviously be the exact opposite of the error that underlies basis of the rumor.[65]

3) Link the rumor to an origin or attitude that is unacceptable to society in general or incompatible with the reigning corporate culture. This means that you should highlight the contradiction between what is known to be true and what everybody thinks and the specific rumor. The public has not realized that this contradiction exists. For example, proving that behind every rumor there are attitudes that the directly related public does not share; that it is a racist rumor that some competitor has launched ... Then everybody will distrust the institution that launched it even more than the rumor itself.

4) When you are faced with a rumor whose content is true, you will have to explain why the information was not disclosed earlier.

5) Point out, if you know the facts, the person who intentionally started the rumor and what exactly their goal was in doing so: attacking the institution, manipulating public opinion regarding an issue, etc. Most of those spreading a rumor act in good faith and when they realize that they have been manipulated, they most certainly will never do it again; but make sure you have irrefutable proof before accusing someone.[66]

---

milk, jelly, bread, etc. It would be like saying the following: this claim has to be false because this ingredient is in everything that we eat. (Let's take for granted that Fresh-Cola is harmless. My point here is that when you are trying to deny a rumor, telling the truth is not enough.)

[65] For example, if a person is accused of anti-Semitism, a simple picture of him or her walking around town with one of the local Rabbis would be enough (it would be even better if we could get them in a picture together wearing casual clothes and conveying the message that, "we are such good friends that we even go hiking together".)

[66] In April 2017, Laura Boldrini, chairperson of the Italian Parliament, suffered an attack on Facebook claiming that her sister benefitted from a state pension at the age of 35 and that she had stolen money assigned to supporting migrants. Boldrini explained that the information was not only false, but also that her sister had died a few years previously.

6) When rumors involve safety, chemicals, physical conditions of a facility or environmental issues, they must be taken seriously and thoroughly and promptly investigated.

7) It is better not to pursue rumors that involve employees, love affairs, and personal issues, unless the organization might be directly affected.

8) Every rumor about possible criminal activity or financial impropriety must be taken seriously. Law enforcement should be contacted immediately to determine the scope of any necessary investigation. A legal counsel can advise on what constitutes due diligence, based on internal and industry precedents.

Leaks

Leaks create different situations from rumors, although a common characteristic is that we are dealing with *incomplete information*. This is the case when someone gives the press part of a document, rather than the complete version, or when an unconfirmed appointment of someone is leaked to the press. As is also the case with rumors, there is some truth in what is being published by these reporters. But as the information is only a part of the whole (the information may be correct, but it is taken out of the context), this means that the information is false.

Leaks are harmful because *they damage relationships with primary stakeholders*. These stakeholders feel they have the right to be properly informed by the institution in the proper way and at the proper time; and when this does not happen, whoever should have provided this information, is going to lose prestige. Furthermore, it shows a clear lack of internal unity, because a leak is always to the detriment of the established authorities. On the other hand, the whole issue is hard to stop and once a leak has happened, it is quite common to see a "counter leak" to try to counterbalance the original.

Leaks occur in practically every possible arena: business, culture, politics, religion.... As Shaw states:

> Why do people leak information? There is a wide range of reasons and sometimes more than one plays a role. You may leak something to get revenge or to punish someone who you feel deserves it. Leaks are re-

leased to gain points with those in the press; to feel or show your power — those who leak information have the sensation that they are the ones in control - and because they have the sincere conviction that the truth must be known and that the authorities are covering it up. But, although the desire to serve the truth is admirable indeed, it may coexist with an inflated sense of self-importance or even being overly fanatical. Many times, those who are leaking information justify it by claiming the only thing they want to achieve is to let the truth be known, when that is far from being true. Normally subordinates are to blame and are responsible for the leak. Yet many times it is a top manager who has leaked the information.

Behind any news leak there lies the beginning of a rebellion. Therefore, even in a case of minor importance, we should never shrug our shoulders and look the other way. Leaks are similar to flat tires: inflating is not enough; you have to see where the hole is and repair it. And with a leak, you have to fire the "spies" (those who instigated and participated in the leak).

But you must do all this by using strictly legal methods. Otherwise, the biggest problem will not be the leaks themselves but rather the illegal methods you used to uncover who was behind the leaks.[67]

Risky issues

In general terms, we could group conflicts that could easily end up triggering a crisis in three major categories: corporate errors, which are highly sensitive in the arena of public opinion; conflicts due to a clear discrepancy between the organization's val-

---

[67] In 2005, HP's CEO had to address a series of leaks coming from the board that were aimed at sabotaging her plans. To uncover who was behind the leaks, the CEO illegally tapped the phones of seven board members, nine reporters and two employees. She was prosecuted and had to resign. The whole operation against the leaks ended up causing HP more damage than the leaks themselves.

ues and activities and its social and cultural context; and clashes with the law. Let us look at each of them separately.

Big little mistakes

Every organization makes "little mistakes" that normally do not lead to major problems. Nonetheless, some small errors may cause a crisis because of external factors.

The prime factor which makes a conflict much, much worse is if it has happened before. Perhaps the trouble is minimal, but it is not the first time that the stakeholders had suffered it. It matters little whether the errors were caused by the organization itself, by a competitor or by a company from a completely different sector; if it is the same error, people will begin to suspect that the repetition is not the fruit of pure coincidence but rather a deliberate and conscious decision against their interests. So they will become very angry indeed, although the incident itself may be relatively minor. They will say in a fit of annoyance: "this is not the first time this has happened".

Whether the conflict is due to the institution's poor management in their due diligence, or because they failed to create a solid win-win relationship with all their stakeholders, this disproportionate reaction shows that there is a latent conflict within the institution's social environment.

In these cases, the right step — prevention! — consists of avoiding this type of friction and — since everybody makes mistakes — learning the best way to react and with immediacy. *Having a full deposit of good will, preventing mistakes and reacting immediately* are the three main elements which will ensure that; though problems may arise, we will not have to address a full-blown, long-term crisis.

The second factor that may convert a minor problem into the starting point of a crisis is that it is related to areas in which stakeholders' perceptions are extremely sensitive because there is already a latent conflict. Research regarding latent conflicts should always be based on an analysis of the most commonly shared social values, because they will show us what the public reaction will be, if they feel that these values are being challenged.

Each company's field of operations is different; so risks will vary from corporation to corporation: for instance, the pharmaceuticals and luxury industries should worry about the treatment of animals, which is of marginal importance to the tourism sector. However, in my view there are four issues which can affect all type of organizations: sexuality, power, money and secrecy. (If you speak Italian, you can use a trick to easily remember them: *sesso, potere, quattrini e riservatezza* form the Roman SPQR).

Sexuality

Sexuality (or to be more precise, sexual behavior which is deemed to be unacceptable in a defined social environment) is always a conflictive issue for any organization. The sexual revolution that took place towards the end of the 20th century has radically transformed the parameters of what is socially acceptable in Western societies. Today, sexuality is a private matter and any behavior between freely consenting adults is none of an organization's business. (At least this is what people say; but one thing is what people say in public and something completely different is what they really think and feel. The voice of natural morality – and other times, Puritanism – never stops talking).

We should add that any person in a position of authority should behave in a more exemplary manner than that which is expected of others. Additionally, the contradiction between what is being said and what is actually being done is often more important than the behavior itself.[68]

If we add the natural public curiosity about any subject related to sex to the aforementioned contradiction, we will indeed have a very explosive combination, that will certainly catch the media's attention and lay the ground for a potential conflict.

While always respecting individual freedom and intimacy, institutions have *to do everything in their power to avoid inappropriate behavior*, in terms of place (in the organization's facilities), of time (during working hours) and of persons (for example, between people who are working together). Society requires institutions to be

---

[68] For example, years ago an American congressman was forced to resign when several of his sex-related texts that had been sent to underaged males were published. This case produced an enormous scandal not only because of the nature of the facts themselves, but also because he had been a strong opponent of gay rights in Congress.

diligent in this matter. Being diligent means being even more careful when the relationship is not among equals: perhaps between a boss and one of his/her direct reports, with underage employees or, in general, whenever the age or position gap may mean near-zero freedom.[69]

So — and we are talking about *prevention* — job interviews should always be carried out by two people; there should be separate dressing rooms for males and females; precautionary measures in high schools and universities should be established regarding online communications and joint trips; filters should be in place to restrict Internet access while on the job, etc.

Power

Power (or should we say, the abusive use of it) is another latent conflict. Power has an *enormous ability to expand.* Most of those who are in power do not want any control mechanism, checks or limitations to be in place; and, when they are, those who have responsibilities tend to see them as mere obstacles. Aware of this reality, Western societies have implemented a system of checks and balances for those who are in positions of power, in both the public and private spheres. The system tries to ensure that power is not exercised arbitrarily and requires certain decisions to be taken after listening to specific people's advice, meetings to be held at certain places, and these consultations to be well documented. As Rudolf von Ihering, one of the most heralded civilists of the 20th century, wrote: «fulfilling procedures is the sworn enemy of arbitrariness and freedom's twin sister.»

---

[69] In November 2019, McDonald's board of directors decided to discharge CEO Stephen Easterbrook following an investigation into his consensual relationship with an employee in violation of internal protocols. The company pointed out that the termination of the contract was "without cause" considering that the violation was not so serious as to deprive him of the exit compensation, which amounted to 54 million dollars. Brian Krzanich, CEO of Intel, was not so lucky: when he left his post in 2018 due to a violation of "no-fraternization policies." In his case, it was he who resigned, and the technology company did not recognize his right to compensation.

The tendency of power to extend is so great that formal barriers alone will not be enough to stop it. A personal commitment is required for justice to survive, because the more power a person has, the easier it is for them to be unfair. In any event, formal rules, although they will never be completely effective, will always make the abuse of power much more difficult and less frequent, which is what prevention aims to accomplish.

The proper exercise of power also includes the ways it is used. It is not nearly enough to simply make the right decisions if power is applied in an authoritarian and despotic manner. The way power is used is critical, and especially so when the decisions made have a negative impact on people. Changes in organizational procedures that demand more from the staff must be carried out and communicated in such a way that they do not worsen the problem: for example, learning a new IT application, moving the offices to a business park far from the city center, restructuring business units and so on: and this is especially true when people are either being made redundant or having their working hours (and earnings) drastically reduced,.

The last piece of advice concerns decisions that may be interpreted as censorship; for instance, prohibitions regarding speaking about certain topics.[70] There is nothing more sacred in today's

---

[70] Attempts to remove or censor elements of information very often backfire. When someone asks for something on the internet to be deleted, it attracts interest and ends up increasing the number of people who access the information. It has even a name: the "Streisand effect", after American entertainer Barbra Streisand. In 2003, Kenneth Adelman photographed the whole California beachfront to document coastal erosion. One of his 12,000 photographs showed Streisand's mansion. The actress sued Adelman and his company, demanding US$50 million and the removal of the picture from the publicly available collection. Before Streisand filed her lawsuit, that picture had been downloaded from Adelman's website only six times; two of those downloads were by Streisand's attorneys. As a result of the lawsuit, more than 420,000 people visited the site over the following month. In addition, the lawsuit was dismissed, and Streisand had to pay Adelman's legal fees, inadvertently drawing attention in this way to something you want to hide also happens to companies. For instance, in December 2013, a YouTube user uploaded video proof that his Samsung Galaxy S4 battery had spontaneously caught fire. When Samsung learned of the YouTube video, it demanded certain conditions before honoring its warranty: it required the YouTuber to delete the

society than freedom of expression. This is the case when people claim they were censored to get public opinion's traction. Please avoid falling into that trap.

Money

Money is a bottomless pit which is full of risks to any sort of organization, big or small, regardless of how well the organization is managed. We are talking about money in the broadest sense and thus it includes any type of material goods. Greed is one of the forces that make the world go around.

The problem does not really refer to what is mine but rather to everything that does not belong to me. That is why both private and public institutions have implemented economic control mechanisms to oversee those who manage the organization's goods, because we all realize that temptation is always present. Perhaps the clearest example would be a bank, an entity whose mission is precisely to take good care of other people's money. The number of preventive measures that exist in banks and financial institutions is as long as your arm; the closer one is to money, the greater the precautionary measures have to be (how much a person is allowed to authorize, for what reasons and who else must authorize this type of transaction, simultaneous (both the where and the how) and post-transaction authorization (auditing, yearly P&L reporting, etc.).

However it must also be said that the tendency is to not reduce these checks but to increase their frequency and intensity; and *economic transparency has become a true global trend* for governments, public institutions, corporations, and non-profit organizations.

It is relevant to mention this trend in favor of transparency in the specific context of prevention. *When the proper prevention measures are in place, the likelihood of an issue becoming a crisis is much*

---

video, to promise not to upload similar material, to officially absolve the company of all liability, to waive his right to bring a lawsuit, and to never make the terms of the agreement public. The user decided to share online Samsung's settlement proposal and his original video drew 1.2 million views in one week.

more remote. Let us put it more graphically: if the precautionary economic measures work properly, top-level management has one less item to worry about.

In addition, it is worthwhile having other prudential measures, such as clear reporting procedures, that emphasize the fundamental precautions which are necessary when administering goods that belong to others.

Examples of this type of precautionary measures would be the proper usage and control of inventories, which should be double-checked whenever top-level managers in any division are replaced or transferred to another position; double signature bank accounts; full reporting at the end of a pre-defined period; audits after projects or events have been terminated; and, last but far from least, the need for excellent administrators who are aware of their responsibilities.

Secrecy

Secrecy, understood to be an excessive tendency to overemphasize secrets, is closely tied in with the previous categories; it works as both a conceptual framework as well as a *safety net*. Power, money and even decency (as Brits ironically say, *there is safety in numbers*) are better controlled by measures of transparency. Additionally, transparency is the first communication criterion when addressing problems that arise in those areas in which the stakeholders are hypersensitive. Acting with transparency avoids errors and, in those cases in which they have not been avoided, communicating with transparency will help to limit the damage. In the words of Louis Brandeis, Justice of the US Supreme Court: «sunlight is the best disinfectant, and electric light is better than police.»

From a legal point of view, transparency is based on a simple principle, included in the legislation of most countries, under the technical name of *Freedom of Information Acts*. This principle states that all information that public authorities keep, with the exceptions of those that correspond to individual privacy or the fundamental interest of the State itself, is public information. The basic idea is that, in a democratic system, citizens have the right to have access to this information in order to control the public powers and to participate in public decisions in an informed and conscious manner.

Legislation concerning transparency is certainly nothing new. Actually, the first law covering administrative transparency was passed in Sweden in 1766. In the second half of the 20th century, this type of legislation has been approved all over the world, first in the Anglo-Saxon world (USA and the Commonwealth of Nations). Recently, new laws as have been passed in Poland (2001), Germany (2006), the USA (2009) with a far-reaching law that was among the first bills presented by the first Obama Administration, and in Spain.

Transparency is certainly one of the most far-reaching, ongoing developments in the world of public administration, as well as in corporations. According to Rubio: «The concept of open government is being built around such principles as collaboration, participation and transparency, all being understood as being values which per se enhance the overall quality of democracy and are much more in tune with our times and citizens' concerns.»

Transparency goes far beyond any field of interest of stakeholders. In a democratic context, all institutions have to be transparent as a clear sign of their "service to society's mindset." The transparency obligation that exists today regarding public administration has far exceeded its original scope and *has spread to institutions of all types, both public and private.* Our societies have now fully accepted transparency as the general rule and stakeholders feel that the only reason for not applying transparency is the desire to hide something, which is either negative or corrupt in nature.

It is true that transparency does have its limits; transparency cannot be applied equally to everyone, or in every situation to the same degree. There are personal and professional spheres in which secrecy is not a choice but rather a serious obligation, which must be kept. There are other circumstances (a wartime situation, in the midst of a terrorist threat or a widespread epidemic) in which some of the accepted transparency policies are automatically suspended. However, these are only the exceptions that confirm the rule. The authorities cannot suspend these civil rights of their own accord, but only with the consensus of the parliament (in other words, the voice of its citizens).

In my view, these compulsory norms on transparency are a social response to the increase frequency of abuses in this area. They who control information do not need to be persuasive, nor do they have to negotiate; they have absolute power. If a mistake is made, I can decide to solve it the way I think best; but I can also decide not to fix it. Moreover, I could also cover up irregularities and mistakes made by colleagues (doctors, judges, engineers, police officials, members of their political party or union) and friends in general, triggering a never-ending chain of favors. This arbitrary power is what transparency tries to avoid.

Meanwhile, technology has made it very difficult indeed – or perhaps even impossible – to impede leaks of highly sensitive information, as we have all seen in the WikiLeaks case. Anyone who has a smartphone can tape a conversation, film people without their knowledge, copy all sorts of documents and post everything on Facebook, YouTube, Flickr or Instagram in a matter of seconds. The measures that are available to stop such actions are ineffective; law enforcement is much slower than criminal activity. Besides, as we will see in chapter 8, if the case finally ends up before a judge, there is a more than 50% chance that freedom of expression will win against the right to protect one's image and personal privacy.

Another reason to beware of secrecy is the legislation in favor of *whistleblowing*. This term describes the case in which an employee publicly denounces some criminal or unethical activity within his own organization. Many countries have passed laws to protect people who have taken these steps against any internal punishment; authorities have even offered immunity in cases in which a crime has been committed or covered up and there are cases in which economic rewards have been paid for such collaboration. Not small money at that. For example, in 2013, the Securities and Exchange Commission offered US$ 14,000,000 to whoever provided information that could be used to recover the money embezzled in a financial corruption case.

Yet, the rewards on offered are not the most critical factor; many secrets have been revealed for revenge or simply because the whistleblower's conscience did not allow them to sleep well. The fact is that, for one reason or another, when more than one person is aware of something this "secret", it's like TNT: it may blow up at any moment.

Confidentiality agreements are no longer sacred either; and when they are broken – and they are broken very often indeed – disclosed information revealing highly negative actions or omissions will seriously harm the company's reputation. Such agreements are normally viewed as an attempt to buy someone's silence. Once this confidentiality has been broken, both parties, the victim and the institution who paid him or her, are going to have mud on their face, but this is especially true in respect of the organization (remember, people are always on David's side and against Goliath). Even if an individual breaks the secrecy agreement in bad faith (for instance, a victim of any corporate error) in order to demand more money and blackmail the company, the party who will suffer the most will be the company. This is valid for any type of institution (political, corporate, cultural, sporting, etc.).[71]

We live in a risky environment, in which there is nothing worse than being perceived as being secretive. Many institutions — some willingly and others because they feel they do not have a choice — have opted for transparency with their primary stakeholders. Whatever their attitude may be, sincere or forced, the fact is that transparency has become the general rule in all organizations which see themselves as being socially responsible.

This general principle of transparency, however, has many exceptions: these tend to be tied to respect for people's intimacy, a professional pledge of secrecy, non-disclosure of anything regarding issues sub iudice, national security secrets, etc. These exceptions do have precise reasons. The prudent decision on whether the right thing is to be transparent or to keep something secret depends on the corporate mission and culture and what the relationships with its primary stakeholders are. In other words, *transparency is not just a communications gadget but also a corporate policy, to be carefully consid-*

---

[71] In 2002, the Cuban and the Spanish governments agreed to free Angel Carromero, a Spanish member of the Popular Party, who had been accused of being responsible for the deaths of two Cubans, leaders of the Christian Liberation Movement, Oswaldo Payá and Harold Cepero, who were killed in an automobile accident. In spite of the fact that all the evidence showed that the accident had been caused by Castro's police, Carromero declared he was guilty and that he would not say anything further about what had happened in exchange for being able to spend his time in jail in Spain. Yet, once he had arrived in Spain everything changed, and he gave several interviews and press conferences. As a consequence, in November 2013 the European Union requested the United Nations to open an official investigation as to what had happened, to the detriment of the Spanish government's interests.

ered by top management and to be consistent with the organization's identity.

In respect of crisis prevention, it is worthwhile to point out
that people have great expectations regarding transparency. Most
consider that they deserve to have access to all information as an
undeniable right. This perception has even been reinforced by
several public scandals which have shown that secrecy in the corporation played a vital role. Those scandals arose *because of* opacity,
but became more harmful, longer lasting and more widespread
because of their secrecy.

Therefore, whoever is governing an organization must be
aware that any intentionally hidden fact that stakeholders may
think they deserve to know, is a danger which may blow up into a
crisis. If the secret is made public, stakeholders will forgive the
company only if it convincingly explains that keeping the secret
was justified in the stakeholders' own interest, not in that of the
company or those who decided to withhold the information. In
addition, companies should have a full and persuasive explanation
ready, in case it is needed. It is critical to release complete information quickly.

These comments regarding prevention in these four spheres
(sexuality, power, money and secrecy) point to one clear conclusion, *the best way to prevent a crisis is to be exemplary in our behavior.* In
the same way that a person should not only behave properly but
also be seen to be doing so, an institution should not only behave
properly in order to enhance its own image but also because it has
a strong internal conviction to do so. But, at the same time, we
should not overlook the fact that acting in an exemplary fashion is
the most prudent policy and a very solid basis for credibility and
good will.

ESG, the new frontiers

The ESG risks triad (Environmental, Social & Governance)
has entered large corporations (the Fortune 200) with force and is
advancing steadily in medium-sized companies. Each of these three
elements integrates two others: the chapter on the environment
includes energy issues and the carbon footprint (and, more broad-
ly, climate change). The social chapter examines those issues in

relation to employees' rights and to human rights in respect of external stakeholders. Finally, governance examines shareholder rights and integrity (or, in negative terms, measures against corruption).

Taken separately, none of those components are new. Each has a different trajectory. What is new is their aggregation under the same umbrella, so that they are managed – analyzed, measured and reported on – in a unified way.

What do elements as heterogeneous as respect for human rights or the carbon footprint have in common to make it useful to integrate them?

Two reasons make this integration advisable: mindset and vision. A preventive mindset gives growing attention to these values and responds to common risk analysis and measurement procedures. Measuring them in the same way and acting on them offers many beneficial ways to transform what underlies all ESG themes: corporate culture.

Second, vision: integrating these elements is useful when working with a more long-term perspective. If strategic planning goes beyond a 3-year horizon, integration has many advantages because it allows us to see the big trends in action.

In that sense, ESG is a new way of looking at issues management. Perhaps the most salient difference is in respect of who exerts the pressure. In ESG, the driving force for change is no longer grassroots activist movements, which persuade public opinion through the media, and from there to legal regulation. Here, the cycle begins with a new sensitivity among investors, who demand from companies that they respect good ESG practices as a precondition for investing. As the UN document *Global Compact* (2015) points out, «Failing to consider all long-term investment value drivers including ESG issues is a failure of fiduciary duty.»

In other words: Having a good position in an ESG ranking facilitates access to cheap finance; a bad one makes funding much more expensive. Therefore, it is not surprising that the main promoter of ESG strategies in many companies is the CFO.

Another good incentive to take ESG risks seriously is the fact that a good rating when competing for large projects convened by States is increasingly relevant. A good position in the ranking is certainly a competitive advantage; a bad one blocks your participation in large international biddings.

In the context of investment funds and large contracts, it is well known that companies that pay attention to ESG risks are more resilient, and that better financial and commercial treatment are therefore reasonable. A good ESG index, Peacock notes, «is often a good indicator of acceptable levels of risk and quality in management.»

This is not the appropriate place to go into detail regarding ESG risk management, which is a discipline in itself. I mention it because ESG risks are today fundamental issues of crisis prevention; and in this field, communication plays a major role, since of the three components of any ESG strategy (*know* the risks that may affect you; *show* what is done to your stakeholders; and *grow*, set continuous improvement goals), one of them is communication.

Conflicts regarding values: controversies

Many different conflicts can arise between the principles and values of an institution and the predominant opinions of the social-cultural context in which it operates. In chapter 1 we emphasized that institutions must try to live in harmony with their neighbors and with society at large. When the relationship is poor, communication becomes very difficult and the risk of crisis increases substantially.

A conflict that is ideologically based is called a controversy. According to Carroggio, controversies are «systematic public discrepancies about ideas and proposals that tend to generate confusion in contents, tension in their relations and rejection of their proposals by their interlocutors.» This author calls them *media controversies*, so as to differentiate them from the classic use of the term in academia, which is actually a rhetorical method to advance in philosophy and other disciplines.

Differences between controversies and crises

Controversies and crises are two separate realities. Crises are centered around facts while controversies focus on principles, values and proposals; crises can be totally unexpected, whereas controversies are the result of a process and are more predictable. Crises require institutions to take immediate, short-term action in order to limit damage, while controversies require a more profound and longer-term response. Crises are extraordinary, while controversies are a part of normal daily life.

Once that has been understood, however, we should add that controversies are in fact quite similar to crises. Firstly, because some controversies lead to crises; and at times the borderline between a heated controversy and a crisis is blurred. Secondly, controversies are also a situation of risks and opportunities: a danger in the relationships with priority stakeholders and an opportunity for the organization to make its voice heard. We could say that *a controversy is a crisis' little sister.*

Controversies happen often because of technological and health risks (atomic energy, petrochemical industries, biotechnology, and sugared soft drinks); because of social and cultural transformations that question long-established customs and traditions, such as bullfights in Spain and foxhunting in the UK; or because of ideological, political changes, etc. These changes create new environments and a new social consensus.

I am not saying that controversies must be avoided at all costs. Controversies are, to a certain degree, unavoidable in today's democratic world; what companies must do is to manage them effectively, limiting their negative effects and taking full advantage of the opportunities that they yield. Controversies may help the organization to better explain its identity, both internally and externally, and — if necessary — to change. In this sense, controversies and even crises can be quite healthy, if management knows how to use them: they may help to promote change, overcoming the inertia that blocks alterations in the status quo.

Companies have to decide what they stand for and, thereafter, be consistent: if they choose to defend certain values that arouse controversy because they constitute their principles, it would be a contradiction to change those values for commercial reasons. That would mean that those values were just "marketing values", a way to promote products in certain places, because it was fancy and cool.[72]

Perverse effects of a controversy

Controversies hinder good relations with our stakeholders and make communication with them difficult. They are factors of disunity and dissent and tend to intensify further. That is why we must try to actively manage these situations, without letting the problem grow.

There are five harmful effects of a controversy, and they tend to feed back.

In the first place, they *generate tension* in our relationships with stakeholders, because no type of compromise can be accepted on values. We see the other as an enemy, as a stereotype, making bad assumptions and gross generalizations.

---

[72] Until 2012, the Swedish furniture company IKEA was well known for its gender-equality position. The company ran an ad in 1994 widely considered as being the first commercial featuring a homosexual couple as part of a larger campaign about "non-traditional" families. Especially since 2006, IKEA has used gay and transgender themes in its advertising in different western markets: same-sex couples in the US, Australia and the UK; a girl and her two daddies in the Netherlands; transsexuals in Spain, France and Thailand; and a bisexual man in Austria. Similar ads were also used in more traditional countries like Italy, Portugal and Poland and IKEA kept them in spite of some criticism from conservative groups. IKEA's corporate answer was: «Homosexuality is one of the elements of life in modern society. Our company cannot ignore this. Family life is changing ... welcome to the new era». However, IKEA succumbed in 2012, when it deleted all images of women in its catalogue for Saudi Arabia (afterwards, they recognized that it was their own decision; Saudi authorities did not ask for that change. The company later said it regretted the move but did not change the catalog); and in 2013, an interview with a lesbian couple in the Russian version of their magazine in 2013 was pulled due to Russian anti-LGBT legislation. My comment here is that principles are sacred everywhere. If you bend them for commercial reasons, they are not principles but something else. It is hard not to agree with Sweden's equality minister, Nyamko Sabuni, who commented that although IKEA was a private company that made its own decisions, it also projected an image of Sweden around the world; and «For Ikea to remove an important part of Sweden's image and an important part of its values in a country that more than any other needs to know about Ikea's principles and values, that's completely wrong»

Later, they *provoke the systematic rejection* of all the other party's proposals. Nothing from the enemy can be good, and therefore they are refuted en bloc, without entering into discussion.

Third, they create *confusion regarding the content*, because the messages are distorted beyond recognition by the other party. Sentences are taken out of context, and caricature, irony, and satire dominate.

Fourth, it is also easy to *get confused as to who are the real interlocutors*. Companies should address their priority stakeholders in the first place to attract them to their position; and then those who are undecided or indifferent. Trying to convince the opponent is a waste of time.

Finally, there is the danger of apathy. Controversies are usually much broader areas of discussion than that of a specific organization, so its managers may think that the problem is too big for them, or that they are not entitled to speak on behalf of everyone. I feel like a sergeant leading a platoon in the middle of a chaotic battlefield without generals. In that situation, it is easier to be reactive than proactive, leading to dire consequences.

But not everything in a controversy is bad. *Controversies raise the level of awareness and interest* in the media and in public opinion. This means that whoever is involved in a heated public debate will be given the stage to explain their ideas, communicate their messages much more openly than they would be able to do without that controversy. Being involved in a controversy is the same as if someone has given you a microphone and then asked you: what do you think about this? In fact, many organizations never have the chance to make their voices heard, except in times of controversy.

A debate about a controversial issue has all the elements of a good story: a heavy dosage of tension, serious consequences, and clear impact on the future. That is why they become news. Organizations should learn from activists and lobbyists; for them, a crisis is an excellent opportunity for their message to be heard in the public arena, to get a place in the media and promote their own agenda with the public authorities. Controversies do not affect organizations directly involved in the issue but are rather a universal call to action for whoever is concerned about the issue. If you want your position to be heard, do not remain silent, because the other party will not. Let's see how.

Guidelines to intervene in a controversy

Addressing a controversy implies being able to publicly defend the company's position and avoiding the four malfunctions that we mentioned above as hindering communication policy: tension, outright rejection of the other position, confusion in respect of contents and interlocutors, and losing the initiative.

Confusion over what the company stands for is the most serious distorting effect of a controversy. Four steps may be taken to address it: use a positive approach, be extremely clear in contents, properly identify your interlocutors and clearly explain all contents.

A positive approach to the issues being discussed helps to overcome the rejection triggered by a controversy. Therefore, companies need to generate a compelling narrative regarding the topic. This narrative must develop *valid arguments from a logical point of view* (believable, well-documented reasoning, based upon facts) and *persuasive from a psychological viewpoint* (presented in an empathetic and well-versed manner, which includes numerous clarifying examples) covering all aspects of the controversial issue. The first task for corporations involved in a controversy is being able to ensure that the institution has a sustainable public narrative.

An important part of this sustainable discourse is its framework. Don't use the same framework based upon the same values, language and symbols as your opponent. The framework is like a railroad track: once you are on it, it will take you wherever the track leads. So it is critical to create your own symbolic context and language.

Context is truly a critical factor. Without context any statement which is made may be misinterpreted or only partially understood. Therefore, companies must explain the contents of their own statements, because within the inherent chaos in a controversy, in which your opponent will exaggerate and ridicule your position, you should not leave any stone unturned. The context states who I am, why I am more than qualified to talk about the issue and why I should be listened to. The problem is not with the text but rather with the context. Without the context, it is very hard indeed for anyone to pay attention to the truth; in other words, to pay attention to what you have said.

These transversal messages should also be well defined, because they are at least as important as the informational content.

Examples suggested by Czarnecki: «we are aware of the situation and are responding to it; this is an urgent matter for us and we are on top of it; the human situation of the people involved is important to us; we are competent, accountable, and responsive, and other responders are working with us as a team; we don't speculate nor assign blame; we will keep you informed as more info becomes available, etc.» In other words: *make your implicit position explicit.*

Choosing the context is very similar to picking the battlefield and where to place our own troops. One place is not the same as another. Dezenhall & Weber suggest we choose *the highest possible moral position*:

> Ronald Reagan once advised: "Wrap every argument in a principle". So every effective communicator must know how to do it. Essentially, it means taking an issue, position, or call-to-action and associating it with a timeless value — something most people cherish or hold sacrosanct. Security. Justice. Privacy. Choice. Safety. The rights of the underprivileged. Fighting oppression. Doing so adds enormous authority and weight to one's claim. You are not just espousing a selfish point of view; you're standing up for something noble. Not only does it win people over to your side, it enables them to justify their position to others.

Explicating the context also implies providing the data that will properly place the discussion in its real dimension.

In addition, decide whom are you talking to. In a controversy, it is a waste of time and money to try to convince your opponent. It is simply impossible. Your attention should be placed on those stakeholders who are undecided or in doubt. Dezenhall & Weber suggest rewriting the old refrain and "do preach to the choir." The first ones we should be persuading are those nearby rather than the contrary. The right strategy in a controversy is to act within concentric circles and address those who are nearest to us (employees, fans, customers, benefactors, etc.) and mobilize them in defense of our organization.

Taking the initiative is also a must. Striking the first blow has many upsides. The media tend to pay more attention to those who are leading the fight and the framework of the controversy is often set by their reporting. A news story always begins with an accusation and it is only at the end that the one who is being accused is going to be allowed to defend oneself. If you are on the defensive, when a reporter finally gets around to asking you to give your version of the story, 90% of it has already been written. Additionally, defending yourself requires many more resources and is much less effective than being on the attack. If you force your opponent to "play defense," you lead.

Conflicts with the established authorities

Conflicts with the social environment may reach a higher level, when they are about issues that are in the phase of crystallization. If society as a whole has reached a consensus and the public authorities have legislated accordingly, restricting the scope of autonomy and freedom of corporations and other organizations, and imposing sanctions, those who still do not accept the new rules, become "anti-social rebels".

In these conflicts, public authorities are not the only adversary. Other actors also play a role in these dispute: people and institutions who carry *the flag of progress*, proclaim themselves the true defenders of what is politically correct and attack all the organizations whom they think threaten social consensus.

The leeway to maneuver in this phase of a conflict is much less than that which exists in a controversy. Here organizations only have three options: adapting to the reigning environment, by changing the values that they had always defended; leaving this field of activity or geographical area; or fighting the battle in the public opinion arena and/or taking the issue to court.

The same advice offered when we discussed issues management, is applicable here. We will also provide further recommendations in chapter 7 when dealing about legal confrontations.

I would like to stress the importance of having a socially sustainable discourse once again and presenting it in a calm and peaceful dialog with positive reasoning. These guidelines may lead to a social dialog and, thus, to reducing the heat inherent in this type of controversy.

Reasoning in this way will certainly not resolve the basic problem, because controversies do not disappear, nor do they remain static; they are in constant evolution (sometimes for the better, but normally for the worse). Therefore, leading organizations have to become catalysts for social change.

If one institution takes the initiative, others with the same basic orientation may be encouraged to address these same threats together in clear coordination, whether they are in the same or different countries. Working together also provides the advantage of being able to split tasks and share resources. Your communication effort and prestige tends to be strengthened by international initiatives.

In short, institutions must pro-actively engage in conflicts with the authorities; this may be the best way to create a new social consensus and democratic change in current legislation, when it is considered unjust and detrimental to society.

The History: Facebook and the Rohingya[73]

Respect for and the promotion of human rights are another key line in crisis prevention. Companies are judged with ethical criteria not only on how they operate within their facilities with their employees, but also whether it is possible to take advantage of their products or services to violate people's rights.

Since 2017, Facebook has been under severe criticism for being instrumental in the ethnic cleansing of the Rohingyas, a victimized ethnic group in Myanmar, considered by United Nations as "the most persecuted minority in the world."

In that Southeast Asian country, the words Facebook and Internet are synonymous, and half of the population are daily users of Facebook. Its widespread usage together with the lack of checked information and the high level of illiteracy made Facebook the ultimate weapon against this minority, which culminated in the exodus of more than 700,000 Rohingyas to Bangladesh.

The Rohingyas are an ethnic group in the western part of Burma. Most of them are Muslims, while a few are Hindu. When Myanmar gained independence in 1948, it did not acknowledge

---

[73] Case documented by José Pocholo Sebastian.

the Rohingya as an indigenous ethnic group. Since that moment, they have not been considered citizens of the country. To begin with, military forces launched "Operation King Dragon", embodying human rights violations such as a systematic rape, destruction of property, open violence, and arrests. Fearing for their lives, the Rohingyas fled to Bangladesh. This was followed up by "Operation Clean and Beautiful Nation," a similar campaign that drove another 200,000 Rohingyas out of Myanmar. To this day, the Rohingyas are officially illegal immigrants in the country. That means that traditional constitutional rights (such as education) are not granted to them by law.

In 2017, a group of Rohingyas fought for their rights and resisted the government's oppression by attacking the Myanmar army. This triggered further hatred towards them and led to another wave of persecution, which again led to a significant number of Rohingyas being violently driven out of Myanmar to seek refuge in Bangladesh: satellite imagery showed that 340 villages were burned or destroyed, by the Myanmar's military.

Before these events, about one million Rohingyas lived in Myanmar. However, about three quarters of those people had fled to Bangladesh by 2018. Independent analysts and NGOs asked Facebook to do something about it. So far, Facebook CEO Mark Zuckerberg has been consistent in giving polite and compassionate answers on different occasions.

For instance, in early April 2018, he answered in an interview: "The Myanmar issues have, I think, gotten a lot of focus inside the company, and they're real issues and we take this really seriously." After acknowledging that anti-Rohingya people were using Facebook to «incite real-world hatred,» he continued: «This is certainly something that we're paying a lot of attention to. It's a real issue, and we want to make sure that all of the tools that we're bringing to bear on eliminating hate speech, inciting violence, and basically protecting the integrity of civil discussions that we're doing in places like Myanmar, as well as places like the US that do get a disproportionate amount of attention.»

Then, he went on to say that the systems that Facebook had in place were quite effective in the context of the country's situation. However, six NGOs took offense to this remark and in an open letter to Mark Zuckerberg, showed examples of oppressive messages being spread through Facebook Messenger, and suggesting specific measures to handle the situation.

Mark Zuckerberg responded to the letter, saying: «Thank you for writing and I apologize for not being sufficiently clear about the important role that your organizations play in helping us understand and respond to Myanmar-related issues. In making my remarks, my intention was to highlight how we're building artificial intelligence to help us better identify abusive, hateful or false content even before it is flagged by our community.»

Facebook then commissioned Business for Social Responsibility (BSR), a global nonprofit organization, to perform a Human Rights Impact Assessment (HRIA) between May and September 2018, using a methodology based on the UN Guiding Principles on Business and Human Rights. The report, which was dated October 2018, confirmed NGOs claims, saying:

> Facebook has become a useful platform for those seeking to incite violence and cause offline harm. Though the actual relationship between content posted on Facebook and offline harm is not fully understood, Facebook has become a means for those seeking to spread hate and cause harm, and posts have been linked to offline violence. A minority of users is seeking to use Facebook as a platform to undermine democracy and incite offline violence, including serious crimes under international law; for example, the Report of the Independent International Fact-Finding Mission on Myanmar describes how Facebook has been used by bad actors to spread anti-Muslim, anti-Rohingya, and anti-activist sentiment.

On November 5, 2018, Facebook released a statement of admission through a post by Alex Warofka, Product Policy Manager, which read: «The report concludes that, prior to this year we weren't doing enough to help prevent our platform from being used to foment division and incite offline violence. We agree that we can and should do more. Over the course of this year, we have invested heavily in people, technology and partnerships in order to examine and address the abuse of Facebook in Myanmar, and

BSR's report acknowledges that we are now taking the right corrective actions.»

In fact, Facebook removed 18 accounts and 52 pages associated with the Myanmar military, which promoted hatred against the Rohingya. However, the United Nations disputed that the right corrective actions were being taken. It called for Facebook and other social media platforms to independently and thoroughly examine how their networks had been leveraged to spread hatred.

The UN acknowledged Facebook's pledge to improve but has noted that it has not provided any specific information about hate speech on the platform and that it would be necessary to assess the gravity of the problem and develop an adequate solution. The UN also suggested that Facebook should perform a due diligence on the ethnic climate in any market that it chooses to enter in order to take the necessary measures to avoid a repetition of what happened to the Rohingyas in Myanmar.

CHAPTER SEVEN

Preparation: the crisis manual

In the previous chapter, we analyzed the advantages of a profound understanding the context and its trends, in order to manage issues that may arise and take the appropriate decisions. Nevertheless, this is not always enough. Anticipation and prevention do avoid many crises and reduce their impact in all cases, but they do not totally avoid such situations. *Organizations may not always be able to avoid a crisis – even if it was foreseen.* For that reason, they should always be ready to face a crisis.

Crisis preparation is the third element of crisis management. Companies need to flesh out a full-scale set of measures to apply immediately before potential crises. These must be set out in writing in a formal document called a *crisis plan* or *crisis manual*. This plan will be the sole focus of this chapter.

Crisis plan: its nature and objectives

A crisis plan may be defined as being the operational program that an organization should follow both during and after a crisis, to either avoid or lessen its negative effects. The document that contains this operational program is also called the crisis plan.

In the same way that we have differentiated crises from accidents and emergencies, we must also avoid confusion between a crisis plan and an emergency plan. The latter is part of crisis management, but it is simply its technical element: the institutional response to an operational contingency. A hospital, for instance should apply a series of measures in the case of an electrical outage in the operating theater (an emergency plan) as part of the measures — not only the technical ones — that they should take in unexpected circumstances (a crisis plan).

Many reasons explain the need for such a program. Firstly, crises happen in every industry: they are not a remote hypothesis, but a likelihood with a greater or lesser chance of happening that can never be totally eliminated. The question to be asked is not if a crisis could occur but rather when it will happen.

Additionally, the organization will be better prepared if all those who can contribute to solving the problem consider in advance the best response, in an atmosphere of composure. As Caponigro says, «it's easier to make smart decisions when you don't feel the pressure of a guillotine hovering over your head.»

Thirdly, a well-prepared organization will respond as one body, with the speed and efficiency of readiness: everybody knows what they are supposed to do and why they are supposed to do it. For instance, in a crisis plan for a school, if children have practiced beforehand how to evacuate the school in case of fire, their speed and organization will undoubtedly better. The same with non-technical aspects like communications: only with preparation and training can an organization become a source of information for good news or for bad.

A fourth reason: looking ahead gives the decision-maker extra time to think about how to regain the initiative rather than being subject to other players. It is rather like a game of chess: the best players do not react to their opponent's moves, but rather develop their own strategy and adapt it to their opponent.

Fifth, planning is the most economical solution. Undoubtedly, getting ready does have its costs, but the fact is that if there is no emergency, I can purchase at the best moment and from the best supplier.

Lastly but probably the most important reason: the plan is a governing and control tool for top management to ensure that the corporate response follows the guidelines and priorities it has set out in advance. In effect, it is quite frequent for a crisis to provoke absolute chaos and a break-down in communications. If everybody knows what the bosses have decided should be done, there will be no power vacuums.

The existence of a crisis manual is becoming much more commonplace. Some people might find it surprising or even out of place that "inoffensive organizations" (small companies, startups or even NGOs) have a crisis manual. Perhaps part of the problem lies in the term "crisis plan", which could be considered as pessimistic or scary. If that is the case, use another, friendlier name, but get ready for both technical and managerial problems.

Allow me to insist on the upside of having such a plan in your drawer. It seems to me somewhat incoherent that a company is prepared for possible material damage in the case of emergencies (fire exits, theft insurance policies, or simply a lightning rod), does not foresee or take any preventive measures regarding damage to their corporate reputation deriving from a crisis.

Crisis plan models

Up until now, we have been focusing on the *crisis manual* as if it were a single concept, but there is not only one model. How formal or informal it is depends on the characteristics of the organization: its structure, environment, size and corporate culture. In very structured companies with a clear definition of competencies, their crisis plan should have this same structure and clearly point out responsibilities and procedures. In more flexible organizations, on the other hand, their crisis plan can be more orientational in the form of guidelines.

The right type of plan has to be consistent with *the organization's governance* and its division between decentralized decisions and centralized control. For example, if in a textile firm operating in numerous countries, the decisions regarding models, prices, advertising, etc. are made locally to adapt to the circumstances in each country, then crisis response should also be managed at a local level; on the other hand, if all the decisions are made at the corporate HQ and the affiliates have very little operational initiative, the same principle should be applied to crisis management. *Crisis management is a part of the organization's culture.*

The crucial point here is to adapt to reality, not to charts. Some organizations claim that practically everything has been delegated down to branch level, but the instructions coming out of HQ are so detailed that the local people have no leeway whatsoever to take any sort of initiative.[74]

Industry and social context also have a say in this. Organizations that develop activities perceived by society as risky (chemicals, for instance) require crisis plans that have been approved by the authorities and appropriately communicated to local communities. The key here is to follow social perceptions, since they may change and what was considered a harmless activity at one point, years later may be seen as dangerous. For instance, the food chain issue has now become an issue in itself, and so prominent restaurants (restaurant chains, three Michelin star restaurants, etc.) need to be ready to explain where each ingredient comes from, its practices regarding hygiene, etc.

Regarding crisis plan format, there are three basic models:
1) A long, detailed document covering all possible problematic situations, and offering a thorough response to each one. The only thing that is left to be done is to simply follow the instructions to the letter.

---

[74] At the beginning of 2016 summer holidays, Barcelona-based Vueling, a low-cost airline owned by IAG (and named "Best low-cost carrier" in 2015 by the trade journal *Air Transport News*), cancelled more than 60 flights and delayed many others, affecting almost 35,000 passengers. The company's first official explanation was that the cause was a strike by French air traffic controllers. In reality, its bad planning was also partly to blame. According to one of its pilots, «Vueling assumed more flights than it could perform.» What made the situation even worse was the company's slow reaction: Vueling hired 6 planes, 32 pilots and 130 people for its customer services department on July 4th, only when forced to do so by pressure from Spanish regulators. Its communication was also poor: although the problem affected the airline's hub, it was handled from IAG headquarters in London; local leaders went into hiding, and it took four days for them to speak up and apologize. For 11 days, the company did not provide any information at all on social media. This episode shows the importance of handling a crisis where the action is, and the consequences of a poor communication structure in which local management has no power or responsibility on how to communicate with their stakeholders.

2) A general guidebook that facilitates an organized response for any critical, unexpected situation. The focus here is not the various crisis scenarios but rather how the ordinary governance rules adapt to these exceptional situations. According to those who defend this model, this type of plan better adapts to the corporate culture.

3) As an intermediate approach, a general guideline valid for any type of crisis, with specific instructions for the most probable scenarios. In this manner, we have an itemized guidebook for the most likely cases and do not lack a manual if something unforeseen happens.

Each model has advantages and disadvantages: for instance, general guidelines tend to be more versatile and easier for managers to put into practice, while the itemized plan is preferable for technically complex situations or when there is a breakdown in communications, because your employees know exactly what to do.

A good plan has to be tailor-made. The first decision to be made is which model works best for my company; i.e. *to consider the type of organization*. If the company is small and the number of people who are involved is not large either, a generic plan is likely to be the best option. On the other hand, a large organization tends to need a more complex and detailed plan (also because people expect a better crisis response from larger, well-known organizations).

The second criterion regards *the type of risks that the institution is exposed to*. If the firm's activity represents a danger for the population, the emergency and mitigation measures are a critical part of this manual. As González Herrero points out, "the protection against possible personal harm should be the prime aim of all planning efforts, especially in the cases in which we are dealing with accident prevention. The organization's social responsibility should outweigh its profit goals, so as to place its employees', its clients' and the community's well-being and safety ahead of protecting any and all property and the company's assets."

The third criterion is tied to *legal requirements*: it is necessary to have an emergency and crisis plan for each scenario that the law demands for each industry.

The final consideration is cost: *to consider the available resources*. The more complex the plan is, the costlier it is going to be to put it into practice. The key word is proportionality, as not all inherent risks can be foreseen: you have to decide what your priorities are and what the likelihood is that each of these events could actually happen. The other side of the coin is that if the plan is overly long and drawn out, management will most likely never approve it, considering it a waste of time and money — and perhaps rightly so!

These criteria will help determine which model will fit your company. Perhaps a good approach is to ask yourself how it should be used, if and when the time comes. As Czarnecki warns, "There is such a thing as over-planning. Your action plan should be something people can keep in their heads in the midst of havoc. No one has time to begin digging through a two-inch binder, Reading procedures, in the middle of a crisis. Everyone needs to know the plan, and it has to be simple (and therefore flexible) enough for that to be possible."

In closing, let me add a dose of common sense in relation with the benefits of having the plan in place. *The plan alone cannot save an institution from crisis.* It is just *one more piece* in the puzzle of crisis management. It has proven its usefulness on many occasions, but by itself it does not guarantee to provide the solution for every problem. Nor does it have to be irrationally followed to the letter. As General Dwight D. Eisenhower once said: «in respect to war preparation, my experience is that making plans is useless, but the planning stage is completely indispensable.»

The plan does not aim to substitute leadership: it just compliments it. It is like a solid sword, such as those made in the Spanish city of Toledo, which have the following words engraved on the blade: «Trust me not if you lack bravery.» At the end of the day, the *plan is only meant to orientate leaders and is never etched in stone.* Its real usefulness lies in the hours and hours of thinking that are required on the part of the institutional managers in preparing it. As stated by Dezenhall, «If given the choice between a thorough plan and a good leader, go with the leader, because people rarely separate the event from the personalities that dominate the event.»

How to prepare the crisis plan

Why have a plan?

The first step in creating a crisis plan is, quite obviously, making the decision to generate it. This decision is not at all easy to take and what proves this is the fact that the vast majority of organizations do not have a crisis plan in place. The main obstacles that have to be overcome fall into one or another of the following categories:

a) Top management doesn't see the need: things are going along very smoothly: we don't make many mistakes, do we? And even when we do, we make the required corrections before anybody notices. The danger of a crisis is so remote that preparing for one would just be throwing money out the window. Why should we assign resources to this useless task when they may be used in another activity which is much more profitable?

b) OK, a crisis may happen, I will accept that; but if and when it happens, we will be ready for it. Naturally, many managers are fully confident that when the crisis hits, they will be able to handle it without missing a beat, thanks to their skills and experience.

c) A crisis may be a real possibility, or even quite likely; but preparing for a crisis is harmful as it will trigger an environment in which fear and a lack of trust prevail; it will encourage criticism and pessimism, distracting people's attention, making them take their eye off the ball and missing the institution's true aims. "Think positive" is our motto!

d) A crisis may happen and we accept that we are ill prepared for it and that to be prepared would certainly be a step in the right direction but we are so busy right now. The day-to-day takes up all our time and we cannot think about something like that, which may or may not happen sometime down the road. There are more urgent issues to be addressed right now.

All of these are serious, real obstacles: if crisis planning is not done properly, it may end up being a useless exercise, a waste of money and even have a negative effect on the organization itself. It is therefore crucial to adapt the crisis plan to the institution and prepare it at the right time.

In response to those objections, we could answer as follows:

a) Any institution may be hit by a crisis. Just read any newspaper, any day of the year. Learning from others' mistakes is less painful and much cheaper than having to learn from our own. Well-prepared organizations do not view crisis management as an expense but rather as a strategic decision, that provides a competitive advantage. As Stocker says, «the potential cost of poorly managing a crisis far outweighs the losses due to a fire or a major IT crash. Finance people refer to it as "reputation," the marketing people call it "brand loyalty" and the stock market puts a dollar and cents value to it.»

b) Complacency on the part of those who have underestimated the chance of being wrong and who have refused to consider that there may be something that they are unable to control is one of the most common factors in a crisis. Surprise is in itself one of the most dangerous factors in most crises.

c) Pre-planning the crisis response may only be damaging if it is poorly executed: without a constructive approach, without the participation of those who should be consulted, without limiting the issues, nor following priorities, without having chosen the most appropriate crisis plan model, or without communicating it internally.

d) Crisis planning is like any planning, as important as having fire insurance or a back-up IT system. Whoever is responsible for strategic planning thinks that looking into the future is as important as doing things for the present.

e) Finally, *the decision to prepare a crisis plan is a prudent strategic measure*: it is a clear sign of the top management's capacity to focus on the future, further consolidate the institution and show their employees, clients, stockholders and society in general their sense of responsibility.[75]

---

[75] On December 10, 2002, a terrorist attack by a group linked to Al-Qaeda in the tourist district of Kuta, on the island of Bali, left 202 dead, of whom 164 were foreigners, and 209 wounded. It was a «massacre in paradise», as the media called it. The economic impact was enormous. But the government and local businesses were determined to learn from the episode, introduce many security changes and make Bali a

Who should draw it up?

Once the decision to generate a crisis plan has been made, these are the steps to follow:

1) First, *designate the proper person to generate it, or* better still coordinate its preparation, since every department should be playing a role.

2) Then, the project leader should talk with those in charge of every operational area within the institution and ask them: what is the worst thing that could happen in your department? What internal and external factors (for instance, the fact that someone who is absolutely indispensable happens to be on vacation or sick) could worsen the whole situation? How can we anticipate something terrible that could happen?

3) The next step is to make a list of the possible crises that could happen considering the following two factors: the severity of the consequences and the likelihood that it may actually happen. By cross-referencing these two criteria, the planning stage will firstly tackle those possible crises that are the most likely to happen and have the highest degree of severity.

4) The following step is to develop scenarios, according to the degree of detail that we wish to give to the plan itself, but always considering the worst possible hypothesis. Later we will look at how to carry out this task.

5) Lastly, *we have to write up the document.* The crisis plan should be put into writing and approved by the organization's top management. A written document will facilitate the crisis plan being put into action when a crisis hits. Additionally, in the best-run organizations, important things are always in writing and in that way, nothing is left to improvisation and we are not counting on someone having the memory of an elephant.

Generating a crisis plan, or at least outlining its general ideas, should be done in a place which is tranquil and far removed from day-to-day battles; there should be enough time to be able to finish it without worrying about some impossible deadline or constant

---

safe place. This resilience has allowed it to become a top tourist destination once again.

interruptions. The best approach is to go someplace out of town and away from the office to think, to calmly bat around the various options and to reach a consensus without any rush about the best way to address each possible situation. You may not return to the office with a finished document with every tiny detail in every single section, but at least you will have a draft of the possible scenarios and the main responses to each of them.[76]

Contents of the crisis plan

The contents of a crisis plan depend greatly on the model that has been chosen: a generic plan has fewer elements than a detailed crisis plan for several potential crises. Keeping that in mind, let us look at the most frequent elements of crisis plans for all types of organizations.

The manual has two parts: the general part, which applies to all types of crises, and the special part, which contains a collection of different scenarios with specific indications.

The first element of the general part is *a positive statement defining an organization's culture*: its identity and mission. This declaration of principles is far from superfluous as it inspires a response to the crisis: it helps the reader to understand how serious the problem is and who the priority stakeholders are. For instance, stating, "Client wellbeing and satisfaction is our top priority", or "employees' safety is the first responsibility of our managers", help to take a quick decision regarding a toxic product recall or an accident at the workplace.

The classification of crises by families and by grades follows, for this is what allows the assignment of competencies. For example, in a multinational, the usual categories are harm to clients, danger of death, financial damage and criminal attack. In each of them a threshold is set, which determines in each case whether the local,

---

[76] Allow me to give an example taken from my experience. The crisis plan preparation for World Youth Day 2011 Madrid started with a three-day-long workshop of the entire organizing committee in a summer house on the Galician beach of Nanín, to consider the different scenarios and draw the fundamental lines of response.

regional or central office is responsible for dealing with the issue, and what autonomy it has: what it can decide on its own and who has to be kept informed; and for what decisions authorization has to be requested.

It is also often useful –especially in emergencies– to assign color codes, as many hospitals do: code blue is cardiac arrest, code red is fire, code black is bomb threat; etc. With two words it is possible to give a signal of the type of problem, its severity and the degree of urgency, which even determines the speed at which the team is notified. Doctors also lead the way: if they use the word stat, they mean immediate notification (from the Latin statim, without delay).

The plan must also determine the *crisis threshold*, the point in the process of deterioration of a situation at which the plan must be implemented. The objective is to give clarity and objectivity to the action, because sometimes the worsening is progressive and when you are very close to the problem, it is not always easy to realize the seriousness of the situation, or fear of the truth slows you down, wasting precious time.

For example, the manager of a fast-food restaurant has to know how many customers have to get sick after eating a burger with fries in order to call a crisis and apply the plan. The threshold helps to distinguish between isolated cases or the beginning of a major outbreak of food poisoning. If the threshold were to be five customers per hour, up to that point, cases would be handled one way; and once that threshold had been exceeded, the manager would stop selling burgers, contact the health authorities and follow their instructions.[77]

---

[77] On November 11, 2017, the Argentine submarine ARA San Juan (S-42) disappeared in the South Atlantic with 44 crew members on board. The Argentine Navy officially announced its disappearance on the 17, in accordance with the Emergency Protocol, and the Secretary of Defense announced on Twitter that President Macri «agrees to use all available national and international resources to find the submarine». Eighteen countries collaborated in the unsuccessful search and rescue operation, which lasted 15 days. Among the many useful lessons that the case study provides, Callero and Elorza highlight the importance of clearly setting the threshold from which an alarm should be raised. The protocols established 48 hours of waiting before declaring a submarine

After deciding the threshold, the plan should determine who in the organization (certainly more than one person) has the authority to *declare* the crisis and call the first Crisis Management Team meeting. Everyone else in the organization needs to know who to contact in case of a serious threat, so the news arrives fast to whoever is in charge.

Next, *the composition of the crisis team*: its members and who leads it; their competencies, distribution of tasks, their specific procedures and how decisions will be taken; its headquarters, in terms of place, equipment, people and financial resources (where the task force will work, with the necessary equipment, support staff, etc. and how to replace whoever is absent or unable to attend, and the amounts of money assigned in the budget).

In general, the crisis center requires special infrastructures only in organizations with a high level of technological or industrial risk, or at large events, where the scale of attendees may prevent access to the meeting area. Otherwise, a normal office is more than enough, where you can work without distraction, meet, exchange information, answer the phone, maintain a web page, answer e-mails, etc.

In addition, the plan should contain a plan B secondary location, in case the main one is not available for any reason.

The internal and external information channels must be determined to fulfill a variety of functions: how to reach the people who must be informed (employees, authorities, opinion makers, etc.); which data must be taken into account if a press conference has to be called, a statement sent, etc.; which informative material will be

---

missing, but the Chief Admiral of the Navy failed to report that the captain of the submarine had reported a battery failure as the reason why the vessel was returning to Mar del Plata ahead of time, information which he retained for five days. There were also contradictions: the US Navy reported that it had detected a noise, but the Argentine spokesperson described it first as *biological noise* from the sea; later, as a *hydroacoustic anomaly*, and as of the 23rd, as an *explosion*. The communication flow was also inconsistent: very reduced at the beginning, as a result of the underestimation of the problem; and then it went to the other extreme, spreading unconfirmed data that generated expectations that later caused frustration among the families of the crew members.

needed to respond to the demand for information; which member of the team will act as spokesperson, etc.

It is very useful to compile information on the external resources that may be required: who to turn to for professional assistance from physicians and psychologists, legal advisers, cybercrime and security experts, ransom negotiators, etc., and external experts to perform the investigations.

Next, procedures must be established to evaluate the effectiveness of the planned measures, drills and emergency simulations. As we will see later, simulations are essential elements in natural and technological crises: they are a profitable investment both economically and communicatively.

After the general part, there follows a description of the various scenarios and the response sketches to each of them in the way described in the next section.

In any event, this list should meet the requirements of the specific institution, considering its type of activity and size, its social context and potential media impact, its track record, etc. A ten-person task force for a regional art museum is just as out of proportion as a three-man team would be for a multinational firm operating in many countries.

How to design scenarios

The technique of designing scenarios is extremely useful: it helps us to fully understand the dynamics of a crisis and to anticipate decisions that will help us gain precious time when the crisis explodes. These scenarios are like flight simulators: they provide the stage on which one's theoretical intelligence is judged and practiced until the application of specific tasks to specific situations without risking anyone's life becomes second nature. As Eugenio D'Ors put it, "experiments should be made with soda", not with a bottle of ten-year-old Albariño wine.

A scenario is *the description of a potential damaging situation plus a response plan.* As Elizalde states, it is "a hypothesis or a conjecture aiming to define the guidelines that will improve people's actions and responses in a potential situation that may really happen someday." Another way of looking at it, in medical terms, would be to compare a scenario to the *description of the findings, along with a diagnosis and general guidelines for treatment of the pathology*:

a) The description includes how the crisis began, what events triggered it, how it develops, who the main players are and what position each one adopts, and how the crisis might evolve in accordance with a timeline (minute one, first few hours, the next day, etc.) The scenario will correspond to a likely-to-happen situation: it does not make any sense to generate a scenario for a risk that is highly unlikely.

b) A diagnosis that identifies the nature of the problem, its causes, and the potential risks. It does not have to be a thorough, detailed analysis, but rather a description of the essence of the problem along with a series of questions (somewhat like a checklist) with the most important elements that should not be overlooked.

c) A treatment, in the form of a draft of the corporate response to this specific case, including: control measures to avoid further damage; contingencies limiting the radius of the damage (for example, so there is no further contagion) and mitigation, to reduce the negative consequences for the victims involved in the crisis (how to meet their needs, etc.); who should be informed and how, etc.

The writing of the description of these scenarios has to meet four basic requirements:

1) Clarity, to avoid any misunderstandings or shadows of doubt.

2) Brevity, so that people will read it. Anything over three pages may be perceived as being too long or trying to cover too much ground.

3) Thorough, with all the elements that are needed to fully understand the situation, the main players and their roles.

4) Emotional, in a style more similar to that of a novel than of a refrigerator manual written by an engineer: it must explain the emotions this situation may produce, the tension each stakeholder may experience, etc.

The purpose of these scenarios is to *be able to anticipate the response*.[78] In this sense, the scenario is really the heart of crisis preparation because it provides the most suitable context for understanding the problems and individualizing the best possible responses; and it does this in such a way that everyone who can contribute to defining the best solution is able to do so (including those who are outside the organization itself).[79]

The Crisis Management Team

Mission and composition

The Crisis Management Team, or CMT, is the task force in charge of facing a critical situation and coordinating the operational effort required by the institution to overcome it. While the name could change to reflect the characteristics of the culture or style of the institution (e.g., crisis unit, operational committee,

---

[78] In 2010, an air traffic controllers' strike hit Spain at Christmas, one of the busiest periods for air travel. The battle between the controllers' union on one side, and the public company Aena (Spanish Airports and Air Navigation) and the Spanish Government on the other, ended with a historic success for the authorities, who managed to terminate an abusive situation and set up a new agreement that met EU standards and rules. The key to this success was that Aena had envisaged four possible scenarios, prepared a detailed plan for each one of them, and then obtained government approval for these action plans in advance. Thanks to these plans, they were able to take the initiative and respond to the incoherent moves made by the less prepared (and somewhat arrogant) air traffic controllers' union.

[79] Robert McNamara, Secretary of Defense under President John F. Kennedy during the Cuban missile crisis revealed many years later, in an interview for the documentary *War Rumors*, that the American response had been planned six months beforehand. The scenario that had been generated did not contemplate missiles – no one had the slightest idea about their existence at that point in time – but rather it had been designed as a plan to be carried out in the event that a pandemic made it necessary to isolate Cuba from the rest of the world quickly and to avoid any damage either to the island or to any other country. McNamara stated: «without this scenario, the decisions that were taken during the crisis would have been much slower, with much less confidence and much more hesitant».

emergency team, etc.) the name itself is of little importance; the key factors are its tasks and responsibilities.

We should distinguish between the group of people who have generated the crisis plan and the CMT, who are the ones in charge of putting it into action: the committee is eminently executive in nature. The aim is to react quickly and implement a whole range of actions on various fronts.

The CMT should also be distinguished from the team that deals with a technical emergency (rescue teams, computer analysts, engineers, etc.), which is usually called the Incident Management Team, or IMT. The mission of the latter is technical, while the CMT deals with political decisions and relationships with stakeholders.

Having a well-prepared team to put the plan into action without hesitation will be a major advantage for the organization. The technical skills and the professional expertise of the task force members will avoid the cognitive limitations of having only one individual in charge of the problem.

The decision regarding the composition of the committee should guarantee two basic factors: transversal competence and authority. Firstly, the committee should be interdisciplinary in nature and include people from all the key areas within the organization. Designation is provisional: when the crisis hits, the team will have to be reviewed and name all the people that are required to face this specific crisis.

Another way of organizing the CMT is differentiating between the permanent team (general manager, communications director, finance director, legal affairs department) and a variable team according to a given crisis: a technical crisis would require technical experts, a financial crisis needs financial experts, etc.

The crisis unit should be on the small side: large committees are not very efficient. Other people can help in executing each task but they are at a lower level: for example, the press office manager or the webmaster will follow the communication director's guidelines, but it is not necessary for them to participate in strategic meetings, although they must attend operational meetings.

The primary responsibility for this task force is to resolve the crisis as soon as possible. Therefore, if the task requires working full time, it will be necessary to name substitutes to temporarily cover the daily tasks of others. The institution cannot possibly stop its normal activity due to the absence of so many key people in each department. In these situations, stakeholders will be looking closely at the institution and so it must be able to demonstrate its capacity to continue working as usual to prevent the crisis itself from becoming bigger.

The CMT must also have the authority to adopt enforceable decisions and not mere recommendations. This is the main advantage of having top management included on the committee. If this is not the case and the CMT director does not belong to the «dominant coalition», as Grunig calls it, they must report to at least one member, know what decisions they can make on their own and which will have to be approved by the executive committee.

Who should lead the CMT?

Many experts have stated that the company's CEO has to be a part of the committee. In a true crisis, the survival of the organization itself could be at stake: what else is more important than that and would require his attention? Furthermore, his presence on the committee indicates the seriousness of the situation to the entire institution. In a crisis, the task force must have the authority to make decisions at the highest levels.

Thus, for Dezenhall & Weber, «the CEO has to lead the crisis team; and if not the CEO, at least the head of the affected unit: the decisive thing is that he can make radical decisions. It is essential to have the power to make the necessary decisions: order the withdrawal and collection of a product or the closure of a plant, negotiate with a prime minister or the mayor, speak with the majority shareholder or with the bank, etc.»

This is reflected in the Incident Management System, a standard applied by many companies and governments, which indicates that the CMT is made up of five to eight people. In its most reduced version, it includes the CEO, the Dircom, the head of the affected department, and the head of HQ. To these four can be added: the HR director, the financial director and the legal advisor.

Others, on the other hand, underline the CMT's operational mission, and argue that the top manager should guide the committee as they lead the rest of the corporate divisions, but without taking part in a formal way. If this is the case, the director of the CMT should be one of the top manager's close collaborators and have direct access to them.

What is clear is that top management doesn't lead the IMT. Emergencies are often best handled by technicians. For example, it would not make sense for the mayor to personally take over the direction of firefighting operations in a fire: they must trust the firefighters.

Whether the top manager is part of the CMT or not, they have a few specific roles to play. First, by deciding (or approving) the policy lines of the corporate response. There are decisions that can only be made by senior management: setting priorities, allocating resources, calling meetings of the team, ensuring a sense of responsibility, compliance with regulations (accountability & due diligence) and transparency, ensuring that all employees take crisis preparedness seriously, and finally ensuring that the committee has the human and material resources to resolve the crisis.

The top manager must also lead communication. Ulmer, Sellnow & Seeger say: «leaders must be actively engaged during a crisis. They should be visible and accessible to the media. They should be responsive to the needs of victims. This communication helps to increase the impression that the crisis is being actively managed and reduces the impression that the company has something to hide. Being available and sincere in times of crisis is one of the most evident characteristics of good leadership.

Everything else depends on the type of organization and its corporate culture as well as on the specific crisis and its circumstances. At the end of the day, what is important is not the chairperson's physical presence but rather that the rest of the managers and employees understand that the CEO backs the team and that everything is under control.

Let me insist one more time: the roadmap is merely a flexible guideline. If there were any reason to add someone to the task force who had not originally been included or to remove someone that originally had been included, whatever the plan says should not be an obstacle for what will be perceived as a prudent decision in this specific case.

The danger of group-thinking

The committee should not be homogeneous but rather integrate people of various types: optimists and pessimists, those who are theoretical and others who are practical, strategists and managers, etc. In addition, if the specific crisis being addressed has been caused by a conflict among different parts within the same organization, then the prudent manager will know how to leverage having people with various ways of thinking among his advisors.

What must be avoided at all costs is what sociologists refer to as "groupthink", which means the behavior pattern in which individuals who are deeply involved in a highly cohesive group work extremely hard to remain unanimity within the group rather than to achieve a realistic review of possible lines of action. As Janis says, with a pinch of humor, «intelligent and even brilliant men are led to make unanimous stupid decisions resulting in a fiasco».

It is true that the crisis team must be close-knit, but this is valid for any decision that has been made, not for the prior deliberations: all should feel free to express their own opinions.

Lastly, many companies include external advisers in the CMT. «No matter how hard we try, we cannot put ourselves on the other side of the mirror. Only someone from the outside can tell us how others see us. And since public perception is so important in many crises, someone outside the organization should be at the committee's disposal», say Meyers & Holusha.

González Herrero recommends integrating the ideas, perceptions and expectations of our main stakeholders in the CMT, using different listening tools: frequent meetings with environmentalists, consumers, journalists, etc., and then transmitting their comments to the CMT.

But there is an even more radical approach: including one of them in the crisis team. This step would ensure that the priority stakeholder's point of view would be heard and listened to. This is the case, for instance, when a school's crisis committee includes a couple as representative of the PTA.

Crisis management specialists may also be included in the crisis committee. The only way to learn how to handle crisis management and communication is through practice, and when the organization lacks this expertise, experts could lead crisis preparation and provide advice while they are solving a real crisis. We will soon be looking at this subject in greater depth.

Organization of the CMT

The crisis committee is by nature a task force. Katzenbach & Smith have described these teams as «a small number of people with complementary skills who are committed to a common purpose, performance goals, and approach for which they hold themselves mutually accountable».

The more complex the team, the greater the need to define precise operational procedures in order to interact efficiently. A crisis unit requires authority and a precise methodology: it requires an almost military degree of discipline in order to act quickly, with rigid coordination and a high degree of mental agility. This strict order will not resolve the crisis by itself, but it is an indispensable requirement. Experience has shown the excellent result attained by using deadlines, timeframes, regularly scheduled follow- up, and monitoring meetings— they may be quite brief but should be held frequently.

Organization of the CMT depends greatly on its functions. Its first priority is dealing with the crisis itself and the people who are affected. Its second priority is communicating effectively about the crisis. So, Leighton & Shelton suggest it be organized in mouth, brain and hands. The mouth is the spokesperson; the brain is the team itself led by the head of the committee; and the hands are those who implement the committee's decisions. Each crisis will determine how many hands are needed.

It is critical to know how to delegate. I highlight this point because quite often, CMT members end up trying to do things by themselves that are not necessary or could be done much better by others. The committee leader may have to meet with the victims or visit the site of the event in order to visibly show his commitment. However, they may be able to delegate the victims' ongoing care to some other person who, while qualified to fully represent the institution, is not actively in charge of solving the problem.

Lastly, *the decision-making process must be defined,* especially if the committee director is not the organization's top executive. Leighton & Shelton comment:

The simplest way is that the committee must be in a majority agreement for all actions. However, this might not be the optimal approach. As Margaret Thatcher (ex-British Prime Minister) said, «consensus is the negation of leadership». We can tell you from our experience, if the leader is ready to lead, and the others in the team are also on board with this manner of decision making, then this is the most effective and efficient manner in which to operate during a crisis.

And finally, communication channels must be ensured, so that CMT members can be in contact with each other and with the rest of the organization. Anyone who has been through a crisis knows that a crisis can only be managed if you can communicate.

External advisors

External advisors, regardless of whether they are independent professionals or experts belonging to a consulting firm or a PR agency can make major contributions and be a big help to the managers of the company under siege, both in the prevention and planning stages as well as at the moment of execution.

In fact, the large consulting firms (Deloitte, McKinsey, Pwc, etc.), international communication agencies (Atrevia, BCW, CSG, Edelman, Llorente and Cuenca, Omnicom, etc.), and many other smaller firms, as well as some marketing and advertising agencies, offer crisis management consulting as one of their most valued (and most expensive) services to companies.

The choice between an independent consultant and an agency depends on the nature of the problem. If it is reputational (for example, how to handle a harassment allegation), the organization only needs advice to make decisions, but it is then able to implement them on its own. In contrast, in more complex crises (for example, a data theft attack), an agency can provide experts in all facets of the problem: programming, legal, HR, media, social media.

We already mentioned earlier how these experts can help in the institutional preparation, with their experience and tested methodology, to prepare the crisis plan, to train the company's executives and to design and conduct simulations and drills. Their role could also be useful during a crisis, as they *are able to see the institution from the outside and this enables them to be much more unbiased.*

Their role is advisory: to give their honest and educated opinion. It is then the company management that decides what is best. Each company has to find the way to integrate these specialists into the institution, but it is not recommended that all responsibilities be completely delegated to them. *These external advisors should never replace the company's management.* They may lead the creation of the crisis plan, the simulations and staff training but the execution of the plan should then be in the hands of the internal manager.

Even when the board does not end up following the advice of external advisers, they are at least compelled to consider alternatives and pay attention to issues that they would not have seen otherwise. In fact, advisors' thoughts will help to clarify the organization's basic assumptions, an indispensable step in successfully addressing the crisis.

The presence and input of a third-party adviser can boost the overall level of attention of business leaders. Nevertheless, it is not always easy to fully leverage their assistance. Sometimes it is due to *a lack of expertise of those requesting their advice,* as they simply do not know what they want, do not provide the advisor with the information they need to carry out their work or they are simply not the proper person to promote the change; the case could even arise in which advice from an outside source is being requested simply to justify decisions that have already been made by others.

There are other times when results are poorer than expected *because the staff does not fully collaborate with external advice.* In fact, some people think that the advisor is someone who has come from outside to tell those on the inside what they should be doing simply to be able to invoice an outrageous sum and then be off. If this is the reigning mindset, it will be difficult indeed for the advisor to expect to receive the information they need or the support they require from these employees.

On other occasions, the advisor lacks the required expertise: they propose outdated solutions, do not have any experience/training in a specific field in which they are being asked to help. Sometimes they may try to prolong the relation with the institution unnecessarily and/or try to sell other services. Gayeski regrets, «unfortunately anyone may claim to be an advisor, and even more so in respect to communication issues, a field in which it is extremely difficult for the client to judge his skills. Many communicators, who otherwise would not be able to earn a living, rent an office, claim to be experts and offer their services.»

Companies should therefore have *a clear idea of what they want from advisors before they call them*. Not all advisors carry out the same role: some are technical experts that deliver a finished product (for example, a crisis webpage); others investigate and gather all the information that may be necessary to make a decision (for example, a survey among reporters after the crisis in order to know what they thinking about the company or how affected the company's reputation has been); and others will be asked to diagnose a problem which the institution is aware of and recommend a valid therapy, but will not be involved in its solution; while others will be asked to help in implementing decisions that have already been made or specific programs (a media training program or a forensic report, for example).

The same may be said, to a certain degree, about agencies. Even if they have in-house experts in many specialties, it is far from certain that the specific professionals assigned to an organization will be the ones really needed. Larger agencies that operate in a wide range of countries and cultural contexts have the clear advantage of offering *global access and local focus*. For instance, Kraus recommends that foreign companies wanting to expand into the U.S. market need local help: «To be successful they need an education on how our market works, what is reputation and how to build it and who are the people they need to know to have 'permission to operate' in both a formal and informal sense. Many of these companies also have to overcome the fact that they are from countries that are misunderstood or feared by the U.S., such as Russia and China.»[80]

---

[80] In 2010, Foxconn, the China-based technology manufacturer which produces smartphones for Apple and other tech companies, had a major corporate-reputation problem after twelve workers committed suicide as a result of overly strenuous working conditions. With no experience in speaking with the media and consumers or anything resembling a communications strategy in its 35-year history, and hav-

But, according to Cutlip, Center & Broom, «ten of the twenty largest agencies in the world belong to advertising agencies, acquired to be able to offer a full turn-key service and this may mean that marketing outweighs this aspect, both in respect to their approach and monetary issues.» Hence, these experts argue in favor of using smaller but more specialized boutique firms.

It is therefore advisable to ensure the competence of the advisor in relation to the specific case. Many advisers are competent in their own specialty, but it is not uncommon for them to present themselves as near-universal experts, which is impossible in such an interdisciplinary professional setting. Robert L.Dilenschneider, former CEO of Hill & Knowlton, says that the seven deadly sins of external agencies are:

> To promise too much, to do too much self-promotion, to give too little service, to tend to the fastest (and most superficial) solution, to apply to institutional communication the principles and practices of marketing or law, and to violate ethical standards.

Lastly, we will have to define who the advisor reports to, who will be in charge of providing them with the data and access that they will need, who they will be handing their reports to and how they will present the conclusions of their work.

The key is clarity: the conditions of every external advisory service must be precise, detailed and in writing, even before they begin to work. The organization must determine precisely what is expected of the advisor and then how the advisor will develop the assignment. The advisor, on their part, must accurately present their true competencies. These prudential measures are of course applicable for any advisory service, but they are more critical in crisis management; precisely the rush in which they have to begin

---

ing set its sights on establishing a bigger presence in the U.S., Foxconn found itself in the middle of an international PR nightmare. It turned for help to WPP's Burson-Marsteller. Its expertise on the inner workings of American media, advertising, politics and government affairs helped Foxconn to cope with a crisis which was bigger in the US than in China. For instance, Burson-Masteller's advice resulted in an all-access *Bloomberg Businessweek* cover story, which included interviews with Foxconn's chairperson and with employees about working conditions.

to work may seem to be a reason to postpone this agreement. If the company says, "we will talk about that later. Let's get to work and solve the crisis," it may certainly regret it later on — when it is too late.

Nevertheless, there are situations in which calling in an external agency may not be beneficial. Firstly, *when discretion and confidentiality are absolute requirements*, and the relationship with that specific agency is far from solid. In these cases, management and staff will not be clear about the real problems at hand, and that lack of trust may become an insurmountable obstacle.

Secondly, *when the institution has a strong and unique personality* and has reasons to doubt if an external agency would be able to fully grasp their perspective and their core values. If the agency were unable to understand and assimilate the institution's identity it would then present a series of proposals that may be valid in most cases but certainly not in this specific case; and the result would be poor or even harmful, results. For instance, I doubt whether Rolls-Royce, faced with a crisis, would follow the same guidelines as Ford. In such cases, the institution would benefit from advice referring to tactics and the execution of specific projects, but not about strategy, which it should not delegate.

Assessing the plan: drills and simulations

The preparation phase is not complete if the validity of the plan is not checked. The best way of learning is by actually going through a crisis and the only way of verifying our preparation is through a test. Experience has shown that this type of testing is very productive and educational.

Beyond the normal assessment methodology in institutional communication, such as focus groups, surveys, the use of prototypes, etc., crisis communication uses two specific methods of assessment and measurement: simulations and crisis committee work sessions.

Drills

Drills are the prime method for evaluating the validity of a crisis plan. A plan will never be complete unless its usefulness has been proven through practical exercises, involving various levels within the organization. At the end of the day, the crisis plan is simply an operational guideline to be used in the middle of a truly complicated situation, but it is also used as an instrument to teach and train people through drills and simulations. During these exercises, people will gain experience, without running the risk inherent in real life situations, in much the same way as those who are studying to become pilots begin their training in a flight simulator and not in a real-life airplane full of passengers.

The usage of drills is extremely useful in respect of contingency plans. Your staff will learn exactly what they are supposed to do at any given moment: how to evacuate the building, how to recall contaminated products, how to avoid contagion in case of an epidemic, how to behave if there is a kidnapping or an armed-robbery, etc.

Simulations are indispensable because in crisis and emergencies many people will have to act in a well-coordinated way. Without a team exercise, how would you ever learn by yourself what you are supposed to do with others? Besides, people learn practical things by doing them, not by studying about them. In addition, there is no other way of knowing if the plan is going to work except by putting it into practice. For instance, only in a fire drill can we truly verify if the emergency exit signs are visible and located in the right places; if the fire extinguishers are working properly; if the fire escapes are wide enough for everybody to get out in a reasonable period of time and/or if the emergency lighting is bright enough.

Drills must be believable and realistic, because behavior observed in a well-designed simulation does not differ fundamentally from that in a real incident. Drills are a profitable investment as they give you a return when you least expect it.[81]

---

[81] In 2004, the Hurricane Charlie hit Cuba, causing the evacuation of 224,000 people and four deaths. That same year, not far from there, Jamaica suffered Hurricane Jeanne, basically as severe as Hurricane Charlie. Due to a total lack of pre-advice and preparation, there were 2,000 fatalities. The most notable difference was that every year before

It is clear that simulations interrupt people's daily work and if poorly done, they may exasperate and even embarrass the participants. So, Caponigro suggests that they be done in an entertaining manner (with prizes and all) to make the exercise as enjoyable as possible and to ensure your employees collaborate wholeheartedly. The organization's management should try to associate what is perceived as an obligation with an enjoyable exercise, especially when we are dealing with younger people (school children for example).

In order for them to be effective training tools, drills should be arranged in concentric circles: first the members of the crisis committee; then the managers; and after that, the whole staff. Some of the drills should be unannounced in order for the test to be real-life. In this sense, the best exercise includes elements of real surprise, to further test the committee. However, never at the very beginning because a surprise drill could have dreadful consequences.[82]

Lastly, the drills' results should be analyzed with its participants, to evaluate its strengths and weaknesses, define the areas to be improved and update the plan.

Crisis committee exercises

Committee members have to devote time not only during a crisis period but also on a permanent basis. It is beneficial for the team to meet regularly (once per quarter, for instance) for practice sessions and to be ready to go immediately if and when required. These exercises are more important than the drills: they are indispensable not only in the resolution of emergencies but also in the handling of all types of crisis.

The best approach is the case method. The team considers a real case and discusses in depth what should be done if that prob-

---

the typhoon season begins all Cuban school children are taught in their own classrooms what they have to do if a Hurricane strikes.

[82] In 2015, a prestigious Kenyan university organized a drill simulating a terrorist attack. Because it was its first drill and no prior announcement was given, students thought real terrorists were assaulting the campus; and one student died and several more were injured when they jumped out of the windows to escape the attack.

lem were to affect their organization. They can be real life cases, or simply two or three press clippings about real cases that have happened in similar organizations.

The situations can be quite different: What would we do if the TV crew from an investigative program were to set up outside the front door of our CEO's home? What if we were to receive a bomb threat? What if one of our teachers was accused of misconduct by one of his female students? What if a former secretary tried to blackmail her ex-boss? What if a number of people claimed they got sick after eating one of our products? What if the company is fined for having fired a pregnant woman? And what would we do if the leading morning radio station were to disclose a series of secret documents?

Another possibility is to use *simulation-based training* (SBT), using digital simulators to replicate a crisis, in which crisis teams have to react in a full-scale interactive environment. SBT may enhance the work that the team actually performs during critical situations. There are numerous software programs available on the market, which are extremely useful tools to train the CMT.

In any event, *these sessions should be held behind closed doors*. It is vital to be able to face real problems and evaluate the validity of the team's responses without running the risk of demoralizing those who make mistakes and much less create embarrassing rumors. Additionally, a committee member should be named to make a report about the conclusions arising from the exercise and introduce all the pertinent changes in the respective crisis plan.

These sessions should be called on a regular basis. Leaving the first or next session for tomorrow indicates that the company is not convinced how useful the exercise is.

Another common methodology is to assemble a group of experts to train our management in crisis management and communication. This system is highly recommended for those institutions that lack the necessary expertise or past experiences to carry out these exercises on their own, or when the organization is in a very delicate and worsening situation in which managers have no time to lose in preparing these exercises. It also has advantage of being able to video your training sessions as the group of experts will normally include a *media-training* module.

In closing, the crisis plan should be reviewed from time to time, either to an agreed schedule (once per quarter) or whenever the circumstances require this to be done: the HQ being relocated, major shift in top management, a new legal configuration, changes in the internal communication channels, etc.

The History: emergency plans[83]

On 8 March 2014, Malaysia Airlines flight MH370 connecting Kuala Lumpur and Beijing, carrying 227 passengers from 13 countries and 12 crew members, lost communication with air traffic control and disappeared from their radar. The search for the plane and its passengers caught the world's attention and lasted for months.

While Malaysia Airlines took many positive steps, a weak communication strategy defined its response. It was CNN who broke the news, not the company; the tone used by the Malaysian government (which, unfortunately for the airline, led the response) seemed cold and distant; the official information shared was completely insufficient when compared to the intense media coverage, and the abundance of groundless rumors which spread through the social media.

This scarcity produced the perception, especially among relatives, that the company was not transparent and was also unable to anticipate the ethnic-based cultural and behavioral differences among the families of the victims. As the Malaysian Prime Minister Najib Razak admitted a year after the crisis, «in the first days after the plane disappeared, we were so focused on trying to find the plane that we did not prioritize our communications».

Many analysts have compared their reaction unfavorably to Air France's behavior after the loss of flight AF447 in 2009. That plane disappeared in mysterious circumstances while flying from Rio de Janeiro to Paris, and the wreckage of the plane was not found for nearly two years. Air France's response focused quickly on family members, showing their empathy at all times; empha-

---

[83] Episode documented by Tom Kitteredge and Paul Tutzer.

sized transparency and collaborative work with the media, providing timely information whenever possible; and did not neglect other *stakeholders*.

By taking responsibility for the disaster from the outset, even without all the details available and focusing on the victims, Air France was able to maintain public benevolence and avoid the intense scrutiny and criticism Malaysia Airlines received. As Zafra assesses, «The lack of information was present in both cases, and the international media expected answers. While unable to explain the mystery of the disappearance of their flight, Air France managed to gain media sympathy because it provided them with constant and regular updates and also because it accepted responsibility for the crisis even without knowing its cause, which made a favorable impression on its stakeholders.»

After the crisis, some commentators alleged that Malaysia Airlines had no crisis protocols. Fuad Sharuji, emergency director for the MH370, flatly denied this. He reported that the airline's emergency committee organizes a crisis drill each year, and that they had had one a few weeks before the disaster. «The stage envisaged a 737 starting from Kuala Lumpur, had an engine failure and crashed in the Strait of Malacca [...] Our [operations] center may not be sophisticated, but our emergency plans are very comprehensive and detailed.»

In fact, the surprise came from the human element of the crisis planning: the CMT director had to be replaced because he could not handle the stress of the situation. «You can have a person who walks like John Wayne and speaks like Tom Cruise in peacetime, but during the war it may be like Mr. Bean», Sharuji said. That is why he insisted that the CMT director should be «strong and very level headed, and very composed and calm even in extremely stressful conditions, and that is not easy to find.»

While a crisis plan provides the basis for responding to a disaster, it is also crucial that response teams adapt quickly to unexpected scenarios.

CHAPTER EIGHT

Action

Prevention is the key to excellence in crisis management and communication: the crisis which has been avoided is the one that has been resolved best. Nevertheless, it is simply impossible to avoid all crises: some will be completely unforeseen while others will be inevitable. Therefore, it is necessary to be well prepared to weather crises if and when they do happen.

In this chapter, we will study how to define the corporate response in seven steps, when a crisis affects the organization, and how to apply what we have learned about principles, stakeholders, and crisis planning.

First, convene the crisis team

The first step is to convene the crisis team, in other words, the people who are in charge of drawing up and implementing a solution to the problem. When a crisis plan exists, this call will be practically automatic; if there is no crisis plan, the managing director will be the one to convene the team.

As we know, this plan is a flexible guideline: there may be reasons, arising from each situation and its circumstances, to include someone in the crisis team who had not originally been a member or, on the contrary, to exclude someone who had originally been included. For example, if the problem is related to taxes, an expert in tax matters will have to be added to the team, even though that professional is not mentioned in the crisis plan.

In this first meeting, the intervention of the corporate CEO is critical since his thoughts on what has to be done will provide the proper framework and to reinforce the unity of the team in respect of the core values which will be inspire the institutional response.

The goals of this first meeting are: to recall how the CMT will work, to define which members of the team are going to be responsible for each aspect, to collect all the information available, and make a stakeholder map for this specific situation.

In the meanwhile, if the situation involves imminent risks to persons or property, the team will need to immediately implement the contingency plan (the part of the crisis plan concerned with emergencies: evacuation, care of victims, calling police or firefighters, etc.).

Distribution of tasks

At the first CMT meeting, the Director usually begins by recalling what is expected of each team member: how they will communicate within the CMT, how issues are studied and decisions are made, who is the sole channel of communication with rescue teams, and who is the interlocutor for each stakeholder.

From the beginning, it is good to appeal for serenity and a collaborative spirit. A CMT may have to work under a sword of Damocles: if we don't do it right, not only will the company go under, but lives may be lost. Anxiety and nervousness will be intense.

Whoever coordinates the team must actively promote a calm atmosphere, not completely free of stress (a moderate dose of adrenaline is necessary to give the best of oneself in a critical situation), but calm and serene. This is the only way to avoid clashes and tension, which are frequent in extreme situations due to the serious risks and uncertainty, overwork, and the confusion of the moment. Those who allow their emotions to influence their actions have less mental clarity to understand the situation and create consensus. As Elizalde describes, «feelings that are too strong will block my rational process and that of the other agents, who remain locked in their emotional states.» Anything that encourages team spirit will be a good idea (in fact, CMT colleagues in a crisis often end up being friends for the rest of their lives).

This effort becomes especially necessary when the source of the crisis is within the institution, or when things have gone wrong because someone has not reported a relevant event when it should have been... The time to assign responsibilities will certainly come, but later. The priority now is to prevent the situation from deteriorating even further, that more people are affected, etc.

Distributing tasks among committee members does not mean that, from that moment on, each one works on their own. In fact, it is precisely at that moment that true teamwork will begin, since defining and implementing the institutional response must be done by all concerned.

In all this, the key pairing is that of the director and the coordinator. The first guides all the work of the CMT, but always remains free: they listen, contribute, decide (or pass on proposals to whoever is responsible) and gives support wherever it is needed, but they have no specific task: the CMT director must delegate everything, because they must have time to think and to anticipate.

The coordinator becomes the Director's main collaborator: the coordinator keeps the logbook, prepares the minutes of the meetings, writes down the decisions and checks that they are carried out according on schedule, etc.

Collecting information

One of the team's ongoing functions is to collect information about what has happened in a systematic way. The team must work from what is known in order to get a complete picture and be able to confirm exactly what has happened (it is probable that not everything that has been said or written is true: in a crisis, rumors, exaggerations, etc. abound). It is important to find out how, when and why the incident occurred, what is certain and what is still unconfirmed. A timeline of events also needs to be established.

While we have to know what happened, we also need to know what did not happen. Checking out possibilities helps both to focus the search and to communicate better.

As we receive more information about the events, we should complete the timeline, with as much detail as possible: for exam-

248 ◄ STEERING COMPANIES THROUGH STORMS AND CRISES

ple, annotating not only what happened, but also when it was learned.

Afterwards, the crisis team should make a map of the stakeholders of this specific crisis. The crisis team must find out what they know, what harm they have suffered, what their fears and expectations are, and how they perceive the role of the organization and its responsibility for the incident. The success of the response depends largely on having a good understanding of these stakeholders.

The *particularities of each stakeholder* need to be described as precisely as possible because these differences will affect the way the organization communicates with each of them. It is usually helpful to create a profile of each stakeholder which sums up their specific features.

Putting yourself in the stakeholder's shoes also means considering the country's culture and local customs. Corporations operating on an international level should be familiar with the local symbols, body language, history, and traditions in all the places where they are present in order to ensure that the actions they take in a critical situation are not misinterpreted.[84]

Check the contingency plan

The CMT must confirm that there is a contingency plan in place. It would make no sense to wait for the CMT to meet to call the fire brigade, evacuate a building that is in danger of collapse or take an injured person to hospital: the contingency plan is initiated ex officio by whoever has that responsibility, according to the established protocol. What the CMT must verify is whether it is working properly, or whether it needs to be reinforced with complementary measures, above all to protect people and facilities: for example, the hiring of a security company, in the event of a violent attack; the sending of a legal support team, etc.

---

[84] In 2000, Firestone suffered a crisis that had been triggered by a major defect in one of its models that was marketed in the United States. Its corporate response was managed by the mother firm, Bridgestone in Japan. According to Cohn, many mistakes were made, perhaps due to a lack of understanding of American consumers, who tend to react very differently from Japanese consumers in a similar situation.

Ensuring the flow of information

Without open communication channels, you cannot manage a crisis. Therefore, the first steps must include measures that ensure fluid communication.

The CMT needs immediate access to what is happening on the ground. Sometimes it will not be possible to have a local agent, because everyone there will be busy dealing with the problem and may think that keeping headquarters informed is a distraction from their immediate responsibilities. That is why it is often better to send an agent, whose fundamental task is to act as a liaison.

For example, if there has been an accident and the injured have been taken to a hospital, the CMT should have someone at the hospital, who will inform them of the evolution of the injured, the state of mind of the relatives, the presence of media, etc.

Second, think before acting

The key phrase for the first committee meeting *is to think before acting*. We will have to resist the temptation to react before we have clarified our ideas; such a temptation is very powerful indeed, as we have seen earlier because crises tend to lead to a destructive sensation of urgency.

With all the information that is available at this point in time, crisis team members have to think about who they are, what the problem is, whose problem it is, how the situation may evolve, and what the right tone to use with its stakeholders should be. Thinking through those questions will help the company to understand what is at stake and define its position. Let us look at each of those points one by one.

Remember who you are

The institution's identity (its principles, founding values, and the service it provides to society) must be the source of inspiration the CMT draws on to solve the problem.

Moreover, I suggest asking not only who I am, but who I want to be. Faced with a crisis that emerges before a company, the *we* disappears. Senior management has to make decisions in the first person singular.

This focus will help ensure that the response is based on the organization's identity and sound ethical principles. For example, when a bank's top executive has committed an offense, how should you respond: as a prestigious financial institution, faithful to its principles of social responsibility, accountability and transparency, or as an entity in which the loyalty that counts is towards those who hired us? Of all my stakeholders (employees, clients, shareholders, the Central Bank of Spain and the ECB, the media, etc.), which one should I give priority to?

Define the problem

Sum up the essence of the conflict with priority stakeholders in a single sentence. You need to look at the problem through the eyes of these stakeholders: their perceptions, their fears, their expectations, their past experiences: what it means to them.

Crises always follow a narrative, in which the characters have archetypical roles: the hero, the villain, the victim, the witness, the sheriff, the wise man, etc. Defining the problem properly will eventually provide useful guidelines regarding the corporate response.

The definition of the problem is full of legal and communicative nuances. An accusation is not the same as proof; a false accusation is not the same as a true one; a wrong decision by the company board is different from an illegal behavior of one of its managers, hidden from the management. Each case has a different answer, because the organization can be considered responsible by its stakeholders and at the same time be the victim of the real culprits.

Also, in some cases there is more than one problem. For example, today's accusation may reveal a previously poorly resolved problem. If I separate the problems, I will see that each one has a different priority audience with a different response schedule.

Identify whose problem it is

Even if the incident happened in your institution, it may not be "your problem." It may be something that needs to be dealt with by health authorities (an epidemic), the police (a robbery), homeland security (a bomb) or firefighters (a fire). On other occasions, it is a problem in which you may share responsibility with other parties, in which case you need to immediately seek their agreement and collaboration.

Identifying who's responsible for the problem will help you determine if the first thing you need to do is report the incident to the appropriate authority, assuring it of your full cooperation, and applying only containment measures until those actually responsible take charge of the matter.

For instance, if a plant manager is accused of sexual harassment, the organization has to check objective facts (people and circumstances) in order to make sure the accusation is plausible, and if so, immediately report the case to the authorities and put in place preventive measures (suspending the accused, etc.). It would be a mistake to go beyond that and initiate a quasi-criminal investigation within the organization.

Anticipate how the situation may evolve

It is important to focus not only on the present. You need to imagine how events may unfold in the coming days and weeks. Further damage may come to light; some containment measures may prove ineffective; some people may react in a surprising way, etc. Thinking ahead will help you to see that the current facts are not necessarily definitive, and that it is better not to make categorical statements if the information you have is uncertain.

Critical situations are fluid. There are more things we don't know than we do; and even - as Donald Rumsfeld would say - there are many things that we do not know that we do not know. Remembering this at the beginning will help us not to be overoptimistic triumphalist when there are apparent signs of progress, as they can change and make us lose credibility.

Choose the right tone

Take a moment to decide what would be the most appropriate tone to be in sync with the context and with your message, so that you will be able to show concern, sadness and compassion, decisiveness..., depending on the situation. In all cases, the response must be extremely calm and objective. It is important to avoid the almost instinctive urge to immediately blame someone else. Blaming someone else diminishes our own moral category: it is better to simply state the facts and let people reach their own conclusions. There is no place for accusations, especially at the beginning of a crisis. It is not for the institution to point the finger of blame at anyone.

These five points will have to be done as *quickly as possible*. This is precisely why having properly prepared for the crisis is so important: corporate managers can devote more time — which is very scarce during a crisis — to the most critical aspects, without wasting it in trying to define procedural and secondary questions that could or could have been resolved beforehand.

Third, decide on the corporate position

The institutional position concerning the problem must be determined according to the points outlined above: What does the crisis mean to you, and what should you do about it?

The first corporate response is critical, because it guides the activity of the institution from that moment on. For this reason, if the participation of the top management is always important, at this moment it is essential.

To respond to the crisis, the organization has to adopt a strategic line, which has three elements.

The first is a look at the present, today and now: How serious do we think the problem is, and what role should the organization play *in solving it* right now? If the problem is ours, what are we going to do to solve it? If not, what steps do we need to take to report it to the appropriate authority and put ourselves at their disposal?

The margin is very wide: from simply informing whoever is competent, and then staying on the sidelines; up to thousands of different ways of making ourselves available to those who need us.

For example, if the river near one of our factories overflows and causes a flood, should I consider building a hospice or a school, although obviously I am not responsible for torrential rain? Remember, we have certain duties that are not based on the law but on expectations.

Of course, if we were responsible, then that first attention to the victims is our responsibility. If it is a public emergency, we will not be the ones to coordinate the rescue work, but undoubtedly there are many support tasks that we can and must undertake. Ask the firefighters, the Red Cross or the mayor how you could help!

The second requires focusing on the past. What role did the institution play in the incident? The institution must assume responsibility based on the evidence. This means taking responsibility for everything that has been proven, but not for anything that remains unproven. The relevant categories are not legal, but ethical:

a) If the organization's responsibility is not in doubt, accept this and issue an apology immediately even if no legal judgment has been given (or if this is impossible, for example, because the time limit for prosecution has expired).

b) If the opposite is the case and it is certain that the organization is being wrongly accused, there is a moral obligation to present a defense.

c) If there is uncertainty about the events and their causes, an investigation should be launched to clarify what happened and the organization should communicate its readiness to take appropriate action based on the conclusions reached. This means a general acceptance of the findings. Until liabilities and damages are determined, there should be no talk of possible sanctions, specific financial compensation, etc.

d) Finally, if a company is accused of something partly true and partly false and the matter is so complex that it is not easy to give a short and clear answer, the best solution is to carry out a complete exercise in transparency. Neither simplified answers nor lengthy, technical explanations will work: they will be perceived as an attempt to muddy the waters. Instead, leaving it to the judgment of the stakeholders is a much more effective means of conveying the company's real desire to be part of the solution.[85]

---

[85] In June 2014, Edward Snowden, the former American official who the previous year had published secret documents about the US government's mass surveillance programs, revealed specific ways in which the CIA and NSA, in collaboration with the big tech companies, were eaves-

Finally, we have to ask ourselves about the future: what changes will the institution need to make in so that incidents of this kind cannot recur? At the start of the crisis, the only thing that needs to be decided (and then communicated, *in that order*) is that when the organization knows exactly what has happened, the necessary changes will be made.

Those three elements define the framing of the corporate response. Everything else will be based on those early decisions.[86]

---

dropping on phone calls and emails all over the world. The news had a particular impact in countries like Germany, where citizens have a high regard for privacy, and protests began. The initial response from the technology companies was defensive: deny it, downplay it, say they didn't know, or keep quiet. This was not strange, because it is an area where national security is part of the small print in contracts. Vodafone decided on a different strategy: to be completely transparent. The company released the Law Enforcement Disclosure Report, which explains the legal conditions that technology companies have to accept in each of the 29 countries where it operates, what kind of information they have to pass on to the respective governments, and the number of official requests received throughout the year. The report was partnered with the NGO Privacy International. By doing so, Vodafone not only put the focus where it had to be put – on spying governments – but also led the change in the sector, gained the appreciation of their clients and created an alliance with groups of privacy activists, which have continued the battle.

[86] In 2013, when the horse meat crisis started in Ireland and spread to the UK, the Swedish food company Findus decided to run some DNA tests on several of their products. Findus discovered that 32 products contained horse meat. The scandal involved the whole food chain, from slaughterhouses to processors, was economically driven (horse meat is cheaper than beef) and many food brands were implicated. Findus' reaction was responsible and fast: on Jan. 30 they found there was horse meat in its lasagnas; the next day they launched DNA tests on all its products, contacted its suppliers and found out where the problem was; two days later, Findus informed the authorities. The next working day it recalled all its products and opened an online platform and a call center to answer consumers concerns. Then it organized a press conference. The information frame was also well constructed: first, they underlined the non-hazardous nature of horse meat for health; then, they widened the scope of the crisis to the whole sector (and in doing so they managed to change its name, from "Findus case" to "Horsegate"); and third, they explained their role in the problem, first as another victim (fooled by its suppliers), and then as a hero, because thanks to them the fraud was discovered.

Fourth, define the corporate response

If previous decisions define the strategy, now is the time for tactics. These are the specific steps to be taken defend the position that has been assumed; or, as far as the public is concerned, the answers to their explicit and implicit questions.

My recommendation is to follow the following blueprint because it responds to the usual demands and expectations of stakeholders, but also to the principles already seen in crisis management.

Repudiate the damage caused by the crisis

The first element of the response consists of connecting emotionally with the public, expressing in an eloquent way that it repudiates the harm done and expresses regret about the incident and the damage caused. The public wants to hear a rejection of what has happened — not an admission of guilt or responsibility, but an expression of sorrow.

In this initial moment, it is also appropriate to connect what is happening with the corporate identity and purpose. That is to say, we not only regret that suffering has been caused but that this affects us, because we defend the value that has been injured in that suffering: it hurts us that a worker has been injured because he is one of ours, but also because for us the safety of our employees is fundamental.

Depending on each crisis, the principle which we appeal will be different: freedom of expression, diversity and inclusiveness, rejection of any form of discrimination, caring for the environment, etc.

This mention is important because it provides the framework for interpretation (in other words, the incident was neither intentional nor frequent, but an accidental exception), not only for those outside the organization but also for those belonging to the organization.

The facts

The next point is the explanation of what happened, which serves as an official interpretation of events ("this is how we see the problem"). A logical and chronological narrative of what has happened must be provided to those who ask. During a crisis, there is a certain degree of competition between different versions of events. It is important that the institutional version take hold among the stakeholders because this narrative will condition the interpretive framework and the role of other actors in the public arena.

As we saw above, in a normal narrative, the usual characters tend to appear: the hero, the villain, the victim, the witness, etc. Assuming a certain role immediately defines my rights and duties in the public scene.

The public does not process data but emotions. Sometimes people ask: what happened here? But deep down, the thought tends to be: which side do I take? This is why it is so important to provide the data with a narrative.

We recount what happened in chronological order, distinguishing what we know for sure, what is more probable, and what we do not yet know but we are going to investigate.

We must not be shy about admitting ignorance: on the contrary, we should reject the temptation to present ourselves as if we were in control of the situation.

Operative decisions

Afterwards, it is the time to define the concrete actions the organization has taken, or is considering taking, to deal with the crisis. They are at the same time actions and communication: they are taken and communicated, because only then are they effective.

Resolve

Measures must be taken to *minimize negative effects* on victims and stakeholders and prevent a domino effect. These might include ensuring that victims are being taken care of and that no one else will be harmed, stopping production of a product under investigation and announcing the recall or collection of items already sold, relieving any allegedly implicated employees of their duties as a precautionary measure, etc.

Dealing with material things is important, but the emotional elements are no less crucial. I emphasize this because people often forget about them, or managers think that organizations should not be involved in such private and delicate areas. That is a mistake. When employees, neighbors, etc., feel the acute pain of the loss of loved ones, companies should facilitate grief, which is partly private and partly public. This is well known by public institutions (state funerals), but less so in companies. Therefore, while respecting people's privacy, religious freedom and wishes, we must know how to offer them compassion, and let them decide what, how and when.

Research

These measures aim at finding out the facts. When the events and their causes are unclear, it must be decided and announced (*in that order*) that an investigation will be launched to clarify what happened. If there is any suspicion that people in positions of authority in the organization may bear responsibility for the incident, because of their actions or omissions, the investigation should be entrusted to an independent investigator or committee.[87]

When the leadership in a crisis corresponds to a public authority (a train accident, for example), that authority is also in charge of the investigation. In those cases, the organization commits to and announces (in this order) its full collaboration with the official investigation. Internal investigations are only possible for aspects not directly linked to the accident.

---

[87] In 2015, Nestlé suffered a crisis in India regarding its main product in the country, Maggi Noodles. In a routine food test at a government laboratory in the northern state of Uttar Pradesh, the results showed the presence of MSG (monosodium glutamate), an ingredient which is prohibited but which experts recognize as safe for consumption; Nestlé says it does not add MSG to this product. The core of the dispute was around the validity of the tests: Nestlé did not accept the official results because they were the outcome of incorrect testing techniques undertaken with obsolete equipment, while the Indian food-safety regulators rejected Nestlé's internal and third-party tests. In the end, Nestlé had to destroy more than 30,000 tons of noodles... When the dispute regards very technical questions, it is crucial to reach an agreement regarding the findings; otherwise, there is no common ground for both parties to work together for the sake of the public interest.

For example, the railway transport safety entity will investigate whether the crashed locomotive had passed all the usual service revisions and whether the spare parts were certified, while the owning company will have to investigate why original spare parts were not bought and by whom. The same goes for fraud: the police will investigate whether the company administrator had accomplices when he stole money from the strong-box, but the organization will review the selection, hiring and training process of the administrator, to discover whether there had been negligence, or simply to learn and improve those processes.

When the facts are private, responsibility to investigate does correspond to the organization. However – as mentioned before –, if there is any suspicion that the organization's managers may be implicated by action or omission, the investigation should be carried out by an independent party. Otherwise, the investigation will not reach any conclusion which is accepted by all, others will carry out other investigations which yield different results, and therefore the money and time spent will have been wasted.

Reform

The third set of measures is aimed at making whatever internal changes are necessary to ensure that similar incidents cannot recur. Such measures are always more effective if individuals from different positions (internal and external) are involved in working out what changes need to be made.

Reform also includes ensuring that, once responsibilities have been proven, those guilty by action or omission are punished. Bear in mind that punishing those who erred is not an option but an inseparable part of justice.

Sometimes the sanction that a company imposes can be strictly symbolic: withdrawing an email address, an award, a street name... but symbolic sanctions are extremely important, because they speak eloquently of my priorities.[88]

---

[88] In 2016, Mexican journalist Carmen Aristegui accused President Enrique Peña Nieto of having plagiarized at least 30% of his law degree thesis submitted to the Universidad Panamericana in 1991. The case was complicated: when the events occurred, UP degrees were issued by

Restitution

The fourth set of measures aims to alleviate, help, and compensate those who have suffered the consequences of activities carried out by the institution.

Some of them involve taking care of the victims: ensuring their medical and psychological care, organizing programs that promote their social integration after the trauma, etc.

Others aim to repair the damage caused by offering compensation. For example, if a meat processing factory had polluted a river, it would have to clean it up and rehabilitate it.

Moral restitution should not be forgotten: to restore the honor of those who were unjustly offended.

Rather than simply offering money, the organization should indicate its willingness to make a fair restitution, which should be determined through negotiation or by an impartial third party.

Renewal

The last group of measures aims to renew the corporate culture: to recover the fundamental institutional principles and values that gave rise to the institution. These measures are necessary when the actions that caused the crisis were very serious breaches of pub-

---

the National Autonomous University of Mexico; the degree thesis professor involved was no longer at the university but held an important position in the judiciary; the UP disciplinary regulations were post-event, and did not apply to former students; and twenty-five years had passed. As the UP tried to explain in a statement, it was «an unprecedented case in which there are no provisions in the regulatory texts applicable to this degree procedure», so that «we are facing a conduct that we cannot examine». This answer did not satisfy many of the university's stakeholders, starting with faculty members and students, who were the victims of the implicit accusation: the UP is an academic center where it is enough to have money or power to graduate. The criteria behind the UP position were only legal (prescription, non-retroactivity, unforeseen conduct, etc.), when in reality a simple message of disapproval would have been enough: «yes, there has been plagiarism, and although a penalty would have been a just punishment, no effective sanction is now possible.» It would have demonstrated the dignity of an institution that calls things by name and speaks truth to power.

lic trust. In this case, we not only have to reform, but also proceed to a kind of re-foundation, which provides a new vitality and a renewed sense of mission to the staff and the rest of the stakeholders in consonance with the original identity of the institution.

As mentioned before, each of these five sets of operational guidelines do not stand alone but are complemented by the corresponding communication initiatives. Each step must be communicated (or better still, agreed upon, since victims and other stakeholders have a voice in this process) to the priority audiences in the appropriate way in each case. Doing good and not making it known would make it difficult to heal the wounds left by any serious crisis.

In Chapter 9 we will see how these elements are articulated in certain types of crisis: due to mistaken values or to illegitimate behavior, etc.

Fifth, formalize the message

The institutional response is articulated in three written documents for internal use by all spokespersons. These documents serve as a guide for all statements and ensure that the institutional response is always consistent and up to date. The first two are always present, while the third is optional. Let's look at them one by one.

The position document

The position document sets out concrete facts, basic principles, and interpretations that will guide the institution's operational response. It is brief and sums up key points: a limited number of messages, written in something close to an advertising style to form easy-to-remember slogans. It should be understandable even for those unfamiliar with the institution or the events.

Let's look at two examples, one for a company and the second for a non-profit organization. If a supermarket chain realizes that one of its dairy products is contaminated, the institutional positioning should be as follows:

- We deeply regret the damage that has been caused by a product that has been on sale in our stores and we will do everything possible to recall it as soon as possible.
- We are fully cooperating with the health authorities and following their instructions in order to limit the number of people affected.
- Our customers' health is our prime concern and consequently we have removed this product from our shelves along with all other products manufactured by this supplier. All other products suspected of having a lower standard will also be removed.

We would like to point out once again that we more than fulfill all our legal obligations regarding food products and hygiene, but we have also decided to carry out an internal investigation to identify the causes of this incident.

The second example is for an NGO. If, in the context of a judicial investigation, the name of an NGO involved in development promotion appears as the alleged recipient of funds from drug trafficking, the institutional position could be:

- The principle that inspires all the activities of this NGO is service to those in need, and we battle daily with all our strength against the consequences of drugs, which cause so much suffering and misery.
- The balance sheet of the NGO is audited by XX, released every year and available to all interested parties. We enforce a strict rule of never accepting anonymous donations.
- Our NGO's operating principle is to always act in accordance with the law and the authorities, and for this reason we are also fully willing in this case to collaborate with the courts and the police.
- Specifically, if in the course of the investigation a falsehood is discovered, the money would be returned immediately (or: pending the result of the investigation, the NGO has established a deposit with the funds involved, which will not be used until the judicial authorities have ruled on the matter).

Question and answer (Q&A) document

Once the positioning has been defined, the Q&A document further develops the institutional position. This communication tool is a valuable support because it defines the lines to link the questions that the public is asking with the message that the company wishes to convey. Thus, it is written bearing in mind the questions that stakeholders would like to ask regarding the problem. Moreover, as it will be in the hands of all of the institution's spokespersons, it is an excellent tool to ensure that the response is articulated with one sole voice.

All the members of the crisis team will participate in preparing this Q&A document. This type of *brainstorming* will also be extremely useful to increase the mental cohesion of the whole team: it will ensure that all the committee members are up to date on what each stakeholder perceives. The questions and answers are then formulated and unified by the director of communications and later approved by the crisis team leader.

To put oneself in the stakeholders' shoes helps to identify their questions. In much the same way as we mentioned in relation to crisis prevention (it is always better to be ready for the worst), it is also better to have the answers for both the simple as well as the more difficult questions , although the latter may not be raised.

The Q&A document is dynamic in nature: it should be updated every time new evidence comes to light, or when a decision is made, or an unforeseen question has been raised, etc.

Argumentaire

In some cases, a third document called an argumentaire may be added. As its name indicates, this document includes facts, evidence and legal reasoning in relation with the controversial issues underlying the conflict: the roots of the whole problem.

The contents of this document have to be as objective as possible. Hence, when we are dealing with data, statements within official documents or publicly stated comments, it is very useful to quote the sources, especially in those cases in which the source is beyond any doubt.

This document is helpful especially in chronic crises, that arise repeatedly; or when the complexity or the vastness of the subjects under discussion are such that spokespeople need additional support. It usually deals with legal questions (for example, it could explain the differences between aggression, abuse and sexual harassment in criminal law), political questions (which authority is competent in a matter shared by several public administrations), historical questions (the origin of a complex situation), technological matters (for example, what data about customers does a telephone operator keep, and for how long), or medical questions (how is meningitis spread), etc.

The argumentaire is an instrument of communication, and therefore it is written with the intention of giving clear explanations about complex phenomena. That is why it is worth taking inspiration from scientific dissemination techniques: using slogans, giving examples, short sentences, colloquial language, etc.

These three documents are valuable tools for anyone who is going to be in contact with the stakeholders, from the institution's top management down to the telephone operators, to ensure that everyone gives the same answer to the same question. This unity of discourse is even more important when different stakeholders have conflicting interests. For example, while employees will not welcome the announcement of a reduction in staff, financial analysts will most likely view it as good news. For that reason, a single and accurately prepared institutional message to be conveyed to everyone will avoid friction and conflict.

For the same reason, these documents are even more important in crises which affect institutions that are present in a wide range of countries, in which the cultural differences, languages, time zones, etc. may be obstacles to establishing a single voice conveying a single message.

These three documents (the position paper, the Q&A and the argumentaire) are *texts for internal usage.* Their purpose is to be guidelines for all institutional contacts with the stakeholders, but they are not aimed directly at the public, for example, as are press releases, institutional statements, etc. Therefore, they are distributed only to those people who are going to have, in one way or another, a role in the management of the crisis. As has been explained earlier, their prime purpose is to guarantee that the institutional response will always be coherent and up to date. Nevertheless, it would certainly not be surprising for these documents to be leaked; the author(s) should therefore bear in mind when writing them that they may end up in the hands of the general public.

Sixth, take the initiative

An enormous number of variables may cause you to lose control of the crisis. It may appear that others are making the decisions about how these events are going to turn out in the end and therefore all you can do is react.

If that is the case, a major step must be taken to change this state of affairs: you must regain the initiative. The prime purpose of crisis preparation, planning and training is precisely this: to be able to take the initiative as soon as you possibly can.

Let us see some operational principles that may help management to take the initiative in an effective way.

Become a source of information

The first way to take the initiative is by becoming a source of information as soon as possible. How fast you react is one of the most critical factors in respect of having a positive impact on the company's stakeholders. All crises create an information vacuum. If the organization is able to fill it, the damage may be considerably limited; it will win the battle for the stakeholders' esteem, when all of them - our own staff, journalists and the public authorities - demand information. Whoever achieves control of the information flow will also have control of the overall crisis.

Becoming a source means calling everyone, one by one. Faced with the void of reliable information, we have to fill the void with *empathetic engagement*, as Peacock calls it.

Becoming a source of information improves relationships with the organization's stakeholders: in a highly competitive environment, remaining silent is usually interpreted as a negative signal by customers, associates, benefactors, etc. When there is a lack of information, stakeholders may start to have doubts and drift away from the institution.

Speaking out as soon as possible has many upsides not only when you are the one providing the information but when you are apologizing as well. The key to successfully asking forgiveness is to do it immediately. Immediate signs of regret have a much greater impact. If you wait until there is no other choice except to express your regret and ask for forgiveness, the impact of your action will be much, much less.

Information must be disclosed without waiting until people begin to demand it. Offering this information decreases the possible damage to the institution's image. Generally speaking, people tend to feel that accidents are inevitable, but this tolerance quickly vanishes when the organization takes too long to provide the information they are expecting. When a company does not make an effort to state all the facts immediately, it is perceived to be hiding information, and anyone who does that is guilty. If the institution wishes to retain the trust of all of its stakeholders (not just that of the media), it must act as an immediate source of reliable information: precise, thorough, coherent and believable answers, which take into account all the circumstances involved.

Becoming a source also allows corporations to play a key role in the framing of the whole controversy. An immediate comment, whether to deny, to express an opinion or to inform about palliative measures will become a part of the first version of the story and contribute to its initial interpretation framework. As Lukaszewski states, «It does not matter how technically perfect your response is. Remaining silent about the issue is poisonous for your reputation and integrity». A brief, incomplete statement that is published immediately is much more effective than a longer, more thorough text that is made public 24 hours later.

For instance, if someone accuses the institution of wrongdoing and threatens to take them to court unless the institution pays them off, why shouldn't the institution simply call the media an hour beforehand to explain why the attack is totally unjust?

Paradoxically, many managers adopt attitudes that are the exact opposite of what they should be doing to win over their stakeholders' trust, and precisely when there is the greatest need to provide favorable signs and the proper information. In a crisis, managers must act diligently, and acting means speaking. These are times of abundant rumors, arguments and opinions of all shades in the media. If the organization does not respond in a reasonable manner immediately (not by simply denying everything), public opinion — which is already shocked by what has happened — will interpret that silence as an admission of guilt.[89]

Crises have always developed rapidly but in today's world of social media the rate at which events happen has multiplied exponentially: everything is instantaneous, or at least things that used to take days now take place in a matter of hours and even in minutes. Now the mainstream media are no longer the gatekeepers of social discourse; the average person has become fully informed of the situation and sets both the agenda and the timeframe.[90]

Beyond any doubt, taking the initiative means doing all you can to make contact with your stakeholders, informing them as well as listening to them. Instead of sticking your head into the

---

[89] In 2016, the Korean company Lotte, the fifth largest conglomerate in the country, suffered a boycott in China, where it had 99 shops and 16 department stores. The cause of the problem was that the company had agreed with the Korean Government to transform a golf course in Seongju-gun into a military base, in order to install a missile-defense system. In two weeks, Lotte's call center and Weibo's profile were filled with more than 20,000 comments protesting and calling for a boycott; and Chinese local authorities, using different procedures and justifications, closed 55 out of 99 Lotte stores. Lotte's communication blackout was complete: it did not communicate anything related to the deal, all those boycott messages in Weibo remained unanswered; their websites were put offline, because they feared the public outrage; and there were no internal communications with the employees at the stores in China, which led to rumors and confusion. This episode is a further proof that silence does not work. It might be true that the company did not have a choice, but you have the duty to explain your position. Otherwise, if you say nothing, public opinion will think you are guilty. In fact, no other Korean enterprises were targeted in China.

[90] On July 6th, 2013, Aviana flight OZ214 crashed on arrival at San Francisco airport from Seoul. The first social media post was made 30 seconds after the accident, and the first post made by one of the passengers was actually available 17 minutes later. Only the organizations that were well prepared in advance (the airport, the US Air Traffic Authorities and other airlines) were able to provide information to passengers in transit and other interested third parties. Aviana, on the other hand, remained silent: its first public statement was made 4 hours and 17 minutes after the accident, and its first press release was 9 hours and 15 minutes after the impact. The consequences of this long silence in its relationship with its customers and investors were very grave indeed. The slowness also impeded Aviana from playing a role in media coverage: journalists simply ignored the company.

sand, you have to contact them immediately and let them know that you are fully available. Being available is sharing all the information you have; but also talking with them even when you have no news to offer. Effective crisis communication involves listening to your stakeholders.

In closing, just one more word to the wise: responding quickly is the golden rule, but you should refrain from confirming something unless you are absolutely sure it is true.[91]

Be creative

Taking the initiative automatically implies promoting actions that may have an impact on events. The institution should not simply provide brief and objective information about what has happened but also intervene regarding any fears that might have been created, concerning the damage incurred and in respect of the overall context. The stark facts may not be enough to explain the organization's position and therefore it is better to be proactive and apply measures that demonstrate the organization's social concern.

For example, if a humanitarian organization were accused of having one of its refugee camps involved in illegal human trafficking and the evidence was overwhelmingly damning, the institutional response should not only address the actual facts but should

---

[91] Sung & Hwang have documented an interesting story. In 2012, a lady wrote both in her blog and on her Twitter account that she had been attacked by a female employee in a restaurant belonging to a well-known Korean chain with 270 franchisees throughout the country. This lady described herself as being 6-months pregnant and stated that the employee had kicked her in the stomach after she had complained about the poor service. Within 48 hours the whole story had gone viral on several online platforms, becoming front-page news in the national media. Even a well-known singer harshly criticized the company on social media and shared the bad experiences they had had in those restaurants. Public feeling was enraged, and a boycott was called. In order to stop the boycott, the company published an apology on behalf of their CEO on the corporate website. But a day later, the company published a press release, stating that, in view of the restaurant's security camera footage, the customer's accusation was false. This was later confirmed by the local police. In the end, the lady finally admitted that she had made up the whole story.

also put the facts in their context, accentuating the success of the many projects that this organization has carried out in favor of migrants.

Creativity is also needed when facing an adversary who is determined to cause major damage to the company. Instead of allowing the other party to lead the public agenda, the timing and the topics of discussion, the organization should use imaginative actions to balance out what is being said, and redirect its stakeholders' attention to focus on those aspects that are truly relevant.

Preparation and planning are indispensable, but they should not eclipse creativity in the search for valid solutions. Knowing how to improvise is also needed. In fact, a critical situation normally requires extraordinary measures which had not been foreseen until this very moment, measures that may even be unique and challenge the institution's daily routine. In a crisis many things may have to be done that in a normal situation would never even be considered. Furthermore, many crises have been caused by the fact that normal procedures did not work properly and therefore that new ideas have to be implemented.[92]

Use gestures and symbols

Symbolic communication means using certain communication techniques based on emotional and dramatic contents rather than on rationalizing the problem. We must always *think visually,* but even more so in a critical situation. Any message needs visual impact because the words do not have the substance... and because the public does not listen all that carefully.

Images and symbols are more powerful than reasoning, in both a good and a bad sense. This is why people in power may arrest someone with a high public profile and also call their friends in the press to be there: they are fully aware that a picture of a per-

---

[92] For example, if the accusation involves suspicion regarding hidden practices, a crisis may be the time to allow the local TV cameras to follow the top corporate manager around for 24 hours. Perhaps in the past such an action had never been authorized and it may never be done again but the critical context the company is undergoing may make it highly recommendable.

son in handcuffs with policemen at his side sends a clear message and leaves a mark on that person for the rest of his life.[93]

This translates into assuming an exemplary role, an eloquent attitude, a maximalist position, in order to crystallize the emotions of public opinion around the institutional position, which in itself personifies a positive value. It is about attracting attention in an eminently visual and immediately effective way.

It is not the same to proclaim from an office in a city sky-scraper that an institution is committed to the protection of children or to the eradication of poverty as to say the same thing in a school surrounded by children, or in a shanty town. It is not the same.[94]

Symbolic communication is frequently used by organizations such as Greenpeace, environmentalist movements, PETA, etc., but less so by mainstream institutions. As Ogrizek & Guillery point out, «symbolic communication is therefore a tactic with high stra-

---

[93] An example of successfully using symbols in managing a crisis is the case of the 33 miners trapped in a Chilean mine due to an explosion, in August 2010. President Sebastián Piñera understood immediately the importance of the accident and considered it a "national issue". Piñera delegated everything related to the technical aspects of the rescue and assumed his role as the head of the country: he was always present when he was needed, and very close to the miners' families; he provided the full collaboration of state-owned companies with expertise in mining, with no budget constrains; and he made a call to the international community for help (instead of the more frequent answer "thanks but we can handle it on our own"). His leadership through the crisis meant that the rescue became the highest point of President Piñera's approval rating during his mandate.

[94] In 2018, two African Americans were arrested by the Police at a Starbucks in Philadelphia (USA). They had been reported by the store manager who panicked thinking they were going to attack him. In footage of the scene, which went viral, it can be seen that the two had done nothing wrong nor resisted authority. The company immediately apologized via Twitter but went further: its CEO Kevin Johnson self-invited himself the next day to participate in *Good morning America*, one of the highest-rated newscasts, to apologize again. Not only that: he took the opportunity to recognize that the episode showed that his staff was not prepared for episodes of this kind, and he announced that the ten thousand Starbucks in the country would close for a day to be trained on how to manage these situations.

tegic potential in a crisis, both outside the company and internally. It is, however, very hard to implement for industrial managers who are not at ease with the emotional dimension and still wish to reassure the public with rational technical arguments». It is possible that these managers feel that this approach is merely a charade. However, the fact remains that it is no less serious in nature and much more human.

Control the dimension of the problem

Do not make the problem bigger than it is. In some cases, the institution should avoid reacting in a way that increases the significance of what's happened and should keep the response at the local level; in others, the importance of the crisis needs to be recognized and it should be managed centrally.

For example, if a bank branch had a problem and the regional office were to make a public statement, the implicit message would be that the branch manager is not the decision maker, but rather that all decisions are being made at the regional office; consequently, the regional office would be considered to be the true culprit for what happened, by either wrongdoing or omission.

This recommendation is not intended to suggest that the parent company hides behind the subsidiary. That would contradict the ethical principles defended in this book. We propose that each should shoulder its own responsibility: if the relationship with the stakeholder is carried out locally, having someone from the central office step in because they are better prepared is a lack of respect. It is logical to help the country manager, even by sending a support team, but to advise him, not to replace him.

Therefore, if the presence of a multinational in a given country is nothing more than a commercial or purchasing office, it is more than logical for the headquarters to take control of the situation, with the help of a local communication agency.

The same is true when the crisis affects a small brand that is owned by another, larger company. For the public (starting with employees, customers, the media and regulators), the ultimate responsibility lies with the mother company, and therefore it is better for them to assume direction of the response, because it will affect the company's reputation. Keeping the problem in its right dimension also means limiting it to its own scope. It does not make sense for a company to reach out to stakeholders that have not been aware of the problem.[95]

Asking for help from your friends

Taking the initiative also *means having the intelligence and bravery to ask for help*. As we have seen, managers are normally tempted to try to solve the crisis by themselves. In reality, crises are better resolved when the organization receives external support. Mora states,

> In communication, in much the same way as in economics, endorsements are vital. The co-signing of a mediator (an expert in this subject, an unbiased observer) represents a guarantee for public opinion. A person or an institution can never impose its prestige: they must earn it with socially responsible actions. In other words: nobody is able to endorse itself.

In this sense, it is better for us to win allies over to our side. Better still, try to get the institution's current allies involved: a crisis is not the best time to start winning new friends but rather it is when your oldest friends should help you.

If, for example, an epidemic breaks out in a hospital, a public statement by its director regarding the quality of its healthcare would have very little impact: 'what else could he say?' people will

---

[95] An example of this point happened in 2012 at Domino's Pizza. Two "smart" employees posted several videos on YouTube in which they were preparing the pizza in a very unprofessional manner, totally ignoring the company procedures and the current legislation in respect of food handling. These videos went viral before the company was able to block them. The company's reaction was immediate: the two employees were immediately fired and reported to the police. Domino's chairperson apologized for what had happened and fully explained the steps that had been carried out to ensure that this would never happen again. However, the most interesting aspect of this case is that Domino's decided "to let whatever happened on internet to stay on internet". Thus, its press release, the chairperson's statement and all the rest of its initiatives were posted on the chain's website but not sent out to journalists so as to avoid the news reaching its *analogical customers* through the traditional media.

say. But if the directors of other hospitals, and hopefully the Regional Health Minister publicly defend that hospital, stakeholders will trust their statements – because they are unbiased – and public opinion will view what has happened more as a mere incident rather than a major crisis.

In this light, we would do well to pave the way for local authorities, industry experts, unbiased organizations (consumers, professional associations, international think tanks, etc.) and community leaders to provide their support for the institution. It is possible, or even likely, that their comments will be less than 100% positive, but this show of being unbiased will most certainly be helpful to the institution.[96]

Paving the way does not mean sitting back and patiently waiting for something to happen. Sometimes it will happen by itself, but other times it will be necessary to take the initiative and request help. We must bear in mind that one of the most negative effects of a crisis is that the institution becomes isolated socially. Some of those who might be willing to defend us will not do so

---

[96] Theranos was a privately-held health technology and medical lab company founded in 2003 by Elizabeth Holmes, who was hailed as the next Steve Jobs, and – according to Forbes – «the youngest self-made female billionaire in the word.» The company promised to make it easier for patients to get blood tests with less pain, no prescription necessary, with access to their own data via an app and at extremely low cost. This vision ultimately earned the company, at its highest, a valuation of around $9 billion. It is worth noting that the company was very secretive about their proprietary technology, never explaining how it worked in public for fear of it being copied. In October 2015, in an article entitled "A Prized Startup's Struggles", *The Wall Street Journal* accused Theranos of deceptive business practices, and also of cheating on the proficiency tests from the FDA. These accusations, although rejected immediately by Holmes on the TV show *Jim Cramer's Mad Money* and in other media outlets, continued to grow, and little by little partners, associates and sponsors withdrew their support. Finally, the SEC announced it was investigating Theranos. Two lessons can be learnt from this episode: Holmes' strategy of denying everything, not taking any blame and picking a fight with the WSJ had disastrous consequences. Second, as Edma Perini states, the same secretive nature of the company that helped both the company and its founder to reach success, made it impossible for it to receive any support from the medical community.

because they are unsure whether their help will be welcomed. You have to ask them to help.

Along the same lines, academic media observatories may be able to provide objectivity in respect of misleading or biased media coverage; and another approach, which may be helpful, is to contact the readers' ombudsman which some media have.

Lastly, and especially in the case of crises in which public perception does not point at the institution as being responsible, it is useful to lead the recovery by requesting the help of whoever wishes to lend a hand. Research by Vieweg, Sutton, et al confirms what everyone has seen with their own eyes: during a crisis, people feel compelled to help. Their generosity not only benefits the victims, but also those who help, because they will be in a better position to comprehend the enormity of a dramatic or emergency situation.

Manage the timing

One of the most difficult aspects to manage in a crisis is the question of times. I use the plural, *times*, because each stakeholder involved in a crisis (the victims, personnel, public authorities, neighbors, etc.) has their own timing, a diverse perception of when things should be done. Elizalde suggests: «analyze the action timing in accordance with the reactions and perceptions of each of the players who are participating in the crisis. Without identifying the timing requirements of each of them in the potential crisis situations it will be impossible to fully grasp the severity of the crisis.»

In a normal situation, informing people immediately implies acting before all the data has been collected. The first communication does not necessarily have to be complete: it is enough to provide all the verified information that is available. Furthermore, incomplete information provided by an institutional spokesperson is considered to be a lesser inconvenience than the *immediate perception of their good will in being helpful, informative and available.*

Speed is the most important factor. When the crisis hits, managers can imagine any number of valid excuses: "it is necessary to gather all of the information, to fully understand all the facts, to ensure that everyone agrees." Quite often, these pretexts lead to a major waste of time. On the other hand, the manager who is well prepared will have the right people, the right tools, and the right channels available to focus on what is truly decisive.

Managing the timings also means *not waiting for someone to request the information.* Responding immediately generates both credibility and trust, while delays and management absence from the scene generate a lack of confidence and suspicion and lead to — and in some cases, even trigger — witch-hunts.

Another clear sign of good time management is to keep people *constantly informed.* Don't stop informing simply because you think the worse has already happened, but maintain an informative attitude: how the injured are progressing, new discoveries in respect of the incident, how the recovery of the site is developing, how many donations the victims have received, etc. This ongoing flow of information, through channels such as periodic newsletters, a specific section in your website, regularly scheduled meetings with the local communities and other affected parties, etc. will reinforce your relations with stakeholders.

Finally, reacting quickly also has consequences when it comes to asking for forgiveness. As Benoit says, an immediate admission of guilt even before the facts are discovered, combined with efforts to make amends for wrongdoing, is much more effective than belated excuses.

In much the same way, actions such as asking for forgiveness must be repeated several times for the stakeholders to fully accept them. Apologizing once is not enough; it has to be done as many times as necessary.[97]

Lastly, proper time management also includes *anticipating what is going to happen next.* Just as the detonation of a crisis requires the urgent solution of certain aspects, it is also essential for the crisis team to not focus all their attention on the short-term issues, but imagine how the situation is going to evolve over the next few days

---

[97] Xifra has documented how the defense strategy used by Dominique Strauss-Kahn, who at the time was the chairperson of the IMF, in respect of with the sex scandal in which he was involved in 2012, failed miserably. One of the main reasons of this failure was that it was based solely on a single TV appearance instead of a well-planned recovery approach, consisting of actions articulated within the framework of a campaign.

and/or weeks. It is always possible that further damage may be discovered, that some palliative measures are unsuccessful, or that some stakeholders have unexpected reactions.

Seventh, communicate

It might seem surprising that, having repeated that management and communication are always linked in a crisis, communication is only the seventh and last step. Well, communication comes at the end only if it is understood as being simply the transmission of a message, but there will be no surprise if - as advocated in these pages - it is considered as being the relationship with all stakeholders and consists more of listening than of speaking.

Designate spokespeople

The first step in the dissemination of the message that has been prepared with so much care is the choice of the spokesperson, that is, the person capable of transmitting the message of the institution to the various stakeholders.

Being a good spokesperson is far from simple: many psychological studies have proven that the fear of public speaking is the strongest and most widely spread fear of all. For this reason, crisis manuals quite often have a full section devoted to preparing spokespeople. This approach has many practical advantages but training a spokesperson once the crisis has already hit is *far too late*. Those skills cannot be improvised or learned on the fly.

In my opinion, preparing the spokesperson is not a part of crisis management but rather a part of corporate communication in general, because the institution requires well-trained managers in all circumstances. Furthermore, the hardest times are certainly not the best circumstances for a media-training course. Learning how to interact with the media in a negative context, when no positive relationship has been established, may encourage a reactive mindset.

On the other hand, we should stop and look at how the best spokesperson for a crisis should be chosen. In general, terms, the decision depends on several factors: the type of crisis (technical or human based); its degree of importance, severe or mild; its scope, general or local; its length, short-lived or chronic.

In severe crises, it is indispensable for the organization to show its concern and commitment. Thus, the highest possible executive should represent it: the managing director or CEO, the president of a university or a foundation, the director of a hospital, the secretary general of a political party, the school principal, etc. In contained crises, the director of communications may handle this role. In technical crises, a product expert or the manager of the department that is most closely involved is the most competent and will thus be more credible in his public appearances. In addition, in emergencies, the best spokespeople are those who are in charge of the rescue teams.

When it is foreseeable that the critical situation is going to last for some time, it is a good idea to think of splitting the spokesperson's role and having one spokesperson at a higher level for major developments and significant changes, and another for updates and regular press briefings.

Whoever is named as spokesperson must meet the three following requirements:

a) Be able to articulate the organization's message, both in general terms and in terms of the organization's response to the specific crisis.

b) Be able to convey credibility and trust, through their personality, their position in the institutional organization chart and their inherent degree of responsibility.[98]

c) *Be able to show compassion, warmth, and patience,* and know how to listen and perceive other people's concerns. Thus, they

---

[98] In 2019, Caritas Internationalis was hit by a crisis when CNN reported that the director of Caritas in the Central African Republic, a Belgian national, had abused minors. Although the problem was local, it affected the international matrix, because public and private benefactors financing its projects around the world suspended aid until the situation was clarified. In these circumstances, Caritas Intl. hired an external spokesperson to serve the media during the crisis without involving those who were truly responsible. Not surprisingly, the credibility of the NGO suffered.

should have a calm personality and never display an excess of emotion when faced with a distressed audience.

In short, *they must have authority.* Journalists or any other stakeholders will immediately realize if the spokesperson is merely covering for their bosses. As a result, the institution will lose its stakeholders' trust since they have demonstrated that they have tried their best to avoid their own responsibilities.

The oft-repeated principle of *audience-centric thinking* may also be applied at this point: the best spokesperson is the one who best communicates with his priority public in a specific crisis. Moreover, in order to communicate well, it will often be indispensable to speak the language of that public.[99]

The same thing can be said regarding its mindset.[100]

Lastly, it is critical to guarantee the unity and consistency of the organization's message. For that reason, *there should always be one spokesperson.* In the case that this is not physically feasible (for example in a crisis that involves several distant facilities) at least there should be a head spokesperson to coordinate the work of the

---

[99] In 2013, a train loaded with oil derailed and exploded in Lac Megantic (Canada), causing 24 deaths and the disappearance of 26 others. According to Jane Shapiro, the railway company made a major mistake in choosing the chairman of the company, who only spoke English, as its spokesperson. «It is conventional wisdom that in crisis communication the highest-level executive should be the corporate spokesman when a severe crisis occurs, especially when there has been a loss of human lives. That's right: top management has to be visible. But it is equally important that the spokesperson be chosen taking into account his language, culture or background. On the contrary he will not be the organization's best representative and will only end up creating distractions. [...] Inexplicably the company did not name a French-speaking spokesperson when in this whole area and in the whole province the official language is French, and everybody uses it every day». The local community was very negative when spoken to in English.

[100] Speaking the same language might not be enough: the cultural context also has to be taken into account. In fact, among the number of errors made by BP during the Gulf of Mexico crisis (2010), the experts have pointed to the fact that they used British spokespeople to talk to the American public: what they were saying, the words themselves, was fully understood, but «all they had to hear was that British accent to make them think that they were trying to pull the wool over their eyes», stated a member of the US House of Representatives.

whole team: they will provide the tools that are required to guarantee message consistency and to ensure that the company says the same thing to all its diverse stakeholders.

Choose the right channels

At this point the company has defined the message to convey, the spokesperson who will give a human face to the organization and the operational guidelines with which we will go forward. It is now time to study how to carry it out. We will begin with some comments which are valid for all types of channels and then look at a few of them more closely.

General guidelines

In the previous chapter, we saw how a crisis is certainly not the best time to open up new communication channels with the various stakeholders. Companies should use those that are already open and strengthen them as much as possible. This does not mean that it is impossible to create new channels to meet the information demand coming from all angles. Nevertheless, these tools should have been foreseen and prepared in detail beforehand: they would be new for the stakeholders but not for the company. For example, the institution may have an internet crisis website already but unavailable to the public until it is necessary.

Existing channels do need to be strengthened. A crisis requires investing resources in coping with the increased demand for information. If when you have an IT breakdown, you automatically call in an expert, that same approach should be applied in respect to communications.

This thought may seem to be rather obvious and in fact it is. But in several cases I have seen how institutional authorities, without batting an eyelid, did not hesitate to bring in a high-powered attorney to defend one of their managers against a criminal accusation; but they debated for ever and ever before deciding to use a crisis communications advisor, although what is at stake is much more serious. (Actually, from time to time I wonder whether it would be good for the overall prestige of crisis managers (as well as being good for our wallets) if communicators were able to charge the same amount for our professional advice as the best lawyers do... but never mind).

The second comment I would like to make here is that in a crisis, the most effective communication approach is to be direct, interactive and straightforward. For instance, in a crisis in which many people are affected, it is commonplace to immediately provide a toll-free telephone number. This channel may be used both to provide information to others as well as to receive their comments: it is essential to monitor the number and contents of calls, the types of concerns most frequently expressed, and any other items of information that may be helpful to the crisis committee.

Generally speaking, the corporate team acting as the institution's ears may also be the people who receive the claims (with the addition of temporary new staff, if necessary). In any case, it is obvious that there is an acute need to carry out this preparation before the crisis hits: neither the technical requirements nor the training for those who are going to be operating the telephones can be done on an ad hoc basis.

Using this same reasoning, *today's social media is the most suitable channel for communicating with the stakeholders during a crisis period:* the message can be personalized, it is delivered instantaneously, and it is cost effective and nearly universal in its reach.[101]

---

[101] SpaceX, short for Space Exploration Technologies Corporation, an American aerospace manufacturer headquartered in California and founded by Elon Musk, suffered a serious accident when in 2015, its Falcon 9 rocket exploded, and all its cargo was lost. Following the incident, SpaceX including its CEO Elon Musk took to the social media to talk about the event. Both the corporate website spacex.com/news as well as the SpaceX twitter account @SpaceX and Elon Musk's @elonmusk were directly used to inform stakeholders of the terrible event. A press conference was organized the same day to answer the biggest questions and start the investigation about the failure of the rocket. In the following 24 hours, Musk took to the social media again to share all public information that the company had and could help to explain the disaster. One week afterwards, Musk posted updates to the events stating that the conclusion of the investigation should be available by the end of the same week, and that customers and the Federal Aviation Administration (FAA), would be briefed first before any information was posted on the internet. Three weeks after the explosion, the company revealed that the report of the accident was finalized, both on the social media and on SpaceX's own website. SpaceX's com-

There is only one condition: that the priority stakeholders who are involved in this specific crisis have to be users of these specific media. This means that the media may be valid for conveying some urgent information to the fans of a specific football team but may not be as effective to communicate with the members of the team's steering committee.

At the same time, problems that are international in scope require communication in the social media that are popular in those countries where the affected stakeholders live.[102]

In today's world, it is a pleonasm to say that «The internet has rapidly become the definitive resource for information during a crisis situation», as Barton stated in 2000. However, it is necessary to remember that using internet requires a certain amount of personnel to respond to the incoming messages, update web contents, monitor the statistics about the number of times the posted information has been visited, and to translate to and from other foreign languages, etc.

A third generalization is related to how the channel may be personalized. Personalized channels are much more effective than generic channels. Therefore, *the more important a stakeholder is, the greater the personalized attention they should receive.* The word "important" refers to the level of priority given to that stakeholder, which will depend on how involved the stakeholder is in this specific crisis.

To avoid mistakes that tend to happen because of the turmoil which is produced in any crisis, the institution's crisis manual should clearly define who is going to call who and in what order so as to avoid any inconvenient errors.

---

munication department did a very good job by sharing the information strategically, but also the crisis management team and the investigation collaborated very effectively with the authorities to solve the dilemma. And in all of this, the drive and motivation of SpaceX's CEO was vital in making all of this happen.

[102] In the case of the plane crash mentioned earlier, Asiana used primarily Facebook and Twitter, but the majority of the passengers were Chinese and Korean. It would have been more logical to have used services such as Weibo, which are more popular in those countries.

In a crisis period there is no time to waste nor should energy be wasted in collateral or secondary activities: *the most effective channels will have to be used.* Nevertheless, the choice of which media to use is not based simply on which one is more effective but is a declaration of principle: *the chosen channel publicly states the institution's self-perception.* My decision defines who I am and what my values are (who I would like to be). It is certainly not the same to announce bad news through a formal communication channel or a press release, as to announce it by means of a hand delivered personal letter.

Additionally, *the choice of which channel should be used conveys a message about top management's priorities.* For instance, a teleconference may be — from the content's perspective — as effective as making a trip to the site, and much faster and cheaper. But if the managing director takes time out from his busy schedule to travel to the disaster site and give a personal hug to the persons who have been affected, or visit them one by one in their hospital beds, it will underscore how important these people and the specific problem is for the institution and for the leaders themselves. His actions truly convey his concern.

Lastly, every institution requires *an integrated, custom-made plan for all the channels covering all their various stakeholders,* which identifies the strengths and weaknesses of each tool. In this sense, it may be necessary to use more than one channel in order to successfully reach a specific stakeholder. For instance, in respect to journalists, Twitter may be the best solution for alerts and for calling press conferences, etc.; the main content should be communicated through one of those press conferences; and the text and documents should be made available to all journalists with the proper credentials, whether they have or have not been able to attend your press conference.

Let us look now at the most suitable tools for specific stakeholders.

The social media

The social media, along with the devices that have made them so accessible, have totally changed the way personal relationship are both created and maintained, as well as how social groups are formed and interact among themselves. These changes have the dimensions of being a true revolution in respect of our younger generation, who were born into this digital world, and who *do not use* these technologies but *are themselves digital*: they think, feel and live within these categories.

White defines social media as «forms of electronic communication through which users are able to create online communities to share information, ideas, personal messages and all other types of content». These various types of communication have changed the way we work, family relationships, entertainment in general, politics and sport. And these changes are only just beginning.

In chapter 1, we discussed how the social media have brought about a social transformation. In this chapter we are going to focus our attention on digital platforms as communication channels to be used during a crisis period, bearing in mind that online and offline are both real and companies should act in both worlds.[103]

As we have just seen in the previous point, the social media have to have three basic attributes to be deemed as effective communication channels during a crisis: direct, interactive and able to be personalized. Furthermore, they are rapid, and function in real time, in a cost-effective manner (they are free) and with efficiency. No other channel can provide the specific, desired information to a group of specific, desired people at a specific, desired moment as well as Internet does.

Moreover, the social media continue to function when other communication channels may have broken down.[104] This speed

---

[103] In footnote 86, we summarized Findus' response to the Horsegate crisis in 2013. It is worth mentioning that although its strategy of full transparency, collaboration with the authorities and social responsibility was correct, they missed out the online world entirely. Findus decided to communicate only through traditional media: they deleted all comments on Facebook and closed their twitter account.

[104] During World Youth Day 2011 in Madrid, its official website suffered a DDoS attack, which was most likely caused by Anonymous; it came at the time when the greatest number of participants was accessing the website. All traffic slowed down considerably and the website itself stopped working from time to time. But the problem did not affect the management of the event because communications were able to be handled through the profiles of several social media that were already operational.

and adaptability to all circumstances be make them especially useful in creating informational environments in real time, an absolutely vital factor for whoever is going to manage an emergency. In fact, the media have become the prime channel in technical crisis management, for communicating both with external and internal stakeholders and the emergency teams. They are, in fact, an integrated crisis communication tool, to be used in the phases of prevention, preparation, response and recovery.

Effectively, when online communities have been formed and the channels work properly, the social media are able to both send and receive preventive information and to provide the correct guidelines for the rapid intervention teams.

They are also being used more and more frequently as channels to request help, and it is likely that those who use the social media for this purpose expect to get a response. They are also being used during the recovery phases: years ago, the funds and the material that were needed for the disaster areas when an earthquake or some other natural disaster had taken place, were raised by phone; later SMSs were used and nowadays we have a special donation app which can be downloaded to our smartphones.

In this sense, *the social media have radically changed the methods used in crisis communication* because these channels are much more efficient. Social media penetration in Western societies is so advanced that very soon it will be practically universal. At the same time, I must add that *the changes affect all channels, but not the principles or our strategies.* Crisis communication is the same as always. The only thing that has changed is how we receive and convey it.

In this sense, best practices in digital crisis communication coincide with those which we developed throughout these pages: establish the rules of risk management and crisis communication beforehand; plan the pre-event logistics; during the crisis, share information with the stakeholders who are entitled to know about the possible risks that they are addressing; listen to the stakeholders' concerns and know your audience (you have to listen to and act with them, taking into account their perception of the risk and its uncertainty and maintain a social dialogue before the crisis explodes). Communicate honestly and openly. Work closely and coordinate with reputable sources. Receive the press and accept their requests. Communicate with compassion, concern and empathy. Accept uncertainties and ambiguities. Provide messages that will enable your stakeholders to protect themselves.

Nonetheless, online crisis management is not a simple task. It is really much more complex than simply designing a beautiful home page or sending tweets out to reporters instead of old-fashioned e-mails: it demands major changes in the approaches being used by communicators and corporate management, because it implies decisions that affect the essence of traditional corporate cultures. The difficulty does not lie in adapting to a new technique but rather in being able to carry out the cultural change within the whole organization.[105]

The fact that they are now the main channels does not mean that they are the only channels. Let's bear in mind that the effectiveness of a channel is measured from the stakeholders' point of view. Social networks do not reach all stakeholders and therefore the use of other channels is recommended; and even when the social media do reach a specific public, they may be less effective than others for one reason or another. White warns that even when a message meets your public through social media, they may not interpret it as it was intended. For example, some stakeholders may not take a call to action as seriously as if it had been presented via a more traditional media.

There are clear upsides, as well as more than some downsides. Firstly, there is a lack of reliability. As is true with any other complex technology, the systems may collapse and in fact they do from time to time. Therefore, companies must always have a contingency plan ready to go.

---

[105] In fact, statistics show a certain delay in implementing those best practices. A survey among the Fortune 500 revealed the following findings: out of these 500 leading companies, 309 (61.8%) have their own page in Facebook; but a mere 28 (9.4%) communicate with their stakeholders in times of crisis; and only 9 post responses to personal messages. Ki & Nekmat, authors of this survey, concluded, «The Fortune 500 companies generally are making very little effort to communicate through Facebook with their stakeholders during a crisis». This data is quite revealing, as in most cases, the largest companies are the first to implement innovative technological solutions; so it would seem reasonable to think that if we surveyed SMEs the percentages would be even lower.

Furthermore, the social media present other issues and major risks that may be hard to overcome: threats to personal confidentiality; danger of unqualified people unethically trying to play a role in technical circles; limits to content quality due to scarce or non-existent entry control; dire consequences of the digital gap between techies and those people who know hardly anything about the new technologies; problems derived from the irritability inherent in the digital environment, etc.

This is certainly not the proper place to examine digital communication strategy and techniques in normal times. We will simply underline a few guidelines about how to address communication in the social media during periods of crisis.

The first step *is to have a fluid social media presence in normal times before* the crisis hits. Crisis managers inherit the current communication channels that are being used. If this is the case, the digital communication architecture will be better structured and will meet the institutional needs during a crisis: roles and access authorizations (as administrators, guests, participants, etc.); types of communities (open or public, closed or private; and secret); or degrees of confidentiality.

In fact, if the organization does not use digital communication channels, it would be worthwhile to create a system in case a crisis arises; but once it has been put into practice, it would be absurd to not use it for normal communications. Another reason is that the social media are an effective channel only when they are used regularly. It's a road through the jungle: Mother Nature is so active that unless it is used constantly, the jungle will soon smother what was has been paved. In this sense, the channels can be kept open with preventive and preparatory crisis messages: simulations, updates to the crisis plan, etc.

As is true in real life, in the digital world it is essential to segment the stakeholders. The greater your segmentation has been, the better your communication with them will be. In fact, we should bear in mind that online groups are very similar indeed to offline groups, so *institutions should maintain separate channels for separate stakeholders*. For example, using Facebook terminology, a fan page is helpful to spread information throughout a very large community; on the other hand, if we wished to create an area for collaborative work (with experts, third party advisors, etc.) it would be better to open a group page.

Once these profiles are operational, the next question that must be addressed is: what can I expect from the social media during the crisis period? The danger is expecting too little because the possibilities offered by the social media are truly enormous. They are helpful in respect of risk analysis, listening to neighbors, recruiting volunteers, validating proposals from a specific public and many other such tasks.

Another question that should be addressed is: what threats may endanger the institution? This strategic approach, which has already been discussed in the chapters covering risk analysis, scenario designing, etc., means creating flow charts to be used for communication throughout the crisis. It would be naïve to assume that a single tweet will go viral: we should assume exactly the opposite. We must decide what accounts and what groups must be created, how to use the @mentions, etc. It may be a bit tedious, but it is an absolutely indispensable task.

These flowcharts include the fact that not all social media operate in the same way: some are one-to-many (blogs, e-mail), others are many-to-one, while there are others that are many-to-many (Facebook, Twitter). So the plan must be a tailor-made mix of social media based upon what we wish to accomplish. To transmit information to many, Twitter may be the most suitable channel, complemented by a blog offering further information. If we are seeking feedback, Facebook will give us the best results. In situations where information is lacking, a Wiki would be very practical in articulating public collaboration. Skype would be great for communications in which listening is a plus, as is emotional feedback. Flickr is best for pictures, etc.

Each one of these channels has its advantages according to what our objectives are. Companies should decide which ones to use in an emergency, and which ones to use in a crisis. For example, experts in the digital world point out that the greatest novelties that the social media have contributed are those related to joint task forces. Therefore, if the institutional problem requires two-way communication – an emergency due to a catastrophe, for example – the best channel will be a system that enables collective intelligence. As Linstone & Turroff point out, «we are entering into the age of participation where whoever is able to help may do so: it no longer matters where they are or whether it was planned for them to intervene or not.»

These new developments also provide the upside of remote online problem solving, in which many people participate. As White points out, «during an emergency situation there is a real danger of thinking that in the eye of the crisis there are people involved in its coordination, aligning needs and offers of help that are coming in from many different places, while, in all reality, ordinarily, there is nobody left.»

In any event, collective intelligence – and its related tools – is not as effective in an ethical crisis, for example. In these situations, you should neither state nor do what the consensus recommends but rather create a consensus around the ethical decision whether it is popular or not.

Web pages

Web pages are the backbone of corporate crisis communication, and quickly become the focal point for all information: press releases, tweets from the official account, webcasts with interviews and press conferences, newsletters, etc.

Nevertheless, their easy usage and high effectiveness for conveying information should not lead us to overlook several possible basic drawbacks: if a web page is poorly used, instead of helping to solve a problem, it may end up making it worse – broader in scale and faster in development. In this sense, companies should avoid any automatic mechanisms, such as "publishing everything on our site," or the opposite, "close down the site": each initiative should be well thought out in advance.

The company's decision whether or not to post an item of news about a crisis on its webpage should be based on the institution's sense of public responsibility and how much trust it wants to generate in its stakeholders. In some cases, it will not be necessary, while in others the public nature of the organization will lead it to make all information available, even its own crisis plan.[106]

---

[106] Many universities and an increasing number of schools have their emergency response plan uploaded to their websites.

Some organizations prefer to inform through their normal web page, while others decide to create a specific website oriented to one or to a certain number of stakeholders (local community, reporters) but not to all of them. These *crisis websites* are uploaded specifically for this situation; they are operational as long as they are needed and then taken offline once the crisis has been overcome. It would be nonsensical to leave material online that was helpful in a certain timeframe but later on could actually be harmful.

In closing, the website (or the app) has clear upsides compared to the traditional press kit, which until very recently was the main tool used in crisis communication: it is faster, easy to update and much cheaper.

Internal communication tools

For many organizations, the most efficient internal communication tool is their institutional intranet, which combines the advantages in an internal informational vehicle with the virtues of accuracy, immediate real-time information, access from anywhere, from the next cubicle or for someone a thousand miles away, etc., virtues that are all inherent in today's global digital society. There are even some organizations that have uploaded their crisis manuals onto their intranet and anyone who has been assigned a password can access them.

In those organizations whose main internal communication channel is a magazine or newsletter to all staff members, this means may be an effective tool for keeping both management and employees up-to-date during a crisis period as long as it is truly an informational vehicle: in other words, this publication provides timely and thorough information about current events and the news reaches everyone before it becomes well-known through the company grape-vine. If the internal publication has a reputation of being objective and of promoting the staff's interest, it may actually become the backbone of our internal communication procedures, *even* in a crisis period.

Audiovisual material is an excellent internal crisis communication channel as it is especially effective in conveying emotional content. Nevertheless, the quality of the product itself must be guaranteed and must avoid the impression of being amateurish.

Nowadays, YouTube has completely changed the name of the game: on one hand, many companies have taken advantage of it by creating their own corporate channels for internal communications. Many have tried to limit access as a security measure (by using access passwords, etc.) but if these passwords have been distributed to a wide range of people, sent out via e-mail or made available on the social media, their videos will soon be available for practically the whole world.

In closing, in addition to these two tools we could mention several others depending on the specific circumstances: teleconferences, internal meetings to provide relevant information to staff members, single-issue meetings and/or postings, etc.

Best practices in customer communication

As we stated earlier, during major crises, organizations should try to maintain a low profile. The best time to try to improve your corporate image is not when the organization in the public eye for the wrong reason, and if the company needs to reconstruct its reputation, this cannot be done through a series of TV commercials or fancy ads. So, advertising campaigns tend to be cancelled as they draw attention to a company when it looks its worst,[107] the additional attention acting like a boomerang on the company and its reputation.

On the other hand, a chronic crisis – in other words, a controversy that is going to involve the organization over a long period of time – is not a justifiable reason to suspend ongoing advertising campaigns, or much less to try to stay out of public view. In this sense, it is a good practice to place advertisements at strategic times

---

[107] Otherwise, it may happen that the campaign becomes a reason for social rejection. This is, according to Valvi & Fragkos, what happened to BP after the oil spill in the Gulf of Mexico: its campaign in the press, radio, TV and online media, in which the company invested 50 million dollars, was criticized by many people including President Obama, who said they should have spent the money on the cleanup instead of on advertising. That forced BP to specify that the money had not been detracted from the cleanup costs.

and in strategic places to convey all the company's point of view and all the information that is indispensable for the public interest. The organization should not assume that the media will accurately convey the message.[108]

Along with spreading basic information through direct channels, buying advertising slots has also been deemed as being positive in conveying the company's ideas during controversies.[109]

Effective channels for journalists

The most commonly used tool in dealing with journalists during a crisis is the press conference, since it allows the company to give abundant information to many people simultaneously. In a critical situation, it is absolutely impossible to attend to all reporters one by one, but a press conference is the right forum for them to ask questions and to ensure that the same message is being given to all.

Obviously, press conferences do have their pitfalls: no journalist wants to have exactly the same information as their colleagues, and much less will that journalist show their own cards by asking a specific question that could provide a hint to their competitors about what they are planning on saying in the next day's newspaper. There are even risks for the spokesperson: if a few reporters think that the institutional responses are either unsatisfactory or simply wrong, their disappointment will be contagious, and the overall atmosphere at the press conference may even turn ugly.

The use of press conferences should be limited: they are useful when the other possible tools to divulge information are unavailable: press releases, one-to-one interviews, etc. As Velasco has recommended, «the severity of the crisis is not a sufficient condition to justify calling a press conference. Organizing one should not be an automatic mechanism linked to severe accidents. In fact, re-

---

[108] In case of food poisoning, it is a responsible action to buy ads to explain to the general population what they should do to protect themselves and to specify what to do with the contaminated products.

[109] Schmertz, who at the time was one of Mobil Oil's top executives, remembers the editorial ads campaign promoted by his company in the 80s to explain the organization's point of view during an ongoing crisis period, with very good results.

porters don't request a public appearance, but rather a fast and factual response to their enquiries.»

In addition to the habitual guidelines about press conferences in normal times (prepared down to the last detail; only when there is relevant information; timetabled in accordance with journalists' deadlines, etc.), during a crisis period, it is better to place strict limits on your available time. The shorter they are, the better.

We should also emphasize other tools which are effective with reporters, according to reporters themselves: e-mails with very descriptive subjects, so the content is obvious at first glance (yes, journalists still use e-mails), Twitter or WhatsApp alerts about new contents uploaded to the website's media section, a summary of the previous press conference on video, the availability of pictures and footage, etc.

Interviews in times of crisis

Interviews are also frequently used during a crisis. Let us have a look at some specific guidelines for interviews in the context of a controversy or a crisis.

The first criterion – relating prudence – is based on *the identity of the interlocutor and his professionalism.* Managers should always know who they are talking to, and never speak to a journalist unless they know what outlet the journalist works for, especially if the interview is over the phone.

It doesn't make sense to arrange an interview with a reporter who has *an ambiguous sense of ethics.* Everybody understands this, even the journalist's own colleagues. An interview is a dialogue and if you know beforehand that the journalist is not planning to respect the pre-agreed conditions, why should you run the risk?

Secondly, think in advance about its context and focus. Will the interview be useful in conveying the institutional message or will its context make it impossible to convey anything? There are always radio and TV programs in which serious people and/or institutions cannot possibly take advantage of: they would simply be ducks waiting to be shot at by the commentator, other participants, or even the spectators themselves. I certainly believe these controversial, satirical or scandalous programs are completely legitimate; but I do not recommend prestigious companies to accept their invitations to participate.

There are other programs that address controversial subjects but are a forum for debating ideas. In these cases, we must certainly avoid being naïve. Kerchner has provided the following thoughts:

> Throughout my professional career as a media trainer and crisis consultant, I have encouraged my clients to be open-minded and collaborate with reporters in this type of program. Lately, however, I have changed my mind and I have found that other colleagues are thinking the same way as I am: arranging an interview on shows such as 60 Minutes, 20/20, Dateline, Inside Edition and American Journal is rather doubtful if we want it to be helpful. Their approach of talking about a subject and their methods of gaining audience automatically make them look at the institution from a negative point of view. Even if you are thoroughly prepared and although your reasons are solid, your chances of achieving your goals of avoiding the perception that the institution is "guilty as charged" for its actions or its negligence are very unlikely indeed.

Thus, the decision to accept or not to accept their invitation will depend on circumstances. There may be situations that are so negative that *we have nothing to lose* and then going ahead and participating in this program might be the lesser of evil. In those cases, in the midst of a profound crisis — when a scandal has been uncovered, for example — it is probably better to go ahead, knowing full well that the best outcome you can hope for is to be perceived as *being a very normal person* without horns or a tail and as having the nerve to have appeared on a program like this.

Thirdly, not all the media are the same as far the organization is concerned. During a crisis period, time is very scarce, so companies should identify which media reach its priority stakeholders. Examining the specific situation will show us whether it is useful to speak to a newspaper reporter, to participate on a well-known TV program or a popular morning radio show, or to give an interview with a very specialized blogger.

The format is also relevant. In general terms, and unless the format is going to be a written Q&A interview (which is not really an interview), we should keep in mind a fact that slightly contradicts intuitions: with the written press, the risk of feeling misinterpreted is greater than with the audiovisual media. The print media interviewer is in full control: the readers will neither see nor hear the interviewee, and the reporter is able to cut and select freely what to publish, and even to include their own perceptions and thoughts, in such a way that the interviewee may not even recognize themselves.

Other thing being equal, (in other words, when the TV reporter is as reliable and relevant as the one from the written press) and there is not enough time for everybody, it is a good idea to give priority to the audiovisual media. TV interviews have a much greater impact than those published in newspapers and magazines, and in a critical situation – in which the emotional aspects have greater importance – radio and TV do a much better job of conveying feelings.

Fourthly, a maximum length of time for the interview should be agreed upon. Shorter is better: the longer the conversation is with the journalist, the more information will be left out. This means that the journalist will have a greater leeway in picking and choosing and, hence, the corporate spokesperson has less control over the outcome.

Additionally, any good interviewer wants the interviewee to be frank, sincere, and spontaneous and preferably to say something completely new and dramatic. To achieve this goal, the interviewer will be overly friendly. It is true that many reporters are genuinely nice and honest people, but not all of them are (as in every profession, also in journalism there are black sheep and even grey sheep) and it is certainly not easy to realize at the drop of a hat if that person's attitude is sincere or if they are trying to fool you.

Sometimes, the exact opposite may happen: the reporter may be intimidating and ask unfriendly questions in an attempt to pressure the interviewee into saying something that they did not plan to say. Regardless of whether it is a sign of true aggressiveness, because the reporter is angry, or whether they are simply pretending to be, the spokesperson's reaction should always be the same: cool, calm and collected.

Serene, relaxed and far from being upset. On TV, whoever gets angry automatically loses any credibility, even when they have been pushed to the limit. So, the more aggressive the person asking the questions is, the cooler the person answering them should be.

These guidelines are not only valid for live, in-person interviews but also for those that are being taped for later showings. In the former, the audience will also be aware of how impertinent a question may be, perceive the bothersome interruptions, the lack of politeness, etc., and automatically sympathize with the person who is being treated inconsiderately, especially if they react with great composure. On the other hand, when an interview is being taped, you must remember that the provocative question may be omitted, and this means that the audience will see you being extremely agitated and have no idea why.

There are many, many ways in which they may try to trick you and you had better be ready for all of them. Let's take a look at one or two:

- Do not legitimize excessively harsh language used by the moderator, by using it in your response, trying to either deny their accusation or to prove otherwise. On the contrary, you should never use the same incendiary terms that they have.

- Do not allow the interviewer to interrupt you too frequently. You must impose your will; keep on saying what you want to say, perhaps raising your voice slightly: most reporters will let you go on and realize that they have gone too far.

- Do not allow hypothetical questions or those referring to future scenarios. On the contrary, strongly reiterate that you never speculate along those lines and much less so in a critical situation such as this.

- Do not deviate from your own stance. Don't think that if you are asked the same question in two different ways, you have to give two different answers. Reporters quite often repeat the same question for several reasons: because they have not been listening, because the response was not well taped due to some interference or a noise, because the answer was too drawn out and boring... or because they are trying to get some further information. When you are sure that what you have said is the proper answer, you should simply repeat it one more time.

- Do not talk too much. The more direct the question was, the shorter the answer should be: the more straightforward your answer is, the fewer chances there will be for opening the door to additional probing.
- Don't feel offended because the reporter asks questions about highly confidential subjects or very personal in nature. The primary instinct of all journalists is to try; but it is the interviewee who decides what to say and what not to say.
- Do not expect the interview to have finished simply because the videographer has stopped filming or because the reporter has closed their notebook. The interview begins from the very first second that you say hello to the interviewer and does not end until you walk out of the door. Quite often the most incisive questions are raised at the very last second, waiting for the elevator, when you think everything has finished and that there is no reason whatsoever to be alert.

These tricks of the trade may seem hard to handle, but with a little practice (that is why you are taped during your training courses), you will win out. In any case we will finish this section with an Italian proverb: *fidarsi è bene, non fidarsi è meglio* (trusting others is good, but not trusting others is even better).

The History: true leadership[110]

On 9 February 2018, one of the largest and most prestigious global NGOs, Oxfam, was hit by a severe crisis when the London newspaper *The Times* accused its British branch of covering up the fact that it had paid women survivors of the 2010 earthquake in Haiti to have sex with NGO executives in charge of the rescue work. The source, as is often the case, was an internal whistleblower.

What followed next was the revelation of a succession of frequent and serious managerial errors. A corrupt internal culture came to light, to the point that this episode has been called "the non-profit version of the Enron case.

[110] Episode documented by Yi Fei Lu and Shuhan Tsan.

The results of this scandal undermined the NGO's relations with *its main stakeholders*: financially, it lost 7,000 regular donors worth to the tune of 14 million GB pounds, and 20 million more in government funds over the next 18 months; many ambassadors and volunteers left the organization; and internal demoralization was profound.

The scandal was a complete disaster for its reputation: at the end of 2017, Oxfam was the fifth most trusted public institution in the UK, but the scandal destroyed that public trust. Unlike for-profit companies, which can undergo a time of bad repute and still generate revenue, charities rely only on their reputation to attract funds and donations. It is likely to be years before Oxfam GB can recover donors.

One of the many lessons learnt as a result of this crisis is the role of headquarters in a reputational crisis. Oxfam is an international non-governmental confederation of 19 independent charities. Each affiliate is an autonomous organization with its own areas of activity and projects, which contribute its own strengths and experience to the confederation to achieve shared objectives.

Theoretically, the mission of the Oxfam International Secretariat is to help coordinate affiliates and provide support to collaborate on joint projects. Fortunately for the confederation, the International Secretariat immediately understood the consequences of the scandal across the organization worldwide. Realizing that the British branch was making the situation worse with hesitant and contradictory responses, HQ intervened to convey the appropriate messages. With the "Plan of 10 Oxfam points", it indicated the way to the English branch and all the others, and promoted the renewal of the local senior management. It was an effective manifestation of true leadership, defending the identity and interests of the confederation by going beyond its statutory power.

The Oxfam scandal yields another valuable lesson: crises hit not only individual institutions, but their sector as a whole. Less than a month after the article in *The Times*, Haiti's president called for an investigation into the work in his country of another NGO, Doctors Without Borders (MSF). Suspicions had been raised by the fact that MSF had hastily repatriated 17 foreigners working for the NGO just after the *The Times* exposé.

Meanwhile, the former executive director of Save the Children appeared in media headlines about three claims of inappropriate behavior against the NGO's personnel about which he had been notified while working at the charity; and on that occasion, the organization revealed that in 2016 it had investigated 56 allegations.

The British Red Cross also admitted a «small number of reported harassment cases in the UK.». Finally, on February 23, 2018, twenty-two aid organizations said they were "very sorry" for the abuses and mistakes made in the sector.

For this reason, we can talk about a before and after in international cooperation and the world of NGOs, with increased scrutiny from regulators and benefactors, and even beneficiaries. It is significant that Haiti, one of the world's poorest countries, has banned Oxfam's staff from entering. Dignity is a more important element than we might think.

CHAPTER NINE

Situational guidelines

Crisis management and communication handbooks devote special attention to earth-shattering crises that have had a devastating impact on human lives, such as natural disasters, a leakage of some harmful chemical, a terrorist attack, etc. In fact, public institutions and corporations need a well-defined program to handle any recall required if one of their products is found to be a potential public health hazard, or an action plan prepared to carry out a full-scale evacuation of an area at risk, etc.

Nonetheless, action plans in case of an emergency are strictly regulated and, in the majority of cases, they are basically technical. In such circumstances, the emergency plan is of greater importance than the crisis plan in itself: if there is a fire, the most important step — and most urgent one — is to extinguish it, not to stop and call every investor or reporter you have on your speed dial. Therefore, emergency response is really of lesser importance in a book like this, which is aimed at managers and communicators.

The same could be said of situations that have caused so much social alarm that the institutions have been forced to self-regulate, issuing rules that enumerate to the very last detail what the corporate response to a crisis should be; furthermore, regulators have dictated protocols with which everybody has to comply. For this reason, we will not go into issues where compliance is the essence of the crisis, such as child abuse in schools, sports teams, etc.: every institution dealing with minors is obliged to have protocols in place.[111]

Instead, it makes more sense here to study specific situations in which decisions have to be made and for which, while involving institutions of any kind, there are particular orientations that we have not yet seen.

These situations are of six types: crises in which the institution is faced by an antagonist - public opinion, a court of law, a boycott, or a criminal aggressor; conflicts that have internal corporate causes; and scandals. Best practices in emergency communication are suggested in each case. Let us examine them separately.

Facing a declared enemy in public opinion

Episodes of this type happen when either an individual or a group of people reach the conclusion that the institution is responsible for what they perceive to be as some sort of injustice and, as a result of this conviction, they become an active player ("active" is the key word here as this phenomenon is known as "activism") seeking social change against everything that the institution stands for, or is doing, in clear and publicly declared defense of the common good.

---

[111] In 2020, the online release of *Hide and Seek*, a Polish documentary film on sexual abuse by Catholic clergy, showed not only horrific sexual abuse of children, but also the abuse of power by a bishop. It tells the story of a family whose two sons were abused by the local parish priest. When the parents found out, they first confronted the priest, who told them to keep silent. Then, they went to the local bishop to report the priest, only to receive a reprimand: «These are lies and you have to leave now», the bishop answered. Only one hour after the documentary was released, the Primate of Poland reported the case to the Vatican asking for an official investigation, in accordance with the protocols approved by the Catholic Church in 2019 regarding cases in which a bishop had not followed the norms on these abuses. A few weeks later, the bishop was removed. Protocols created in 2019 helped to take the right decision rapidly and without hesitation (which was quite different from the past).

The opponent's prime objective is to call attention to what they feel is the supposed injustice being committed by the institution and to exert as much pressure as they possibly can on the institution in order to force it to redress the situation. To achieve this goal, they use all available measures to influence public opinion in order for the general public to pressure the political authorities, in the hope that these authorities will then force the institution to change its unacceptable policies — if they have not already done so earlier of their own accord. Examples of these activist groups are Greenpeace, PETA or SNAP (Survivors Network of those Abused by Priests).

According to McFarland, activists are differentiated from other lobbies in that they claim to represent general interests and are transversal while lobbies seek to defend the interest of specific business groups. Generally speaking, these activists begin as temporary organizations linked to a well-defined objective (the battle against some clear and common enemy, for instance). However, it often happens that they end up becoming permanent institutions with their own structure and a professional staff.

People become involved with these groups in several ways: as followers, subscribers to their bulletins, benefactors, part-time volunteers, and activists: the latter are the most committed members, who are ready to go to war for the association. The percentages vary greatly between one type of involvement or membership and another.

The most specific trait of these groups is that *they follow a well-defined plan to attain social support.* Each group has its own style and strategy but in general, we could say that they are based on the element of surprise, irreverence, highly dramatic and fast-moving action and tactics. Their repertoire is wide indeed: sidewalk tables where they explain their point of view to passers-by, claims taken to court, street fairs and protests stopping traffic for hours on end, chaining themselves to the gates of "the enemy", parades and any other sort of surprising act they can think of to attract people's attention.

Their main objective is to attract the attention of the media. Activists require media support in order to legitimize their proposals and accelerate the process of getting the public and the authorities involved. Everything they do is therefore aimed at becoming newsworthy. Quite often, they also aim to be provocative. Their goal is to be on the front page and to accomplish this they are more than willing to dress up as if they were going to Mardi Gras, march down the street, shout at the top of their voices, etc. They actually choose the tactic that they are going to apply on any chosen day by asking themselves: what can we do today to ensure that we attract reporters' attention?

Activists are very familiar with the use of symbols and rhetoric. They claim they are the underdogs, philanthropists, romantic idealists, fighting the ordinary man's battle against the powerful who are only interested in making more profit. It also helps them to be perceived as being those who have nothing to lose. Having very few resources forces them to be highly creative.

They seem naïve, but their naturalness is well–studied and anything but spontaneous. Behind every action there is a well-developed tactic, the result of a thoroughly prepared strategy and hours and hours of work, as explained as far back as 1971 by Alinski in his classic work entitled *Rules for Radicals*. Since then other books have explained how it is done and how it should be put into practice: *Making the News, the Activist Manual* and more recently *Prime Time Activism*.

Institutions have to be aware of these tactics in order to be able to successfully confront them. Lerbinger suggests the following operational guidelines.

Firstly, companies must absolutely recognize that there is a clear confrontation between the two parties: feigning indifference or reacting with indignation or looking down your nose at them is exactly the reaction that your adversaries are expecting (and hoping for) because that puts the organization in a bad light with the media and in the court of public opinion.

Once you have accepted the fact that there is a confrontation, the next step is to get to know who the rival is, what they seek, what their strengths and weaknesses are and how they normally act. This information is required in order to make the first decision: is it wise to openly accept the confrontation in the arena of public opinion or should we be more defensive in our approach and wait for our adversary to make the first move.

The next step is for the organization to evaluate its own vulnerability, both objectively (examining its own nature and activity) and subjectively (in other words, what are the chances of being targeted in a direct campaign orchestrated by one of these groups?). Activists are always looking for well-known institutions to fight, because it will give them greater visibility. For instance, the protests of the so-called "No global" tend to choose easily recognized worldwide companies, such as McDonalds, to be their targets because of the international media echo that such companies guarantee.

Other factors that will increase an institution's vulnerability are its economic strength and geographical expansion (it is poor taste to attack a smaller, weaker local company), its reputation of being progressive (activists think that institutions who like to project a progressive image will be more likely to yield to popular pressure) and its field of activity: those who produce and market consumer goods are more vulnerable.

Experts suggest that dialogue should be accepted with the well-consolidated groups, those who have a certain reputation and are seriously perceived as defending legitimate interests. Whoever refuses to accept these channels will be viewed as arrogant and anti-democratic. On the other hand, if the adversary is being provocative and their request for dialog is just manipulative, it is better to think twice because this dialogue may simply serve as a springboard to gain legitimacy and provide them with an excellent public platform to present their complaints.

Once again, there are certainly no hard and fast rules and it will all depend on each specific case. Even when it has been proven that our adversary is acting in bad faith, it does not necessarily mean that we should reject any attempts at dialogue: perhaps this will be the best strategy to weaken their demands in the face of public opinion.

Jackson has recommended avoiding confrontation in the following cases: when the issue is too complex and impossible to explain in a brief and clear manner to the general public; when the rival clearly has the upper hand; when the adversary is not really seeking to reach any real, specific goal but rather is simply seeking publicity; when the organization — according to an unbiased audience — is clearly in a position of absolute superiority and does not want to concede legitimacy to their protests. In all other cases, the debate should be accepted, to fully explain the legitimacy of our own position and to demonstrate that the organization is not afraid to explain its identity and activities.

If it is planning to go ahead, the organization should carefully choose the most appropriate representatives in accordance with the type of confrontation and with who their interlocutors are going to be. Their representatives should have mediator skills and be perceived as being calm and constructive, levelheaded, friendly, etc. in their attitude. The mediator must have authority but cannot be the institution's CEO. His role as mediator primarily consists of facilitating communication between the institution and the adversarial group. Acting in this way will buy the organization extra time and lead the way to a calm and objective decision-making process.

Sometimes activists' protests look like criminal acts: insults, verbal aggressions, mockery, ugly rallies on people's homes, disobedience, or damage to individuals and/or property. In these cases, the institution should definitively weigh up the possibility of calling in the police or going to court. Nonetheless, keep in mind that starting legal action may only prolong the crisis or make it worse for everybody. The real battle is winning public opinion; the legal battle has many other characteristics and its own timeframe. It is always wise to listen to your lawyers, but you should not make your decision based solely on legal reasoning. The same thing is true with respect to calling in the police: other weapons in the fight for public opinion are often much more effective than brute force, especially considering that the public (at least in Europe) often takes the side of the peaceful protestor over the aggressive law enforcer.

Another option that usually bears fruit is using third parties, which act as mediators. A person or institution of repute could intervene and promote consensus.

Lastly, we should weigh up the advantages and disadvantages of negotiating. You must decide if it is better to yield to your opponents' demands and thus lessen the pressure, or if, by accepting his demands, you will only be opening the door to greater demands in the future. Experts recommend that you should be firm but have an open attitude: *we cannot accept everything, but we are certainly willing to talk* is a good way to start the conversation and may even help you to better understand the person who is sitting across the table.

As is true in any crisis, companies have to take the initiative. Confrontation is a media event, and you should never allow your adversary to monopolize the media, as that will only deepen the crisis. If that happens, the general public will end up believing that those who are demonstrating on the streets are absolutely right. Therefore, the best approach is to take a moderate, positive and creative attitude and express your own stance from the community's perspective: defending general interest, not a selfish one.

Facing your adversary in court

The tension surrounding a conflict heats up considerably the instant that either an individual or an institution goes to court to defend its rights and/or expectations. This tendency is especially true in countries like the USA, but it is really global in nature and clearly on the rise. Not even NGOs are immune from this tendency, and more and more of their disagreements with individuals or other legal entities end up in front of a judge.

Earlier, in chapter 3, we saw how organizations have to face conflicts and controversies by blending legal and communication aspects: and we emphasized the idea that top management has to be able to manage two points of view that are inherently contradictory. In this section, we will be studying to what degree communications criteria should exert influence, at the moment when the critical decision is being made about whether or not to go to court to defend our interests. We will also look at how communication efforts are actually able to complement legal actions.

Most communicators encourage consensus and defend a peaceful path to agreement. They strongly recommend doing everything possible to avoid going to court as a method of resolving a conflict. This means, above all, trying to avoid it by all possible means.

For example, Lukaszewski recommends that whenever any misconduct or unlawful act has been discovered, either within or outside the institution, it should be immediately and decisively reported. Later on, if the problem has not been avoided, every peaceful effort must be made to negotiate a win-win agreement acceptable to both parties, before the case is actually taken to court, if necessary using unbiased mediators . In order to achieve this, it will be helpful to follow the guidelines explained in chapter 5 about conflict management, including the managerial experiences referring to potential conflicts: the assignment of staff and resources to exert influence on the social agenda.

At the end of the day, we should explore every possible avenue to reach an agreement. In most cases, the damage that is perceived by the stakeholders is very great indeed and so it is better to be creative in exploring ways to reach a settlement that will not harm either party.

If the other side absolutely refuses to engage in dialog or its offer implies a major, obvious injustice, perhaps there will be no other choice than to accept legal proceedings to defend our rights. In any event, we must be aware that the legal system is never perfect, so we shouldn't be surprised is sometimes it does not work. Therefore, there are occasions where recourse to the law can be counterproductive: for example, it may not be wise to start legal proceedings if winning in court is very unlikely or if the trial will be very long and most probably end in stalemate.

It may be effective to go to an international court or file a claim for international arbitration (for example, the International Center for Settlement of Investment Disputes, ICSID, of the World Bank). This would be a logical step: huge sums are often at stake; these courts have the impartiality that many governments lack; and they deal with matters which are so complex that public opinion remains on the sidelines.[112]

Legal actions tend to be very ineffective whenever they are related to an issue related to the internet. Obviously, if a company thinks that its domain name has been violated, it can go to the authorities in charge of this type of issue. At first glance, it is tempting for any of us who have faced such a crisis, but there are

---

[112] In 2012, Repsol appealed to ICSID against the expropriation of 51% of YPF by the Argentine government; but it sued the oil company Chevron (who had reached an agreement with the Argentina government to take Repsol's place). Repsol filed a lawsuit in a federal court in New York. In this way, Argentina was forced in 2017 to recognize the Spanish company's right to receive USD 5B as compensation for the expropriation.

times when it is virtually impossible to pinpoint who is responsible. Then even if you do find out who it is, the conflict may become the typical "David vs Goliath" case that we have seen earlier, at least in the eyes of public opinion. And, beyond that, the problem may not even be resolved: in the world of the internet, you can never really make your enemy disappear.[113]

Digital activism tends to go hand in hand with a large number of websites which seem to love attacking institutions. These are called *anti-websites, rogue sites* or *suck sites*. They are normally set up and maintained by infuriated former clients or employees and use a mix of real complaints and irony – they can be very funny – which may be damaging. According to González Herrero and Smith, «It is never easy and there is no general consensus about how to focus these problems. The alternatives range from starting your own blog, if you do not have one already; contacting other bloggers and asking them for their help; launching an online information campaign, responding with your own ironic response or deciding to proceed with some sort of legal action, depending on the concrete situation.» As always, the most effective approach is prevention, buying all the most significant similar domains, and even the anti-sites: in the long run, it is both cheaper and more effective.

Another type of legal nightmare is when the public authorities have applied some type of administrative measure against the institution that may be deemed harmful to them or restrictive of their fundamental rights. This is normally done under the pretext of ensuring public safety and order, or in the social interest. In these cases, says Banacloche, «the best way of resolving the controversy is to go to court.»

These conflicts are even harder to manage, as public authorities (judges, law enforcement officials, controllers and supervisors) tend to leak information to the media as a way of pressuring those

---

[113] This is what happened to Dunkin' Donuts: a dissatisfied customer set up www.dunkindonuts.org as a site to receive customer complaints. The company reported it and in the end the customer had to give them the domain. But, lo and behold, a new domain popped up - dunkindonutssucks.com... The moral of the story is that the audience will always find one place or another to be heard.

being investigated. In this way, the media do their dirty work for them and it is very hard to win in this type of situation.

A fourth type of legal conflict happens when the right to honor and the reputation of an institution and of the people linked to it (and sometimes also the right to privacy) clash with the exercise of freedom of expression in its various forms: freedom of criticism, freedom of artistic creation, freedom of education, or freedom of information.

In the current legal context in Europe, freedom of expression prevails over the right of people to their image and reputation, except in cases of danger to public order. It is a global trend in jurisprudence and legislation as well. More and more countries have abolished the crime of defamation from their Criminal Codes. [114]

Maintaining the general principle that *the legal route is rarely beneficial*, there are cases in which it is advisable to go to court to restore justice: for example, when the defamation has had great impact due to its objective content or because of the diffusion which it received, it is highly probable that the judge will rule in favor of the institution. In these cases, taking this route serves to prevent similar situations from recurring in the future.

Let us insist once again: before going to court, one must assess the situation from the point of view of public opinion and present the initiative as a peaceful exercise in the defense of rights that are

---

[114] This trend is a global tendency in both jurisprudence and also in the most recent legislative actions. More and more countries have recently abolished the crime of defamation: for instance, in the Americas, Mexico, Panama (2007), Brazil (2009), Uruguay (2009), Argentina (2009), Costa Rica (2009), El Salvador (2011), Granada (2012), Bolivia (2012), and Jamaica (2013). However, today we are witnessing a return of this legal figure. The report *Critics are not criminals*, issued by the Thomson Reuters Foundation, stated that today there is «an international consensus that the law on the crime of defamation violates international standards of freedom of expression, which led to depenalization of many aspects of defamation in various countries. However, in recent years we have documented an alarming resurgence in the use of these outdated provisions to harass critical journalists». Research shows that the former norms (on defamation) are easily instrumentalized by politicians and public officials to harass and silence their critics.

at the basis of all mutual coexistence. In this sense, if what is being demanded is a monetary settlement, we can tell the courts that any amount that is awarded will be given to some worthy NGO, as Banacloche has stated «in order to avoid lesser sentences based upon the supposed economic possibilities of the parties involved.»

When a company does decide to request the court's protection, it has to choose between a civil or a criminal process. Each of them has advantages and disadvantages, from both the legal and the communications perspectives. The criminal approach tends to be faster and exerts more pressure on those who may be declared guilty, because people don't like going to jail, do they? But this route may be perceived as an aggressive attitude by public opinion. On the other hand, civil proceedings tend to be much slower and tedious but they are viewed in a more favorable light by both the general public and, more specifically, by the media. They lead to positive outcomes, as long as the institution wins (a hefty economic sentence will dissuade the other party from ever attacking us again).

In this sense, you have to carefully weigh up the reasons favoring one choice or the other. Are we really sure that the court's verdict is going to be in our favor? How long is it going to take? What will our adversaries be doing in the meantime? How will our stakeholders interpret us if we take our adversaries to court?

Quite obviously when there are doubts about how the courts will rule or it is foreseeable that the length of time required will pave the way and allow for further attacks, or perhaps that the media will once again be paying attention to our adversaries, the institution would do well to avoid falling into the trap of starting legal action, especially when our priority stakeholders do not agree with us.

If, in the end, there is no other choice but to go to court – or perhaps the organization has been forced to by its adversary – the legal battle should be left in the hands of our attorneys; but the fact that there is an on-going legal process does not mean that the problem will be solved in the courts of justice, but rather – as we have seen earlier – there are still two more arenas of negotiations: that which is presented by the legal system itself and that of public opinion. For instance, if we are talking about a case of insults, the legal action will go hand in hand with communications that will, hopefully, impede the law from becoming an element that may cause us to lose support and credibility of the eyes of public opinion.

The same thing will happen whenever the group we are calling "our adversaries" are people in the position of a public authority. Just as we saw when we were discussing controversies, all claims should be presented from the general point of view, and not as the result of exercising every individual's rights.

The third point to be considered is that the legal process cannot be fully separated from the art of persuasion. Judges, district attorneys and members of the jury all form their own opinions, as well as discussing the case with their wives and husbands, reading the newspapers, watching newscasts on TV and talking about it with taxi drivers, etc.

Fourthly, announcing that you have gone to court automatically turns the whole thing into a circus that the media loves, a signal that our adversary is going to try to take the conflict to two separate scenarios and coordinate their actions to gain momentum in both arenas. In this sense, Lukaszewski has denounced the growing tendency that lawyers have of talking to the media, and he states categorically: «in most cases it should be forbidden.»

Boycotts

Halfway between a public adversary and an illegal attack are those who organize boycotts against an organization. A boycott is *a public request made by an individual or a group to not buy an organization's goods and services, because their institutional behavior or attitude deserves social punishment.* This action is undertaken with the hope — and expectation — that the loss of sales and revenue will be an effective motivation for the organization to change.

Vulnerability to a boycott is not limited to companies: public institutions and NGO's may also be victims. Thus, the main aspect is not the monetary issue but rather the whole concept of having a group mobilizing against you until their demands are met.

It should be mentioned here that this type of protest is very rarely successful. In order for a boycott to achieve its goals, five conditions must be met. They are as follows:

1) The accused's behavior is very grave and offensive to society: boycotts will not work against lesser offenses or if the points at issue are not clearly established to be true.[115]

2) The boycott must be against a product or service which normal citizens are in touch with, which they both know by name and tend to use. For instance, you cannot boycott yacht propellers, but you could organize a successful boycott against a well-known brand of tennis shoes.

3) The product or service being targeted has to be easily replaceable, *its substitute must not be more expensive nor lower the quality of life of consumers.* You could boycott a specific soft drink because there are other similar products available at any bar or supermarket, but a boycott against a public water monopoly would never be successful as there is no other possible supplier of this service.

4) The initiative has to be against a large and *well-known institution* in order for people to remember it and to make a conscious decision that it is a good idea to teach the "giant" a lesson that

---

[115] For instance, the 2013 boycott against the TV show *La Noria*, broadcast by one of the leading TV networks in Spain (Tele 5) was successful because its policy of paying delinquents and/or their relatives to go on one of their programs to discuss the crimes they were committing was considered intolerable. After unsuccessfully trying to get the station to remove the program, the promoter of the boycott posted the following note in his blog: «these are the brands that are sponsoring the criminal's mother», triggering a civic movement against those brands, which ended up removing their advertising from the program. The TV station's terrible strategy is itself another lesson to be learned. If, instead of attacking the blogger, they had accepted their mistake and apologized, they could have led the movement to reform TV programming and restored their tarnished reputation. The brands acted responsibly by removing their advertising dollars, and publicly promising to never advertise on any program that paid delinquents in the future and to pay more attention to where they placed their advertising. This resulted in changes within the TV network itself; they not only removed the program but modified their whole schedule to improve its criteria in respect of both content and advertising. The TV networks as a whole have learned the lesson that today's consumers have a voice that must be listened to. The case underlines the fact that a boycott may well be successful whenever it is directed against some type of scandalous behavior.

they won't forget. It is essential to have a certain amount of David vs Goliath to be successful.[116]

5) *A boycott should not be overly demanding on sympathizers.* A boycott should never count on a high level of active participation: it can only assume a serious personal commitment from its own activists, that is, those within the organization that is promoting the boycott. It can tell people 'don't buy this or that' but they cannot expect people to be out marching for hours on a rainy day.

Some experts mention a sixth condition: that *the communication media has to support* the boycott: without the legitimacy provided by the media, boycotts are doomed to fail. The media are the referees in the battle between those organizing the boycott and those being boycotted, and they play this role by placing the news in one context or another, for or against the organization. Furthermore, if the media no longer pay attention to the boycott (because there is simply not enough news to be reported, or if the media's agenda turns to some other conflict that it deems to be more newsworthy) people will suddenly forget about supporting the boycott and return to buying and using that supposedly evil product or service.

The need for media support is well documented in most publications, yet there are cases in which the opposite has been true.[117]

---

[116] For example, in 2010 Greenpeace launched an internet campaign against companies that are using palm oil, because cultivating this product adds to the overall destruction of the tropical forests in Asia and harms the protected species that inhabit them (orangutans). As Greenpeace needed notoriety, they chose the most well-known company on their list, Nestlé, which was using this type of oil to make their *Kit-Kats*. As Fronz explained, «unfortunately for Nestlé, it was chosen even though the oil used to manufacture that specific candy bar comes from a completely different place, and it is the only product in which Nestlé uses that type of oil, and the company is highly respectful in relation to any and all environmental issues».

[117] This is the case of the Danone boycott that was launched on January 10, 2001 in France by left-wing parties, trade unions and other leftist groups. The corporate response was straight out of a textbook and so the media reached the conclusion that the crisis had finished – among other reasons, because not a single boycott had ever been successful in France. Yet the reality was that the food giant's P&L showed that the boycott had actually worked and in less than two years, the section that

In this sense, the traditional doctrine about the need for media support may well have been made obsolete by the emergence of the social media. Nowadays stakeholders have channels available to reach an agreement about some issue without needing the help provided by journalists.

In fact, the internet has led to a dramatic increase in the number of digital boycotts, which are quite different from the traditional type: they are shorter but more intense in nature and without the need for mass participation in the social media. In these cases, the people promoting the boycott do not have to totally destroy the company in order for their protest to achieve results. A marginal drop in sales or the loss of a couple of points in their stock quotation is enough to show the company's managers that they have lost control of the situation and to force them to revise the company's policies.

It is far from easy to accurately evaluate the real effectiveness of a boycott because very few organizations will ever publish the degree of damage that a protest has had on their bottom line. However, the fact that companies normally give in to this type of actions is a clear sign of their effectiveness as agents of change. In fact, a 2% decline in the sales of a clothes manufacturer, a food company or a well-known transportation firm would represent a negative gap of millions of dollars in their yearly results.

Faced with a boycott, it is critical for the institution not to over-react. Time is the main adversary for those who are promoting the boycott. In addition, boycott promoters are the ones who have to prove that they have justifiable reasons for what they are asking; the onus is not on the institution itself. So if the organization over-communicates, it will be playing directly into the hands of their adversaries by giving the boycott further notoriety. In these circumstances, it is better to maintain a lower profile in the public arena and reduce the brand's visibility. Thus, all advertising campaigns

---

was responsible for the crisis was sold off to another company for a song. According to Hunter, Menestrel & Bettignies, the secret of the success of this specific boycott was the use of the internet by its promoters: it enabled them to coordinate their actions despite not having any coverage at all in the media. In this sense, they anticipated what the social media would allow people to do ten years later.

314 ◄ STEERING COMPANIES THROUGH STORMS AND CRISES

should be stopped, all promotional activities cancelled, and any new product launches or initiatives that could be associated with the boycott delayed.

During a boycott, internal communication becomes your number one priority: straightforward, intense and personalized. It should explain why the accusations are false and then what exactly the organization's position is on the issue. It is also necessary to intensify communication with the other major interested stakeholders, including the authorities and, above all, consumers.[118]

Before responding to a boycott, it would be helpful to ask yourself what reasons are behind it, and whether an ethical element in your activity has provoked these protests. You should not exclude the possibility that after carrying out this self-examination you may uncover some practices in your organization that should be changed. If that is the case, your first action will have to be to rectify what is being done wrong.

The guidelines that we have just described will also be useful if and when you are planning to organize a boycott: for example, when a consumers' organization wishes to call a boycott against a company to try to force them to remove their advertising from a TV program which they feel is not showing respect for women, etc. Before launching the boycott, they had better be sure that their assumptions on which their reasoning is based are as solid as they think.

Illegal attacks

We are referring to incidents that are *illegal or criminal acts against the institution, carried out by external agents*. The most frequent type of incident is intentional contamination: the aggressor ma-

---

[118] In the Nestlé boycott that we mentioned before, the YouTube campaign was very harmful indeed: the Greenpeace video was watched by 1,500,000 viewers and more than 500,000 people actually signed a document against the use of palm oil. Fronz reached the following conclusion: «the Nestlé campaign to raise awareness about its environmental protection campaign and its corporate responsibility programs in those countries was much less successful than Greenpeace's campaign».

nipulates a product or service to create social panic, which they will be able to use to blackmail the company, economically or political- ly. However, there are other types: fraud, the kidnapping of em- ployees, the marketing of plagiarized goods, theft of documents, cybercrime, etc.

Thieves and other violent people do not only rob banks. The everyday workplace is becoming one of the most dangerous places for one's physical and moral well-being — and even one's very life. In fact, violence has invaded such (until recently) peaceful places as schools, to the point that firms and advisors specialized in prevent- ing violence in educational institutions are now in great demand.

Criminal attacks have no claims to public legitimacy, and therefore there are no particular indications. The key is preventive protection: perimeter fences, access control, security forces, anti- hacking systems, etc. No wonder security companies are booming: there is no shortage of felons, so it is better to protect yourself be- forehand than afterwards. It would be serious imprudence if man- agers use the same itineraries to drive to work every day in a coun- try where kidnapping is frequent. Also, in a country where terror- ism is ever-present, it would be wise to ensure that the mail de- partment knows how to differentiate between an envelope carrying a bomb and a normal one. We are responsible for the consequenc- es of these crimes if we do not follow what prudence and common sense advise.[119]

---

[119] On December 6, 2016, a man fired a semiautomatic rifle at full blast in the Pulse nightclub in Orlando (USA), killing 49 people and wound- ing 53 more. Disney World is fifteen miles away. In recent years, after the terrorist attacks of San Bernardino and Paris, the theme park had reinforced its security measures, with more guards, dogs, metal detec- tors and the latest technology, less visible but very effective. These precautions proved their effectiveness when the police reviewed the recordings of the security cameras of the entrances to the park and discovered that the nightclub murderer had prowled around the park entrance only hours before, with two semiautomatic weapons hidden in a baby carriage. Everything indicated that his first objective was a massive concert inside the park. Thanks to Disney World's strong secu- rity measures, he left the venue to go to the nightclub. An attack at the concert would have claimed many more victims.

In other cases, criminal attacks could have a communication element: for instance, when an organization is attacked by terrorists or by hired thugs aiming to take hostages, place bombs on university campuses, destroy works of art, etc. in order to gain notoriety for their particular cause or movement; or to intimidate an institution from looking for a solution to a social injustice or simply out of pure hatred.

Managers and corporate communicators tend to be more affected by the type of attacks that are carried out to help a *cause*: that is, the use of violence to gain increased visibility for political, ideological, or social demands. We could describe this type of action as being "violence with a message," since the aggression is carried out as part of the overall communication goals. In this sense, terrorism is — according to Ranstorp & Wilkinson — an instrument used «to create and exploit a climate of fear between a broader social group than that of the victims themselves, to increase public awareness of their cause and to force society in general to yield to the terrorists' demands.»

This type of aggression tends to follow the same script: first, the threat is announced, either in clear terms or as a vaguely disguised possibility, followed by a demand to the specific institution or to society in general. For this reason, communications play a significant role in terrorist-related episodes. Canel and Sanders consider that terrorist attacks belong to the field of crisis communication, for three reasons: first, because the attacks are certainly crises; second, because they have an important communicative dimension; and third, because they damage the reputation of the institutions.

If the demand is aimed against the institution itself, the vulnerability will depend greatly on the institution's financial capability to meet the terrorists' ultimatum, as well as on its type of activity: organizations that are more susceptible to this type of attacks are the ones which have *innocent* products, such as food and candy for children, medicine, etc.

Crisis management in this type of situation should aim to achieve three basic objectives: maintain personal safety and security, act within the realms of social responsibility and never overlook the fact that, in addition to solving the problem itself, we should also be paying maximum attention to our communications.

Thus, companies should never give in to any sort of blackmail but should rather work hand in hand with the police unit in charge of the situation; they should recall the product that is under threat and immediately establish communication with the priority stakeholders - relatives of the people who are affected, our own employees and the media.

Lastly, the institution should take all *measures to diminish the damage that has been caused or could occur*: evacuating all personnel, recalling contaminated products, etc. These measures effectively show that the institution feels that public health, and especially their stakeholders' welfare, is most important (at the same time it reduces the risk of people later making monetary claims in court).

Barton gives three pieces of advice in respect of violence are three:

a) Threats should be taken seriously. The exact content of messages should be written down, provided to the authorities promptly and investigated promptly.

b) Fears should be shared. If an individual fears that a coworker, neighbor, or schoolmate is acting abnormally or could pose a threat to themselves or others, a call to an emergency response agency is warranted.

c) Response guidelines should be tested in practice. When a threat emerges, it is paramount that organizational leaders test how they may respond to an actual incident. Crisis teams should meet to discuss the content of a threat, who should be notified, who will monitor the actions/statements of the perpetrator, and how all departments will coordinate and communicate with each other if and when an escalation of the case occurs.

As far as communication is concerned, here again there are two separate negotiation tables: a public table, which is daily news in the media; and a private table, between the authorities and the aggressors. The institution that is suffering the attack must be fully aware of this dichotomy and act accordingly. Knowing that terrorists are seeking notoriety as their prime objective is a good starting point when the time comes to adopt the proper measures in re-

318 ◄ STEERING COMPANIES THROUGH STORMS AND CRISES

spect of stakeholders.[120] Coordination with the public authorities must be very close indeed and affects not only their crisis management but also their communication throughout the whole process.

In closing, I would like to point out how important mobilizing public opinion is in this type of circumstance. The pressure of public opinion is the fastest, and in many cases, the only way for national and international authorities to get involved in the issue.

Financial crises

Companies that are listed and traded on the stock market are always at a greater risk, as any action could lead to a drastic fall in their trading prices. Sudden changes or an ongoing decline in the market may have a long-lasting negative impact on the organization.

Two factors may trigger highly negative consequences: firstly, poor economic results; secondly, some extraordinary event that has a major negative repercussion in the overall worth of the company. The value of each individual share traded in the stock market, its variable worth, is defined by its real value or by the anticipation of future profits, but to an increasing extent share value also has non-financial components. Therefore, when a crisis has a negative impact on the corporate reputation, it is only natural for it to be reflected in the company's stock market quotation.

When the company suffers a loss in its stock market capitalization, this opens up two separate fronts that the management has to address. Firstly, it creates concern among both institutional and private stockholders; and consequently, other powerful stakeholders such as investment analysts and the financial media. At a lower

---

[120] For example, 9/11 was clearly carried out in such a way as to ensure maximum news coverage. As Richards states, «the timing of the two New York City attacks was planned in such a way that the crash on the first tower would ensure that many more TV cameras would be on the scene to record the crashing into the second tower.» That's why, in the worst years of IRA terrorism, Irish institutions and news media worked closely to differentiate between what was indispensable information about the terrorist attacks as such and what was helping terrorists to spread terror among the general population.

but still quite relevant level, the company's top management is affected and their morale will be impacted because their bonuses depend greatly on share value. In this sense, financial crises are institutional or corporate governance crises, as they create conflicts with their internal stakeholders: their top management and shareholders.

The current tendencies in today's stock markets create further risks. The stock market has become much more short-term focused than ever before, as the more sophisticated usage of technology enables analysts and investors to have access to more information than was humanly possible before. Now the institutional investors (pension funds) are the main players, and their declared goal is to attain higher yields than the stock market average.

There are four clear consequences of these major changes: firstly, many investors take short-term positions. According to Wallace, «It is estimated that the average stock mutual fund today turns over its complete portfolio every year.» This means that the relationship between any organization and its shareholders is strictly and solely financial in nature. As we stated in chapter 1, the most relevant activity in crisis management and communication is to strengthen the relationship of the organization with its stakeholders. However, with this type of shareholder, there is no relationship to preserve, simply because no true relationship exists.

The second change is the direct participation by the shareholders in the corporate management function. In today's world, its most powerful form has less to do with an annual meeting gadfly or a socially responsible investing advocate, than with a giant public pension fund, discretely but forcefully expressing its discontent to management and the board – often through coalitions with other major shareholders, who, together, wield a very big stick, says Wallace.

Thirdly, there are more and more alliances among shareholders to defend their own common interests. The newest phenomenon is that such alliances now include smaller shareholders who used to be isolated but nowadays are more and more united on platforms to defend their own rights.

Fourthly, and as a natural extension to the changes which we have described above, there is now a phenomenon called *shareholder activism*: large investors - usually hedge funds - identify underperfoming and undervalued companies, buy a major equity stake (big enough to get inside information and to have a say in the company), and design quick-fix solutions to boost value for shareholders (for instance, dividing the company, or selling some assets). If their desires are not met, these investors often engage in a proxy fight to place their representatives on the corporate board of directors, quickly creating an institutional crisis or a major governance issue.[121]

This type of activism is certainly not a positive trend in the world of business in general and, more specifically, not for those companies who are preyed on, because it gives even greater extra weight to short-term results and far over-estimates the value of mathematical metrics. But institutional investors play into their hands as the results are beneficial for them, with the result that this tendency has spiraled and enlarged its sphere of influence, and, unless experts are wrong, is here to stay.[122]

From a communication perspective, the response to a financial crisis should avoid some basic errors that happen all too frequently. Let us look at some of them.

The first basic error is when the *Investor Relations* (IR) and the *Public Relations* (PR) departments are separated and do not report to the same person. Wallace states:

> Investor and public relations are, of course, artificial divisions in the communications function, necessitated by the fact that it is hard to find the combination of strong financial and communication skills in one individual. It is never an ideal arrangement, especially

---

[121] For instance, this is what Carl Icahn, the billionaire investor, did when he teamed up with powerful mutual funds in order to get a seat on the Blockbuster Entertainment Board of Administration, and once he was there he imposed a completely different corporate strategy from that which the company had followed until that point in time.

[122] Wechtell, Lipton, Rosen & Katz have documented with precision more than 200 activist campaigns that all took place in one year (2013). According to the information published by Hedge Fund Research, the total amount mobilized by these activists was over $ 93 billion only in 2013, nearly triple the figure that they managed in 2012. And the more available the funds are, the greater the chances will be of them gaining control of larger and larger corporations.

these days when IR executives often manage financial media enquiries. Nevertheless, in normal times, with a strict delineation of responsibilities, companies make it work. The intensity of a crisis, however, often awakens the latent conflicts between two independent external communications functions coexisting under one roof.

Many journalists are unaware of these differences (or if they are, they try to take full advantage of this "latent conflict") and raise questions to the PR people that are financial in nature and then talk to the IR folks about general business issues. The replies are inevitably inconsistent, the information provided is incomplete and, in some cases, reserved information may be disclosed. For these reasons, the best solution is to integrate IR and PR, making them both report to the corporate communications manager. However, this step must have been taken before the crisis hits: during a crisis, you will never be able to join their functions.

The second source of errors is the divergence in approaches suggested by the communicators and the legal affairs department. The former view communication as a tool to improve the current situation: communication is a profitable opportunity for the institution. However, for the latter group, communication is simply a source of risk and normally does nothing else except create more and more problems.

The most specific aspect of this divergence is that in a financial crisis top management tends to accept the legal response more often than not because corporate governance in companies traded on the stock market is a highly regulated field, with complex legal situations which lawyers tend to understand from A to Z, but which communication people are not nearly as familiar with.

The problem with an overly legal approach to crisis response is that it can encourage a hunker-down position that cedes the high ground to critics and adversaries. Lawyers are usually conservative, and they discourage the kind of calculated risk-taking that lies behind any good communication plan. But successful crisis management strategies are often dramatic. The solution is to assimilate both the legal and public relations perspectives, and to ensure that the two functions are operating together as a team. This is one reason why crisis planning and role-playing, where attorneys and communication professionals practice working as a team in a simulated crisis 'war-game', are so important.

The third possible source of basic mistakes lies in the proper choice regarding the institutional spokespeople and their approach. In a financial crisis, management normally sees the glass as practically full while investors see the exact opposite. According to Wallace, «Most CEOs and top executives are can-do optimists. Unless they are facing a clear and unmitigated catastrophe, their first instinct is often to underestimate the crisis and overestimate their ability to get it fixed. Financial audiences, on the other hand, are often experiencing hyper-reality. They have been surprised, their reputations have been damaged, and they are in the dark.»

Therefore, executives have to make a concerted effort to be both realistic and objective. It is not the moment for rosy optimism and sugary assurances. The corporate spokesperson should be determined, but above all, realistic. Furthermore, financial audiences will probably never be as prepared as they are at this moment to hear and bear the worst. Put out all the bad news that you know. Show suitable emotion. Admit what you do not know. If you think it could get worse, say so. Commit to a reasonable and workable timeframe to get answers.

Looking at what we call prevention, a financial crisis once again confirms the principle that credibility is perhaps the most precious commodity. Investors' decisions to hold on or to jump ship are influenced by reputation more than we might suspect. They will ask themselves if they have a basis to trust management to share information and restore order. That is why interaction with institutional shareholders and sell-side analysts is perhaps the most complex and demanding external relationship which public company management has to deal with.

In these situations, implement preventive measures so as to strengthen the corporate reputation: know your institutional shareholders; seek constant feedback from investor audiences; strengthen the IR portion of the website; have clear, written policies, suitable for external distribution, related to insider trading, financial disclosures, corporate governance and other issues; and conduct a periodical communication audit of your shareholders and analysts.

Along with these preventive measures, we must point out the importance of never hiding from the media. The right approach is to strengthen your relationship with them by providing complete, timely and relevant information, as the shareholder activists are highly skilled at manipulating media coverage. The media have become activist allies and activists use them with a high degree of sophistication in both the traditional and digital platform arenas.[123]

At the end of the day, it is quite clear that, even in rather odd situations such as those that we are looking at in this section on financial crises, a crisis is manifested as being an aggression against the organization's internal unity. So, in order to successfully resist the attacks of these activist-shareholders, companies must encourage unity with the board of administration. In order to successfully frame their proposals, management needs this unity which is the result of years of working closely and harmoniously with the board members, building a solid working relationship between the board and the corporate CEO and ensuring the board's long-term commitment with the company.

Misguided values in the organization

The origin of this type of crisis is internal and voluntary in nature: the organization seeks a high short-term yield, even though this may harm or even endanger its stakeholders or the public good. Sometimes these decisions are taken to directly benefit the company's management at the expense of others; and other times, though seeing the inherent risks, leaders will choose a potentially harmful course of action for the company's advantage, in the hope that there will be no adverse effects.

---

[123] For instance, as Balet states, «when Icahn took an activist stake in Apple, he announced it via Twitter. The impact was immediate and shook the markets up – it was a lesson that everyone in the activist community learned and one that is likely to be emulated. When considering pre-emptive activist defense planning, companies need to understand what social media strategies are available both in defense and offence».

It's like driving at 90 miles an hour through a small village. The driver knows it is both illegal and risky, but because they are in a hurry, they decide to do it hoping nobody will cross the road in front of them. What is voluntary is assuming the risk, not the harm (otherwise, it would be a different type of conduct: a killer with a wheeled weapon).

There may be a wide range of varying causes: a company in financial trouble tries to survive by reducing safety measures; faced by a new competitor, a company could decide to reduce the quality of its products so as to retain its overall profit margin; an organization could decide to hide structural deficiencies in a building or an unexpected danger or side-effect of one of their services.

These crises show that the corporate culture is indeed corrupt and needs to be totally reformed. The root of the problem resides in the way the organization is managed and the manner in which its major decisions are made. Consequently, in every case, *when faced with this type of situation, it is mandatory to revise the corporate culture*, looking especially closely at what exactly the corporate spirit is and the values that the decision-making process is based on (quality, service, productivity, etc.)

A clear sign of a misguided corporate culture is when the common opinion of its managers and staff is that they should not be messengers of gloom and that, whenever there is a problem, they are all afraid to communicate it to the authorities.

Other signs of a wayward management attitude may be that they feel that they are only responsible to a specific public. For example, management may heed requests from shareholders while ignoring the best interests of employees; or they may implement production guidelines which provide the highest quality product to customers while exploiting employees beyond any reasonable level; or the extreme opposite, they may unreasonably defend an employee who has committed some sort of wrong-doing to the detriment of a customer.[124]

---

[124] An example of ignoring victims is how many American universities have dealt with sexual assaults on campus. The documentary *The Hunting Ground*, released at the Sundance Festival in 2015, exposed how universities around the country had failed to tackle the problem and even worked together with campus police to hide cases and erase data

This is also the case when bonuses and incentives are based solely on productivity, and do not consider that the efforts required to reach certain targets may affect the quality of their customer care, safety in the workplace and other essential values. If, for example, pizza delivery personnel's pay were based solely on the time it takes to deliver a pizza (the company offers a free pizza if it arrives late, but then discounts its price from the person's salary), this policy would encourage reckless riding and inevitably lead to accidents.

To avoid this type of crisis, it is indispensable to improve the quality in the management team: unless this happens, all of the other measures will be nothing more than simple, misleading cosmetics.

The so-called "political responsibilities" deserve a little more of our attention. This expression usually describes the indirect responsibilities managers have when the illicit behavior was unforeseen when it should have been; or because we were not diligent enough in handling the problem. This means, on one hand, that there is someone who is directly guilty and, on the other, that our stakeholders feel that management is in some way responsible for what has happened: for instance, when subordinates are not sufficiently supervised by their bosses.

This responsibility due to omission is a corporate problem, because stakeholders do not trust managers who have been publicly accused of poor management. At this precise time, when the or-

---

to protect their economic interests and reputation. Data showed that 40% of US public universities did not report any cases of sexual violence in their schools to the authorities. A field in which the problem is more severe is university sports: athletes constitute 3% of students and are thought to be responsible of 19% of sexual assaults on campus. One of the saddest cases concerns a student at Harvard Law School, who was abused before classes had even started. Instead of supporting the victim of a proven abuse, the official reaction was to publicly ridicule the student: in an open letter, nineteen professors discredited the assault survivor and defended the student who had abused her. After a furious controversy, the US federal government stepped in and found Harvard Law School had violated the law (Title IX). Finally, the University issued a new policy and set of procedures regarding sexual harassment, meeting federal standards. Since then, Harvard has taken other measures to address the problem.

326 ◄ STEERING COMPANIES THROUGH STORMS AND CRISES

ganization needs more trust than ever and the on-going help of its priority stakeholders in order to overcome the crisis, managers lack credibility.

In these cases, the most effective measure is to *suspend the executive/employee, whenever there are reasons to believe that the accusation is true.* Acting in this way has many advantages: it conveys a clear message of change and internal reform that everyone will easily understand; it shows that the institution values its stakeholders' perceptions and welfare more than that of its managers; it stops anyone who is under suspicion from interfering in the on-going investigation about the causes of what has happened; it diminishes the inherent tension with stakeholders, because the corporate interlocutor is not among those accused; etc.

Bear in mind that a suspension does not necessarily mean that the company admits its responsibility. As one of the top managers of an Italian company declared in similar case, in respect of his leaving the firm, «it was necessary to show a clear sign of discontinuity». For this reason, it may be a good idea to accept voluntary resignations or encourage a forced substitution when a major issue arises, as this will resolve the problem, at least in the eyes of your stakeholders. Changes in the institutional top management are especially recommended in ethical crises of this type.[125]

If the person involved is discredited to the point that it will be virtually impossible for them to lead the institution during and after the crisis, then the time has come to bite the bullet and ask them to take a temporary leave of absence, at least while the real

---

[125] In 2008, it was disclosed that a broker of the French bank Société Générale had committed a major fraud which led to the bank losing of € 4,9B. An independent Board member of the Bank, who was familiar with the bank from within but, at the same time was able to view the problem from the outside, was appointed to lead the investigation team. In this way, the main problem in the minds of the stakeholders (shareholders, clients, governmental regulators) was overcome: the impression that it was virtually impossible for the broker to have acted on his own without the collaboration of other people. As Pin comments, «Choosing a person from outside, someone with experience and a certain degree of moral authority, was a wise move, particularly when public trust in the organization was at rock bottom».

responsibilities, not simply those which had been perceived are being clarified.

The demands of justice and wisdom in such cases make it imperative that no final decision be taken until all the facts have been proven. In order to reach absolute certainty about what has actually happened, an objective and unbiased investigation carried out by an independent party is required. Thus, unless this absolute certainty has been reached by some other way (the person admitting they are guilty, undoubted documentary or audiovisual proof, etc.), it is much better to only make temporary decisions. If, at the end of the day, it is proven that the person involved was actually innocent, they may be re-admitted to the same position without any further issues being addressed.

In synthesis, both extremes have to be avoided. On one hand, *do not blindly act* according to what your stakeholders say about someone inside. Listen carefully but investigate before acting; otherwise, if the organization just gives up, it will end up being more vulnerable to future protests. Accepting (or even requesting) the person's resignation solely based on external protests and long before having reached any sort of certainty about the veracity of the accusations, goes directly against the basic principle of not capitulating to external pressure or interference solely to gain popularity; it is a sign of being dangerously weak.

The second extreme would be to protect a guilty executive or employee at any cost, as if accepting that the airing of any internal wrongdoing will bring worse consequences. This is also unfair on the company's interests and identity, and is damaging to the rest of honest managers and employees. Companies should be exemplary in respect to the law.

The final decision will be taken when the time comes, considering all the circumstances surrounding the case: the degree of danger perceived by the company's stakeholders, the severity of the facts involved, etc. In short, these crises may end up being beneficial if the causes are recognized and the proper remedies into place. On the other hand, if we simply focus our attention on external causes, or accuse others, the company will miss an excellent opportunity to improve.

Illegal corporate behaviors

In these situations, *organizations intentionally and consciously attempt to deceive their stakeholders* (authorities, customers, employees, shareholders). The premeditation and intentionality differentiate this category from the previous one, in which there was no actual wrongdoing, but only simple negligence on the part of the institution's managers.

Unfortunately, *this type of crisis happens quite frequently*: companies that knowingly sell products with defects; that fail to pay social security contributions which have been deducted from their employees' payroll; companies which build in areas that are restricted due to avalanche or flood risks; which bribe officials in charge of granting building licenses (or political party officials who demand 3% to rig a tender); which indulge in industrial espionage to learn about their competitors' future plans and projects; or companies which resort to blackmail of whatever kind. Whoever acts this way is always lying as well. Nothing happens until these facts are uncovered; but as soon as they are disclosed, the organization's reputation will immediately be in tatters.

There are two very different scenarios. First, the illegal activity can be attributed directly to the organization because it was agreed upon by the leadership and is simply following their normal decision-making processes. In this case, the organization responds in full, in addition to the personal criminal consequences for those who made the decision.

Second is the case in which it was a manager (or a group of managers) who carried out the illegal activity without the knowledge of senior management. Here, responsibilities of the company towards stakeholders are the same, but it is possible that the main injured party is the organization itself. Therefore, it can also present itself as a victim, and act and communicate as such (witnesses at a trial, for example).[126]

---

[126] Petrobras is the largest Brazilian corporation in terms of revenue, and a symbol of pride for Brazilians. The Lava Jato scandal, which began in 2014, is the largest corruption scandal in the history of the world, with illegal payments exceeding 5 billion dollars. A police investigation uncovered a massive and systematic network of corruption

In both cases, all strategies start from the same point: *stop doing what is wrong, apologize and change your behavior*. Without fulfilling these mandatory requirements, companies will simply miss the point. Leadership in these circumstances is shown by taking the bull by the horns and changing direction without delay.[127]

So, the attitude which is called *damage control* (trying to resolve an image issue, without addressing the real problem) is completely wrong. Faced with the moral dilemma of choosing between putting yourself first or acting responsibly, the only valid ethical response is

---

involving businessmen and powerful politicians. Some Petrobras executives overpaid the construction of offices, drilling rigs, refineries and other infrastructure, and their contractors spent part of it on bribing politicians and political parties, and the rest went into their own pockets. In its response to the crisis, Petrobras correctly defined its position as a victim of the scandal, and promised to support the investigation to clarify what happened. Despite the fact that the scandal created much turbulence within the company, it was clear to top management that these corrupt executives were not the company. In addition to collaborating with the official investigations, it collaborated with prosecutors in the trials to recover part of the amount stolen from the company and to rebuild Petrobras' reputation. It also strengthened supplier selection policies; trained all employees on compliance standards; took disciplinary action against employees who were involved in internal misconduct; created an independent, confidential and outsourced channel for receiving internal and external complaints; strengthened its internal communication to rebuild employee confidence and morale; became a reliable and proactive source of information for the media; and implemented a reputation recovery plan with advertising and participation in social networks. The objective was to defend the company, reinforce its importance for the country, and publicize its actions to prevent similar conduct in the future. All these measures were consistent with the identity assumed by the company of having been the victim.

[127] This is what the president of Apple did in February 2012 when it was discovered that FoxConn, its main supplier in China for their iPhones, was intentionally violating the local labor laws and had employees who were younger than 14. According to Pin, «He reacted promptly and resolutely, asking the Fair Labor Association to conduct an inspection at the manufacturer's plants and allowing television cameras full access». Cook also responded publicly to accusations, saying: «It's extremely rare in our supply chain, but our top priority is to eliminate it totally. We've done that with our final assembly vendors and are now working down into the supply chain. If we find a supplier that intentionally hires underage labor, it's a firing offense».

to tell the truth, remedy the situation and accept your own responsibilities.[128]

Hence, *the first thing that needs to be done is to apologize*. Normally pardon is granted whenever it is requested with sincerity and humility, when it is apparent that the company involved truly wants to repair the damage that has been done and changes his behavior to ensure that this issue will never arise again.

It must be made perfectly clear that they radically reject what happened and they are fully aware that they have misbehaved, both in words and in actions. This rejection strives for a total change of standards and a new approach: management (normally, new management) has to convincingly show that it will overcome these problems not with a new set of rules, but rather with a new set of virtues. Stakeholders must understand that the organization will never again be wishy-washy if and when it is faced with this type of poor behavior in the future.

The second valid element in this type of case is the *company's commitment to respect the law and to cooperate with public authorities*: judges, police departments, monitoring agencies. Open and frank collaboration proves beyond doubt that a major change has taken place: it is clear the company has moved from a position in which criminal conduct was overlooked to one in which there is a sincere desire to behave properly.

Thirdly, the company will have to separate itself from the accused, both in terms of legal defense and in communications: different lawyers and different spokespeople, so they could implement different strategies.

Fourthly, the company should *adopt an open, collaborative attitude with the media*. This attitude is always advisable in any type of crisis, but that recommendation is even stronger in this case be-

---

[128] Earlier we mentioned the Firestone case in which the company reached financial settlements with those who had sued the company but did not recall the sub-standard product from the marketplace. Cohn reached the following conclusion about that episode: «One of the most significant early lessons of the tire-recall crisis points directly to top management. It shows what happens when companies believe legal settlements will cost less than fixing problems. When problems become public – and they do – companies face a much bigger hit to the bottom line».

cause there is a major temptation to remain silent or to try to cover up responsibilities. Coming out of this only with egg on your face is not what is at stake in this case. You might end up in jail.

Work closely with the media, recognize the error that has been committed, provide information, apologize and clearly manifest the desire to change – this is the attitude which will be most warmly received, which will lead to the critical moment being overcome more quickly and, looking back on the situation, it will also facilitate your recovery. On the other hand, whoever hides and says nothing, is sticking their head in the sand, in the belief that if we ignore them, the problems will simply disappear.

Once everything has been done to remedy the wrong that has been committed, the next step is to address *internal reform*. All internal control processes should be reviewed: the supervision procedures, the way risks are analyzed, claim management. Companies must find out why the warning alarms did not go off when money disappeared; why people were hired with no security check; why reasonable claims and protests from users or clients were not taken seriously: in other words, why the prevention measures were insufficient or ineffective.

Even though we will look at how to conduct the internal reform in the next chapter, it is worth mentioning here that in this type of corporate crisis, what is required are measures that attack the root of the problem and are never superficial in nature.

Actually, in cases of human error, companies tend to pay more attention to mistakes of leadership and personality rather than to other key factors: the institutional environment (how corporate governance is implemented) and the nature of this organization's followers. Nevertheless, a single misguided leader cannot drag the whole organization into a crisis, even though they may be very smart or very evil indeed: they need the help of unbalanced or unmonitored internal structures and a group of wrongly motivated followers.[129]

---

[129] Thoroughgood & Padilla have made a thorough study of the sexual abuse scandal that occurred at Penn State University, in 2011, in which the main cause of the lack of institutional reaction to abuses for many years was a corrupt internal culture.

In respect of the fines that should be levied from the person who is guilty, a wise decision would take into account a number of factors: the degree of responsibility that they have, their ties with the company, the seriousness of the accusations themselves, the solidity of the evidence against the accused, the sensation of danger that is perceived by our stakeholders, etc. At the same time, the same recommendation that was made in the previous section is valid here as well: *while the facts of the case and is the people responsible have not been fully proven, decisions referring to people should be provisional.*

For example, if a judge charges one of the managers, it would be the time to study whether, for the good of the corporation, they should be immediately suspended from all their functions, as a clear sign that their behavior is rejected and that the door is open for proper investigations. On the other hand, suspension may not be absolutely necessary in the case of an employee who does not have any contact with the stakeholders: people who are presumed to be guilty should only be removed from those positions that are deemed dangerous.

This suspension is a preventive measure, with no long-term effects: the institution should not be the ones who judge whether the person is guilty or not; that is the task of the judicial system. What is important here is that whatever measure is taken should be effective and, at the same time, not be offensive: it is always necessary to keep the window open just in case the accusations prove to be false, regardless of what appears to be the case at this point in time.

Lastly, some scholars suggest that *a crisis presents an excellent opportunity to implant an ethics code into the institutional culture*, establishing new quality and service standards. It is clear that a written text does not solve the problem: wrongdoings are not avoided by multiplying the number of norms. But it does have some advantages: it is an internal training and prevention tool (no one will be able to claim later on that they were unaware of the rule); it graphically proves that the proper measures have been implemented; and in some countries, such as the USA, it will reduce the sanctions determined by regulators, who look favorably on these types of self-control tools. Nevertheless, one must guarantee that adopting an ethical code will mean an authentic transformation of the corporate culture, and not simply a cosmetic gesture.

Corporate scandals

According to Webster, a scandal is «a circumstance or action that offends propriety or established moral conceptions or disgraces those associated with it.» In management, though, a scandal has a more specific meaning. As Fronz states,

> Literature has the same definition for a scandal as for a crisis, but in addition there will be a revelation of a moral misconduct committed by an individual (regardless of whether it was actually committed or if it is merely a presumption), and the indignation as a consequence of this revelation.

The feeling of indignation may be either a true feeling or simply a false sign of regret. It is clearly false when someone shouts out, "what a scandal!" as a way of calling attention to the fact, or protesting against some sort of out-of-date values, etc. More than a scandal, this type of reaction is a marketing tool.

A true scandal therefore means that there has been *a transgression of a fundamental ethical norm because it directly attacks the basic principles of the community.* Whoever creates the scandal is attacking the social identity and therefore should be rejected as an enemy of society, and it is indispensable to punish the guilty person and even to expel them from the community.

Scandal triggers a strong, emotional, negative reaction: such a behavior is perceived as being so grave that it cannot be pardoned. Additionally, as the aggression has been general in nature, anyone who is part of the community feels legitimately that they are entitled to oppose the scandal. Thus, if a conflict is limited in scale and a crisis is larger, a scandal may be described as being a *universally superlative size.*

This universally superlative size may have been caused by a very serious mistake or perhaps by an attempt to resolve a crisis in an illegitimate manner: by denying it, by corrupting journalists or bribing police officers to cover it up, etc. In this sense, any attempt to hide a problem tends to be more serious than the problem itself,

because it is a free and responsible behavior.[130] In this sense, scholars like De María define corporate scandal as being «the public
exposure of an organization which has not responded well to a
crisis.»

It is worth highlighting that *scandals refer to specific social environments*. Each community has its own fundamental principles and
so it is perfectly possible that something that is scandalous in one
geographical or cultural context may not be deemed that way in
another.[131] For example, as the [French] psychiatrist Serge Hefez

---

[130] On September 9, 2014, the British pharmaceutical giant Glax-
oSmithKline was found guilty of bribery and fined nearly £ 300M, the
largest ever corporate fine in China at that point (prior to this case, GSK
had been involved in many legal issues in different countries: in 2010,
its subsidiary in Puerto Rico pleaded guilty to criminal charges of pro-
ducing adulterated drugs; in 2012, it pleaded guilty in the United States
to criminal charges including the promotion of a drug to unapproved
users, the failure to report safety drug data, false best prices, etc., and
paid a USD 3B settlement; in 2013, the company was under investigation for bribery in Jordan, Lebanon, Iraq and Poland...). In addition to
the fine, GSK's medicines suffered a 61% drop that year. The reason for
that heavy punishment could be related to three elements: first, during
the different stages of the official investigation, GSK statements were
continually disproved by later investigation results; second, David
Cameron, then UK Primer Minister, publicly defended the British company, and this infuriated the Chinese government, which took it as an
intolerable interference; and third, the company started a private investigation, which is illegal in China. This case shows that a bad crisis
response transforms a problem into a scandal-level problem; and the
importance of understanding the political, cultural and legal differences
of each country, and to respond to the crisis in a way that works both
locally and globally.

[131] Football in Italy is a very serious business. The Federazione Italiana
Giuoco Calcio (F.I.G.C.) manages both professional and amateur football, starting from the "Serie A" down to regional tournaments across
the whole country. It was established in 1898, and nowadays the FIGC
includes almost 14,000 clubs and 60,000 teams and manages around
600,000 football matches per year. The role of the President is paramount in the association. In 2014, Carlo Tavecchio was elected as President of the FIGC with 63.63% of the votes. He has the reputation of
being a good manager, an expert in the sport industry, a skillful politi-
cian and a troublemaker. On several occasions he has made totally
inappropriate statements characterized by racism, sexism, xenophobia,
and homophobia. During his campaign to be reelected, he made racist

has pointed out, «The French are not like the Americans. They are totally capable of tolerating someone with an intense sex life as long as there is no abuse of power or violence.»

The fundamental point is that you must know whether certain behavior is scandalous for some of the institution's priority stakeholders; and you must adapt the strategy designed to repair the institution's image in the local environment. What may be necessary in some countries may be practically suicidal in others.[132]

Scandal creates an *unstable and complex situation*. On the one hand, all stakeholders are offended, both those from afar, because what you have said or done is intolerable, and your friends, because although they know that you are not like that, your mistake is likewise unpardonable.[133]

_____

statements against foreign football players. Three samples: talking about women in football on a television show, he said: «In the past, it was believed that women were handicapped persons compared to the male athletic expression. However, we realize now that they are very similar». Again, in another interview he commented: «I have nothing against the Jews, but better to keep them under control». Third, talking about another person on an open mike, he said: «But is it true that he is a homosexual? I have nothing against "them" but keep them away from me. I am absolutely normal». Despite this unacceptable behavior, neither the FIGC, nor Italian sports regulators nor the media found it deplorable. In fact, in 2017, he was reelected with 54.03% of votes.

[132] A comparison of the defense strategies of Bill Clinton and Silvio Berlusconi in reference to their own sex scandals, according to García, clearly shows how the culture, the way politics is played and the attitude of the media in respect to those in power in the USA and in Italy are so completely different that both politicians ended up with the same result (political absolution) by applying completely different approaches.

[133] In April 2014, the American National Basketball Association (NBA), was struck by a crisis with regard to the racist comments of Los Angeles Clippers owner, Donald Sterling. The website TMZ released a 9-minute taped conversation in which Sterling made deeply offensive comments about African Americans. The Clippers' first response took a legal approach and underlined that «We do not know if it is legitimate or [if] it has been altered. We do know that the woman on the tape — who we believe released it to TMZ — is the defendant in a lawsuit brought by the Sterling family alleging that she embezzled more than $1.8 million, who told Mr. Sterling that she would "get even."» Sterling also said that the contents of that recording does reflect his views, be-

On the other hand, emotions may run so high that they can often trigger uncontrollable reactions. Whoever reacts against a scandal is acting as if they feel that the aggression against the community is so serious that they have the necessary authority to oppose it, using verbal and even physical violence. They are not only legitimized to act but they are forced to do so to protect society.

Recognizing the warning signs of a scandal is fundamental in order to avoid minimizing its severity. The emotional explosiveness of a scandal goes beyond the control of those involved and drags all the other stakeholders into it. In normal circumstances, they would feel close to the organization but in the face of the fury that has been unleashed by some, they join in with the protests, or, at best, remain silent.

The response to the scandal should aim to reduce the negative emotional tension by articulating a sincere, eloquent and serene request for pardon and by showing a true feeling of regret. An institutional response that is overly rational, that tries to give explanations, would be counterproductive: it is perceived as trying to justify the facts or attempting to minimize responsibility. Feelings are so high that there is a danger that the emotion's shock waves will lead to a consensus that the aggressor is unaware of the severity of his acts, and that the only acceptable solution is to eliminate them (either symbolically or tangibly), in accordance with the dy-

---

liefs or feelings, and he apologized to anyone who might have been hurt by them, and also to Johnson, the woman in litigation with Sterling. There was intense negative public reaction, including comments by President Obama during the following days, which was intensified by the release of a second recording. Then, everybody (other teams' owners, famous players and celebrities, Clippers' players and coach, sponsors, etc.) asked the NBA to respond appropriately. Just 4 days after the incident occurred, the NBA commissioner announced that Donald Sterling would be banned from the NBA for life. He would also be fined US$ 2.5M (the maximum allowed according to league guidelines), and the other owners would move forward with a plan to remove Sterling from ownership, forcing him to sell the team for violations of rules of the NBA's constitutional by-laws. Two weeks later, the Clippers had another CEO, and a few days later, the former Microsoft CEO Steve Ballmer bought the Clippers after medical experts deemed 80-year-old Donald Sterling to be «mentally incapacitated». This episode shows how quickly things can evolve in a scandal, and that the fast and rigorous NBA reaction was a key factor in containing the problem.

namics of a scapegoat: an animal that is sacrificed to recover social harmony.

In this sense, a scandal is like a gas leak: it is a potentially explosive situation in which the first thing we have to do is to make sure that there are no sparks in the vicinity. Being aware of this fact will help us to see that the response has to be quite different than that which would be appropriate for this same accusation if it were not tainted by this scandal.

The corporate response to a scandal should be based on five elements:

1) An *immediate reaction*, before the emotional shock waves turn into a heavily damaging tsunami.
2) An *emotional attitude in full harmony with our priority stakeholders*, keeping in mind that in a corporate scandal, emotions run much deeper across a wider group of stakeholders.
3) A total rejection of the root of the problem: the company should manifest explicitly that it shares the social condemnation of what happens, and consequently asks for pardon.
4) Begin an independent investigation.
5) And never, never, never lie: otherwise, stakeholders' attitudes will explode when they perceive in the organization's response any hint of lying, deceiving, misleading or even confusion and hesitation.[134]

A combination of all five elements may act as a shield against an overheated public opinion.

A short-term response taking into account these five elements tends to be enough to prove that the institution sincerely regrets what has happened. This is sufficient for its stakeholders to believe that it has learned its lesson and is ready to once again become the player it has always been within its social environment. Apologizing (a clear and explicit recognition of responsibilities and a public request for forgiveness) is indispensable to surmount a scandal. As

---

[134] An example of this type of crisis is the Australian Wheat Board scandal, which originated in acts of bribery. Top level civil servants in the Saddam Hussein regime were bought off and acquired wheat at a very favorable price from Australian suppliers and in clear violation of the UN-imposed sanctions. As Grebe points out, a false response to a scandal may lead to a secondary or double crisis.

Coombs states, «The severe damage of a corporate scandal requires some form of atonement from the organization. The response should therefore seek to soothe the public, not antagonize them further.»

What we should never do is to try, on the contrary, to examine the causes of the issue from a cold, scientific perspective, making comparisons with other episodes that were more or less similar, etc. If we were to act in that way, we would be lighting a match right beside the proverbial gas leak.

In the long term, the only valid response to a corporate scandal is to completely transform the organization: reconstruct it, addressing the causes that provoked the scandal and carrying out any internal reforms that may be required. That is why some authors have used the expression "redemptive organizations," with obvious religious connotations.

Corporate scandals cannot be managed superficially: management cannot simply attempt to limit or avoid their responsibility. As we will see in the following chapter, the reforms must reach the deepest roots of the problem.

Communication experiences in emergencies

An emergency due to a disaster may be defined with Palttala as «a situation that threatens to harm life and health or the environment, for which public authorities and non-governmental organizations are the main responders, because of its magnitude and severe consequences.»

In chapter 2, we differentiated crises from emergencies, underlining the technical aspects of an emergency and emphasizing that the most critical step in those situations is to address the immediate problem. In a rural fire, for instance, the first step is to contain the blaze, evacuate those in jeopardy, set up traffic detours, etc. As Barbara Reynolds, of the Center for Disease Control (USA) puts it, «90% of crisis response is communications.»

Public authorities are often afraid of causing panic, a concern that may lead them to withholding information. However, if information is made available, people can make better-informed choices.

Unfortunately, in large emergencies what is frequently missing is.... communication. Palttala and his team have found that, for different reasons, communication is not a relevant part of emergency management even in the case of disasters. The communicators' role is understood differently in the organizations involved in the emergency response and is limited to setting up and managing the information channels, or including a media strategy and assessment measures. Secondly, the various organizations involved tend to be very reluctant to share information, so there are numerous gaps in the information flow. Third, their cooperation policies determine how to integrate information, but these policies do not cover common operational principles, which are the basis for deciding what information should be shared and what should not. These divergences are quite frequent, especially when cooperation is between international and national organizations, or between military and civil organizations. Fourthly, very rarely is there any assessment or evaluation after the crisis, and if there is, the results are not shared or discussed by the various participating organizations.

Crisis management and communication principles and general practices are fully applicable in emergencies. Let us add a few more specific suggestions:

As always, the first step is prevention. As anticipated when dealing with risk communication, prudence recommends that communities affected by the danger should be told about its nature and the signs leading us to believe that it is imminent, in order for them to become familiarized with self-protection measures. Familiarity lessens uncertainty in a crisis, while new and so far unexperienced threats are more frightening. Also, freely and consciously taken risks may be perceived as less harmful than those which are out of people's own control.

These preventive tasks involve listening to citizens' concerns and needs before the crisis occurs. Many past experiences show that trying to do this after the crisis will run into insurmountable problems, principally because of a mistrusting environment.

It is also useful to harmonize response strategies and communication channels among those institutions that normally work closely together in emergencies: police, firefighters, civil defense,

Red Cross, etc.; and in the communication training that is given to emergency workers.

In emergencies, the tone and approach of everybody involved is vital. As Palttala recommends,

> Building trust requires not just professional expertise to rescue people and mitigate harmful consequences, but also openness and empathy, explaining decisions and alternatives. Crisis messages should tell people what can and cannot be done by the authorities, what people can and cannot do for themselves, and where to get more information about the crisis event.

These comprehensible messages should contain data about what has happened, as well as perspectives of action (what can be done?), and significance (what does it mean to you?).

In respect to the attention given to the media during a disaster, the communications department staff should be present in the emergency coordination center but also at the disaster site itself. Reporters need to hear their comments from the site itself, and not from someone working in an office hundreds of miles from where the problem lies. Being on site is where they can give assistance: providing access to people to be interviewed, getting permission to film, and contributing information and comment that help reporters to understand the scope of the catastrophe.

In addition, media relations face another difficult challenge: when the crisis is over (and sometimes even earlier), the "blame game" starts. Reporters will either accuse the organization of being responsible for the disaster or they will claim that it has been too slow in its response or ineffective in its rescue and emergency support. Knowing this in advance is critical in order to avoid being taken by surprise and to be able to respond prudently.

Lastly, even though in an emergency the technical aspects are paramount, communication tasks are also crucial for the emergency to be resolved satisfactorily. What happened in 2010 in Europe in response to ash emitted by a volcano in Iceland could be a helpful example.

In spring 2010, a volcano poetically named Eyjafjallajökull erupted, creating clouds of ash that blocked practically all European air traffic for two weeks. The initial European reaction was immediate: it closed off its air space following the protocols as established by the International Civil Association Organization, which had a contingency plan in case of a volcano erupting. It was a technical decision that was made immediately in accordance with the pre-approved rules and based on the principle that security is the prime consideration above any other.

Nonetheless, as the days went by and the technical criteria continued to indicate that half of Europe was unsafe for flying, discrepancies began to appear: the airlines were the first to raise their voice, as they were losing money hand over fist, and arguments were presented which called into question the scientific lines of thought and the operational measures within the contingency plan.

When the blanket closure crept into its second week without any sign of relenting, the whole dynamic of this specific crisis changed significantly, not only due to the pressure being exerted by the airlines but also to the overall blockage of the economy by the airspace closure. There were appeals for a change in the technical plan to introduce criteria that were much more politically oriented. The first countries that decided to change their strategies were the UK and Ireland, which set up a series of flight zones depending on the scale of risk. Immediately after that, the whole Eurozone decided to split its airspace into three zones, depending upon the degree of pollution caused by volcanic ash.

This crisis taught us several lessons: the first is that pre-defined plans are extremely useful in cases which are technically very complex and which cover several environments, because they indicate the measures that must be implemented immediately to protect public security and safety. At the same time, plans that are based on purely rational technical criteria are insufficient if the crisis is prolonged over time: political, social, etc. criteria must be incorporated due to the complexity of the scenario.

The second is that crises and risk management typically take place under uncertain and ambiguous conditions. In these situations, as Christensen and his team state, "the prevalence of rational choices characterized by clear, stable, and consistent goals, a fair understanding of available goals and means, and an apparent center of authority and power, is not realistic. [...] In these situations, flexible political and administrative coordination may be a reasonable alternative to action based on calculated planning."

In a nutshell: crises are managerial problems, not technical issues; and therefore they should not be left solely in the hands of technical people. Large emergencies have such a wide range that they automatically involve the authorities. In such situations, public leaders have to address three separate challenges: manage the operational response to the crisis, clearly communicate with their stakeholders, and resolve the political in-fighting generated by the operational response to the crisis. Bear in mind that of these three elements, only the first is technical in nature and so can be delegated to others.

How to apologize and be forgiven

Let's finish this chapter by considering best practices in corporate apologies, which in many crises are an indispensable step in the corporate response and mark the beginning of a post-crisis recovery.

As we have all experienced firsthand, it is not easy to ask for forgiveness. If it were, Adam and Eve would have apologized, and now we wouldn't be bald, fat and ugly. But it just isn't. It means getting embarrassed, putting yourself at someone else's mercy, and accepting a punishment. That's why we resist and look for excuses: I'm not entirely sure it was *only* my fault, it was almost *impossible* to avoid it, deep down he provoked me, etc.

However, it is essential to learn to ask for forgiveness, because it is good for those who ask for forgiveness even more than for those who receive our excuses. Moreover, because mistakes are inevitable, authentic forgiveness not only resets the marker to zero, but improves the relationship with those we have offended. In that sense, asking for forgiveness is almost as good as preventing an error.

Apology aims to obtain forgiveness from those hurt by our improper behavior. In that sense, proof of its effectiveness is whether it achieves that goal. If we are not forgiven, we should better think that there is something more to be said or to be done.

That is why it is so important, when asking for forgiveness, to listen, to learn if the shot was on target or missed, by insufficiency or by excess. If this were the case, it would be better to rephrase the request quickly and in the right way, so the episode is closed as soon as possible.[135]

If you're going to apologize, do it right away - as soon as you realize you have some responsibility in what happened. If your *stakeholders are right there in front of you*, don't wait to know the chapter and verse of everything that happened, but apologize immediately. The speed of apology is a manifestation of sincerity: if it takes time, people think we have been forced to do it, or that we have done it out of interest.[136]

---

[135] In 2009, Amazon discovered that it had mistakenly sold two George Orwell books without the corresponding rights. It deleted the books from the server, refunded the money received, and then informed customers what had happened. It was a perfectly legal decision, outlined in the Kindle User Agreement. However, it violated user expectations, and many of them demanded explanations. An official Amazon spokesperson then intervened, explaining the facts again. However, the lack of any apology and his distant and cold tone produced rejection. Therefore, the following week, the CEO of Amazon apologized in these terms: «This is an apology for the way we previously handled illegally sold copies of 1984 and other novels on Kindle. Our "solution" to the problem was stupid, thoughtless, and painfully out of line with our principles. It is wholly self-inflicted, and we deserve the criticism we've received. We will use the scar tissue from this painful mistake to help make better decisions going forward, ones that match our mission. With deep apology to our customers, Jeff Bezos, Founder & CEO».

[136] At the 2017 Academy Awards (the Oscars) ceremony in Los Angeles, one of the Pwc partners in charge of the results gave the presenter a wrong card, which announced that the award for best picture was going to the wrong movie. According to Pedowitz, there were two delays: the first was because the people responsible took several minutes to realize their mistake and correct it, by which time the acceptance speeches of the producers had already begun. The second and more serious was that Pwc's public response came a day later. It was a serious mistake not to immediately correct that blunder committed live on a global stage in front of hundreds of millions of people watching on tv or on the social media, and even more so, in front of the producers and actors who suffered the error. If any of the Pwc partners responsible for the process, or any other representative of the firm had taken the stage and apologized gently and humorously for their personal mistake, they would have won the goodwill of the audience, the damage would have diminished, and the noise would have lasted less time. As is often

Occasionally we hear a manager saying, after a mistake: «At the time I thought I was making the right decision, but now I see it the way others saw it, and I understand why people got angry and frustrated. I'm so sorry I caused that anger, which I certainly didn't mean to.» Such a phrase (which looks as if it came from a good lawyer's pen) is not an acceptable request for forgiveness, because no mistake is acknowledged nor request for forgiveness made. It's just an elegant way to try to get out of trouble without taking any blame.

Excuses must be rooted in the local culture, in the concrete mindset of the participants and audiences to which they are addressed. Not all cultures value requests for forgiveness the same way. Numerous studies show notable differences between Eastern and Western cultures: for example, Chinese sensitivity is different from European, and a bad response is worse than the absence of an answer: «Eastern cultures are more tolerant to an attitude of silence and reserve to accusation», says Lee. Other studies show that there are also differences between Central and Northern Europe from the south and west of the continent.

To summarize, we could say that a good request for forgiveness has the following elements:

- An expression of personal repentance (I'm *sorry*). Words and gestures have to say it. As always, nonverbal language is much more effective than verbal language. You have to do it in person, if possible.
- A specific explanation of what went wrong (*I apologize because I, we...*). Saying "mistakes were made" is not an apology, but a simple explanation, unable to turn the page. An apology is well done when the offended nod to the description of the facts.
- A recognition of responsibility (*it was my, our fault*). We ask forgiveness when we have done something wrong, willingly or unwillingly. Expressions such as "I'm sorry you felt offended"

---

the case in crises, this episode also revealed the true character of the people involved. For example, La La Land producer Justin Horowitz navigated the chaos in style. His serenity, in explaining the situation, easing the uncomfortable tension and confidently but humbly announcing that he would wait on stage until the winners arrived to personally present them with the award, made him the MVP of the night.

are not real apologies, because they dodge responsibility and pass it on to the other. They are perceived as thinking, "I haven't done anything special, but you're so sensitive..." The more accountability is shown, the easier it is to forgive, whereas if we try to diminish it with excuses and explanations, we are perceived as denying that we feel responsible.

- A statement of repentance *(I will change whatever is necessary so that it never happens again)*. Deeds are more important than words. My behavior is what really shows that I'm sorry.
- An acceptance of penance *(I accept the penalty, if any)*. Let us remember a fundamental principle: punishment is an inseparable part of justice. Only the victim can freely decide not to apply a penalty. Culprits cannot absolve themselves.
- An offer of repair *(so I will compensate for the damages and restore the situation to the original state, if possible)*. It is proof that we are really responsible (other than guilty: reparation is not a punishment but an obligation).
- A commitment to follow up on the reform plan *(I will keep you posted of how the changes proceed)*. It's a manifestation of availability.
- Finally, a request for forgiveness *(will you forgive me?)*. We cannot forget that forgiveness is a gift from the offended, which depends only on their generosity. Therefore, we must avoid speaking with arrogance, like demanding to turn the page. On the contrary, forgiveness is saying sorry as many times as necessary, until the victim says it is enough.

The extent of each point depends on the circumstances of the case, but in general, the shorter and more direct, the better.

Learning how to ask for forgiveness sincerely and honestly requires empathy and trial and error. An organization in which it is practiced frequently shows a healthy corporate culture, in which bonds between people and trust are strong.

The Story: Shareholders said, enough is enough[137]

In late 2015 and early 2016, pharmaceutical and agribusiness industries went through several M&A because it was considered that only giants could survive on a globalized stage. Dow Chemical and DuPont, the two largest chemical groups in the U.S., announced their merger.

In this context, the German company Bayer tried to acquire Syngenta, but it failed. ChemChina, China's state-owned chemical company bettered its offer.

Fearing to become the target of an acquisition, at the end of 2016 Bayer signed a UD$ 63B acquisition agreement with Monsanto, which was implemented in mid-2018. Monsanto, one of the world's leading manufacturers of genetically modified seeds, produces Roundup, the herbicide used by most farmers in the United States, known as "the Weed Killer."

The acquisition was a poisoned candy. In August 2018, just a few months after the merger was completed, a court determined that the herbicide caused cancer, and ordered Monsanto to pay US$ 289M ($39M in compensation and $250M in punitive damages).

In January 2019, the French authorities banned Bayer from selling Roundup in France. In March 2019, another lawsuit ended in a conviction to pay US$ 80M. In April 2019, the supermarket chain Costco removed Roundup from its shelves. In May 2019, a jury in Oakland, California, ruled that Monsanto had to pay a billion dollars to a couple who fell ill.

Finally, in June 2019, Bayer ran an ad saying, «We've heard and learned. From today we will raise the bar.» The company announced a €5B investment in Research and Development for alternatives to herbicides. The company also reported that it would set up a special committee to address its legal problems due to numerous pending lawsuits.

What had happened? The crisis had reduced Bayer's market value by about € 5B: now the company was worth less than before acquiring Monsanto. Dividends per share decreased from 8.29 in

---

[137] Episode documented by Ileo Mbanianga.

2017 to 1.80 in 2018. The acquisition of Monsanto one of the worst operations in the history of German corporate finance. Its CEO, who had been with the company for more than 30 years, became the first executive chair of the German company to lose a vote of confidence in the assembly. Shareholders began asking the company to separate the agrifood business from the pharmaceutical sector. They had gotten tired of waiting to see what was going on and forced management to change strategy.**Error! Bookmark not defined.**

CHAPTER TEN

The post-crisis period

The crisis is over. The emergency has been resolved, the activity of the organization has resumed, the employees and managers have returned to normal work, the media are no longer giving us their full attention. A few threads remain: compensating the victims, appealing the fines, preparing the defense against legal complaints, etc., but that will take time and does not halt the activity of the management.

We would like nothing more than to turn the page as soon as possible, and be back to business and profits.

Well, we can't. Trying to forget what happened is a legitimate wish, but it's wrong, at least until we have learned everything there is to learn from what happened and from our behavior during the crisis.

Why? Because the past crisis has left the institution more vulnerable, and a second crisis is not only possible, but would be much more damaging. Looking the other way now would prevent us from preventing a relapse, which is usually more serious than the first time we got sick.

It is often said that something can be learned from any crisis, but this goal is not always achieved. There are institutions that do not learn from a crisis and make serious mistakes again. The reverse situation is also possible: some companies emerge successfully from a crisis, but do not learn its lessons (sometimes things go well by sheer chance, in the same way that sometimes things go wrong even if things are done well), and the managers mistakenly think that they are already prepared for any crisis.[138] Finally, there are intelligent and prudent institutions that have managed to learn from the crises suffered by others, and, by taking the right decisions, have successfully avoided them.[139]

For this reason, the post-crisis period is a time that must be approached with rigor and method. Evaluation is a fundamental part of any planning, and it should not be done only at the end but in each of its parts. Each part of a project should include an element of control, to ensure that the objectives have been achieved and, if necessary, the appropriate changes should be introduced without waiting for their implementation to be completed.

The same is true after a crisis. Plans and actions are developed dynamically, adapting to changes in attitudes and behaviors of the stakeholders. Do not wait for the post-crisis period to make improvements to the plan: do it as soon as you discover them. For this reason, we have already studied some evaluative elements in the previous chapters: analysis of the environment, predisposition to active listening, monitoring, drills and simulations to check the plan, etc.

The only issue pending is the general assessment at the end of the crisis, and the guidelines for planning the post-crisis period. The following pages are devoted to these two topics.

---

[138] According to Mitroff & Anagnos, Johnson & Johnson masterfully managed the Tylenol crisis in 1982 (one of the historical cases of crisis communication) but later on, its response to minor problems throughout the 1990s was less than exemplary.

[139] in the 90's, Nike suffered several boycotts due to the accusation that they had been using under-aged workers in Southeast Asia, until they finally changed their internal outsourcing policies with suppliers from outside the United States. Adidas and Reebok – who were in exactly the same situation – didn't wait to introduce the same changes before coming under attack by these activists.

Declaring the end of the crisis

One of the defining signs of a crisis is that it is difficult to decide exactly when it has concluded: the line marking the end is vague and blurred, and may not even be the same for all the various stakeholders. For instance, clients may feel that this critical situation is over once the organization has implemented measures to protect them, but if the staff are aware that the problems have not yet been fully resolved and do not share their clients' point of view, then there are still steps to be taken before we close it and say that the crisis is over.

In that sense, Coleman prescribes that it is not the time to initiate public recovery if victims are still suffering damage or new victims continue to appear; if the crisis is not under control, but continues to grow; if operational normality has not been returned to within the organization; or if the climate of public opinion does not allow it, because they are still thinking about the present and not yet about the future.

Looking at it from another angle, the severity of a crisis may also be measured by the length of time that it has lasted: the sooner it is finished, the lesser the ensuing damage will be and the easier recovery will. Thus, we should know when we can *declare the crisis to be finished* in order to remove all the special measures that had been implemented and return to our normal operations.

I would like to emphasize this active term "closing" because it is often hard to understand when the crisis is finished. It is the corporation's task to publicly and clearly announce that the crisis is over and the situation that had initially triggered it has been resolved. Everyone knows that good news is usually less newsworthy; that type of news is always placed on page 15, never on the front page. Therefore, communicating it effectively is even more necessary. On the other hand, there is always the risk that our stakeholders have only heard about the problem and not the solutions that have been implemented. If that is the case, personnel and other stakeholders may think they still are under the effects of a crisis, and that will hinder renewal initiatives and new projects.

At the present time, this is even more true because of social media. On the internet, anything that has happened in the past is still present from the very instant that someone starts a search: the results are not going to be chronological but depend more on the number of visits to the site. This means that the items that appear first are not necessarily the ones that best reflect the truth or the most up-to-date situation. Therefore, we must declare a crisis to be finished and publicize the news that it is over as much as we can.

The moment must be chosen with care: it cannot be too soon, when the crisis has not really ended; nor can it be too late, when people have already forgotten about it.

The ending of a crisis may be communicated in several different ways, according to the type of crisis in question and the degree of awareness prevalent among our various stakeholders. If, for example, it was related to a public health or safety issue, it should have the same degree of publicity which the announcement of the problem had at the very beginning. In some cases, the managing director may communicate it in an op-ed, an interview or even through an advertising campaign underlining the company's strong commitment to their consumers and the internal reforms implemented by the company.[140]

This step must be taken, not because these campaigns will convince those who have felt offended (an ad can hardly change ingrained perceptions based on personal experiences), but because they will be effective for those people who really support the institution: they are eager to see how the organization is "fighting back" rather than giving in. As we explained in detail in the chapter referring to controversies, you have to communicate in concentric circles, starting with your own choir.

The decision to declare that the crisis is officially over should not emphasize the problems that have taken place. Its purpose is to

---

[140] Pepsi Cola did this in their famous syringe scare case. In 1993, a woman took them to court for having found a syringe inside a can of Pepsi that she had just bought. Soon afterwards, several other cases appeared in numerous places around the United States. Even though Pepsi proved time after time that it was impossible, the crisis was not over until an in-store security camera caught a person secretly trying to put something into a can. This graphic image turned the whole crisis around. In order to declare that the crisis was over, the company placed a dramatic announcement: "Pepsi is pleased to announce… nothing," were the only words in the advertisements that were placed in hundreds of newspapers all over the United States.

publicly certify that any shadow of doubt that was hanging over the company no longer exists. Everyone who is aware of the situation is going to perfectly understand what we are talking about and those who did not know anything about it will not realize that there was ever any bad news.

So more than a public declaration that the crisis is over, there are many cases in which it will be advantageous to use a symbolic communication: in other words, clearly express that the problem has been resolved without having to say so literally. For instance, you might organize some sort of event to present a project in the name of the two parties who were in conflict earlier on.

Remember also that crises should be understood as both problems and opportunities. The news that a problem has been properly resolved is a golden opportunity to reestablish the corporate reputation in the situation created by the new circumstances.

Measuring the overall effects caused by a crisis

Once a crisis has actually finished, companies should devote some time to analyze in depth what effects the crisis has had on the organization as a whole.

The subjective element

Often the first thing you want to assess is the objective damage to the organization: economic losses, decline in sales and market share, additional costs for more expensive financing, etc.

My advice is start with the subjective element: with the people. The staff will be physically and emotionally exhausted. These have been very intense days, weeks or months from all points of view, with very long days and a roller coaster of emotions. Physical collapse and depressions are not exceptional.

Furthermore, the work environment may have become rarefied. Some will be demoralized, with a loss of commitment and internal cohesion. The blame game will have left its mark, and there may be contained anger against the guilty and against those responsible, either individuals or entire teams. "*They* have gotten us into this," is thought and even openly said. And all this happens when we most need people's energies, commitment and creativity.

My first tip is to plan your break. Now that you are starting over, it's easier than when the machines are at full speed: organize a schedule so that people can rest by shifts (if you can't make it a week, try at least some looooong weekends). Investing in your people is always profitable.

It is also necessary, as we saw previously, to organize the mourning duel, if there were victims, both corporate and personal. Pain and sorrow have their times, and you have to know how to adjust to them with flexibility.

The internal audit

The first step to learn is to look inwards. Learning from one's own mistakes goes beyond generic self-criticism. You have to objectify what happened. «It is extremely important to learn from experience, and that can only be achieved with a careful and detailed analysis of what happened, how and why», says O'Rourke. Every crisis is a lesson from which something can be learned. You have to learn from all mistakes: it is painful, but very effective in the long run. [141]

It is not superfluous to insist on the need to strive to learn from experience, because in many organizations the prevailing wisdom opposes reviewing past events, especially if they have been negative or senior managers have been implicated. But the contrary

---

[141] An example from my beloved Italy: on hearing about the power outage that happened in the New York City on August 14 and 15, 2003, the national power company's chairperson stated that «a similar power outage in Italy is practically impossible because the quality of our own power network is much greater.» Unfortunately, this was proven to be untrue a mere 43 days later: on September 28, Italy had a major power outage. However, Rome was able to learn its lesson: after what had happened in New York City due to the outage, the Rome City Hall had had a meeting on September 2, to prepare a contingency plan that would prevent the Italian capital from becoming totally paralyzed due to a lack of electricity. This plan saved the whole city from being severely affected by the power outage. The Mayor, Walter Veltroni, said afterwards, «If many things did work properly last night, it was because of that meeting on September 2.»

is true: learning from experience will prompt executives to improve their skills. In fact, well-run organizations learn from crises.

Unfortunately, a report on crisis communication in Spain published a few years ago indicated that crisis committees met to analyze the crisis a posteriori in only 43.2% of the companies surveyed, and the percentage of those who put into writing what they had learned was even lower: 26.3%.

This global balance sheet of the crisis (damages suffered and missed opportunities) must be *limited to describing the facts*. It examines what happened, what worked well and what did not, what the impact of the crisis was on the relationship between the institution and its stakeholders in the short, medium and long term; this report will also foresee that certain negative consequences may appear much later. At this moment, the facts and their causes are of interest, not how to avoid something similar in the future. This audit is about *knowing the real causes and consequences of the problem*.

The report is the starting point to face the future, and that is why consensus must be reached on this matter. Otherwise, if the effects of the crisis are mixed with proposals for change, those who do not share the proposals could reject the baseline data to defend their personal position.

Some authors recommend that the evaluation be done promptly, no later than five days after the crisis has been overcome. Otherwise, overall impressions tend to evaporate.

The method is simple: prepare an online (but confidential) questionnaire, and ask managers and employees to describe their experiences in writing in the most objective way possible, making it clear that the aim is to evaluate the processes, not the people. A person or a team is then commissioned to write the final or forensic report. It can be commissioned from an external party, with a commitment to confidentiality, especially if advanced technical knowledge is required (in the event of a cyber-attack, accounting forgery, industrial failure, etc.).

These accounts of the crises suffered are an invaluable instrument for the future of the organization. Archiving written reports of these episodes will provide those who come afterwards a useful point of support should the crisis reoccur years later and none of those who intervened at the time work at the institution any longer. For these reports to achieve their objective, they should be written for people who were not witnesses to the events, and therefore they must provide contextual data so that the situations are well understood.

The external audit

The next step is to look beyond the walls of your own institution. Listening to your stakeholders is a fundamental aspect of the immediate post-crisis period.

It is convenient not only to provide the public with the information they ask for, but above all to take the time to listen to their concerns and answer their questions. These listening sessions offer the institution an opportunity to clarify grey areas, explain what happened, apologize, and reduce the distances between the parties.

Crises create confusion, and in the end it is more than likely that the fundamental data will not remain clear in the memory of the public. It is the institution's task to give the official interpretation of the facts.

On the other hand, listening to the public in live debate is a great opportunity for institutional learning and should not be rejected, even if in the process they give us a piece of their minds. As Ulmer, Sellnow & Seeger say,

> In training sessions, we often explain how organizations should keep their friendly stakeholders close and their disgruntled stakeholders even closer. However, many organizations feel compelled to keep their unhappy stakeholders at a distance and only communicate with and listen to stakeholders with whom they agree. This, in our opinion, is a mistake.

Also, you have to dare to measure. It is convenient to quantify and translate the effects into figures and data: how many messages have been received, and of what type (complaints, solidarity, concern, congratulations); what has the informative coverage of the media been like; what do employees think about it, etc. Only through reliable factual information can the status of the different stakeholders be known.

One of the most serious effects of a crisis is that it ends up being obsessive. The opinions, judgments, feelings and concerns expressed by different stakeholders, sometimes expressed bitterly and aggressively (demonstrations and protests, boycotts on social networks, insulting letters and even anonymous threats) and through the media, could prevent the institution from talking about something not crisis-related. Stakeholders seem fixated and monothematic, and the institution cannot disconnect from the problem or talk about other things... This listening will allow us to talk about institutional renewal, an unavoidable transit to close the crisis.

The internet has introduced new factors that play a role in all post-crisis situations. The overall effects of crises last much longer nowadays than before. Organizations have to accept the fact that it is virtually impossible to delete all negative postings on the internet, even though the crisis has been over for years. The internet perpetuates bad news. Understanding crises as "one single day of bad news" is when the only media were the mainstream media. Nowadays, bad news may be seen and revisited by anyone and forever. So an evaluation to define and confirm the solution of the crisis is much more important than ever before.

Plans of reform

Once we have the forensic report specifying what happened with all the gory details, the company must determine what changes must be made to avoid a recurrence and to eliminate vulnerabilities.

The reform plan comes after the external audit because public perceptions will give us many clues about what we need to change, how much time we have to change, and how to change. As a wise and holy Englishman, John Henry Newman, once said, «what others say about me teaches me a lot about myself.»

Certainly, the general lines of the reform may be clear in advance: in fact, we have already communicated them in the midst of the crisis, as a fundamental part of our response. I am referring to the small print of these changes and how to implement them.

This is the right moment to make specific proposals on how we should act from now on. These proposals are debatable: an error can be eliminated in more than one way. That is why it is important to separate this phase from the forensic report, to avoid the proposals being inseparably associated with facts.

Managers and staff must also contribute to this process: on many occasions, no one knows the facilities and processes better than they do. Not listening to them is equivalent to ignoring how much they can collaborate (and also inciting a lack of commitment).

It is also useful to bring in experts from each sector, because in this way the crisis becomes an opportunity for a qualitative leap for the organization. Resistance to change is much lower after a crisis: take advantage of it.

This new phase in the life of the organization must be faced with a constructive spirit. Furthermore, if the recovery strategy is correct, in a few months the organization may have recovered all the lost ground and even improved its previous situation. For this reason, not a few organizations have taken advantage of a crisis to introduce more or less profound changes, since crises produce the awareness that it is necessary to change something (or many things); they provide an opportunity to break the inertia of those who think, or, as they say in Italy, *squadra che vince non si cambia*. For this reason, some managers provoke a crisis in a controlled way, so that they can guide the reform of the organization.

Along with the reform plan, a new risk analysis will also have to be carried out.[142] Crises displace organizations in their environment, and therefore the risks are different, or they may at least have changed in degree.

The next normality

Once a crisis has hit an organization, *nothing will ever be the same as it was before*. This is the case whether or not the organization is responsible for the crisis. For instance, after a terrorist at-

---

[142] In 2003, the SARS epidemic (another coronavirus) showed the vulnerability of major sporting events. Organizers of the Wimbledon tennis tournament decided to take out an insurance policy costing 1.5 million pounds a year to cover themselves in the event of an epidemic. When Covid-19 arrived, the organizers received 114 million.

tack has taken place, the organization is certainly not the same, nor does it go about its daily activities or organize events in the same easy-going way as it had always done before. But, if the crisis is an ethically based issue, there is an even greater need for the organization to be renewed, to go back to its original principles and to fully recover any of its basic values that may have been lost along the way.

Borrowing a term coined to describe the consequences of the 2008 financial crisis (and which has become widespread thanks to the coronavirus), it could be said that from now on there is "a new normal". Other experts prefer to use "the next normal", in order to underline the accelerated changes in our world.

Both expressions are very appropriate in my view: you have to unlearn a number of habits and learn to do things in a new way. In other words, after a crisis it is not enough to implement a reform plan, as if it were a functional change: as if we were moving from one headquarters to another. No, the corporate culture changes. Simply "learning from the crisis" is not enough; *a full breakaway from the past is always required.*

The damage to the company's name could be so irreparable that its owners even have to change it.[143] But that would just be cosmetics, not a profound transformation.

At the end of the day, more than recovery, perhaps we should be talking about renewal, understood as «a fresh, determined and frontal approach to work in the period in which an organization

---

[143] In 2013, the so-called Horse-gate crisis hit the whole European food trade. In note 86 we summarized the corporate response by Findus, one of the players involved, who acted responsibly with transparency and in full cooperation with the authorities. On the other hand, the French meat processing company Spanghero did the opposite: when the laboratory test results showed that they were one of the food chain suppliers using horse meat instead of beef, its chairperson denied all accusations and threatened legal action against those accusing them; one month later, new tests showed that they were not only using horse meat but also a forbidden process on sheep; they then argued logistical mistakes; finally the company recognized its wrongdoings because of price pressure from consumers. Its chairperson was dismissed, and the company was sold and changed its name: "Spanghero" had appeared so many times in the media associated to the Meat mafia fraud that the new owner had no other choice than change it and start over.

emerges after a crisis», suggest Ulmer, Sellnow & Seeger. The way to do this is to take advantage of the global analysis of the crisis, described in the previous section, and start from what happened: what controls failed, what distorted values inspired the decisions, what procedures have been shown to be ineffective, etc. .; and above all, what changed outside.

Knowing what happened and why is the best way to convince yourself that you have to change. Any serious change begins by persuading yourself of its need. Nystrom & Starbuck say:

> It is very rare for staff to change their values and customs solely because others are better or more effective. They are aware that both institutional values and customs come from previous rational decisions and experiences of success, and therefore it should be clear to them that those values and experiences were seriously distorted, before thinking that they would have to change them.

In this phase, it is interesting to discover why danger signals are not heeded. It can be done in various ways. Veil has developed The Mindful Learning Model, a method that helps organizations recognize danger signs and act to prevent errors and crises. It is about overcoming the obstacle to learning represented by routine and about limiting the negative effects of confidence in expectations. This method is beneficial because it is preventive in nature: much of what is learned in a crisis is concentrated in the post-crisis moment, says Veil, while the conscious learning model studies the barriers to improvement in the period before the crisis, and draws conclusions about the way organizations perceive and manage danger signals.[144]

---

[144] The Brazilian mining company Vale S.A. it is the world's largest producer of iron and nickel ore; it also produces manganese, ferroalloys, copper, bauxite, potash, kaolin, and cobalt. On November 5, 2015, an iron ore dam in Mariana, Minas Gerais, suffered a catastrophic failure, and floods destroyed the village of Bento Rodrigues, killing 19 people. The Mariana disaster is considered the worst environmental disaster in the history of Brazil: around 60 million cubic meters of iron waste flowed into the Rio Doce, causing toxic flows of brown mud that contaminated the river and the beaches of the river mouth when they

Post-crisis reconciliation

Internal reform, compensation and apologies are the first steps in the renewal process. The objective of this task in the period following the crisis is not to restore its image, but to renew the organization from within. We have to act from the inside outwards, and not the other way around.

Then comes the recovery of public confidence, which looks a lot like reconciliation. Having put our house in order is not enough; it is necessary to face the consequences of what happened in the perceptions of the stakeholders. The crisis could have included «very serious behaviors, such as fraud, deception, incompetence or exploitation of others – says Gillespie – difficult to repair». In other cases, the fault may have been less, but the damages suffered by victims make it costly to turn over the page. In these circumstances, the prevailing climate is one of mistrust, which Gillespie & Dietz describe as the «forced reaction of distance to a distorted behavior on the part of a third party», and therefore the objective of the organization must be to show «competence, benevolence and integrity», which are the foundations of trust.

This way of behaving, when the wound is still open, is vital. What happened hurts, but how the institution reacted hurts too. If the facts or their impact were denied, the state of justice with due reparation has not been recovered or if the public has not been

---

reached the Atlantic Ocean seventeen days later. The disaster created a humanitarian crisis: hundreds of people were displaced, and the cities along the Doce River suffered from water shortages. Four years later, on January 25, 2019, another Vale dam collapsed, nine kilometers east of Brumadinho. The dam released a mass of mud that advanced on houses in a rural area near the city. Two days later, a second dam collapsed as well. At least 214 people died as a result of the collapse, and 91 disappeared. While the 2015 disaster unleashed about five times more mining waste, the rupture of the Brumadinho dam was much more deadly. The impact of this catastrophe on Vale was enormous: compensation, stock depreciation, litigation and fines, etc. However, the company's response to the emergency was "by the book", applying the best crisis management practices in all s aspects. They learned from the previous accident, and at least public attention was focused on how to recover, not on analyzing how the company had handled the crisis.

listened to after the crisis, reconciliation will be much more difficult.

Other factors also influence this gradual process, explains
Tomlinson: the desire on the part of the public to reconcile; the
nature of the relationship between the organization and its stakeholders; and the enormity of the violation committed.

That is to say, there will be a predisposition to reconciliation if
the union between the parties was especially strong for emotional
reasons or because of shared values and objectives, or if both stood
to lose a lot if a reconciliation did not occur, says Boyatzis. These
are elements to be considered, as they can favor or hinder the repair of trust.

Let's remember what we said when talking about consensus:
trust is «the intention to accept one's own vulnerability based on
positive expectations about the other's behavior», say Mayer, Davis,
& Schoorman. In essence, the public has to change its attitude,
something that is possible only because it wishes to, it cannot be
forced to; and it is the consequence of a mixture of elements: of
what I have done to deserve their distrust, and of their desire to get
along again.

Among all the measures which we have looked at throughout
this book, the following activities are especially appropriate:

- Measure the lack of trust: it is necessary to define and evaluate
  in some way the trust that has been lost. As Schoorman says,
  knowing the most damaged element will give us clues about
  how to guide the recovery, focusing on where the transgression
  had the most impact.
- Accepting responsibility is a factor that promotes trust, if it is
  accompanied by a request for forgiveness when there was guilt
  and/or responsibility, or - as Kim points out - when the trust
  was based on competence, and the transgression showed negligence.
- Return to a situation of justice, because the damage has been
  repaired and the culprit has received a proportionate and fair
  sanction.
- Communicate appropriately: Talton has examined how the
  veracity of information is vital in regaining trust, and underlines the role of the quality of the information (the explanations given about what happened are adequate), honesty and

frankness when it comes to communicating, the integrity of the interlocutor, and the channels chosen (for example, "stakeholders are informed in person as soon as possible"). Ultimately, the public want to be able to look the organization's management in the eye, and evaluate what its leaders are made of, and «what they say has changed.»

Every reconciliation process, like any cure, has its own particular rhythm, and strengthening relationships is one important feature of the process. In this sense, the post-crisis moment is a great time for communication. It provides new opportunities to talk about the institution in a hopeful, forward-looking context.

I insist: the objective is not to improve the image of the institution, but to translate the renovation that has been carried out into concrete projects. Communicative content must be given to these projects, since the institution needs to change its image to be useful in the society in which it lives. In short: the measures taken to prevent new cases must be communicatively articulated, showing how the institution has changed. Otherwise, a decisive element will be lacking in overcoming a new crisis: i.e. stakeholders are aware of the changes that have been made.

For this reason, it is necessary to prepare and implement a specific communication plan through the usual instruments: advertising, events, sponsorship and patronage, promotions, etc.

For example, if in a country the figure of the trade union movement has suffered notable damage in public perception as a result of a series of scandals, the unions should study how to present the figure of the trade-unionist in a positive way, first of all to members and then to the rest of society, in a specific program which presents exemplary stories and significant achievements to people through television programs, comics, books, etc. The same could be said of a sports competition tainted by repeated cases of doping, etc.

Finally, it is worth remembering that reconciliation is easiest when a great deal of benevolence has been accumulated over time. That goodwill is obtained with a prolonged effort – in years – of integrity, a job well done, a spirit of service, credibility. Only then will the public give the institution the benefit of the doubt should a problem arise. As we said at the beginning of these considerations, the best way for an institution to protect itself against a new crisis is to improve its relations with each of its stakeholders.

The Story: Rise and Fall of a Myth

Proof that good journalism does not imply good communication was the BBC scandal involving Jimmy Saville (1926-2011), a true television personality. From the 1960s to the 1990s, he hosted two hit BBC programs: *Top of the Pops*, a popular music magazine show, and *Jim'll Fix It*, a program that granted wishes to children who wrote cards to him. Saville was also a philanthropist: he raised approximately £40 million for charity and gave away 90% of his personal wealth. Saville was knighted by Queen Elizabeth II in 1990. After retiring, he often appeared on British television as a special guest on prestigious shows.

After Saville's death in 2011, the BBC decided not to broadcast a program about allegations that the journalist had sexually abused children. Nevertheless, during the Christmas period, the BBC aired several nostalgic programs that paid tribute to its late star.

In 2012, rumors about Saville's child abuse gained momentum, and the following year, rival television network ITV ran a program documenting evidence of his crimes. Other media took the opportunity to return the criticism they had received from the BBC, which considered itself to be above good and evil, and paid a lot of attention to the stories. Soon afterwards, the police opened an investigation and more than 400 of Saville's alleged victims came forward. Today Saville is believed to be the most prolific pedophile in British history.

To make matters worse for the BBC, the police investigation uncovered three damning facts. First, countless cases of Saville's abuse took place on BBC premises, and it became apparent that many station employees were aware of what was happening and simply turned a blind eye. Second, Saville had clearly used the fame that the BBC had brought him and his position as the host of a popular children's show to gain access to his victims (and he would later use this position to force his victims into silence).

Third, Saville was not alone. Several well-known BBC stars were prosecuted for similar offenses and many were found guilty.

The independent investigation found that there was a serious problem with the culture at the BBC during the time of Saville's abuse: employees had their suspicions, but did not blow the whistle; the managers heard the rumors, but decided not to investigate *one of their own*, and together they generated a culture in which Saville's pedophilia was effectively tolerated and allowed.

As a result of these and other mistakes, several senior managers resigned, including the BBC CEO. After his departure, the new CEO rolled up his sleeves, ready to solve the scandal at whatever price, with determination and transparency.

He took responsibility for the mistakes made in the institution and began to rebuild trust with the public. He opened a thorough investigation, and reported his progress frequently, often as a featured story on his daily newscasts; neither he nor the other executives shunned difficult questions from the press, who challenged them severely. Many of these top executives were held accountable and eventually left their jobs. There was even a dedicated section on the BBC website, which remains open and active to this day, and documents the scandal in its entirety.

The crisis was also used as an opportunity to restructure the organization chart, information lines and risk mitigation measures. The new CEO launched other measures that promoted the effective participation of all employees and fought against bureaucratization. He addressed underlying issues and helped rebuild public trust.

In praise of prudence

Dangers ...

I would like to conclude these pages by calling for a good dose of healthy realism. First, not all crises can be avoided. Furthermore, even if what needs to be done is right, the crisis will damage the organization, because the corporate response does not always work. Human limitations, mistakes, ethical weaknesses, and the imperfection of language can make the results imperfect.

In a crisis, much of a manager's job is damage control, and something similar happens with communicators: as Dezenhall & Weber graphically describe, «crisis communicators are the Public Relations traumatologists. While other communicators may flirt with beautiful lies, our business is telling ugly truths».

Second, prudence will advise us not to apply the proposals in this book as if they were immutable truths stolen from Olympus. It is true that they are based on the repeated experience of many cases, but we will never reach certainty about the cause-effect relationship in many episodes. There is a key factor, which is somewhat embarrassing to mention, but it would be dishonest not to: luck. Sometimes you have done everything absolutely perfectly and things still turn out all wrong; and sometimes exactly the opposite, and somehow, out of the clear blue sky, everything is solved when you would have bet your last penny that there was no way out.

368 ◄ STEERING COMPANIES THROUGH STORMS AND CRISES

Third, relying on documented case studies to dictate good practice has a flaw. The problems that were solved well and did not end in a crisis have not left a trace, for a very simple reason: their protagonists did not leave a record of what happened. In some of the best-resolved crises of recent times, the guiding principle was discretion. And if we know nothing, we can learn nothing.

Fourth, serious problems take time to resolve, and solutions must be gradual. Mora says:

> Social trends have a complex life: they are born, grow, develop, change and die. Consequently, the communication of ideas has a lot to do with cultivation: sowing, watering, pruning, before harvesting (...) The opposite of this principle is the haste and short-termism that lead to impatience and often also to discouragement, because it is impossible to achieve entity objectives in short terms.

Processes of such long gestation are not resolved in years, months or weeks. Cardinal Ratzinger explained that our vision of the world usually follows a *masculine* paradigm, where the important thing is action, efficiency, programming and speed. And he concluded that «it is appropriate to give more space to a *feminine* paradigm, because women know that everything that has to do with life requires waiting and that in turn demands patience. The opposite of this principle is the haste and short-termism that leads to impatience and often also to discouragement, because it is impossible to achieve important objectives quickly.

Finally, in crises mistakes are inevitable. Each crisis manager could count hundreds of failed attempts and serious errors. This is normal, because whoever has made no mistakes has probably not done anything at all!

... and opportunities

Let's not look only at the dangers: let's also focus on the opportunities. A crisis is the best opportunity for change.

The need to innovate, to become more competitive, to provide a better service to the public, by adapting to their needs – always in constant evolution– and to discover its own vulnerabilities, oblige an institution to change. If society, the market, the family and people change, institutions must also change to adapt to new situations.

Therefore, it is not surprising that some use the momentum created by a crisis to overcome inertia. In crises the *onus probandi* changes: when managers are faced with a serious problem, the question will no longer be whether to change or not, but how to change.

Whoever manages a crisis is in an advantageous position to facilitate change, which begins by persuading the public of the benefits of change. So instead of meeting resistance the plan will be well received. More communication, less resistance. Cutlip, Center & Broom go so far as to say that «the essential mission of institutional communication is to help organizations adjust and adapt to changing contexts».

The danger may be to overreact, stretching the plant to make it grow faster. In this sense, certain attitudes will be essential: putting oneself in the shoes of others, knowing how to listen, not giving the impression of wanting to expose the fact that others are obtuse, indolent or outdated; not thinking of yourself as the only one with great new ideas; not pushing too hard, being patient, giving more time to people who require it, being open to new data that arises in the process of change.

In reality, change is guided, not managed, and has more to do with leadership than directing. Cotter & Cohen acknowledge:

> Leadership refers above all to the affective part of behavior. It consists of communication, vision, knowing how to form a strong team and create a sense of urgency. It has more to do with how you influence people's feelings and perceptions than with how you present information to them to change their mindset.

In addition, personal talents and certain dispositions of character are required: the serenity to remain calm and know how to withstand the pressure or stress of the crisis without losing equanimity; a constructive spirit, to highlight the positive aspects of each situation; a tendency to seek the opportunities that underlie all crisis situations; and knowing how to work in a team, actively seeking the advice of others. No one is perfect or self-sufficient. We need help. However, says Ariño,

There are many people, especially senior managers, who do not consider asking for help. They unconsciously think that it would imply that they are vulnerable, and that they are not in control of the situation. This is a mistake. Asking for help from our collaborators should be the most normal thing in the world. Asking for help is recognizing that management work is complex enough to require input from bosses and collaborators.

Role of the communicator in a crisis

Regardless of who is in charge of the CMT, the communications director is always part of it, since communication is an essential element in the resolution of the problem. As Fink says, «the most important factor for a communicator in times of crisis is to have immediate access to authority, and the second is that he himself has authority». This is confirmed in practice by the fact that in many institutions of all kinds the communications director has become a senior manager (and in many cases, one of the vice presidents) with direct access to the president.

Sometimes they are entrusted with the leadership of the CMT. Is this a good idea? It depends, as they say in Galicia, my homeland. It can be a good solution if the crisis is highly communicative. But beware: if the real reason was that the top management has not taken the problem seriously, communicators do not usually have a position of such authority as to make decisions that really bind the organization, and in this case the remedy would be worse than the illness.

Experts, scholars and practitioners are unanimous: the advice of the Dircom is a valuable element to anticipate problems, and that – as Bowen points out – «its integration in the organizational structure and in strategic decisions contributes effectively to companies be more ethical and improve prevention".

Edward R. Murrow, one of the founders of the Center of Public Diplomacy, when questioned about reputation management after a failure, replied that if he was to be at an emergency landing, he preferred to be at takeoff as well, that is, when decisions are made that affect critical moments.

In practice, however, things are not so clear. Statistical studies show that in Europe and North America, less than 50% of communication directors report directly to the first executive. But it is interesting to note that one of the most frequent decisions after a crisis is to change the organization chart in that regard. For example, Fronz says that after the crisis suffered by Siemens in 2006 (a case of bribery to obtain new contracts), the company announced the creation of a corporate director of communication directly answerable to the CEO.

It is a fact that in more and more institutions the communications manager is a member of the executive committee. This trend is more intense in organizations that are more sensitive to the perception of their stakeholders: banks, energy companies, technology companies, universities, political parties, NGOs, etc. Certainly, it is not to avoid crises, but it is due to the importance of relations with the public, which are considered a priority.

However, the organic situation is not the most important. It is not enough to sit at the table and report directly to the CEO to ensure effectiveness. As Grunig says, more important than his position is his authority, since it depends on his real influence in the organization. The Dircom should be part of the institution's *dominant coalition*. In short, the real authority does not come with the job title but must be earned.

Hence the importance of the leadership capacity of the institutional communicator, since the crisis puts them in the forefront and able to condition the future of the institution. One thing is for sure: opportunities do not wait. If the favorable circumstances arrive and do not find the communications director ready to facilitate the change, they will be left out, even though many of the decisions have to do with communication. Furthermore, there is no shortage of managers with great vision, who will not wait for their communication managers to propose initiatives: they will go it on their own.

In fact, as Bowen explains, communicators have five routes to 'gain weight' in their organizations and become part of the dominant coalition: an organizational crisis, an ethical dilemma, the acquisition of credibility over time, being on the media's agenda, and as a result of leadership; and of all of them, the most frequent is the first: the crisis. In this sense, crises are not only opportunities for companies that know how to deal with them, but also for communication managers prepared to .assume leadership responsibilities.

All too often, what prevents communication professionals from successfully intervening in the strategic direction of the organization is their passivity and lack of managerial skills. A head of communication who considers themselves as a mere executor or a technician is not going to be able to play a managerial role. Only those who have an overall vision and who propose strategic objectives will sooner or later participate in strategic decisions. Moreover, institutional communicators reach professional maturity precisely when they realize that their role is not limited only to their own office but has to do with the institution as a whole. This is the moment when incorporation into top management should take place.

Unfortunately, many communicators consider themselves to be alone. They see their relationship with managers in these terms: *tell me what you want to say, and I will tell you how to say it.* Certainly, communication skills are essential in this field, but an attitude like this ends up leading managers to think of the communication department as an instrument to implement decisions and not as part of the decision–making process. On the other hand, an institutional communicator who has a wider, overall vision will be able to make an effective contribution to the institution for which they work.

The manager's virtue

All the proposals and experiences suggested in this book highlight the value of prudence, understood as the ability to judge well and choose the best option in each circumstance. This virtue, proper to the one who governs, must characterize managers and crisis communicators, and for that reason I would like to finish the book by praising this virtue.

Prudence is, in my opinion, what rounds off the virtues in people. It is the meeting of science, experience and conscience.

It is no coincidence that the Latin word *prudentia* comes from *providere*, to see from afar, to anticipate, to provide. To be prudent is to know how to identify a just solution. St Thomas Aquinas explains in the *Summa Theologiae* that the three acts pertaining to the virtue of prudence are: to ask for advice, to judge righteously and to decide.

In our field, asking for advice is part of being well trained, and not trusting only our own judgment and abilities. Judging correctly means thinking seriously with enough time. And taking the right decision implies acting, overcoming the paralysis of inaction for fear of making mistakes.

Ordinary language sometimes confuses prudence with slowness or inaction. It is the opposite: the prudent thing, when you see a child drowning in the pool, is not to ask for advice, but to jump into the water immediately, with the sole condition of knowing how to swim ... and sometimes not even that.

I wish that if we were asked the same question that was posed to a newly crowned young Jewish king, «What gift would you like to receive now that you begin your reign?» we would answer in the same way: wisdom of heart to discern good and evil, and not money or glory or a long reign. Because with prudence, everything else will fall into place.

Bibliographic references

Roger AILES & Jon KRAUSHAR (1988). *You are the message: Secrets of the master communicators.* Irwin Professional Pub., Homewood

Saul D. ALINSKI (1971), *Rules for radicals. A practical primer for realistic radicals*, Random House, New York

Can M. ALPASLAN & Ian I. MITROFF (2010), *Swans, Swine, and Swindlers. Coping with the Growing Threat of Mega-Crises and Mega-Messes*, Stanford University Press, Stanford

Peter ANDERSEN and Brian SPITZBERG (2009), "Myths and Maxims of Risk and Crisis Communication", in HEATH & O'HAIR, op.cit.

Peter F. ANTHONISSEN, Ed. (2008), *Crisis Communication - Practical PR strategies for reputation management and Company Survival*, Kogan Page, London

L.M. ARPAN & D.R. ROSKOS-EWOLDSEN (2005), "Stealing thunder: Analysis of the effects of proactive disclosure of crisis information", *Public Relations Review*, 31 (3), 425-433

William ASHLEY & James MORRISON (1995), *Anticipatory Management, Issue* Action Publications, Leesburg

L.M. ARPAN (2002), "When in Rome: The effects of spokesperson ethnicity on audience evaluation of crisis communication", *Journal of Business Communication*, 39 (3), 14-26

G. L. ATKINS (2010), "Organizational networks in disaster response: An examination of the U.S. government network's effort in Hurricane Katrina", in William T. COOMBS & J. HOLLADAY, Eds., op. cit.

Laurence BARTON (2001), *Crisis in Organizations II: Managing & Communicating in the Heat of Chaos*, South-Western College Publishing, Cincinnati

Otis BASKIN & Craig ARONOFF (1983), *Public Relations: The Profession and the Practice*, Wm. C. Brown Publications, Dubuque

Zigmunt BAUMAN (2007), *Liquid Times: Living in an Age of Uncertainty*, Polity Press, Cambridge

Max BAZERMAN & Margaret NEAL (1992), *Negotiating Rationally*, The Free Press, New York

William L. BENOIT (1995), *Accounts, excuses and apologies*, State University of New York Press, Albany

William L. BENOIT & Augustine PANG (2008), "Crisis communication and image repair discourse", in T.L. HANSEN-HORN & B.D. NEFF, Eds., op.cit.

Jonathan BENTHALL (1995), *Disasters, relief and the media*, I.B. Tauris & Co, London

Dieudonnée T. BERGE (1990), *The first 24 hours: A comprehensive guide to successful crisis communications*, Basil Blackwell, Cambridge

Shannon A. BOWEN (2009), "Ethical Responsibility and Guidelines for Managing *Issues* of Risk and Risk Communication", in HEATH & O'HAIR, op.cit.

Shannon A. BOWEN (2009), "What communication professionals tell us regarding dominant coalition access and gaining membership", *Journal of Applied Communication Research*, 37 (4), 418-443

Joel BROCKNER & Erika HAYES JAMES (2008), "Toward an understanding of when executives see crisis as opportunity", *Journal of Applied Behavioral Science*, 44 (1), 94-115

David BUCHANAN (2011), "Reflections: Good Practice, Not Rocket Science — Understanding Failures to Change after Extreme Events", *Journal of Change Management*, 11 (3), 273-288

Judith P. BURNS & Michael S. BRUNER (2000), "Revisiting the theory of image restoration strategies", *Communication Quarterly*, 48, 27-39

María José CANEL & Karen SANDERS (2010), "Crisis Communication and terrorist attacks: framing a response to the 2004 Madrid bombing and 2005 London bombing", en COOMBS & HOLLADAY, op.cit.

Juan Pablo CANNATA, "Gestión de crisis y comunicación: una perspectiva desde la teoría mimética de René Girard", en Isabel DE LA TORRE, José Antonio RUIZ SAN ROMÁN & Leticia PORTO PEDROSA, Coord. (2013), *Organizaciones en tiempos de crisis. Perspectivas, diagnósticos, alternativas y propuestas*, AISOC, Madrid

Jeffrey R. CAPONIGRO (2000), *The Crisis Counselor. A Step-by-Step Guide to Managing a Business Crisis*, Contemporary Books, NTC, Lincolnwood

Clarke L. CAYWOOD, Ed. (1997), *The Handbook of Strategic Public Relations & Integrated Communications*, McGraw-Hill, New York

Michael T. CHARLES & John Choon K. KIM (1988), *Crisis Management. A Casebook*, Charles C. Thomas Publ., Springfield

William Howard CHASE (1984), *Issues Management: Origins of the Future*, Issue Action Publications, Stamford

Cosimo CHIESA DE NEGRI (2009), *CRM — Las cinco pirámides del Marketing Relacional*, Deusto, Barcelona

Tom CHRISTENSEN, Mathias JOANNESSEN & Per LAEGREID, "A System under Stress: The Icelandic Volcano Ash Crisis", *Journal of Contingencies and Crisis Management*, 21 (2), 72-81

An-Sofie CLAEYS & Verolien CAUBERGHE (2012), "Crisis response and crisis timing strategies, two sides of the same coin", *Public Relations Review*, 38, 83-88

Brent COCKER (2014), "Hard for me to say I'm sorry: Seeking brand forgiveness using advertising", *paper* presentado en la *European Marketing Academy Conference*, Valencia 3/6-VI-2014

Robin COHN (2000), *The PR Crisis Bible*, St. Martin's Press, New York

William T. COOMBS (1999), *Ongoing Crisis Communication. Planning, Managing, and Responding*, Sage Publications, Thousand Oaks

William T. COOMBS (2007), "Protecting organization reputations during a crisis: The development and application of situational crisis communications theory", *Corporate Reputation Review*, 10, 163-176

William T. COOMBS & S. Jean HOLLADAY (2012), "The paracrisis: the challenges created by publicly managing crisis prevention", *Public Relations Review*, 38 (3), 408-415

William T. COOMBS & S. Jean HOLLADAY, Eds. *Handbook of Crisis Communication*, Wiley-Blackwell, New York

John P. COTTER & Dan S. COHEN (2002), *The Heart of Change*, Harvard Business School Press, Boston

Vincent T. COVELLO (2003), "Best practices in public health risk and crisis communication", *Journal of Health Communication*, 8, 5-8

Stephen R. COVEY (1990), *The 7 Habits of Highly Effective People: Powerful Lessons in Personal Change*, Free Press

Malcolm CRAIG (2000), *Thinking visually*, Thomson, London

Scott CUTLIP, Allen CENTER & Glen BROOM (2000), *Effective Public Relations*, Prentice Hall

Al CZARNECKI (2009), *Crisis Communications: A Primer for Teams*, iUniverse, Lincoln

W. DE MARIA (2010), "After the scandal – recovery options for damaged organizations", *Journal of Management & Organization*, 16 (1), 66-82

James W. DEARING & Everett M. ROGERS (1996), *Agenda-Setting*, Sage, Thousand Oaks

Eric DEZENHALL & John WEBER (2007), *Damage Control*, Penguin, New York

Roumen DIMOTROV (2008), "The strategic response: an introduction to nonprofit communications", *Third Sector and Communication*, 14 (2), 9-50

M. DUNN (2004), *Survey: NASA workers afraid to speak up*, www.space.com

Luciano H. ELIZALDE (2011), *Estrategias en las crisis públicas - La función de la comunicación*, La Crujía Ediciones, Buenos Aires

Luciano ELIZALDE, Damián FERNANDEZ PEDEMONTE y Mario RIORDA (2011), *La gestión del disenso –la comunicación gubernamental en problemas*, La Crujía Ediciones, Buenos Aires

Raymond P. EWING (1987), *Managing the New Bottom Line: Issues Management for Senior Executives*, Dow-Jones Irwin, Homewood

Jesper FALKHEIMER (2014), "Crisis communication and terrorism: the Norway attacks on 22 July 2011", *Corporate Communications: An International Journal*, 19 (1), 52-63

Jesper FALKHEIMER and M. HEIDE (2010), "Crisis communicators in change: from plans to improvisations", in W.T. COOMBS & S. HOLLADAY, eds., *Handbook of Crisis Communication*, Wiley-Blackwell, Malden, 511-526

James FALLOWS (1997), *Breaking the News*, Vintage Books, New York

Kathleen FEARN-BANKS (1996), *Crisis Communications: a Casebook Approach*, LEA, Mahwah

G. FILIZZOLA & G. LOPEZ (1995), *Victimes et victimologie*, Que sais-je, PUF, Paris

Steven FINK (2000), *Crisis management. Planning for the inevitable*, Universe, Lincoln

Kristin FJELD & Mike MOLESWORTH (2006), "PR practitioners' experiences of, and attitudes towards, the internet´s contribution to external crisis communication", *Corporate Communications: An International Journal*, 11 (4), 291-405

Charles J. FOMBRUN (1996), *Reputation*, Harvard Business School Press, Boston

F. FRANDSEN & W. JOHANSEN (2011), "The study of internal crisis communication: Towards an integrative framework", *Corporate Communication: and International Journal*, 16 (4), 347-361

Sandra L. FRENCH & Tracey Quigley HOLDEN (2012), "Positive Organizational Behavior: A Buffer for Bad News", *Business Communication Quarterly*, 75 (2), 208-220

Monroe FRIEDMAN (1990), "Consumer Boycotts: A Conceptual Framework and Research Agenda", *Journal of Social Issues*, 47, 149-168

Christian FRONZ (2011), *Strategic Management in Crisis Communication - A Multinational Approach*, Diplomatica Verlag, Hamburg

César GARCÍA (2011), "Sex scandals: A cross-cultural analysis of image repair strategies in the cases of Bill Clinton and Silvio Berlusconi", *Public Relations Review*, 37, 292-296

Diane GAYESKI (1993), *Corporate Communications Management. The Renaissance Communicator in Information-Age Organizations*, Focal Press, Boston

Amiso M. GEORGE & Cornelius B. PRATT, Eds. (2012), *Case studies in crisis communication –International Perspectives on Hits and Misses*, Routledge, New York

Richard GIGLIOTTI & Ronald JASON (1991), *Emergency Planning for Maximum Protection*, Butterworth –Heinemann, Newton

Dawn R. GILPIN & Priscilla J. MURPHY (2008), *Crisis management in a complex world*, Oxford University Press, New York

Alfonso GONZÁLEZ HERRERO & Suzanne SMITH (2010), "Crisis Communications Management 2.0: Organizational, Principles to Manage Crisis in an Online World", *Organization Development Journal*, 28/1, 97-105

Alfonso GONZÁLEZ HERRERO & Suzanne SMITH (2008), "Crisis Communications Management on the Web: Hw Internet-Bases Technologies are Changing the Way Public Relations Professionals Handle Business Crises", *Journal of Contingencies and Crisis Management*, 16 (3), 143-153

Alfonso GONZÁLEZ HERRERO & C. PRATT (1996), "An Integrated Model for Crisis-Communications Management", *Journal of Public Relations Research*, 8 (2), 79-105

Alfonso GONZÁLEZ HERRERO (2012), "Hoe to Manage a Crisis Before it Hits", *IESE Insight*, 15, IV-2012, 20-27

Jack A. GOTTSCHALK, Ed. (1997), *Crisis Response: Inside Stories on Managing Image under Siege*, Visible Ink Press, Detroit

Sasha Karl GREBE (2013), Things can get worse – How mismanagement of a crisis response strategy can cause a secondary or double crisis: the example of the AWB corporate scandal", *Corporate Communications: An International Journal*, 18 (1), 70-86

Frank GRIFFIN (2009), "Merck's Open Letters and the Teaching of Ethos", *Business Communication Quarterly*, 72 (1), 61-72

Rachna GUPTA (2011), "Corporate Communication: A Strategic Tool for Crisis Management", *Journal of Economic Development, Management, IT, Finance and Marketing*, 3 (2), 55-67

Joanne E. HALE, Ronald E. DULEK & David P. HALE (2005), "Crisis response communication challenges: Building theory from qualitative data", *Journal of Business Communication*, 42 (2), 112-134

John HARVEY-JONES (1988), *Making it Happen*, HarperCollins, London

Robert HEATH & Douglas ABEL (1996), "Proactive Response to Citizen Risk Concerns: Increasing Citizen's Knowledge of Emergency Response Practices", *Journal of Public Relations Research*, 8, (3), 151-171

Robert HEATH & Richard A. NELSON (1986), *Issues Management, Corporate Policymaking in an Information Society*, Sage, Beverly Hills

Robert HEATH & H. Dan O'HAIR, *Handbook of Risk and Crisis Communication*, Routledge, New York

Robert L. HEALTH (Ed.), *Handbook of public relations*, Sage, Thousand Oaks

Mats HEIDE & Charlotte SIMONSSON (2014), "Developing internal crisis communication – New roles and practices of communication professionals", *Corporate Communications: An International Journal*, 19 (2), 128-146

Carole M. HOWARD & Wilma K. MATHEWS (2000), *On Deadline*, Waveland Press, Prospect Heights

Keith M. HEARIT (2001), "Corporate apologia: When an organization speaks in defense of itself", in R. L. HEALTH (Ed.), op.cit.

Keith M. HEARIT (1995), "Mistakes were made: Organizational apologia and crisis of social legitimacy", *Communication Studies*, 46, 1-17

Keith M. HEARIT (2006), *Crisis management by apology: Corporate response to allegations of wrongdoing*, LEA, Mahwah

Rene A. HENRY (2000), *You'd better have a hose if you want to put out the fire*, Gollygobbler Productions, Windsor

Dan HILL (2003), *Body of Truth*, John Wiley & Sons, Hoboken

Mark Lee HUNTER, Marc LE MENESTREL & Henri-Claude DE BETTIGNIES (2008), "Beyond Control: Crisis Strategies and Stakeholder Media in the Danone Boycott of 2001", *Corporate Reputation Review*, 11/4, 335-350

INSTITUTE FOR CRISIS MANAGEMENT, *Annual Crisis Report*, www.crisisexperts.com

Patrick JACKSON (1982), "Tactics of confrontation", en J. NAGELSCHMIDT, *The Public Affairs Handbook*, AMACOM, New York

Erika H. JAMES & Lynn P. WOOTEN (2010), *Leading under pressure: From surviving to thriving before, during and after a crisis*, Taylor & Francis, New York

Irving L. JANIS (1982), *Groupthink: Psychological Studies of Policy Decisions and Fiascoes*, Houghton Mifflin, Boston

Yan JIN, Brooke Fisher LIU & Lucinda L. AUSTIN (2011), "Examining the Role of Social Media in Effective Crisis Management: The Effects of Crisis Origin, Information Form, and Source on Public's Crisis Responses", *Communication Research*, 41 (1), 74-94

W. JOHANSEN, H.K. AGGERHOLM & F. FRANDSEN (2012), "Entering new territory: a study of internal crisis management and crisis communication in organizations", *Public Relations Review*, 38 (2), 270-279

Jean-Noel KAPFERER (1990), *Rumeurs*, Le Seuil, Paris

Kathy KERCHNER (1997), *Soundbites. A Business Guide for working with the Media*, Savage Press, Superior

Astrid KERSTEN (2005), "Crisis as usual: Organizational Dysfunction and Public Relations", *Public Relations Review*, 31 (4), 544-549

Eyun-Jung KI & Elmie NEKMAT (2014), "Situational crisis communication and interactivity: Usage and effectiveness of Facebook for crisis management by Fortune 500 companies", *Computers in Human Behavior*, 35, 140-147

Rushworth KIDDER (2003), *How Good People Make Tough Choices: Resolving the Diliemmas of Ethical Living*, Harper Collins, New York

Jeong-Nam KIM & Yunna RHEE (2011), "Strategic thinking about employee communication behavior (ECB) in public relations: testing the models of megaphoning and scouting effects in Korea", *Journal of Public Relations Research*, 23 (3), 243-268

Robert W. KINKEAD & Dena WINOKUR (1992), "How Public Relations Professionals Help CEOs Make the Right Moves", *Public Relations Journal*, 48 (10), 18-23

Jill G. KLEIN, Craig N. SMITH & Andrew JOHN, (2004) "Why we boycott: Consumer motivations for boycott participation", *Journal of Marketing*, 68, 92-109

Alexander KOUZMIN (2008), "Crisis Management in Crisis?", *Administrative Theory and Praxis*, 30 (2), 155-183

Patrick LAGADEC (1991), *La Gestion des Crises. Outils de réflexion à l'usage des décideurs*, McGraw-Hill, Paris

R. LASKER (1997), *Medicine and public health: The power of collaboration*, New York Academy of Medicine, New York

William LEISS & Christina CHOCIOLKO (1994), *Risk and Responsibility*, McGill-Queen's University Press, Buffalo

Otto LERBINGER (1997), *The Crisis Manager*, LEA, Mahwah

Jonathan LOW & Tony SIESFELD (1998), "Measures that matter: Non-financial performance", Strategy & Leadership, 26 (2), 24 - 38

J.E. LUKASZEWSKI (2013), *Lukaszewski on Crisis Communication: What Your CEO Needs to Know About Reputation Risk and Crisis Management*, Rothstein Associates, Brookfield

R. LUECKE (2007), *Crisis Management. Master the Skills to Prevent Disasters Mastering the Media*, Harvard Business School Press, Cambridge

Francis J. MARRA (1998), "crisis Communication plans: poor predictors of excellent crisis public relation", *Public Relations Review*, 24 (4), 461-474

Álvaro MATUD (2013), "¿Googlecracia o Googleísmo? Los nuevos desafíos de la libertad en la sociedad digital", *Nueva Revista*, 145, 23-38

Alessandra MAZZEI, Jeong-Nam KIM & Carolina DELL'ORO (2012), "Strategic Value of Employee Relationships and Communicative Actions: Overcoming Corporate Crisis with Quality Internal Communication", *International Journal of Strategic Communication*, 6, 31-44

Thomas D. McCANN (1994), "Win the Legal Battle, lose the Public War: Public Opinion of Corporations", *Management Review*, 83 (8), 43ss.

Andrew S. McFARLAND (1976), *Public Interest Lobbies*, American Enterprise Institute for Public Policy Research, Washington D.C.

Gerald C. MEYERS & Susan MEYERS (2000), *Dealers, Healers, Brutes & Saviors. Eight Winning Styles for Solving Giant Business Crises*, John Wiley & Sons, New York

Ian I. MITROFF & Tierry C. PAUCHANT (1990), *We're so big and powerful nothing bad can happen to us. An investigation of America's crisis prone corporations*, Carol Pub., Secaucus

Susan D. MOELLER (1999), *Compassion Fatigue. How the Media Sell Disease, Famine, War and Death*, Routledge, New York

Juan Manuel MORA, Ed. (2009), *10 ensayos de comunicación institucional*, Eunsa, Pamplona

Edgar MORIN (1993), "For a Crisology", *Organization and Environment*, 7 (1), 5-21

Danny MOSS & Barbara DeSANTO (2002), *Public Relations Cases. International Perspectives*, Routledge, London

Rick A. MYER, Christian CONTE & Sarah E. PETERSON (2007), "Human impact issues for crisis management in organizations", *Disaster Prevention and Management*, 16 (5), 761-770

Kenneth N. MYERS (1993), *Total Contingency Planning for Disasters: Managing Risk, Minimizing Loss, Ensuring Business Continuity*, John Wiley & Sons, New York

Alejandro NAVAS (2007), "Nuevas tecnologías y cultura: ¿acceso sin límites?", in Alejandra WALZER, Marcial GARCÍA LÓPEZ & Juan Carlos RODRÍGUEZ CENTENO, Eds., *Comunicación alternativa, ciudadanía y cultura*, Edipo, Madrid, 209-224

Mayer NUDELL & Norman ANTOKOL (1988), *The handbook for effective emergency and crisis management*, Lexington Books, Lexington

Michel OGRIZEK & Jean-Michel Guillery (1997), *Communication de crise*, PUF, Paris

Stefano PACE (2014), "Social media and consumers´ reactions to brand crisis: The case of Barilla", paper at European Marketing Academy Congress, 3/6-VI-2014

Pauliina PALTTALA, Camillo BOANO, Ragnhild LUND & Marita VOS (2011), "Communication Gaps in Disaster Management: Perceptions by Experts from Governmental and Non-Governmental Organizations", *Journal of Contingencies and Crisis Management*, 20 (1), 1-12

Augustine PANG, Nasrath Begam Binte Abul HASSAN & Aaron Chee Yang CHONG (2014), "Negotiating crisis in the social media environment", *Corporate Communications: an International Journal*, 19 (1), 96-118

Tierry PAUCHANT & Ian MITROFF (1992), *Transforming the crisis-prone organization: Preventing individual, organizational, and environmental tragedies*, Jossey-Bass, San Francisco

Charles PERROW (2007), *The Next Catastrophe – Reducing our vulnerabilities to Natural, Industrial, and Terrorist Disasters*, Princeton University Press, Princeton

Thomas PETERS & Robert WATERMAN (1982), *In Search of Excellence*, HarperCollins, London

José Ramón PIN (2012), "Leadership under Pressure: Communication is Key", *IESE Insight*, 15, IV-2012, 28-35

Marion K. PINSDORF (1999), *Communicating When Your Company Is Under Siege. Surviving Public Crisis*, Fordham University Press, New York

Michael REGESTER & Judy LARKIN (2008), *Risk Issues and Crisis Management in Public Relations - A Casebook of Best Practice*, Kogan Page, London

Claus RERUP, "Picking up the Signals That Trigger Crises", *IESE Insight*, 15, IV-2012, 13-19

Sandra L. RESODIHARDJO, Carola J.A. van EIJK & Brendan J. CARROLL (2012), "Mayor vs. Police Chief: The Hoek van Holland Riot", *Journal of Contingencies and Crisis Management*, 20 (4), 231-243

Régis REVÉRET et Jean-Nicolas MOREAU (1997), *Les Médias et la Communication de Crise*, Ed. Economica, Paris

Barbara REYNOLDS, J. GALDO & L. SOKLER (2002), *Crisis and emergency risk communication*, Centers for Disease Control and Prevention, Atlanta

Barbara REYNOLDS & M. W. SEEGER (2005), "Crisis and emergency risk communication as an integrative model", *Journal of Health Communication Research*, 10(1), 43-55

Barry RICHARDS (2004), "Terrorism and Public Relations", *Public Relations Review*, 30 (2), 169-176

Al RIES & Laura RIES (2004), *The Fall of Advertising and the Rise of PR*, Harper-Collins, New York

Ulien ROSENTHAL, Argen BOIN, Louise COMFORT, Eds. (2011), *Managing crises – Threat, Dilemmas, Opportunities*, Charles C. Thomas Publisher, Springfield

Christophe ROUX-DUFORT & Carole LALONDE (2013), "Editorial: Exploring the Theoretical Foundations of Crisis Management", *Journal of Contingencies and Crisis Management*, 21 (1), 1-3

Rafael RUBIO (2013), "Gobierno abierto: más allá de los principios", *Nueva Revista*, 145, 2-12

Aino RUGGIERO & Marita VOS, "Terrorism Communication: Characteristics and Emerging Perspectives in the Scientific Literature 2002-2011", *Journal of Contingencies and Crisis Management*, 21 (3), 153-166

Charlotte RYAN (1991), *Prime Time Activism. Media Strategies for Grassroots Organizing*, South End Press, Boston

Jason SALZMAN (1998), *Making the News: A Guide For Nonprofits And Activists*, Westview Press, Boulder

Friederike SCHULTZ, Sonja UTZ & Anja GÖRITZ (2011), "Is the medium the message? Perceptions of and reactions to crisis communication via Twitter, blogs and traditional media", *Public Relations Review*, 37, 20-27

Mark S. SCHWARTZ, Wesley CRAGG & W. Michael HOFFMAN (2012), "An ethical approach to crisis management", *IESE Insight*, 15, IV-2012, 36-43

Andreas SCHWARZ & Franziska PFORR (2011), "The crisis communication preparedness of nonprofit organizations: The case of German interest groups", *Public Relations Review*, 37, 68-70

Herb SCHMERTZ (with William NOVAK) (1986), *Goodbye to the low profile*, Little, Brown and Co, Boston

Matthew W. SEEGER, Timothy L. SELLNOW & Robert R. ULMER (2003), *Communication and organizational crisis*, Quorum Press, Westport

Matthew W. SEEGER (2006), "Best Practices in Crisis Communication: An Expert Panel Process", *Journal of Applied Communication Research*, 34:3, 232-244

Mike SEYMOUR & Simon MOORE (2000), *Effective Crisis Management. Worldwide Principes and Practice*, Cassell, London

Fraser P. SEITEL (2001), *The practice of Public Relations*, Prentice Hall, Upper Saddle River

Joanna SIAH, Namrata BANSAL & Augustine PANG (2010), "New Media: a new medium in escalating crises?", *Corporate Communications: an International Journal*, 15 (2), 143-155

S.B. SITKIN (1992), "Learning through failure: The strategy of small losses", en M. D. COHEN & L. S. SPROULL, Eds. (1995), *Organizational learning*, Sage, Thousand Oaks, 541-578

Peter SNYDER et al (2006), *Ethical Rationality: A Strategic Approach to Organizational Crisis*, Sage, Thousand Oaks

Carlos SORIA (1997), *El laberinto informativo: una salida ética*, Eunsa, Pamplona

Betsy STEVENS (1999), "Persuasion, Probity, and Paltering: The Prudential Crisis", *The Journal of Business Communication*, 36 (4), 319-334

Minjung SUNG & Jang-Sun HWANG (2014), "What drives a crisis? The diffusion of an issue through social networks", *Computers in Human Behavior*, 36, 246-257

Lawrence SUSSKIND & Patrick FIELD (1996), *Dealing with an Angry Public*, The Free Press, New York

Nassim N. TALEB (2010), *The Black Swan: The Impact of the Highly Improbable*, Random House, New York

Christian N. THOROUGHGOOD & Art PADILLA (2013), "Destructive Leadership and the Penn State Scandal: a Toxic Triangle", *Industrial and Organizational Psychology*, 144-149

Kathleen TIERNEY, Michael K. LINDELL & Ronald W. PERRY (2001), *Facing the unexpected: Disaster preparedness and response in the United States*, John Henry Press, Washington DC.

Philip K. TOMPKINS (2005), *Apollo, Challenger, Columbia. The decline of the space program*, Roxbury, Los Angeles

Benjamin TOPPER & Patrick LAGADEC (2013), "Fractal Crises – A New Path for Crisis Theory and Management", *Journal of Contingencies and Crisis Management*, 21 (1), 4-16

Robert R. ULMER (2012), "Increasing the Impact of Thought Leadership in Crisis Communication", *Management Communication Quarterly*, 26 (2), 523-542

Robert R. ULMER (2001), "Effective crisis management through established stakeholder relationships: Malden Mills as a case study", *Management Communication Quarterly*, 14 (4), 590-615

Robert R. ULMER (2011), "Creating Opportunities and Renewal Out of a Crisis", *Communication Currents*, 6, (6), www.natcom.org

Robert R. ULMER, Timothy L. SELLNOW & Matthew W. SEEGER (2007), *Effective Crisis Communication –Moving from Crisis to Opportunity*, Sage, Thousand Oaks

Robert R. ULMER & Timothy L. SELLNOW (2000), "Strategic Ambiguity and the ethic of significant choice in the tobacco industry's crisis communication", *Communication Studies*, 48, 215-233

Aikaterini C. VALVI & Konstantinos C. FRAGKOS (2013), "Crisis Communication strategies: a case of British Petroleum", Industrial and Commercial Training, 45 (7), 383-391

Toni G.A.A. VAN DER MEER & Piet VERHOEVEN (2013), "Public Framing organizational crisis situations: Social media versus news media", *Public Relations Review*, 9, 229-231

Richard F. VANCIL (1987), *Passing the Baton: Managing the Process of CEO succession*, Harvard Business School Press, Boston

Shari R. VEIL (2011), "Mindful Learning in Crisis Management", *Journal of Business Communication*, 48 (2), 116-147

Shari R. VEIL, Timothy L. SELLNOW, and Elizabeth L. PETRUN (2012), "Hoaxes and the Paradoxical Challenges of Restoring Legitimacy: Dominos' Response to Its YouTube", *Crisis Management Communication Quarterly*, 26 (2), 322-345

Shari R. VEIL & Rebekah A. HUSTED (2012), "Best practices as an assessment for crisis communication", *Journal of Communication Management*, 16 (2), 131-145

S. J. VENETTE, T.L. SELLNOW & P.A. LANG (2003), "Metanarration's role in restructuring perceptions of crisis: NHTSA's failure in the Ford-Firestone crisis", *Journal of Business Communication*, 40, 219-226

VV.AA., (2004), *Harvard Business Essentials: Crisis Management - Master the Skills to Prevent Disasters*, Harvard Business School Press, Cambridge

Misse WESTER (2009), "Cause and Consequences of Crises: How Perception Can Influence Communication", *Journal of Contingencies and Crisis Management*, 17 (2), 118-125

Connie M. WHITE (2012), *Social Media, Crisis Communication, and Emergency Management –Leveraging Web 2.0 Technologies*, CRC Press, Boca Raton

Jordi XIFRA (2012), "Sex, lies and post-trial publicity: The reputation repair strategies of Dominique Strauss-Kahn", *Public Relations Review*, 38, 477-483

Kaibin XU & Wenqing LI (2013), "An Ethical Stakeholder Approach to Crisis Communication: A Case Study of Foxcomm's 2010 Empoyee Suicide Crisis", *Journal of Business Ethics*, 117, 371-386.

Printed in Poland
by Amazon Fulfillment
Poland Sp. z o.o., Wrocław

72711681R00217